Video Basics 7

Video Basics 7

Herbert Zettl

San Francisco State University

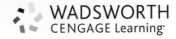

WADSWORTH
CENGAGE Learning·

Australia • Brazil • Japan • Korea • Mexico • Singapore • Spain • United Kingdom • United States

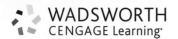
WADSWORTH
CENGAGE Learning·

Video Basics, Seventh Edition
Herbert Zettl

Senior Publisher: Lyn Uhl

Publisher: Michael Rosenberg

Development Editor: Megan Garvey

Assistant Editor: Erin Bosco

Editorial Assistant: Rebecca Donahue

Media Editor: Jessica Badiner

Marketing Program Manager: Gurpreet Saran

Senior Content Project Manager: Michael Lepera

Art Director: Marissa Falco

Print Buyer: Doug Bertke

Rights Acquisition Specialist: Jessica Elias

Production Service/Compositor: Ideas to Images

Text Designer: Gary Palmatier, Ideas to Images

Copy Editor: Elizabeth von Radics

Cover Designer: Gary Palmatier, Ideas to Images

Cover Images: Edward Aiona (people) and
        Panasonic (camera)

Library of Congress Control Number: 2011941996

ISBN-13: 978-1-111-34446-7
ISBN-10: 1-111-34446-9

Wadsworth
20 Channel Center Street
Boston, MA 02210
USA

Cengage Learning is a leading provider of customized learning solutions with office locations around the globe, including Singapore, the United Kingdom, Australia, Mexico, Brazil, and Japan. Locate your local office at **international.cengage.com/region**.

Cengage Learning products are represented in Canada by Nelson Education, Ltd.

For your course and learning solutions, visit **www.cengage.com**. Purchase any of our products at your local college store or at our preferred online store **www.cengagebrain.com**. Instructors: Please visit **login.cengage.com** and log in to access instructor-specific resources.

Printed in Canada
1 2 3 4 5 6 7   15 14 13 12 11

To Alex and Anne

Brief Contents

Contents

PART III   Image Creation: Sound, Light, Graphics, and Effects   123

CHAPTER 7   Audio and Sound Control   124

About the Author

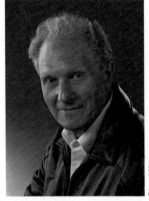

Herbert Zettl is a professor emeritus of the Broadcast and Electronic Communication Arts Department at San Francisco State University (SFSU). He taught there for many years in the fields of video production and media aesthetics. While at SFSU he headed the Institute of International Media Communication. For his academic contributions, he received the California State Legislature Distinguished Teaching Award and, from the Broadcast Education Association, the Distinguished Education Service Award.

Prior to joining the SFSU faculty, Zettl worked at KOVR (Stockton-Sacramento) and as a producer-director at KPIX, the CBS affiliate in San Francisco. While at KPIX he participated in a variety of CBS and NBC network television productions. Because of his outstanding contributions to the television profession, he was elected to the prestigious Silver Circle of the National Academy of Television Arts and Sciences (NATAS), Northern California Chapter. He is also a member of the Broadcast Legends of the NATAS Northern California Chapter.

In addition to this book, Zettl has authored *Video Basics Workbook, Television Production Handbook,* and *Sight Sound Motion.* All of his books have been translated into several languages and published internationally. His numerous articles on television production and media aesthetics have appeared in major media journals worldwide. He has lectured extensively on television production and media aesthetics at universities and professional broadcast institutions in the United States and abroad and has presented key papers at a variety of national and international communication conventions.

Zettl developed an interactive DVD-ROM, *Zettl's VideoLab 4.0,* published by Wadsworth/Cengage Learning. His previous CD-ROM version won several prestigious awards.

Preface

Camcorders, like cell phones and computers, change so fast that what you buy today may be obsolete tomorrow. Right? Well, considering how fast the mobile phone transformed into a pocket-sized high-definition camcorder and a sophisticated communication device that lets you talk to your friend while watching a YouTube movie, you may have a point. Does this mean that this technological advancement brought about a similar fundamental change in video production? No. The basic steps of moving from a good idea to a professional-looking video piece have pretty much remained the same, regardless of whether you use your old camcorder or the latest DSLR camera.

Video Basics is written in the spirit of helping you learn video production from the ground up so that your move from amateur to professional status will be relatively painless but maximally effective. A solid knowledge of the basics of video will also give you the confidence to go beyond the conventional—and to break the rules if necessary for the optimal clarification and intensification of a message.

Don't be bothered by the term *basics*. I was, so I will repeat with slight variations what I wrote in the preface of the previous *Video Basics* edition: Whenever I had to read a book that had "basics" in the title, I felt slightly put down before ever looking at what was in the book. I guess I took *basics* to mean I was automatically classified as inferior or, at best, unenlightened. This feeling grew even stronger when I thought I knew a little about the subject. Now I know better. *Basics* does not imply an evaluation of the reader but describes an essential prerequisite for helping someone acquire the necessary knowledge and skills to master a subject or an activity—such as video production. As a matter of fact, I now get annoyed when I try to learn the basics of a subject but find that many of the fundamental steps are left out.

The content of this book is streamlined so that it can be taught as well as learned in a single semester. Note, however, that reading even this text alone won't make you a hot-shot videographer. Much like learning how to play guitar or piano, video production requires considerable practice.

VIDEO BASICS 7 HIGHLIGHTS: DEFINITIONS

To avoid confusion about what is meant by some popular terms, the following definitions explain how the terms are used in this text. For specific definitions of these and other terms, consult the glossary at the back of this book.

Video

As in all previous editions, *video* is used throughout the text as a more inclusive term than *television*. Video encompasses the full range of today's electronically delivered moving images, from what we normally call "television" to corporate videos and productions done in media departments, to documentaries or digital filmmaking by individuals or a group of friends, to multimedia content and streaming video on the Internet.

Aesthetics

The term *aesthetics* does not refer to the theory of art or what is beautiful but rather to media aesthetics, which deals with the understanding and the control of light and color, two- and three-dimensional space, time/motion, and sound. The few descriptions of some of the basic aesthetic principles are not intended to detract from learning the technical aspects of production equipment but rather to facilitate their optimal application. Traditional media aesthetic factors such as lighting, picture composition, and shot sequencing are relatively independent of technological advances and therefore become the anchor of all successful video productions. How to compose an effective shot, choose the right music, or construct a successful sequence of close-ups must go hand-in-hand with learning the more technical aspects of video equipment.

Digital

Digital, which describes the nature of an electrical signal, has become a catchword for all types of video equipment, quality standards, and even production processes. To clarify some of the often-puzzling terminology of digital television and the various scanning systems, in this edition the scanning, sampling, and compression standards of digital television (DTV) and high-definition television (HDTV) are explored and their major differences are explained. Despite the lure of high-definition equipment, you will find that in many cases learning the actual operation of equipment and production processes is the same regardless of whether the equipment is a small consumer camcorder or a high-end HDTV one.

■ VIDEO BASICS 7 HIGHLIGHTS

To make full use of this text, you should be aware of some its special features. All are intended to help you learn a complex subject in an expeditious and affable way.

Chapter Grouping

To cover the broad spectrum of video production, this book is divided into six parts:

- ■ Production: Processes and People
- ■ Image Creation: Digital Video and Camera
- ■ Image Creation: Sound, Light, Graphics, and Effects

- Image Control: Switching, Recording, and Editing

- Production Environment: Studio, Field, and Synthetic

- Production Control: Talent and Directing

As you can see, the book describes how to move from an initial idea to an effective screen event regardless of whether you are doing a wedding video, a documentary, or large-screen digital cinema. It discusses the people normally involved in the production process, the major tools of video production, and how to use them to get the intended job done effectively and on time.

Key Terms

Each chapter's key terms appear at the beginning of the chapter, in the context of the text, and again in the extensive glossary. They are intended to prepare you for each chapter's terminology and serve as a quick reference as needed. The key terms are also identified in ***bold italic*** in the chapter text in the context in which they are defined.

You should make an effort to read the key terms before moving to the actual chapter text. There is no need to memorize them at this point—they merely serve as the first part of the pedagogical principle of redundancy. Hopefully, they will trigger an *aha!* response when you encounter them in context.

Key Concepts

The key concept margin notes emphasize each chapter's principal ideas and issues and are intended primarily as a memory aid. Once you learn a key concept, it should be easier for you to retrieve the rest of the related information.

Main Points

These summaries recap the chapter's most important points and key concepts. They do not represent a true précis—a precise and accurate abridgment of the chapter content—but are intended as a final reinforcement of the essential points. Beware of thinking that all you need to do is read the summaries. They are no substitute for the in-depth chapter content.

The following information is primarily directed to instructors who are already familiar with previous editions of *Video Basics*.

New to Video Basics 7

All chapters of this edition have been updated and, where necessary, the text streamlined and the concepts clarified. You may still find occasional references to analog processes and equipment. This is done only when comparing the two electronic principles or when a certain concept is better explained in the context of analog processes. The following list highlights some of the major changes in this edition:

- High-definition video (HDV) was eliminated because it has been replaced by true HDTV even in small consumer camcorders.

- Some of the content in chapter 3 (Image Formation and Digital Video) has been rearranged and some eliminated to make this admittedly demanding chapter as painless as possible for the reader.

- Super-HDTV scanning modes, normally used for digital cinema, are introduced.

- Digital single-lens reflex (DSLR) cameras and some mounting equipment are briefly discussed.

- Three-dimensional (3D) video is explained in chapters 4 (Video Camera) and 6 (Looking through the Viewfinder).

- Light-emitting diode (LED) lighting equipment and its studio use are added.

- Tapeless recording media and nonlinear editing are stressed throughout the text.

You should realize that while 3D video equipment is readily available, 3D production techniques are still in a great stage of flux. All of the past and present 3D productions show one thing: you cannot create effective 3D content by simply applying 2D production techniques, even if you use high-end 3D equipment. Whereas we all know that z-axis motion shots, which show objects hurling out of the screen toward the viewer, are quite effective, the assumption that we already know enough about 3D video production techniques to develop valid principles is simply false. For example, the so useful over-the-shoulder shot sequence is no longer effective when used in 3D video.

Such issues, however, should not prevent instructors or students from discussing 3D and undertaking some experimental productions that may speed up our understanding of what 3D video is all about. In fact, video production departments are the ideal platform for undertaking such production research.

SUPPORT MATERIALS

Video Basics 7 offers a wealth of support materials for both instructors and students. These thoroughly class-tested and highly praised print and electronic supplements are available to assist you in making the learning—and the teaching—experience as meaningful, enjoyable, and successful as possible.

For Students

As a student you can reinforce the text with three additional learning aids: *Video Basics 7 Workbook*, CourseMate for *Video Basics 7,* and *Zettl's VideoLab 4.0* DVD-ROM.

Video Basics 7 Workbook   The *Workbook* can test your retention and retrieval of video production basics. When doing the *Workbook* problems, try not to seek the answers in the text until you have finished a particular *Workbook* section. This way you will get a better idea of whether you have a sufficient grasp of a particular production process or piece of equipment so that you can apply it in a variety of contexts.

CourseMate for Video Basics 7   CourseMate for *Video Basics 7* includes an interactive eBook with highlighting, note taking and an interactive glossary, and interactive learning tools, including chapter tutorial quizzes, flashcards, and more. You can access CourseMate and other online resources at *www.cengagebrain.com.*

Zettl's VideoLab 4.0   The *Zettl's VideoLab 4.0* DVD-ROM lets you manipulate production equipment in a virtual studio or field environment and apply various production techniques from the text. For example, you can mix audio, frame shots, zoom in and out, create your own lighting effects, and have plenty of opportunity for editing. All you need is a laptop with a DVD slot.

WebTutor for Video Basics 7   WebTutor is a customized learning solution, keeping you connected to your textbook, instructor, and classmates.

For Instructors

For instructors, the following class preparation, classroom activity, and assessment materials are available.

Video Basics 7 Workbook   The *Workbook* can be used to test student retention and retrieval of video production basics and also serves as a primer for actual studio and field work. I have also successfully used the *Workbook* as a diagnostic tool for advanced production students. Having students do various in-class *Workbook* problems at the beginning of the semester (without the aid of the text) quickly reveals the strengths and weaknesses of their production knowledge and skills.

CourseMate for Video Basics 7   Cengage Learning's CourseMate for *Video Basics 7* reinforces course concepts with interactive learning, study, and exam preparation tools that support the printed textbook. See *www.cengage.com/coursemate.*

Zettl's VideoLab 4.0   Even if you lecture or conduct your lab activities in a studio, you may find it convenient, at least initially, to demonstrate some of the production techniques by first showing the class examples from the *Zettl's VideoLab* DVD. Such a primer seems to facilitate the use of equipment in an actual production or lab situation. *Zettl's VideoLab 4.0* now features Advanced Labs—challenging exercises designed to improve students' ability with the equipment and concepts introduced in the regular modules.

WebTutor for Video Basics 7   The WebTutor provides access to all of the content of this text's rich CourseMate and eBook from within a professor's course management system. CourseMate is ready to use as soon as you log on and offers a wide array of web quizzes, activities, exercises, and web links. Robust communication tools—such as a course calendar, asynchronous discussion, real-time chat, a whiteboard, and an integrated e-mail system—make it easy to stay connected to the course.

Instructor's Manual   The *Instructor's Manual for Video Basics 7 with Answer Key for Video Basics 7 Workbook* includes chapter notes with teaching suggestions and activities, multiple-choice questions, essay/discussion questions, and additional teaching resources. The manual also includes the answers to the exercises in the *Workbook*. Note that for the multiple-choice questions the correct answer is indicated by a > symbol and the page number where the specific problem is first discussed in the text.

ExamView® Computerized Testing   This testing aid lets you create or customize tests and study guides (both print and online) using the test bank questions from the online Instructor's Manual. ExamView offers both a Quick Test Wizard and an Online Test Wizard that guide you step-by-step through the process of creating tests. The "what you see is what you get" interface allows you to see the test you are creating on-screen exactly as it will print or display online.

If you are a qualified adopter of the text, you can order these resources through your local Wadsworth/Cengage representative. You may also contact the Wadsworth/Cengage Academic Resource Center at 1-800-423-0563 or get more information at *www.cengage.com/wadsworth.*

■ ACKNOWLEDGMENTS

As with the previous edition, I am indebted to Michael Rosenberg, publisher; Megan Garvey, development editor; and Rebecca Donahue, editorial assistant. Megan and her assistant were always available to quickly respond to my questions and requests.

Gary Palmatier of Ideas to Images and his team of superprofessionals translated my ideas into this book, as they have done so effectively for all of the previous editions. A big thank-you, Gary! We all—author and readers—benefit greatly from the brilliance and the diligence of my copy editor, Elizabeth von Radics. I am lucky to have someone of her caliber on my production team. Ed Aiona deserves special thanks for his impressive photographs. They help not only illustrate the equipment but also clarify specific concepts.

My gratitude also goes to Mike Mollett, proofreader; Medea Minnich, indexer; Christina Ciaramella of PreMedia Global, photo researcher; and Bob Kauser, Global Rights and Permissions Administration, Wadsworth/Cengage Learning.

I am grateful to the reviewers of the previous edition, all of whom made valuable suggestions: Dr. Nancy F. Kaplan, Hofstra University; Steven Mathena, Tri-County Technical College; Steven Middleton, Morehead State University; Ben Scholle, Lindenwood University; Lewis Trusty, Hawaii Pacific University; Randy Visser, Southern Maine Community College; and Kimberly Wells, Delta College.

As many times before, these colleagues of mine in broadcast education and the industry were always ready to help: Marty Gonzales, Hamid Khani, Steve Lahey, and Vinay Shrivastava of the Broadcast and Electronic Communication Arts Department at San Francisco State University; Rudolf Benzler, T.E.A.M. Lucerne, Switzerland; John Beritzhoff, Snader and Associates; Ed Cosci and Jim Haman, KTVU Oakland–San Francisco; Ed Dudkowski, Producer; Michael Eisenmenger of the Community Media Center of Marin; Elan Frank and Reed Maidenberg, Elan Productions; Professor Nikos Metallinos, Concordia University; and Professor Manfred Muckenhaupt, University of Tübingen. To all, a big thank-you!

This book could not have been done without the many volunteers who helped stage and modeled for the many photos in this edition: Socoro Aguilar-Uriarte, Karen Austin, Ken Baird, Hoda Baydoun, Clara Benjamin, Rudolf Benzler, Tiemo Biemüller, Gabriella Bolton, Michael Cage, William Carpenter, NeeLa Chakravartula, Andrew Child, Laura Child, Renee Child, Christine Cornish, Ed Cosci, David Galvez, Eric Goldstein, Poleng Hong, Michael Huston, Lauren Jones, Akiko Kajiwara, Hamid Khani, Philip Kipper, Fawn Luu, Orcun Malkoclar, Johnny Moreno, Anita Morgan, Tomoko Nakayama, Tamara Perkins, Richard Piscitello, Ildiko Polony, Robaire Ream, Kerstin Riediger, Joaquin Ross, Maya Ross, Algie Salmon-Fattahian, Heather Schiffman, Alisa Shahonian, Pria Shih, Jennifer Stanonis, Mathias Stering, Heather Suzuki, Julie Tepper, Takako Thorstadt, Mike Vista, Andrew Wright, and Arthur Yee.

My wife, Erika, gets a big hug for keeping me—and herself—in a good mood throughout the writing of this edition of *Video Basics*.

Herbert Zettl

Production: Processes and People

Today it is possible for you to use your cell phone and a small laptop computer to create a documentary in high-definition video and sound that will garner you an Oscar nomination. Right? Well, there is always the chance that you get lucky—once. But as a professional in the video business, you must be much more consistent and produce high-quality programs on a more regular basis. To achieve this goal, you must understand not only how a specific piece of equipment works but also how to get from idea to video image efficiently and effectively—the whole production process. You must also learn to work with people—a team of experienced production experts—all of whom must collaborate to create a worthwhile program and bring it to its intended audience. This book will help you become such a professional.

Part I explores how the production process works and how to move systematically from the initial idea to the finished production with confidence and minimal wasted effort. You are also introduced to the standard technical and nontechnical production teams.

angle The particular approach to a story—its central theme.

field production Production activities that take place away from the studio.

medium requirements All personnel, equipment, and facilities needed for a production, as well as budgets, schedules, and the various production phases.

multicamera production The use of two or more cameras to capture a scene simultaneously from different points of view. Each camera's output can be recorded separately (iso configuration) and/or fed into a switcher for instantaneous editing.

postproduction Any production activity that occurs after the production. Usually refers to video editing and/or audio sweetening.

preproduction The preparation of all production details.

process message The message actually perceived by the viewer in the process of watching a video program.

production The actual activities in which an event is recorded and/or televised.

production model Moving from the idea to the program objective and then backing up to the specific medium requirements to achieve the program objective.

program objective The desired effect of the program on the viewer. The defined process message.

single-camera production All of the video is captured by a single camera or camcorder for postproduction editing. Similar to the traditional film approach. Also called *film-style*.

studio production Production activities that take place in the studio.

Production Process

You are ready to roll. You've got a million ideas for shows, each of which is considerably better than what you ordinarily see on television. But how exactly do you get them out of your head and onto the screen? This step—the production process—is the core of all successful programs. It cannot be done intuitively; it must be learned. But don't be dismayed. This chapter provides you with a useful guide to moving from idea to image—your prizewinning masterpiece. It also explains the production phases and leads you through the preproduction steps. Finally, it helps you generate useful program ideas on demand and points you toward the ever-closer convergence of video and digital cinema productions, regardless of whether they are done as single- or multicamera productions in the studio or in the field.

▶ **PRODUCTION MODEL**
Organizing the details for moving from original idea to finished product

▶ **PRODUCTION PHASES**
Preproduction, production, and postproduction

▶ **IMPORTANCE OF PREPRODUCTION**
Moving from idea to script and from script to production details

▶ **PREPRODUCTION: GENERATING IDEAS ON DEMAND**
Brainstorming and clustering

▶ **PREPRODUCTION: FROM IDEA TO SCRIPT**
Program objective, angle, evaluation, and script

▶ **PREPRODUCTION: FROM SCRIPT TO PRODUCTION**
Medium requirements and budget

▶ **MEDIA CONVERGENCE**
Digital cinema and video and single- and multicamera use in the studio and in the field

◼ PRODUCTION MODEL

Don't be dismayed. A model is not a set of absolute rules; it is strictly a suggestion of how to approach and accomplish a difficult task. In this case it is meant to help you organize the many details necessary to move from the original idea to the finished product. The production model is not a foolproof system that works every time you use it but more of a road map for how to get from idea to screen image with the least number of detours.

The production model is based on the realization that the message that counts is not necessarily the one you start with but the one that is perceived by the viewer. This process is a bit like cooking: the final success of your undertaking is measured not by the ingredients you use (the initial idea) but whether your guests like the meal (the message actually received). Wouldn't it make sense, then, to start with an idea of how the meal should finally look and taste and then figure out what ingredients you need to make it?

This production model works on the same principle: once you have developed the initial idea, you move directly to what, ideally, you want the viewers to learn, feel, or do.[1] The **_production model_** suggests that rather than move from the initial idea to the production, you jump from the initial idea to a **_program objective_**—the desired effect on the viewer. Then and only then do you back up and decide on the medium requirements necessary to produce the intended communication effect. Because the final effect is the result of a process between what you present on-screen and what the viewer actually perceives, this all-important message is called the **_process message_**. **SEE 1.1**

As you can see, this model shows four distinct processes: (1) moving from the basic idea to the program objective (desired effect on the viewer) and the angle; (2) determining the necessary medium requirements in preproduction; (3) generating the program objective in the production phases; and (4) distributing the message (the production) to the target audience.

What happened to the process message? You won't really know what the actual process message is unless you observe a viewer watching your show and reacting to it. This is the weakest point in the production of video and broadcast communication. We rarely, if ever, know just what the actual process message is or how close the program objective came to the actual viewer impact.

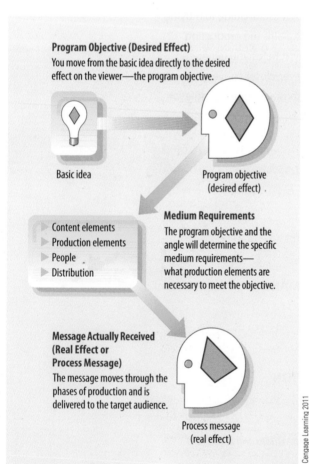

Program Objective (Desired Effect)
You move from the basic idea directly to the desired effect on the viewer—the program objective.

Basic idea

Program objective (desired effect)

- Content elements
- Production elements
- People
- Distribution

Medium Requirements
The program objective and the angle will determine the specific medium requirements—what production elements are necessary to meet the objective.

Message Actually Received (Real Effect or Process Message)
The message moves through the phases of production and is delivered to the target audience.

Process message (real effect)

© Cengage Learning 2011

1.1 PRODUCTION MODEL
The production model shows how to move from the show idea to the finished program with maximum efficiency.

1. This concept is based on the classic instructional design by Mager. See Robert Mager, _Preparing Instructional Objectives_, 3rd ed. (Atlanta: Center for Effective Performance, 1997).

Rating services estimate (more or less accurately) how many people are watching a particular show but not what they actually think, feel, or do while watching it. This is why smart producers of comedy series let a studio audience see each installment before it gets on the air. If a sure-fire joke does not generate audience laughter, it is rewritten on the spot or scrapped. **ZVL1** PROCESS→ Effect-to-cause→ basic idea | desired effect | cause | actual effect

Note: The **ZVL** icons point to related segments on the *Zettl's VideoLab 4.0* DVD-ROM. You can run each module when you see its cue in the text, or you may prefer to wait until you have finished reading the chapter and run all relevant modules at one time. The DVD-ROM is not an essential part of this book; it is meant to reinforce the text and to facilitate the transition from reading to actual practice.

■ PRODUCTION PHASES

Over the years certain routines—production processes—have evolved that can facilitate the complex job of getting ideas translated into effective shows. These processes include chores that need to be done *before* the production, *during* the actual production activities, and *after* the production. In production lingo we call these the preproduction, production, and postproduction phases. **ZVL2** PROCESS→ Process introduction

Preproduction includes all the planning and coordination of details before the actual production activities.

Production starts when you open the studio doors and turn on the equipment or when you load your vehicle with the gear for a field production. In production you actually encode, or translate, the original program objective into a series of video segments. Production involves the medium requirements—the coordination of production and technical people and the operation of the production equipment.

In *postproduction* you select the best bits and pieces of the recorded event, enhance their picture and sound quality as necessary, correct some of the minor production mistakes, and assemble the shots and the scenes into a coherent whole—the video program. For complicated programs that require a great deal of editing, the postproduction phase may take as long as, or even longer than, the preproduction or production period. **ZVL3** PROCESS→ Phases→ production | postproduction

This chapter focuses on preproduction. The details of production and postproduction take up the rest of the book.

■ IMPORTANCE OF PREPRODUCTION

In preproduction you develop the initial program idea, define the program objective, and select the people and the equipment necessary to translate your idea into effective video and audio images.

Meticulous preproduction is a key factor in maximizing your video production efficiency and effectiveness. There is a proven formula that you must not only remember but also always apply, even if the production you are doing is relatively simple: *the more attention you pay to preproduction, the more effective the production and postproduction phases will be.* Remember this advice especially when you are tired of organizing details and are itching to go on-location and start shooting. **ZVL4** PROCESS→ Phases→ preproduction

Normally, the preproduction activities require two distinct approaches: the move from idea to script and from script to production details.

■ PREPRODUCTION: GENERATING IDEAS ON DEMAND

All good productions start with a good idea. As obvious as this sounds, you may be surprised to find that one of the more difficult demands in professional video is coming up with good ideas consistently. Often the calendar or clock dictates when to be creative. Unfortunately, tight production schedules will not tolerate your waiting for divine inspiration. You must call on techniques that help you jolt your imagination even on a down day. Two well-known and effective devices for unlocking ideas are brainstorming and clustering.

Brainstorming

Brainstorming involves freeing your mind of the restrictions you impose on it because you feel, however unconsciously, that you have to think and say something that fits the situational framework and others' expectations. It is a form of "conceptual blockbusting" that ignores or breaks down traditional barriers to creative expression.[2]

Picture yourself for a moment as an observer of a brainstorming session of advertising people who are supposed to think of a "new approach to showing a family car that handles like a high-powered sports car." Six people sit in a circle; in the middle of the circle are two microphones and a small audio recorder. One of the people (P1 = person 1), who is also the team leader, starts with:

P1: "Knock, knock!"

P2: "Who's there?"

P3: "Nobody. It's raining."

P4: "Japanese calligraphy."

P5: "Slick roads."

P6: "Sports car–like handling."

P1: "Bullet-like fast."

P2: "Slalom ski race."

P3: "Replaces space shuttle."

P4: "Calligraphy of haiku poetry."

And so forth.

After a few more go-arounds, one of the participants gets annoyed at person 4, who consistently expanded on the theme of Japanese calligraphy and its aesthetic and spiritual meanings. Person 4, who works as a designer and is currently taking a workshop in Japanese calligraphy, defends herself by saying that this workshop opens up a whole new design world for her—poetry in motion. Some snickers. Person 1, the team leader, admonishes everybody that anything goes in brainstorming and that, initially, all ideas are equally valid. He reminds the idea team that there

---

2. See James L. Adams, *Conceptual Blockbusting,* 4th ed. (Cambridge, MA: Perseus, 2001).

should be no judgment passed as to the relevancy of the utterances, however far out they may initially seem. During the discussion period, person 4 says that she could easily paint a beautiful curvy wet road with one brush stroke on which the new red car could safely speed along. Bingo! This idea was finally translated into a highly successful car commercial: first you see the black road painted on the screen, then the red car moving fast, but safely, along the graceful curves of the shiny black road.

Although there should be no restrictions, successful brainstorming depends on a number of conditions:

- It is best done with several people.

- You start out with a general idea or related image (car commercial) and let everybody call out whatever springs to mind.

- It's important to let all minds roam freely and not evaluate or judge any of the ideas, however irrelevant they may seem.

- Document all ideas by audio-recording them or writing them down.

- In the review stage, recite the list of comments several times to discover novel connections.

If necessary, you can do brainstorming by yourself, but you will need some way of recording it or writing it down. One of the more popular solitary brainstorming techniques is clustering.

Clustering

In the middle of a piece of paper, write a single word that seems somehow central to your basic program idea or program objective and circle it. Now write down and circle another word that is somehow associated with your key word and connect the two. Write down other word associations and connect them to the last one circled.

In a short time, you will have created a cluster of words or ideas. Don't try to design a cluster or be logical about it. Work fast so that you will not be tempted to ponder your associations. Let your mind flow freely. When you feel that your ideas are exhausted, don't force yourself to find more connections or more-logical ones. The idea cluster seems to have a natural limit. You will most likely know when you have enough branches and it is time to stop. If one word or phrase is especially intriguing yet seems out of place, start a new cluster but leave the old one alone. Once you are at that point, look at the finished diagram and search for patterns. These patterns will inevitably reveal some novel connections and relationships that were not obvious before and can serve as springboards for the program objective (process message) and the medium requirements. **SEE 1.2**

As you can see, clustering is similar to brainstorming except that during clustering you create an immediate visual pattern that yields quite readily the major interrelationships of the various ideas.[3] But it is also much more restrictive than brainstorming. **ZVL5** PROCESS→ Ideas

> **KEY CONCEPT**
>
> Successful brainstorming and clustering depend on a free, intuitive, and noncritical flow of ideas.

---

3. Clustering as an idea-unlocking technique for writing was developed by Gabriele Lusser Rico in *Writing the Natural Way,* rev. ed. (Los Angeles: J. P. Tarcher, 2000).

1.2 CLUSTERING

Note that clustering starts with a central idea and then branches out in various directions. Clustering must be done quickly and uncritically; it is much like written brainstorming.

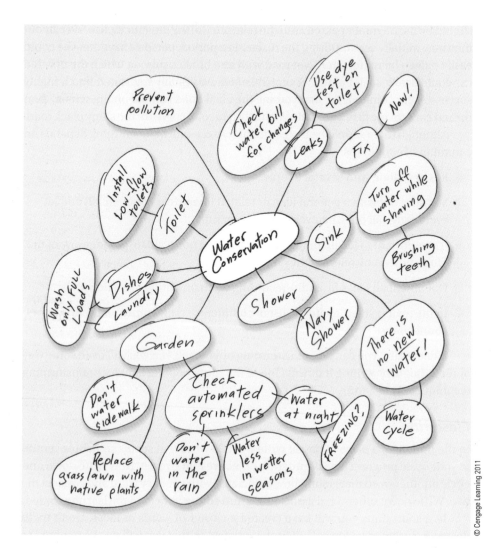

PREPRODUCTION: FROM IDEA TO SCRIPT

You must have some idea of what meal to prepare before starting to cook. The same is true in video production. Running around with your camcorder before deciding on what it is you want to tell your viewers is a wasteful activity at best. An effective production process depends on a fairly clear idea of what you want to communicate. As we all experience, however, most initial production ideas are rather vague and are rarely concise enough to serve as a definition of the desired communication effect—the program objective. This way of thinking is perfectly normal. As a matter of fact, you should weigh the potential effectiveness of several similar ideas before settling on a single one, but you should not move on to specific production details without first having a clear program objective.

For example, suppose you have just moved to Big City, and your daily commute prompts you to "do something about these crazy Big City drivers." You are certainly not ready at this point to plunge into production. Changing your idea to "do a documentary on the crazy Big City drivers" is no improvement. You need to think more about exactly what you want viewers to learn about becoming better drivers. The more precise your definition of the intended effect—the program objective—the easier it is to decide on the appropriate production format and the necessary procedures. **ZVL6** PROCESS→ Effect-to-cause→ basic idea

Program Objective

Exactly what is it that you want the audience to know, feel, or do? To "do something about these crazy Big City drivers" says little about what to do and how to go about achieving that "something." You need to construct a precise program objective.

Rather than tackle all the bad habits of the "crazy Big City drivers," you may want to isolate a single problem that is especially bothersome and that you consider important. As in most learning or persuasion tasks, specific objectives are usually more effective than general ones, and small steps are more easily managed and accomplished by the viewer than large ones. For instance, you may find that the misuse or nonuse of turn signals has become a serious threat to traffic safety. So, rather than address *all* the bad habits of Big City drivers, you can isolate a single objective: *Demonstrate to Big City drivers that turn signals help other drivers react to your changing directions and contribute to traffic safety.*

Once you have a clear program objective, you can start visualizing some possible approaches. Because you are a creative person, you come up with several good approaches to this video. But which one should you choose? What you now need is an effective angle. **ZVL7** PROCESS→ Effect-to-cause→ desired effect

> **KEY CONCEPT**
>
> The program objective describes the desired communication effect on the viewer.

Angle

In the context of designing a show, an **angle** is a specific approach to the story—a point of view of the event. Effective video programs often have an angle that is different from the usual treatment of the same subject and is more relevant to the viewer. Although the requirement of "finding an angle" has been abused by many newspeople in their attempts to sensationalize a basically uninteresting story, it is a valuable and positive way of clarifying and intensifying an event.

In our example one of the possible angles could be to show the terrible consequences of an accident that was caused by a driver who failed to signal his lane change. Or you may show the misuse or nonuse of turn signals from a bicyclist's point of view—one who has a hard time avoiding reckless drivers even during her relatively short ride to campus. You may find, however, that these drivers are not really reckless but simply absentminded or discourteous.

Isn't this now an entirely new angle on how to approach the turn signal problem? Yes, it is. Instead of telling Big City drivers that they are reckless and had better learn to use turn signals because it is the law, you may want to persuade them to be more courteous and helpful to one another and to the traffic around them. To accommodate and assist the less-than-perfect drivers, rather than accuse and attack them, may be a more effective angle for all sorts of traffic education. Instead of using threats as a means to make them use turn signals, you now appeal to their pride and self-esteem.

Unless you are the writer, you will find that scriptwriters often come up with a useful angle. Most writers will be happy to accept suggestions for an angle even if they later discover a better one.

Evaluation

Whatever angle you choose, always ask yourself two questions: *Is the proposed video worth doing?* and *Is it doable?* Despite your good intentions and desire to rival in your production the style of an elaborate Hollywood movie, you will not succeed unless you have the Hollywood budget and the production time to match. Money and time are production factors as real as cameras and microphones.

You will find that your clients—the school board, a big corporation, or a local cable channel—become more and more demanding. They expect you to come up with a superior product in an unreasonably short time for an unbelievably low budget. Give up right now? Not at all! But you may have to scale back your grand intentions and come up with ideas that are realistic, that is, that can actually be accomplished by you and your team and that will provide the client with the promised project on time and within budget.

Don't promise what you can't deliver. It is wise to accompany your creative leaps with the two reality factors: available time and money. You simply cannot do a million-dollar production if you have only $500 to spend. Or, if you have only four weeks to complete a show, don't attempt a production that requires on-location shooting in different parts of the world and two months of postproduction.

Script

You are now ready to write the script or hire a writer. You need a script, even if all it says is "no script." The script is an essential communication device among all nontechnical and technical production personnel. We discuss the various script formats in chapter 17. **SEE 1.3**

■ PREPRODUCTION: FROM SCRIPT TO PRODUCTION

In preproduction the script becomes the key for the actual production preparations. You must now translate the script into medium requirements, which include various people and production elements.

Medium Requirements

Normally, the **medium requirements** are expressed as workflow that includes selecting talent, determining technical and nontechnical personnel, and requesting studio or field facilities and equipment. **SEE 1.4**

As you can see in figure 1.4, the script now serves as the main guide for all further technical and nontechnical production requirements. As the producer your main preproduction contact will now be the director. Under your close supervi-

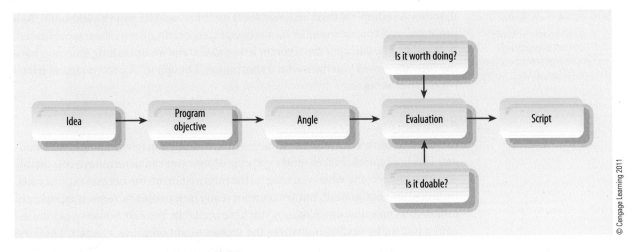

1.3 PREPRODUCTION: FROM IDEA TO SCRIPT
This preproduction phase involves the major steps that lead from idea generation to scriptwriting.

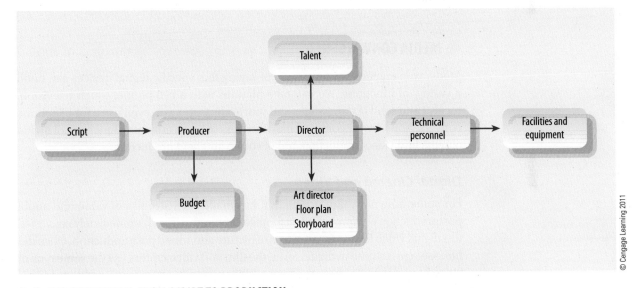

1.4 PREPRODUCTION: FROM SCRIPT TO PRODUCTION
This preproduction phase involves the major steps that lead from the script to the actual production process.

sion, the director chooses the talent, assigns the art director to design a set, and discusses with the technical supervisor the necessary personnel, facilities (studio, location, and postproduction facilities), and equipment (camera, lighting, audio, and video recorders).

Note that who does what in preproduction is not always as clear-cut as the figure implies. For example, you may find that sometimes the producer rather than the director will choose the talent or request a set design from the art director. This is all the more reason for you, the producer, to communicate frequently with all technical and nontechnical personnel involved in preproduction and to make sure that they all complete their assigned tasks on time—and let you know about it. As a producer, insist on having all of your messages, especially all e-messages, confirmed. If, for example, you sent the director an e-mail about an upcoming meeting, have the director e-mail you back with a short note: "OK, got it." *A good producer triple-checks everything.*

Budget

As you determine the medium requirements, you will also have to prepare the budget. This is a typical chicken-and-egg proposition: you can determine a reasonably accurate budget only when you have all the information on the necessary personnel, facilities, and equipment, but you cannot really hire people or request equipment unless you know how much money you have available. You can, however, get started with a budget by finding out where the money might be going. Figure 1.5 lists the typical general budget categories for a medium-sized video production. **SEE 1.5**

Although budgets are extremely important, we won't worry about money just yet but rather concentrate on how to make the video production process maximally efficient and effective.

▉ MEDIA CONVERGENCE

Media convergence is a fancy way of saying that specific digital devices can fulfill a variety of functions. We can take pictures with a cell phone, watch television, receive and send text messages and movie clips, and, yes, even use it for telephone conversations. In our context it usually refers to the overlapping functions of digital cinema and video production and of studio and field production.

Digital Cinema and Video

For some time now, film production has made extensive use of video and audio postproduction equipment. Most footage captured on film is immediately converted to a digital video format for all stages of picture and sound postproduction. Once the film footage is stored in digital form, the film and video editors use the same type of video equipment. To show the final movie version in a theater, the edited video is sometimes transferred back to film, mainly because many movie houses have not changed from traditional film projectors to digital ones. But many movie theaters are now using super-high-definition (HD) video projectors to show the video version without transferring it back to film.

The only part of traditional film production that has partially survived the digital video invasion is the camera. A few old-school filmmakers still insist (with some justification) that film delivers a softer, less in-your-face image than even the best digital cinema cameras.

But even this last holdout faces a serious challenge, if not inevitable defeat, from greatly improved digital cinema cameras. These super-HD digital cinema cameras not only rival or supersede the sharpness of the traditional film image but match other important characteristics, such as color fidelity, as well. You will read more about them in chapter 4.

PRODUCTION BUDGET

CLIENT:
PROJECT TITLE:
DATE OF THIS BUDGET:
SPECIFICATIONS:

NOTE: This estimate is subject to the producer's review of the final shooting script.

SUMMARY OF COSTS	ESTIMATE	ACTUAL
PREPRODUCTION		
Personnel	————	————
Equipment and facilities	————	————
Script	————	————
PRODUCTION		
Personnel	————	————
Equipment and facilities	————	————
Talent	————	————
Art (set and graphics)	————	————
Makeup	————	————
Music	————	————
Miscellaneous (transportation, fees)	————	————
POSTPRODUCTION		
Personnel	————	————
Facilities	————	————
Recording media	————	————
INSURANCE AND MISCELLANEOUS	————	————
CONTINGENCY (20%)	————	————
TAX	————	————
GRAND TOTAL	————	————

© Cengage Learning 2011

1.5 BUDGET SAMPLE
This budget example shows the basic cost summary, which lists the essential preproduction, production, and postproduction categories. Such a summary is normally accompanied by a more detailed breakdown.

Studio and Field Production

Up to now it has been convenient to divide the video production or film process into studio operations and field operations. After all, a *studio production* takes place in the studio, and a *field production* occurs outside of it—and you will certainly have to learn about both. But today more and more field techniques are brought into the studio, such as the use of a single handheld camera, highly flexible sound pickup devices, and low-powered lighting instruments for general, nondramatic lighting. Similarly, many field productions employ studio techniques, such as complex multi-camera and audio pickups of live sporting events and the relatively simple two- or three-camera setup of a wedding or charity fashion show in which each camera's output is recorded separately for later postproduction editing.

As you can see, this convergence of production techniques requires your thinking about not only whether to do your production in a studio or in the field but also whether it will be a ***single-camera production*** that produces all video for extensive postproduction (sometimes called film-style); a ***multicamera production*** in which each isolated, or iso, camera records simultaneously a different angle of the same event; or a multicamera setup for live transmission, in which the output of all cameras is fed into a switcher that allows the director to do instantaneous editing. **SEE 1.6–1.8**

This convergence means that you must be conversant with both systems, even if you later decide to concentrate on one or the other. Initially, you will find that starting with multicamera production—regardless of whether you work in the studio or outside of it—will make it easier for you to work in single-camera production later on. This is because when using two or more cameras simultaneously, you can actually see different camera angles side-by-side and how they cut together. In single-camera production, you see only one camera angle at a time and have to wait until the postproduction phase to find out whether they cut together smoothly during editing.

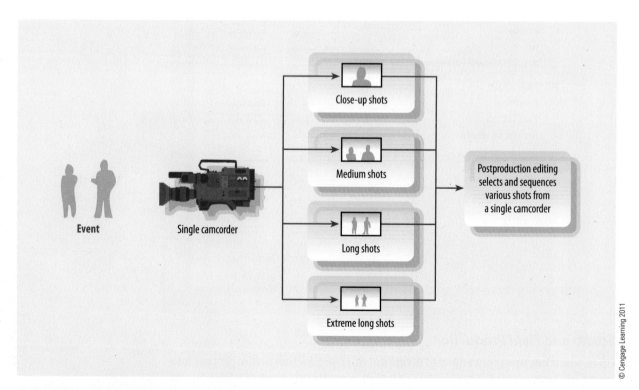

© Cengage Learning 2011

1.6 SINGLE-CAMERA (FILM-STYLE) APPROACH
In this production technique, only one camera is used to record all shots for postproduction.

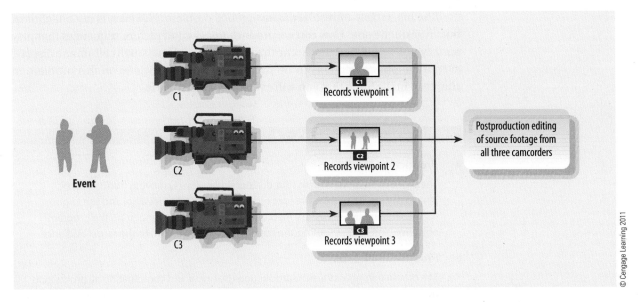

© Cengage Learning 2011

1.7 MULTICAMERA SETUP IN ISO CONFIGURATION
In this setup several cameras are used to simultaneously record the same event from various viewpoints.

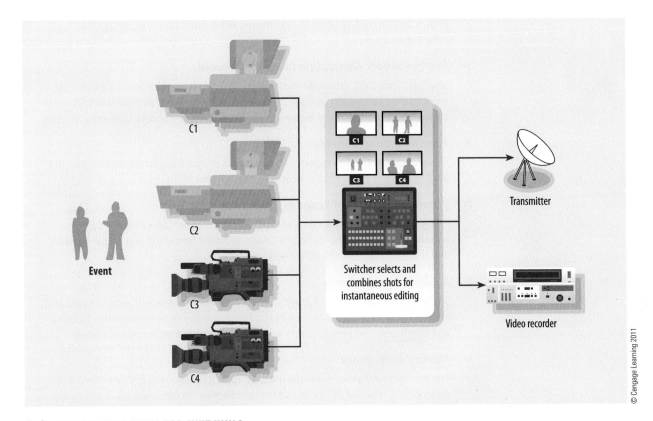

© Cengage Learning 2011

1.8 MULTICAMERA SETUP FOR SWITCHING
In this setup several cameras are used to feed their output to a switcher. The switcher enables its operator to select the appropriate shots and sequence them. This is also called instantaneous editing.

The big, largely unresolved convergence problem, however, is not a technical but an aesthetic one: How can we produce images and picture sequences that play equally well on a superlarge home theater screen and on a small cell-phone display, even if the phone happens to be smart? We elaborate briefly on this problem in chapter 6 in the hope that you will eventually help solve it.

M A I N   P O I N T S

▶ *Production Model*

The production model shows four distinct processes: (1) moving from the basic idea to the program objective (desired effect or process message) and the angle, (2) determining the necessary medium requirements, (3) generating the program objective, and (4) distributing the message (the production) to the target audience.

▶ *Production Phases*

The production phases are preproduction (planning and coordinating all production details), production (encoding the program objective into a series of video segments), and postproduction (selecting and sequencing the best video segments for a coherent video program).

▶ *Importance of Preproduction*

Preproduction is a key factor in maximizing video production efficiency and effectiveness.

▶ *Preproduction: Generating Ideas on Demand*

In video production, creativity means coming up with good ideas on a consistent basis on time and within budget. Two helpful methods are brainstorming and clustering. Both techniques demand a spontaneous and noncritical delivery of ideas.

▶ *Preproduction: From Idea to Script*

This preproduction step includes formulating a program objective, deciding on the angle, evaluating the entire concept, and writing the script.

▶ *Preproduction: From Script to Production*

This production phase concerns all medium requirements as well as the budget. It requires deciding on the nontechnical and technical personnel and on the facilities and the equipment for the actual production.

▶ *Medium Requirements*

The medium requirements include content elements (program objective, angle, and audience analysis), production and postproduction elements (equipment, facilities, and schedules), and people (talent and nontechnical and technical personnel).

▶ *Media Convergence*

The media convergence concerns the overlapping functions of digital cinema and video production and of studio and field production. Multicamera productions are sometimes instantaneously edited through switching and sometimes recorded as iso sources for postproduction. Single-camera productions usually resemble film production in shot acquisition and postproduction editing.

ZETTL'S VIDEOLAB

For your reference or to track your work, the *Zettl's VideoLab* program cues in this chapter are listed here with their corresponding page numbers.

EFP team Usually a three-person team consisting of the talent, a camcorder operator, and a utility person who handles lighting, audio, and/or video recording, and, if necessary, the microwave transmission back to the studio.

nontechnical production personnel People concerned primarily with nontechnical production matters that lead from the basic idea to the final screen image. Includes producers, directors, and talent. Also called *above-the-line personnel*.

postproduction team Normally consists of the director, a video editor, and, for complex productions, a sound designer who remixes the sound track.

preproduction team Comprises the people who plan the production. Normally includes the producer, writer, director, art director, and technical director. Large productions may include a composer and a choreographer. In charge: producer.

production schedule A calendar that shows the preproduction, production, and postproduction dates and who is doing what, when, and where.

production team Comprises a variety of nontechnical and technical people, such as producer and various assistants (associate producer and production assistant), director and assistant director, and talent and production crew. In charge: director.

technical personnel People who operate the production equipment, including camera operators, floor persons, and video and audio engineers. Also called *below-the-line personnel*.

time line A breakdown of time blocks for various activities on the actual production day, such as crew call, setup, and camera rehearsal.

Production Team:
Who Does What When?

I f you are a painter, you can do everything yourself: come up with the idea, buy the materials, prepare the canvas, struggle with form and color, and finally sign and date the finished work. You could even do the selling without other people involved. The entire creative process is under your control.

This is not the case with most video productions, unless you are simply video-recording your vacation adventures or working for a news department that uses VJs (video journalists). A VJ not only determines the best way to report a story but also does the camera work, the editing, and the voice-over narration. Although this is technically possible and saves money, it rarely results in a high-quality product.

Most professional video productions involve a group of people—a production team— with each member performing a clearly defined function.

This chapter focuses on what the people do and how they work together in standard video production.

▶ **PRODUCTION TEAMS**
The preproduction, production, and postproduction teams

▶ **PASSING THE BUCK**
What happens when production people do not work as a team

▶ **TAKING AND SHARING RESPONSIBILITY**
What happens when production people know their functions and work as a team

▶ **PRODUCTION SCHEDULE AND TIME LINE**
How to set up a production schedule and develop a realistic time line

▶ **PRODUCTION WORKFLOW**
How to move from one production activity to the next as efficiently as possible

You may best understand who does what by dividing the team into people involved in the preproduction, production, and postproduction phases. The preproduction team includes the people primarily involved with planning the production; the production team comprises the people who translate the ideas into actual video pictures and sound; and the postproduction people put together all the selected video clips, which contain the optimal video and audio segments, and give the whole production the final polish.

Some production people are involved in only one of these phases; others may be involved in all three. As you can readily see, no single individual has complete control over the entire creative process. Unlike the painter, you must learn to work as an effective team member, which means that you know exactly what is expected of you when assigned to a specific production position and also what everybody else is supposed to be doing. Once you know who is supposed to do what, when, and where, you can establish effective communication among the team members and let them know when specific tasks need to be done. A production schedule and a time line are essential in coordinating the different production steps and the efforts of all team members.

Regardless of whether you are a member of the preproduction, production, or postproduction team, you will find that some team members are more engaged and interested in what they are doing than others and that even the most conscientious team members have an off-day. But it is usually the weakest link in a chain that needs attention, not the strongest one. Rather than complain about the weak contributions of some team members, help them improve their performance. You must also get used to the idea that, in such a complex and high-pressure job as video production, occasional mistakes are inevitable. Fixing blame should then be done not to vindicate the other team members but to define the problem so that it can be avoided the next time.

The primary requisites for any kind of team are that all members respect one another and work for a common goal. A famous football coach and television commentator was once asked how to improve a team's sagging spirit and attitude. His answer: "By winning!" *Winning* in video production means enabling each team member to do his or her best to produce exceptionally good shows on a consistent basis.

▇ PRODUCTION TEAMS

The size and the makeup of the production team depend on the scope of the production. As mentioned before, electronic news gathering (ENG) for simple stories can be done by a single person, the VJ, who simultaneously acts as reporter, camcorder operator, and editor/narrator. While financially profitable for the news operation, this one-person-band approach is very hard on the individual who is doing it, and the results are clearly uneven. Even relatively simple electronic field productions (EFPs) are usually done with three people. The ***EFP team*** consists of talent, camcorder operator, and a utility person who takes care of the lighting, audio, and, if necessary, additional video-recording devices. A big-remote telecast, such as a live sporting event, may keep 30 or more people very busy (see chapter 15).

The accompanying tables summarize the major ***nontechnical production personnel*** and ***technical personnel*** and their principal functions. **SEE 2.1 AND 2.2**

Sometimes the production people are divided into above-the-line and below-the-line personnel. These designations are not clear-cut and have more to do

2.1 NONTECHNICAL PRODUCTION PERSONNEL

PERSONNEL	FUNCTION
Executive producer	In charge of one or several programs or program series. Coordinates with client, station or corporate management, advertising agencies, investors, and talent and writer's agents. Approves and manages budget.
Producer	In charge of an individual production. Responsible for all personnel working on the production and for coordinating technical and non-technical production elements. Often doubles as writer and director.
Line producer	Supervises daily production activities on the set.
Studio and field producers	In large operations, studio and field producers are assigned different producing responsibilities: the studio producer takes care of all studio productions, and the field producer handles all field productions.
Associate producer (AP)	Assists producer in all production matters. Often does the actual production coordination jobs, such as telephoning talent and making sure that deadlines are met.
Production assistant (PA)	Assists producer and director during the actual production. Takes notes of comments made by the producer or the director during rehearsals, which serve as a guide for the crew to fix minor production flaws before the final recording.
Director	In charge of directing talent and technical operations. Ultimately responsible for transforming a script into effective video and audio messages. In smaller operations also assumes the producer's responsibilities.
Associate, or assistant, director (AD)	Assists director during the actual production. Often does timing for director. In complex multicamera productions, helps to "ready" various operations (such as presetting specific camera shots or calling for a graphic effect).
Talent	Refers, not always accurately, to all performers and actors who regularly appear on video.
Actor	Someone who portrays someone else on-camera.
Performer	Someone who appears on-camera in nondramatic activities. Always portrays himself or herself.
Announcer	Reads narration but does not appear on-camera.
Writer	Writes video scripts. In smaller-station operations or in corporate video, the writer's function is often assumed by the director or producer or by somebody hired on a freelance basis.
Art director	In charge of the creative design aspects of show (set design, location, and graphics).
Music director/conductor	Responsible for music group in large productions, such as the band that plays on a variety show. Can also be the person who chooses all the recorded music for a specific show or series.
Choreographer	Determines all movements of dancers.

2.1 NONTECHNICAL PRODUCTION PERSONNEL *(continued)*

PERSONNEL	FUNCTION
Floor manager	Also called *floor director* and *stage manager*. In charge of all activities on the studio floor, such as setting up scenery, getting talent into place, and relaying the director's cues to the talent. In the field the floor manager is basically responsible for preparing the location for the shoot and for cueing all talent.
Floor persons	Also called *grips, stagehands,* and *facilities persons*. Set up and dress sets. Operate cue cards and other prompting devices. Sometimes operate microphone booms. Assist camera operators in moving camera dollies and pulling camera cables. In small operations also act as wardrobe and makeup people. Set up and ready all nontechnical facilities in the field.
Makeup artist	Does the makeup for all talent (in large productions only).
Costume designer	Designs and sometimes constructs costumes for dramas, dance numbers, and children's shows (in large productions only).
Property manager	Maintains and manages the use of set and hand properties, such as tables, chairs, and office furniture (set properties), and telephones, coffee cups, and flashlights (hand properties)—for large productions only. In smaller operations props are managed by the floor manager.

© Cengage Learning 2011

with who pays whom than who does what. In general, above-the-line personnel are people who do not operate any equipment; below-the-line people normally do. **ZVL1** PROCESS→ People→ nontechnical | technical

Let's find out who is normally involved in the three primary production stages: preproduction, production, and postproduction.

Preproduction Team

The primary responsibility of the ***preproduction team*** is to develop the idea for the video and plan its production so that the translation of idea to pictures and sound is as efficient as possible. For most standard EFPs, the preproduction team consists of the producer, the director, and sometimes the talent. In larger field and studio productions, the people involved in this initial idea-generating phase include the producer, writer, director, and scene designer or art director and sometimes the technical supervisor or the technical director.

The original idea may come from the corporate client ("Do a 10-minute video showing that the customer is our most precious commodity") or the producer ("Do a piece on your campus food service"), or it may come from a concerned citizen ("I would like to do a show on the pros and cons of timber clear-cutting"). Often specific show ideas, such as a particular angle for a commercial, are the product of several people's brainstorming.

Producer   Once the general idea is born, it is nurtured through all preproduction stages by the producer, who states the specific purpose of the show—the desired effect on the viewer (the program objective) and sometimes the process message

2.2 TECHNICAL PRODUCTION PERSONNEL

This category includes engineers who are actually engaged in engineering functions, such as installing and maintaining new electronic equipment; it also includes production people and technicians who operate such equipment.

PERSONNEL	FUNCTION
Chief engineer	In charge of all technical personnel, budgets, and equipment. Designs electronic systems, including signal transmission facilities, and oversees installations, day-to-day operations, and all maintenance.
Assistant chief engineer or technical supervisor	Assists the chief engineer in all technical matters and operations. Is often involved in preproduction activities of large productions. Schedules crews and participates in big-remote surveys.
Technical director (TD)	In charge of all technical setups and operations during a production. Does the actual switching in a studio production. Often acts as technical crew chief.
Lighting director (LD)	In charge of studio and field lighting; normally for large productions only.
Director of photography (DP)	Carryover from film production. Takes care of lighting and camera operation in single-camera productions.
Camera operators	Also called *videographers* and *shooters*. Operate studio and field cameras. Sometimes also do lighting.
Video operator (VO)	Also called *video engineer* and *shader*. Adjusts the camera controls for optimal camera pictures (also called *shading*). Sometimes doubles as maintenance engineer.
Video-record operator	Operates video recorders (VRs) during the production. In small field productions, the audio technician doubles as VR operator.
Video editor	Operates video-editing equipment. Often makes creative editing decisions as well.
Sound designer	In charge of creating the sound track of a complex production, such as a drama, commercial, or large corporate assignment.
Audio engineer	Often called *audio technician*. In charge of all audio operations in production and, in the absence of a sound designer, in postproduction. Sets up microphones and operates audio console during the show.
CG operator	Operates the character generator (CG), a computer dedicated to the creation of letters and numbers in various fonts.
Maintenance engineer	A true engineering position. Maintains all technical equipment and troubleshoots during productions.

© Cengage Learning 2011

(the message that the viewer actually perceives while watching the show). The producer also prepares a budget for the entire production.

As soon as the budget has been approved, you, as producer, need to hire and coordinate all additional personnel, equipment, and production activities. You or your associate producer (AP) will then devise a production schedule that indicates who is to do what and the times when the assigned tasks should be completed. This calendar is essential for coordinating the activities of all the people involved in the production.

Writer   The next step is writing the script. The writer interprets the program objective into a video production and writes down what he or she wants the viewers to see and hear. This production step is obviously crucial. It often determines the production format, such as instructional show, interactive multimedia show, or documentary, and the style and the quality of the production. Like the production schedule, the script serves as the guide for all further production activities.

Scripts are almost always revised several times. Sometimes the original content isn't accurate and needs some corrections. At other times the words sound too stilted and pedantic when actually spoken, or there may be some shots that are unnecessary or too difficult to produce. For all of these reasons, good video writers do not come cheaply. Settle on a fee before the delivery of the script. (There are various script samples in chapter 17.)

Director   The director translates the script into specific video and audio images and often selects the necessary production crew and equipment. In large productions, such as a drama for digital cinema, the director is greatly aided in this translation process by a storyboard artist (see figure 12.15). The sooner the director is brought onboard in preproduction, the better. The director may work with the writer early on, for example, to ensure the most effective interpretation of the program objective. He or she may even help the writer with the basic approach, such as changing the original idea of producing a brief instructional video into an interactive multimedia experience, or a documentary into a dramatic format, or a company president's address into a town hall–type forum. The director can also define or change the angle or help with ideas about the specific environment in which the event is to take place.

When directing an electronic field production or a big remote, the director is part of the survey team (see chapter 15).

Art director   The art director uses the script and the director's comments for the set design or specific location for the show. He or she is also in charge of decorating the set and designing the graphics, such as the titles for a show. The art director must create an environment that fits the overall style of the show and that facilitates the anticipated production procedures. Even the most beautifully designed set is useless if there is not enough room for camera movement and microphones or if it cannot be properly lighted. In digital cinema and large video productions, the production designer is responsible for these activities and normally assigns to the art director specific jobs, such as designing the set.

For normal studio productions, the art director prepares a floor plan, which is a diagram of scenery, stage properties (tables and chairs), and set dressings (wall hangings, lamps, and plants) drawn on a grid. (See chapter 14 for a more detailed discussion of the floor plan.) The floor plan is an important preproduction guide for the director and, for large productions, the lighting director (LD), audio engineer, and floor manager as well. With a good floor plan, these people can visualize the principal shots and place the cameras, lights, and microphones accordingly. The floor manager needs the floor plan to set up and dress the studio set.

Technical director   The preproduction team may also include a technical director (TD), or technical supervisor, especially if the production is a live telecast of a special event, such as a parade or the dedication of a new building. The TD can determine ahead of time the major technical facilities necessary for the proposed production.

Small production companies and television stations often combine roles. The functions of the producer and the director, and even the writer, might be carried out by a single person—the producer-director; and the floor manager might also act as art director and property manager.

Large productions may include on the preproduction team a graphic artist, a costume designer, a sound designer, and a choreographer. `ZVL2` PROCESS→ Phases→ preproduction

Production Team

Most routine EFPs are accomplished by a three-person **production team:** the talent, the camcorder operator, and a utility person who takes care of audio, lighting, recording, and transmission. If you use two cameras for a multicamera shoot, you have to add a second camcorder operator. In single-camera EFPs that are more ambitious, the camera operator may also take care of the lighting; this dual job is carried out by the director of photography (DP)—a carryover from film production.

In most multicamera productions, the production team is considerably larger. The nontechnical members include the producer and various assistants—associate producer and production assistant (PA)—the director, the associate or assistant director (AD) if it is a complex show, and the talent. Whereas the major part of the producer's job is in preproduction, in the actual production phase it is the director who is heavily involved. Sometimes there are several producers for a show series: a producer who arranges the budget and negotiates with talent, and a line producer, who supervises the daily activities on the set or in the studio. Some productions have a studio producer who is responsible for the studio segments of a show and a field producer who takes care of the segments video-recorded outside the studio.

The production crew, which comprises technical and nontechnical production personnel, normally includes the floor manager and floor persons (grips or utility persons), the technical director, camera operators, the lighting director, video and audio engineers, the video-record operator, the CG (character generator) operator, and the video operator (VO), who adjusts the cameras during the production for optimal video output. Large productions add an engineering supervisor and a maintenance engineer as well as various costume people, a property manager, makeup artists, and hairdressers. `ZVL3` PROCESS→ Phases→ production

Postproduction Team

The **postproduction team** is relatively small and normally consists of a video editor and the director. The editor will try to make sense of the various video-recorded segments and put them in the order indicated by the script. The director will guide the editor in the selection and the sequencing of shots. If you, as the director, have a good editor and a detailed script, you will have relatively little to do. You may want to see a rough-cut, or an "off-line" editing version, before you give the editor the go-ahead to prepare the final "on-line" video recording. If the project requires complicated special effects or the selection of unusual shots, you may have to sit with the editor throughout the process to select most of the shots and determine their sequence.

Complex postproduction may also include extensive manipulation of sound, called audio sweetening. It consists of remixing, adding, or replacing small or large portions of the original sound track and can take more time and effort than editing pictures. Major sound postproduction is done by a sound designer.

Most producers do not get involved in postproduction, at least not until the first rough-cut is done. Some producers cannot stay away from the editing room, however, and get intimately involved in every decision. Such fervor is, despite all good intentions, not always appreciated by the editor and the director. `ZVL4` PROCESS→ Phases→ postproduction

PASSING THE BUCK

Let's visit a television studio to watch the video recording of a visiting rock group.

When you arrive at the studio well before the scheduled start time, the production is already in the wrap-up stage. Neither the musicians nor the production people look too happy. The PA tells you that the recording session had been pushed ahead three hours because of the band's tight schedule. It becomes obvious that the session did not go as planned. There are small groups of people on the studio floor engaged in lively discussions. Let's listen in on what they are saying.

In one group, the band manager is complaining about poor scheduling and the "static look" of the show, and the lead singer is kvetching about the "bad sound." The executive producer tries to appease the band members, while the producer accuses everybody of not communicating with him. The director defends his overall visual concept and personal style and accuses the musicians of not understanding the "true nature of video." The band manager mutters something about the sloppy contract and the lack of coffee during rehearsals.

Some crew and band members vent their frustrations about technical problems. They argue about which microphones should have been used and where they should have been placed and about light levels that were much too uneven for good pictures. The LD counters by saying that she had practically no time for adequate lighting, mainly because she lost three hours of setup time. The musicians complain that the sound levels were too low, while the camera operators say that the music was too loud for them to hear the director's instructions in their headsets. They felt lost, especially because the director had not briefed them ahead of time on what shots to get.

The floor manager and his crew wonder aloud why they had no floor plan. It would have saved them from having to move the heavy platform on which the band performed from place to place until the director was finally satisfied with its location.

Everyone seems to be passing the buck and blaming everybody else for the production problems. What could have been done to minimize or avoid these issues? Before reading on, write down the complaints of the band and the production members and, by referring to figures 2.1 and 2.2, try to figure out who on the production team was directly responsible for the various problems.

Ready? Now compare your notes with the following recommendations.

Situation: The video-recording session was pushed ahead by three hours because of the band's tight schedule.

> ***Responsibility:*** Producer. He should have coordinated the band's schedule more carefully with his production schedule. Moving up a shooting schedule by three hours forces the crew to work unreasonably fast and causes stress. Most seriously, it reduces, if not eliminates, valuable rehearsal time.

Situation: The band's manager complains about poor scheduling and the "static look" of the show. The lead singer is unhappy with the sound as recorded.

> ***Responsibility:*** Again, the producer is responsible for scheduling and should have double-checked with the band manager about exactly when the band would be available for the studio production. The "static look" complaint is aimed at the show's director; and the "bad sound" is directed at the audio technician, who chose the type and the position of microphones and did the sound mixing. Ultimately, the TD is responsible for all technical processes, including the sound pickup and mixing. The producer should have brought together the lead singer, band manager, and audio technician in the preproduction phase to discuss the sound requirements. The producer should also have arranged for the band manager to meet with the director to discuss the visual requirements and the overall look of the performance. The director could then have discussed his ideas about the "true nature of video" with the band manager. Even if the initiative did not come from the producer, the director and the audio technician should have pressed for such a meeting. Obviously, there was little communication among the members of the production team. The blame for the sloppy contract goes to the band manager and the executive producer, and the PA should have arranged for coffee.

Situation: The choice of microphones and their placement is being challenged. The band members complain that the sound levels of the foldback—during which the sound as mixed was played back to the band members—were too low. The camera operators could not hear the director's instructions because of the music's high volume and were without direction.

> ***Responsibility:*** The type of microphones used and their placement is clearly the responsibility of the audio technician. Again, despite the drastically reduced setup time, a prerecording meeting with the key members of the band could have prevented most of the sound problems, including the low playback levels. The director or TD should have anticipated the intercommunication problems between the director and the camera operators. Even the best intercom headsets

will not function when used close to high-volume sound sources such as the speakers of a rock band. The director could have minimized this problem by meeting with the camera operators ahead of time to discuss the principal shots for each camera.

Situation: The light levels were too uneven for good pictures.

Responsibility: The LD is responsible for the uneven light levels. Her excuse is that she lost three full hours of setup time and that she had no floor plan with which to do even the most rudimentary preproduction planning. She could have contacted the director during the preproduction stage, however, or at least two days before the production, and asked about the floor plan and the lighting requirements for the show. In addition, when time is tight it is more sensible to illuminate the set with a generous amount of overall light rather than with highly specific light beams in limited areas. This would have made the lighting more even. (See chapter 8 for lighting techniques.)

Situation: The floor manager and his crew lacked a floor plan, which resulted in needlessly moving a heavy platform.

Responsibility: A floor plan would have told the floor crew the exact location of the platform on which the musicians perform. It would also have helped the LD decide on the basic lighting setup and the director on the basic camera positions. The lack of a floor plan is a direct result of poor communication among the preproduction team and, therefore, the ultimate responsibility of the producer. The director should have consulted the art director about the set and the floor plan during preproduction and then asked the art director why the floor plan was not done according to schedule. The TD, LD, and floor manager should have asked the director for the floor plan before the actual production date.

As you can see, a production team can operate successfully only when each member knows his or her assignment and all members are in constant communication with one another during the preproduction and production phases. Just as with team sports, if a single member of the production team makes a major mistake, the show goes down despite the superior performance of everyone else. Thorough preproduction could have averted many of these problems.

▮ TAKING AND SHARING RESPONSIBILITY

Fortunately, a subsequent visit to an elaborate multicamera EFP of an MTV segment turns out to be a much more satisfying experience than our studio encounter.

When you get to the location of the MTV shoot, you find a whole section of the street already blocked off by local police, and you have to show your pass. You see action everywhere. The audio technician and his assistants are adjusting the loudspeakers, and the camera operators are checking out some shots. You are greeted by the floor manager and introduced to the producer and the director. Despite the bustling activity, the producer seems amazingly calm and takes time out to explain the concept of the MTV segment: the lead singer drives an old Cadillac convertible down the street to a stop sign, where the dancers mob his car.

Some of the dancers are already practicing their routine, while others are coming out of a large trailer that serves as the talent's makeup and dressing room. Everybody seems relaxed, and you sense purpose and competence in what each team member is doing.

The director checks the time line (the schedule for the production day), posted by the trailer, and asks the floor manager to call for a run-through. There is instant activity: the dancers take their positions, the car is moved to the starting point, the camera operators get their opening shots, and the audio people start the sound track playback. So far as you can tell, the run-through goes very smoothly; the crew and the talent also seem happy with the outcome. Nevertheless, the director calls for a brief meeting of crew and talent to discuss some production problems.

The PA reads the notes that were dictated to him by the producer and the director during the run-through:

- "Dancers in the back can't hear the music."

- "Johnny [the lead singer driving the Cadillac] can't see the mark."

- "Shadows on him are too harsh when the car stops."

- "Need a tighter shot of Johnny."

- "We should be looking up at Johnny, not down on him."

- "Johnny is sweating too much. Light reflects off his nose."

- "Lots of dirt in the dancing area."

- "We can see audio cables in the background."

- "Some dancers are blocking Johnny on a close-up."

Which people would you ask to take care of these minor production problems? Let's look at the notes again.

"Dancers in the back can't hear the music."

Correction by the audio engineer.

"Johnny can't see the mark."

This means that Johnny can't see the mark on the curb that tells him exactly where to stop the car. The mark has to be moved to the stop sign.

Correction by the floor manager.

"Shadows on him are too harsh when the car stops."

Correction by the floor crew under the direction of the LD.

"Need a tighter shot of Johnny."

Correction by the director and, ultimately, the camera operator.

"We should be looking up at Johnny, not down on him."

The producer looks at the director. She turns to the specific camera operator.

Correction by the director and, ultimately, the camera operator.

"Johnny is sweating too much. Light reflects off his nose."

The director looks at the makeup artist. This problem has nothing to do with lighting.

Correction by the makeup artist.

"Lots of dirt in the dancing area."

Correction by the floor manager and the floor crew.

"We can see audio cables in the background."

The audio engineer says that he will take care of it.

Correction by the audio assistant and the floor persons.

"Some dancers are blocking Johnny on a close-up."

Correction by the director and the choreographer.

After this brief meeting, the director calls for a 15-minute reset break during which the production crewmembers go about correcting the problems. After the reset the director checks the time line and calls for another run-through. The following three hours are taken up by more rehearsals, two more such brief production meetings (often called "notes"), and several takes. The floor manager calls for a wrap (the completion of all production activities) a half-hour ahead of schedule.

Unlike the studio show of the rock band, this MTV field production was obviously well prepared in preproduction. During production the members of the technical and nontechnical staffs knew what they had to do, how to communicate constructively, and how to share responsibilities. The notes meetings were an effective and efficient way to identify major and minor production problems and to ensure that the appropriate people took care of them. Some directors in complex productions schedule as much as one-third of the total rehearsal time for notes and resets.

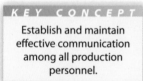

KEY CONCEPT

Establish and maintain effective communication among all production personnel.

▉ PRODUCTION SCHEDULE AND TIME LINE

Like the script, a production schedule is essential to proper production coordination. It shows the specific dates for preproduction, production, and broadcast. Although the terms *production schedule* and *time line* are sometimes used interchangeably, they are quite different from each other and fulfill different functions. The ***production schedule***, compiled by the producer, is the overall calendar for a production, which can span weeks. The ***time line***, on the other hand, is usually drawn up by the director and shows the allotted time segments for a single production day.

Here is an example of a production schedule for a 15-minute studio interview with the president of City College.

INTERVIEW PRODUCTION SCHEDULE

March 1   Confirmation by college president.

March 2   First preproduction meeting. Interview format ready.

March 4   Second preproduction meeting. Script ready. Floor plan ready.

March 5   All facilities requests due, including set and prop requests.

March 9   Production. Studio 1.

March 10   Postproduction, if any.

March 14   Air date (broadcast).

Note the four-day lead-time from the due date for all facilities requests (March 5) to the actual production date (March 9). This lead-time is necessary to ensure that the studio and all facilities requested are available.

The time line for the actual production is much more detailed and breaks a single production day into blocks of time for specific activities. As you recall from the MTV field production, the director, floor manager, and PA periodically checked the time line to see whether the production was on schedule. Following is the director's time line for the interview of March 9, as indicated on the producer's production schedule.

TIME LINE: MARCH 9—INTERVIEW (STUDIO 1)

8:00 a.m.   Crew call

8:30–9:00 a.m.   Technical meeting

9:00–11:00 a.m.   Setup and lighting

11:00 a.m.–12:00 p.m.   Meal

12:00–12:15 p.m.   Notes and reset

12:15–12:30 p.m.   Briefing of guest in Green Room

12:30–12:45 p.m.   Run-through and camera rehearsal

12:45–12:55 p.m.   Notes

12:55–1:10 p.m.   Reset

1:10–1:15 p.m.   Break

1:15–1:45 p.m.   Video recording

1:45–1:55 p.m.   Spill

1:55–2:10 p.m.   Strike

Let's examine more closely each of the time line's activities.

Crew call   This is the time when all production crewmembers (floor manager and assistants, TD, LD, camera operators, audio people, and other equipment operators) are expected to show up and start working.

Technical meeting   This meeting includes the principal nontechnical and technical people: producer, director, interview host, PA, floor manager, TD, LD, and audio engineer. The director briefly explains the program objective and how she expects the show to look (simple interview set, bright lighting, fairly tight shots of the college president). This meeting is also to double-check all technical facilities and the scenery and props.

Setup and lighting   According to the floor plan, the setup is relatively easy for the floor manager and his crew. The lighting is routine and does not require any special effects. The two hours allotted should be sufficient for both activities.

Meal   It is important that everybody be back from lunch at exactly 12:00 p.m., which means that everyone has to be able to leave the studio at exactly 11:00 a.m., even if there are still minor setup and lighting details remaining. Minor adjustments can be made during the reset time.

Notes and reset   If there are no major setup and equipment problems, the period set aside for notes may be considerably shorter. The available time can then be spent on a more leisurely reset: fine-tuning the lighting, moving a plant that may interfere with the person in front of it, cleaning the coffee table, and so forth.

Briefing of guest   While the production crew is getting ready for the first run-through and camera rehearsal, the producer, the interview host, and the PA (and sometimes the director) meet with the college president in the Green Room to go over the program concept. The Green Room is a small, comfortable room specifically set up for such a briefing.

Run-through and camera rehearsal   This run-through is to familiarize the guest with the studio environment and procedures, to check on the camera shots, and to rehearse the show's opening and closing. It is intentionally brief to keep the guest as fresh as possible. Because of severe time constraints, news interviews are normally not rehearsed. The producer may brief the guest during camera setup and lighting.

Notes and reset   The run-through and camera rehearsals will inevitably reveal some minor problems with the lighting or audio. The floor manager may ask the makeup person to straighten the president's tie and put a little makeup on his forehead to hide the perspiration.

Break   Even when working on a tight schedule, it is important to give the talent and the crew a brief break just before the production. This will help everybody relax and separate the rehearsal from the actual video recording.

Video recording The time allotted allows for a few false starts or closings. The fewer takes there are, however, the fresher the interview will be.

Spill This is a grace period to fix things that went wrong unexpectedly. For example, the director might use this time to redo the introduction by the host because the president's name was inadvertently misspelled in the opening titles.

Strike This activity does not refer to a protest by the crew but to the clearing of the studio of all scenery, properties, and equipment.

Such a detailed time line is especially important for an electronic field production. The EFP schedule normally includes additional items, such as loading and unloading equipment and transportation to and from the remote location.

Once you have a production schedule and a time line, you must stick to them. The best schedule is useless if you don't observe the deadlines or the blocks of time designated for a specific production activity. Experienced producers and directors move on to the next segment according to schedule, regardless of whether they have accomplished everything in the previous segment. If you ignore the time limits too often, your schedule becomes meaningless. **ZVL5** PROCESS→ Phases→ production

As you can see, knowing the functions of every member of the production team and coordinating them according to a precise schedule are essential to effective and efficient video productions.

> **KEY CONCEPT**
> Establish a realistic production schedule and time line and stick to them.

PRODUCTION WORKFLOW

Regardless of whether you work for a small independent video company or a television network, you cannot avoid hearing about production workflow. Like other such buzzwords, *workflow* has a variety of meanings. At the most basic level, workflow is how to move from one production activity to the next as efficiently as possible. This process may be as simple as adding transitions and effects to an edited video sequence, or as complex as receiving daily news stories from a number of sources and processing them for multiple newscasts.

An efficient workflow may also require establishing and maintaining effective communication channels. For example, the video editor in Seattle may want to show you, the producer, a specific editing sequence before continuing; the client and her sales staff in Houston would like to see some shots of the product they are advertising so that they can give you some feedback on how it should look; and the executive producer in New York may want to see the rough-cut before allocating more money for the project. Fortunately, in the age of web streaming and smartphones, you can send and receive text, video, and audio files with incredible speed from anywhere in the world. There are companies that specialize in such workflow communication, which can even automate routine channels. They can analyze your workflow needs, assist you in streamlining your workflow, and send high-quality pictures and sound files to the right people at the right time. **SEE 2.3 AND 2.4**

2.3 BASIC WORKFLOW

The basic workflow moves from the script to production and from there to postproduction; it requires reliable feedback channels.

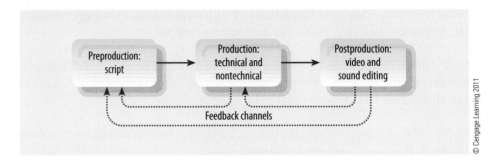

2.4 WORKFLOW COMMUNICATION

The key to a smooth workflow is a multidimensional communication system. All production personnel and other related agencies have access to optimally efficient two-way channels.

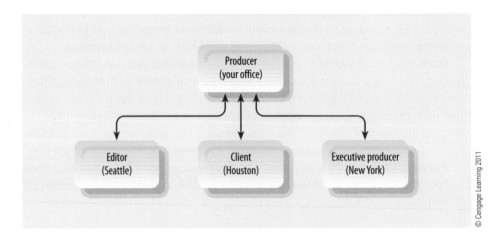

KEY CONCEPT

Efficient production depends on a reliable workflow.

The efficiency of your workflow is measured by the speed and the reliability of your communication channels and how fast you can move from one activity to the next with a minimum of errors and wasted effort.

MAIN POINTS

▶ **Team Members**

The members perform nontechnical and technical functions. Nontechnical people do not normally operate equipment; technical people do. The nontechnical people are also called above-the-line personnel; the technical people, below-the-line personnel.

▶ **Preproduction Team**

These people plan the production. This team normally includes the producer, writer, director, art director, and, occasionally, technical director (TD). Small production companies or television stations often combine preproduction functions to be carried out by a single person, such as producer-director, producer-writer, and video journalist (VJ). Larger productions employ additional preproduction personnel, such as an associate director (AD), a sound designer, and a choreographer.

▶ **Production Team**

An ENG (electronic news gathering) "team" may consist of a single VJ, who not only reports the story but also operates the camera and does the postproduction editing.

The typical EFP (electronic field production) team comprises the talent, a camcorder operator, and a utility person. Larger field and studio productions employ a much larger team. It may include the producer and various assistants, such as associate producer (AP) and production assistant (PA); the director and the associate director (AD); and the talent. The production crew usually includes the floor manager and floor persons (grips or utility persons), technical director, camera operators, lighting director (LD), video operator (VO), audio engineer, video-record operator, and CG (character generator) operator. In preproduction the producer is in charge of coordinating the various people and production details; in the production phase, the director is in charge.

▶ **Postproduction Team**

This team normally consists of the director, the editor, and, in complex productions, a sound designer who remixes the sound track. The director and occasionally the producer guide the editor in the selection and the sequencing of shots.

▶ **Production Schedule and Time Line**

A production schedule, prepared by the producer, is a calendar that shows the major preproduction, production, and postproduction activities. A time line, drawn up by the director, shows a breakdown of time blocks for a single production day.

▶ **Production Workflow**

An effective workflow helps you move from script to screen as efficiently as possible. The key factor is fast and reliable communication channels that connect all decision-making people of the production process.

ZETTL'S VIDEOLAB

For your reference or to track your work, the *Zettl's VideoLab* program cues in this chapter are listed here with their corresponding page numbers.

Image Creation: Digital Video and Camera

After having learned what video production is all about and who does what in producing a program, shouldn't you be able to run out and finally create a knock-your-socks-off movie or documentary? Not quite yet. You must exercise a bit more patience and realize that mastering the art of video capture includes a healthy dose of technical know-how. Before you embark on an ambitious production, learning the technical basics of video, the workings of a video camera, and how to use the camera to capture compelling images will save you time, money, and especially nerves.

Even if a camera's automated features enable you to produce acceptable images, there are many instances in which the automatic video controls work against rather than for you. You probably notice that when you photograph your friends against a bright window, they appear as silhouettes or, at best, look woefully underexposed. As a professional, you need to know how to override the camera's automatic features when the circumstances or your artistic intentions require that you go beyond the default settings.

Part II covers the basics of how an electronic image is formed—a prerequisite to understanding how to use a camera to its fullest technical and artistic potential.

KEY TERMS

480i/480p A scanning system of digital television. The *i* stands for *interlaced,* and the *p* stands for *progressive*. Each complete television frame consists of 480 visible lines, usually in the 4 × 3 aspect ratio, that are scanned as two interlaced fields (480i) or one after the other (480p). This system is generally referred to as digital SDTV (standard-definition television).

720p A scanning system of digital television. The *p* stands for *progressive,* which means that each complete television frame consists of 720 visible lines that are scanned one after the other. An HDTV (high-definition television) standard.

1080i A scanning system of high-definition television. The *i* stands for *interlaced,* which means that each complete television frame consists of two interlaced scanning fields. A high-end HDTV system.

1080p A scanning system of high-definition television. The *p* stands for *progressive,* which means that each complete television frame consists of 1,080 visible lines that are scanned one after the other. A high-end HDTV system.

analog A signal that fluctuates exactly like the original stimulus.

binary digit (bit) The smallest amount of information a computer can hold and process. A charge is either present, represented by a 1, or absent, represented by a 0. One bit can describe two levels, such as on/off or black/white. Two bits can describe four levels (2^2 bits); 3 bits, eight levels (2^3 bits); 4 bits, 16 (2^4 bits); and so on. A group of 8 bits (2^8) is called a *byte*.

codec Stands for *compression-decompression*. Can be one of several compression systems of digital video, graphics, and audio files.

compression The temporary rearrangement or elimination of redundant picture information for easier storage and signal transport.

digital Pertaining to data in the form of binary digits (on/off pulses).

field One-half of a complete scanning cycle, with two fields necessary for one television picture frame. In analog (NTSC) television, there are 60 fields, or 30 frames, per second.

frame A complete scanning cycle of the electron beam. In interlaced scanning, two partial scanning cycles (fields) are necessary for one frame. In progressive scanning, each scanning cycle produces one complete frame.

frame rate The time it takes to scan a complete frame; usually expressed in frames per second (fps). In analog (NTSC) television, there are 60 fields, or 30 frames, per second. HDTV can have variable frame rates for acquisition, editing, and delivery.

high-definition television (HDTV) Includes the 720p, 1080i, and 1080p scanning systems.

interlaced scanning The scanning of all the odd-numbered lines (first field) and the subsequent scanning of all the even-numbered lines (second field). The two fields make up a complete television frame.

progressive scanning The consecutive scanning of lines from top to bottom.

quantizing A step in the digitization of an analog signal. It changes the sampling points into discrete numerical values (0's and 1's). Also called *quantization*.

refresh rate The number of complete scanning cycles per second. Usually expressed in frames per second (fps).

sampling Taking a number of samples (voltages) of the analog video or audio signal at equally spaced intervals.

scanning The movement of the electron beam from left to right and from top to bottom on the video screen.

Super Hi-Vision A video system that produces extremely high-resolution video images. Generally used for digital cinema.

Image Formation
and Digital Video

Digital video is firmly established. All video production is done with digital equipment, perhaps with the exception of some high-quality analog camcorders that are still working and were just too expensive to throw away. Even if the video acquisition is analog, however, all other production steps, such as editing, require digital facilities. Although we are often made to believe that all digital is by definition high quality, you will find great quality differences in digital video. But how can you tell? This chapter answers this question and further explains what digital is all about and why we switched from analog to digital video processes.

These explanations involve a great amount of technical detail, which might become overwhelming rather than enlightening. Just take it step by step and try to get the overall concept of what is being discussed. Eventually, you will become as familiar with such terms and details as you did while exploring the various functions of your computer and its different software programs.

▶ **BASIC IMAGE FORMATION**
   Interlaced, progressive, and digital video scanning systems; and flat-panel screens, including LED, LCD, and plasma panels

▶ **WHAT IS DIGITAL?**
   The on/off principle of the binary system

▶ **DIGITAL PROCESS**
   Analog and digital signals; sampling and quantizing; compression and codecs; and downloading and streaming

▶ **DIGITAL PROCESS RESTATED**
   A user-friendly metaphor to explain analog and digital signals and the digital process

▶ **WHY DIGITAL?**
   Picture and sound quality in dubs, compression, and picture and sound manipulation

■ BASIC IMAGE FORMATION

The basic principle of image formation is dependent on the process of ***scanning***, which is the same for black-and-white television, color television, standard analog television, and digital high-definition television. The basic scanning process is still best explained by using the old standard monochrome (black-and-white) television set that uses a cathode ray tube (CRT) and by a similar color system. The picture formation of the current flat-panel video displays is much more complicated but works on the same scanning and color-mixing principles.

The back end of the monochrome picture tube houses the electron gun, which emits a tiny but sharp electron beam. In an old and heavy television set with a smooth glass screen, this beam is guided through the long neck of the picture tube to scan the inner face of the tube, which is covered with thousands of tiny phosphorous dots. The stronger the beam, the brighter the dots light up. **SEE 3.1** When the beam is too weak to illuminate the dots, the screen appears to be black. When the beam hits the dots at full strength, the screen looks white. In digital television these dots are called *pixels* (a contraction of *picture element*), a term borrowed from computer lingo. A pixel, similar to the tile of a mosaic, is the smallest element of a digital picture that can be identified by a computer.

The heavy analog color set has three electron guns in the back of the tube that emit three separate electron beams. The inner face of the color picture tube has neatly arranged groups of RGB—red, green, and blue—pixels, which are activated by the three beams. One of the beams is designated to hit the red pixels, the second

3.1 VIDEO IMAGE FORMATION
The electron gun in the back of the picture tube generates an electron beam. This beam is guided through the long neck of the tube to scan the thousands of dots covering the inside of its face.

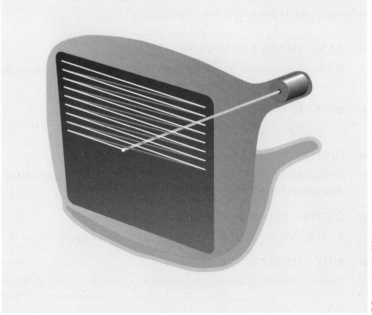

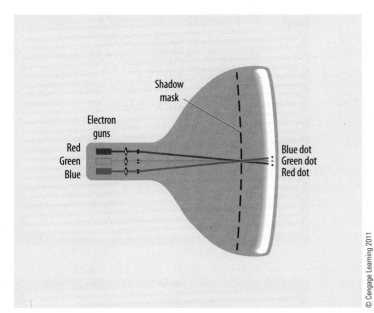

3.2 COLOR VIDEO IMAGE FORMATION
The color receiver has three electron guns, each responding to the red, green, or blue part of the video signal. Each beam is assigned to its specific color.

to hit the green ones, and the third to hit the blue ones. **SEE 3.2** Varying intensities of these three beams provide all the colors you see on the video screen. (See chapter 8 for a discussion of these three primary colors of light and how they mix into all other colors.)

Scanning Process

The electron beam, emitted by the electron gun, uses scanning to "read" the television screen, much like how you read a printed page: from left to right and from top to bottom. There are two basic scanning systems: interlaced and progressive. All standard analog television is interlaced; digital video can be interlaced or progressive.

Interlaced scanning   Unlike a person's reading line by line from top to bottom, in *interlaced scanning* the electron beam skips every other line during its first scan, reading only the odd-numbered lines. **SEE 3.3A** Then the beam returns to the top of the screen and reads all the even-numbered lines. **SEE 3.3B** Scanning all the odd-numbered lines yields one *field*. The subsequent scanning of all the even-numbered lines produces another field. The two fields compose one complete picture, called a *frame*. **SEE 3.3C**

Progressive scanning   In the *progressive scanning* system, the electron beam scans each line in sequence, much like the way we read. The beam starts at the top-left corner of the screen and scans the first line, then jumps back to the left and scans the second line, then the third, and so forth. After the last line has been scanned, the beam jumps back to its starting point at the top left and begins the process all

3.3 INTERLACED SCANNING

A In interlaced scanning, the electron beam first scans all the odd-numbered lines, from left to right and from top to bottom. This first scanning cycle produces one field.

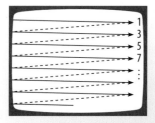

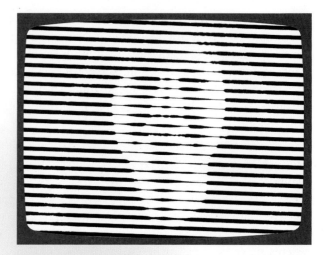

B The electron beam jumps back to the top and scans all the even-numbered lines. This second scanning cycle produces a second field.

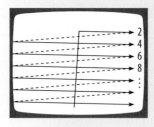

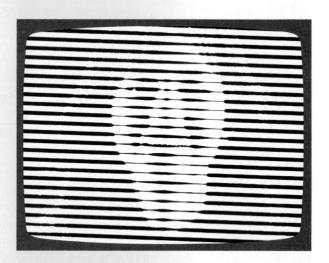

C The two fields make up a complete television picture, called a frame.

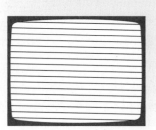

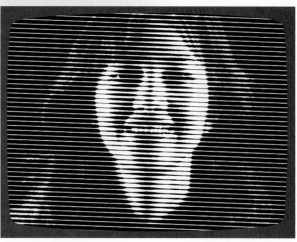

Edward Aiona

over again. The lines are, indeed, scanned in an orderly progression. All computer screens and a majority of digital video and cinema use progressive scanning. **SEE 3.4** Contrary to interlaced scanning, which produces half a frame (one field) for each scanning cycle, progressive scanning reads all the lines and produces a full frame for each scanning cycle. The number of frames progressively scanned per second is usually listed as *fps* (short for *frames per second*) and often called the **refresh rate**.

Digital Video Scanning Systems

Generally, digital television (DTV) has become synonymous with superior picture quality. One of the reasons for the improved quality of digital video over standard television (STV) is that DTV has a higher picture resolution (sharper picture detail), truer color, and a wider contrast ratio (more subtle grays between the brightest and darkest picture areas). Even if digital video is generally superior in quality to analog systems, however, not all digital video is high-definition television (HDTV). You will find that there is some confusion about just what constitutes "high-definition." Let's try to clarify the distinctions.

For all practical purposes, four digital systems have emerged for video production: 480p (*p* stands for *progressive scanning*), 720p, 1080i (*i* stands for *interlaced scanning*), and 1080p. The numbers (480, 720, and 1080) stand for scanning lines we can see on a normal television receiver. As usual, the digital cinema people didn't want to admit that they are now working with HDTV just like the video folks, so they promptly introduced an even higher-resolution standard that uses many more scanning lines for each frame, with thousands of pixels making up each single line.

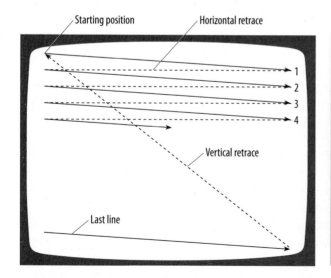

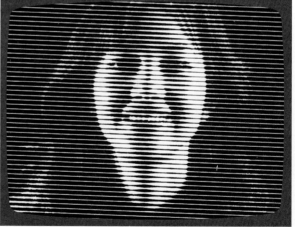

Edward Aiona

3.4 PROGRESSIVE SCANNING

In progressive scanning, the electron beam scans each line from left to right and from top to bottom. This scanning cycle produces one complete frame. The beam then jumps back to the top to start a new scanning cycle to produce another complete frame.

480p system   The picture of the ***480p*** system is composed of 480 visible lines (just about what you actually see of the 525 lines of the standard analog system) that are progressively scanned. It normally produces 60 complete frames (not fields) per second. Because of the striking picture quality, the 480p system is sometimes regarded as HDTV, although technical classifications do not include it in the high-definition category. The main difference of 480p is that it can scan a 16 × 9 (wide-screen) picture area.

720p system   The ***720p*** system produces 720 visible lines that are progressively scanned. Its normal refresh rate is 60 frames per second. The high number of lines results in very sharp pictures that are absolutely high-definition. The 720p system is in the HDTV category. It normally scans a 16 × 9 picture area.

1080i system   The ***1080i*** system uses interlaced scanning to save bandwidth. This means that its signals can be transported through a smaller pipeline than if its scanning were progressive. Although the 1080i system produces only 30 frames (60 fields) or less per second, its extremely high number of scanning lines contributes to higher-definition video than with either the 480p or the 720p system. It is currently the highest-quality broadcast HDTV system. It normally scans a 16 × 9 picture area.

1080p system   The ***1080p*** system uses progressive scanning. All visible lines are scanned for each frame. 1080p video cannot be broadcast because of its excessively high bandwidth. It is usually reserved for digital cinema, which uses the cinematic 24 frames per second; but this low refresh rate is generally boosted to 60 fps during playback (but not for transmission) to avoid flicker.

Super-high-definition scanning systems   These systems, called ***Super Hi-Vision*** or ultra-high-definition television (UHTV), are currently used primarily for digital cinema. Some are firmly in place, whereas others are still in development.

4K system   This system consists of 4,000 or more pixels per scanning line (horizontal resolution) and more than 2,000 scanning lines (vertical resolution). The scanning is progressive and usually varies among 24 fps, 48 fps, and 60 fps (see chapter 4).

8K system   This ultra-high-definition system operates with a horizontal resolution of close to, or sometimes even more than, 8,000 pixels per line and a vertical resolution of more than 7,000 scanning lines. All lines are scanned progressively.

Both K systems are intended primarily for very large-screen digital cinema projection and not for broadcast television. Transmitting such a great amount of video information as broadcast signals is currently neither practical nor necessary because home TV sets could not reproduce such super-high-definition video.

Note that the video quality of all systems depends not only on the number of pixels that make up each scanning line but also on how much the video signal is compressed. The more compression imposed on a signal, the less high-fidelity it becomes. We discuss compression further later in this chapter.

Variable scanning systems   Most high-end camcorders have a variable scanning system that can change the 60 frames per second to a higher or lower *frame rate*. For example, many DPs (directors of photography) prefer a frame rate of 24 fps when acquiring footage for digital cinema, but you can also lower it to 15 fps or boost it to 60 fps or even higher. The very low and very high frame rates allow for smooth accelerated- and slow-motion effects.

Flat-Panel Displays

Almost all digital video is viewed on flat-panel displays. One of the great advantages of flat-panel displays over the old CRT television sets is that the flat panel can get quite large—from the familiar small foldout video camera monitor to a large home theater–type screen—without getting much thicker. Other advantages of flat-panel displays are improved color rendition (colors that are more subtle), greater contrast ratio and more shades in between, and generally a higher resolution (more pixels per square inch). One of the major quality criteria for flat-panel displays is the black level, that is, how black the black looks. The darker the blacks are, the more vivid the rest of the colors.

You may find, however, that sometimes video images on flat-panel displays take on a pasty, almost posterized look, which despite the high resolution smacks of low-quality analog pictures. This usually happens when standard-definition or highly compressed video is shown on the high-definition flat-panel television set. But if you don't get too close to the screen, flat-panel displays make even such relatively low-definition video look surprisingly good.

LED, LCD, and plasma panels   The three most popular flat-panel systems are the LED (light-emitting diodes), LCD (liquid crystal display), and plasma panels. The LED panels consist of many tiny light bulbs, each of which makes up a pixel and is activated by the video signal. The LCD and plasma panels use two transparent sheets that contain, sandwichlike, either a liquid (LCD) or a gas (plasma), which let a backlight shine through in various configurations when a video signal is applied. All produce stunning color video, and you would be hard-pressed to tell one system from the other by simply looking at the image. The advantage of an LED panel is that it uses less power and doesn't run as hot as the other two panel systems.

WHAT IS DIGITAL?

All digital video and the way computers process information are based on a binary code that uses on/off, either/or values for all their operations. The *on* state is represented by a 1, and the *off* state is represented by a 0. These **binary digits**, or **bits** for short, operate on the light-bulb principle: if you have a 1, the light bulb is on; if you have a 0, the light bulb is off. The digital world runs on the either/or principle: either the light is on, or it is off. It does not know any in-betweens.

◾ DIGITAL PROCESS

At first glance this either/or system of binary digits (0 or 1) may seem clumsy and quite contrary to our daily experience, which, as we all know, has many in-betweens. But this rather pigheaded either/or system has as its overwhelming advantage the great resistance to data distortion and error. It also permits any number of combinations and shuffling around—an extremely important feature when manipulating pictures and sound.

Analog and Digital Signals

An ***analog*** signal is an electrical copy of the original stimulus, such as somebody's singing into a microphone. The technical definition is that the analog signal fluctuates exactly like the original stimulus. The analog signal is also continuous, which means that it never intentionally skips any part of the signal, however small the skip may be (see figure 3.5).

The ***digital*** signal, on the other hand, is purposely discontinuous. It takes the analog signal and selects points (instances) at equal intervals (see figure 3.6). These successive points represent the original signal—a process called ***sampling***.

Digital System

In the digitizing process, the analog signal is continuously sampled at fixed intervals; the samples are then quantized (assigned a concrete value) and coded into 0's and 1's.

Sampling   In this process a number of samples (voltages) are taken of the analog video or audio signal at equally spaced intervals. When you take and measure a relatively large number of instances at shorter intervals from the original analog signal, you have a high sampling rate. When you take a reading of relatively few instances at larger intervals, you have a lower sampling rate. A higher sampling rate produces better signals. The sampling rate of a video signal is usually expressed in megahertz.

Quantizing   The ***quantizing*** step in the digitizing process changes the sampling points (instances) into discrete numerical values (0's and 1's) by giving each point a specific number.

Compression and Codecs

The process of ***compression*** includes the temporary rearrangement or elimination of all data that are not absolutely necessary for preserving the original quality of the video and audio signals for storage and transport. The process of rearranging rather than throwing away is called *lossless* compression; the compression that actually deletes redundant data is the *lossy* kind.

Lossless compression   The advantage of lossless compression is that it maintains the original makeup of the digital video and audio signals. The disadvantage is that the system still has to manage overly large files. Such files are usually too bulky for streaming your favorite music for uninterrupted listening or for watching a movie trailer on your computer without having to wait for a prolonged download.

Lossy compression   The advantage of lossy compression is that it can make a large file considerably smaller, which will then take up less space when stored on a computer disk. The files can also be transported faster, which allows streaming. With the help of compression, you can listen to your favorite song from beginning to end without occasional interruptions to wait for the rest of the data to catch up, and you can squeeze an entire motion picture onto a single digital disc. The disadvantage is that higher compression inevitably reduces picture and sound quality.

There are lossy compression systems, such as MPEG-2, that produce amazingly high-fidelity pictures. They are designed to ignore certain picture detail that does not change from frame to frame. For example, MPEG-2 might not bother with repeating the green of the grass from frame to frame when showing a close-up of a golf ball rolling toward the cup but will simply add the digital data that show the rolling ball. Whenever necessary, the compression system borrows the green-grass information from the frame that initially showed the grass the first time. MP3 is a lossy compression system for audio files. The highly efficient and versatile MPEG-4 system operates in quite a few different incompatible configurations, depending, for example, on whether you want to stream your video over the Internet or compress a 3D spectacular.

> **KEY CONCEPT**
>
> Compression rearranges digital data (picture and sound information) or eliminates redundant data to increase storage capacity and speed up signal transport.

Codecs   All such compression techniques are part of different ***codecs***—*compression-dec*ompression systems—which are used for a variety of compression purposes. Apple QuickTime, for example, has several codecs, such as a high-quality, less-lossy one for screening your masterpiece and a fairly lossy one for sending it over the Internet to share with friends. Why worry about codecs when all you want to do is produce a nice video story? Because if your camera operates with a different codec than your computer, you won't be able to view your beautiful footage on your computer much less edit it into the prize-winning documentary.

> **KEY CONCEPT**
>
> A codec is a compression standard.

Downloading and Streaming

These concepts refer to digital signal transport. When downloading, the files are sent as data packets. Because these packets are often transferred out of order, you must wait for the downloading process to finish before you can watch a video or listen to an audio file.

When streaming data, the digital files are sent as a continuous data flow that can be viewed and listened to while the delivery is under way. You can listen to the first part of a song while the rest of it is still being delivered.

■ DIGITAL PROCESS RESTATED

You are probably tired by now of all the technical talk, so let's restate the digital process in a more user-friendly way, using a metaphor that helps explain the important difference between the two signal types and why we go through such technical maneuvers to change an analog signal to a digital one. Note that this metaphor is not necessarily technically accurate but is merely intended to simplify and illustrate the complex digital process.

Analog Signal

Let's look at a graphic representation of a simple analog electrical wave. Such waves, which are normally variously shaped, make up audio and video signals. **SEE 3.5**

Now assume that such waves are quite long, have slightly different shapes (different frequencies and amplitudes), and are made from garden hoses. These hoses (analog signals) must now be shipped by truck to different locations (video and audio signal transport and recording). The requirement is that the original shape of the bent hoses (signals) cannot be disturbed even to a slight degree (no signal distortion) during shipping. But even the most expensive shipping company (high-end equipment) cannot prevent the long hoses from getting some kinks (signal noise) during packing into the long and cumbersome crates (analog recording) and during transport (signal transport). When the hoses with the kinks are then used as models for wave duplication (dubbing), the various distortions from the original curves are not only maintained but often exacerbated by additional kinks (added signal noise and artifacts).

Digital Signal and Quantizing

Somebody very smart in the packing division comes up with a radical idea: why not cut up the hoses into smaller pieces and number each piece before shipping (quantizing)? This way the hoses can be more easily packed and shipped in smaller crates (packets) and in smaller trucks (bandwidth). Because the shipment contains a plan of the hoses' original curves (computer software), the numbered pieces can be reassembled to look like the original hoses (analog signals).

Sampling

An equally smart colleague in the assembly division discovers that when you cut a hose into very small, equally spaced pieces (sampling), you don't need all the pieces to represent the hose's original curves (high sampling rate). If, however, you cut the hose into just a few large pieces to save time and money, they can no longer accurately simulate the original curves (low sampling rate). As a result, the digital representation of the analog signal would be of much lower quality. **SEE 3.6**

Compression and Transport

The sampling gave the person in the packing division another idea: because each piece of hose has a specific number, you may be able to repack the pieces so that all the straight pieces can be squeezed in one small box and the curved ones in another (lossless compression). This would certainly save space (smaller files) and allow smaller trucks to be used for transport (smaller bandwidth). Or, he might even get away with throwing away some of the pieces before packing them, such as the parts that make up long stretches before the first curve, which serve no real function when simulating waves (lossy compression). Nobody would notice the missing parts anyway. The smart packer was right on both counts.

While testing how much he could throw away, however, he also discovered that the more hose pieces (data) you throw away, the less accurate the reassembly of the waves will be (low picture and sound quality).

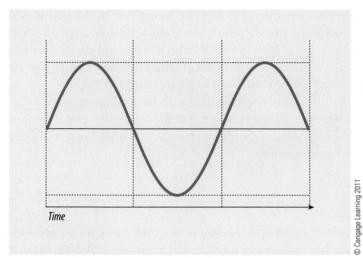

3.5 ANALOG SINE WAVE

This figure shows a visual representation of a simple analog electrical wave.

Time

© Cengage Learning 2011

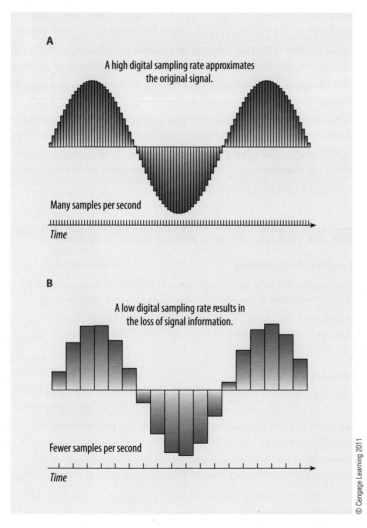

A

A high digital sampling rate approximates the original signal.

Many samples per second

Time

B

A low digital sampling rate results in the loss of signal information.

Fewer samples per second

Time

© Cengage Learning 2011

3.6 SAMPLING

To convert an analog wave into a digital one, it is divided and measured at equally spaced intervals.

A A high sampling rate looks more like the original wave; most of the original wave is retained.

B A low sampling rate looks less like the original wave; not much of the original wave remains.

The transportation manager decided that the pieces can be shipped in two ways. One way is to load all the straight pieces in one truck, all the curved pieces in a second truck, and a mixture of both in a third. With this method the receiver has to wait until all trucks have arrived and all boxes are opened (downloading) before the assembly of the various curved hoses can begin (opening the file).

The second method is to load several trucks with boxes that contain enough pieces to get started with the assembly of some of the hoses. The first hoses are already functional (the beginning of the file can be opened) while the rest of them arrive one after the other (streaming).

◼ WHY DIGITAL?

After juggling all these technical systems, you may wonder why we bother with digital in the first place. After all, we can produce and modulate analog signals that perfectly represent the original stimuli. In fact, the binary process seems rather crude. Because its entire language is made up of only two digits—0s and 1s—it must, for example, write the simple number 31 as 0001 1111. But, as you have just learned, this rather simple on/off, either/or principle is its major strength: the binary either/or principle of the digital system does not allow ambiguities, which would show up as picture and sound distortions. It allows you to make a great number of copies, with the last looking just as good as the original. Copies of an analog recording, on the other hand, get progressively worse.

Another major advantage for video is that you can compress the signals to save storage space and facilitate signal transport. Finally, it lets you manipulate pictures and sound in a controlled way—and even paint pictures and create sounds simply by arranging the pixels in a specific way. The relative clumsiness of the system is more than compensated for by its incredible speed.

M A I N   P O I N T S

▶ **Interlaced and Progressive Scanning**

An interlaced television frame is made up of two scanning fields, which are necessary for one complete frame. Interlaced scanning scans every other line, then goes back and scans the lines that were skipped. Progressive scanning scans every line. In progressive scanning, each scanning cycle produces not fields but a complete video frame. The frame rate, or refresh rate, can vary.

▶ **Digital Video Scanning Systems**

The most prevalent digital television scanning systems are 480p, 720p, 1080i, and 1080p. These systems produce video with higher resolution than standard analog television, improved color, and more subtle shadings between the brightest and darkest picture areas. High-definition television (HDTV) uses the 720p and 1080i scanning systems; super-high-definition digital cinema (4K and 8K systems) uses a higher number of scanning lines, with each line made up of thousands of pixels.

▶ ***Variable Scanning Systems***

Some video cameras, especially high-end digital cinema cameras, have a variable scanning system that can produce the standard movie frame rate of 24 frames per second (fps) or even lower as well as the HDTV 60 fps and even a very high frame rate for slow-motion effects.

▶ ***Flat-Panel Displays***

There are three flat-panel systems: LED, LCD, and plasma panels. Although they operate on different complex technical principles, their pixels are all activated by the video signal. The LED panels are more economical in power consumption and generate less heat than the other two systems.

▶ ***Analog and Digital Signals***

An analog signal fluctuates exactly like the original stimulus. A digital signal is based on a binary code that uses on/off, either/or values represented by 0's and 1's; it is purposely discontinuous.

▶ ***Sampling and Quantizing***

Digital signals sample the analog signal at equally spaced intervals and assign each sample a specific binary number—the process of quantizing. Each number consists of a combination of 0's and 1's. The higher the sampling rate, the higher the picture quality. Digital signals are very robust and do not deteriorate over multiple generations.

▶ ***Compression and Codecs***

Digital signals can be compressed; analog signals cannot. Compression eliminates redundant or unnecessary picture information to increase storage capacity and speed up signal transport and video and audio processing. Lossless compression rearranges the data into less space. Lossy compression throws away redundant or unimportant data. There are several codec (compression-decompression) systems that offer various means and degrees of compression.

▶ ***Downloading and Streaming***

Downloading means that the data are sent in packets that are often out of order. You need to wait until all packets have arrived before you can open the file. Streaming means that you can open the file and listen to and watch the first part while the data delivery of the balance of the file is still in progress.

▶ ***Why Digital?***

The digital process permits a great number of copies to be made without any deterioration to picture and sound quality, various forms of compression and relatively safe signal transport, and the manipulation of pictures and sound. It can also be used to create new pictures and sound synthetically.

KEY TERMS

aperture Iris opening of a lens; usually measured in f-stops.

beam splitter Optical device within the camera that splits the white light into the three additive primary light colors: red, green, and blue.

camcorder A portable camera with the video recorder built into it.

camera chain The camera and the associated electronic equipment, consisting of the power supply, sync generator, and camera control unit.

camera control unit (CCU) Equipment, separate from the actual camera, that allows the video operator to adjust the color and brightness balance before and during the production.

CCD Stands for *charge-coupled device*. One of the popular imaging devices in a studio camera or camcorder.

chrominance channel Contains the RGB video signals or some combination thereof. Also called *color, and C, channel*.

CMOS Stands for *complementary metal-oxide semiconductor*. A high-quality imaging device similar to a CCD.

DSLR camera Stands for *digital single-lens reflex camera*. Basically a still-photo camera that can also produce video footage. It has an optical viewfinder that permits viewing through the lens for still pictures. In the video mode, it switches to an electronic image.

ENG/EFP camera Highly portable, high-end self-contained camera without a built-in video recorder used for electronic field production.

fast lens A lens that permits a relatively great amount of light to pass through at its largest aperture (lowest f-stop number). Can be used in low-light conditions.

focal length With the lens set at infinity, the distance from the iris to the plane where the picture is in focus. Normally measured in millimeters or inches.

f-stop The scale on the lens, indicating the aperture. The larger the f-stop number, the smaller the aperture; the smaller the f-stop number, the larger the aperture.

iris Adjustable lens-opening mechanism. Also called *lens diaphragm*.

luminance channel Contains the black-and-white part of a video signal. It is mainly responsible for the sharpness of the picture. Also called *luma, or Y, channel*.

sensor A solid-state imaging device in a video or digital cinema camera that converts the optical image into electric energy—the video signal. Also called *CCD, chip, and CMOS*.

slow lens A lens that permits a relatively small amount of light to pass through (relatively high f-stop number at its largest aperture). Requires higher light levels for optimal pictures.

viewfinder A small video screen or flat-panel display on a camera that shows the black-and-white or color picture the camera generates. The flat-panel displays are also called *monitors*.

zoom lens Variable-focal-length lens. All video cameras are equipped with a zoom lens.

zoom range How much the focal length can be changed from a wide shot to a close-up during a zoom. The zoom range is stated as a ratio, such as 20:1. Also called *zoom ratio*.

Video Camera

Your friend brags about the new digital camcorder he just purchased. It has a three-chip sensor that allows video capture in both a 4 × 3 and a 16 × 9 aspect ratio, a fast 15:1 optical zoom lens with image stabilization, a high-resolution viewfinder, and a foldout color LCD monitor. Audio is captured with a built-in stereo microphone, but he can also attach an external one. The camcorder uses large-capacity memory cards to record 720p or 1080i high-definition (HD) video, and it connects to the computer with an HDMI or USB cable. He encourages you to get the same model because it produces superior video and audio and is especially well suited for nonlinear editing. But how do you know that these features really justify the relatively high price of the camcorder?

This chapter helps you answer this question. You will also learn how a video camera works as well as the relative advantages of various camera types and systems.

▶ **BASIC CAMERA FUNCTION AND ELEMENTS**
  Function, lens, beam splitter and imaging device, video signal processing, and viewfinder and monitor

▶ **TYPES OF CAMERAS**
  Camcorders, ENG/EFP cameras, studio cameras, DSLR cameras, digital cinema cameras, and 3D camcorders

▦ BASIC CAMERA FUNCTION AND ELEMENTS

Whether digital or analog, and regardless of their size, cost, and quality, all video cameras operate on the same basic principle: they transduce (translate) the optical image that the lens sees into a corresponding video picture. More specifically, the camera converts an optical image into electrical signals that are reconverted by a television receiver into visible screen images.

Function

To fulfill this function, each video camera needs three basic elements: the lens, the imaging device, and the viewfinder. **SEE 4.1**

The lens selects a portion of the scene at which you point the camera and produces a sharp optical image of it. The camera contains a beam splitter and an imaging device that convert the optical image of the lens into weak electric currents, which are amplified and further processed by a variety of electronic components. The viewfinder and the foldout monitor reconvert these electrical signals into video pictures of the lens-generated scene. **SEE 4.2**

To explain this process, we start with how a lens operates and sees a particular portion of a scene, then we move on to how the beam splitter and the imaging device work, and finally to how the video signal is reconverted into a video picture by the television receiver. Why bother with knowing all this, especially since most

4.1 BASIC CAMERA ELEMENTS

The video camera has three main elements: the lens, the imaging device, and the viewfinder.

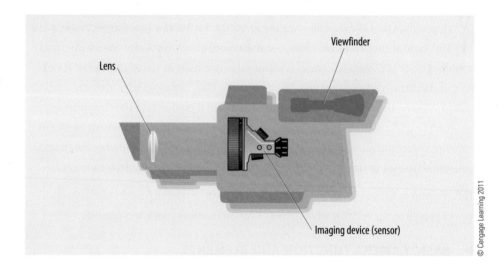

© Cengage Learning 2011

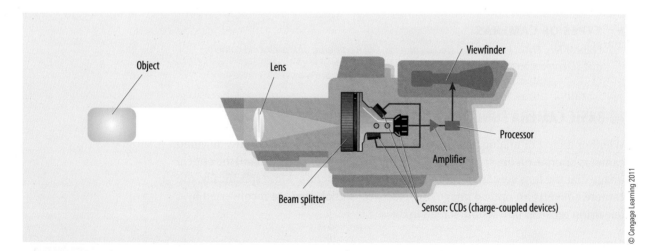

© Cengage Learning 2011

4.2 FUNCTIONS OF THE CAMERA

The video camera translates the optical light image as seen by the lens into a corresponding picture on the screen. The light reflected off an object is gathered and transmitted by the lens to the beam splitter, which splits the white light into red, green, and blue (RGB) light beams. These beams are then transformed by the imaging device (sensor) into electric energy, which is amplified and processed into a video signal. It is then reconverted into video pictures by the viewfinder and the monitor.

camcorders have automatic functions that can produce pretty good pictures and sound? The problem is that such automatic functions produce good pictures and sound only under ideal conditions. But what are ideal conditions? And what can you do when conditions are less than ideal? Knowing the basics of how a camera works will help you decide when and how to override the automatic functions to produce optimal video. It will also aid you in understanding how other production elements such as lighting must be manipulated to meet the requirements of the camera. Most importantly, such knowledge will help you become a video professional. **ZVL1** CAMERA→ Camera introduction

Lens

Lenses determine what cameras can see. They are classified by *focal length*, which is a technical measure of the distance from the iris inside the lens to the plane behind the lens where the projected image is in focus. This measurement assumes that the lens distance calibration is set at infinity (∞). This distance is normally given in millimeters (mm); thus a still camera can have a 24mm or a 200mm lens. Lenses can also be classified by how wide a view you get from a specific camera position. A wide-angle lens (short focal length) gives a relatively wide vista. A narrow-angle lens (long focal length) gives a relatively narrow vista with the background greatly magnified.

The optical quality of the lens determines to a great extent how good the video picture will look. Regardless of the quality of the camcorder itself, a good lens is one of the principal prerequisites for good pictures. This is why the lenses for high-end cameras can cost many times more than your entire camcorder, including its built-in lens.

Focal length   The *zoom lens* on a camera can change from a short-focal-length, or wide-angle, position to a long-focal-length, or narrow-angle, position and back in one continuous move. A short-focal-length zoom position gives you a wide-angle view: you can see more than with a lens in the narrow-angle position. To bring a zoom lens into the extreme-wide-angle position, you need to zoom all the way out. You will see a relatively large portion of the scene in front of you, but the middle- and background objects look quite small and therefore far away. **SEE 4.3**

Zooming all the way in puts the zoom lens in a long-focal-length, or narrow-angle, position. The zoom lens will now give a much narrower, but enlarged, view of

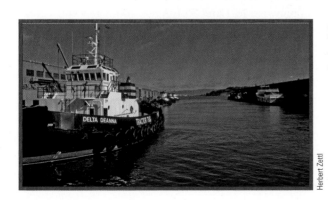

4.3 WIDE-ANGLE VIEW
The wide-angle lens shows a wide vista, with the faraway objects looking quite small.

Herbert Zettl

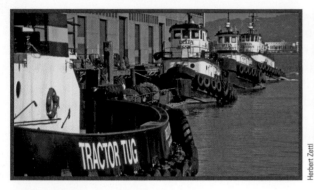

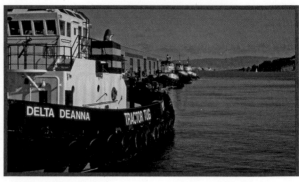

4.4 NARROW-ANGLE VIEW

The narrow-angle, or telephoto, lens shows only a narrow portion of the scene, with the background objects appearing much larger relative to the foreground objects than in a wide-angle view. The tugboats now look much closer together.

4.5 NORMAL VIEW

The normal lens shows a vista and a perspective that are similar to what we actually see.

the selected scene. Because the narrow-angle lens functions similarly to binoculars, it is also called a telephoto lens. **SEE 4.4**

When you stop a zoom in the middle of the zoom range (between the extreme-wide-angle and narrow-angle positions), you are more or less in the normal lens position. The angle of view of a normal lens approximates what you would see when looking directly at the scene. **SEE 4.5**

Because the zoom lens offers a great variety of focal lengths between its extreme-wide-angle and narrow-angle positions, it is also called a variable-focal-length lens. **ZVL2** CAMERA→ Zoom lens→ focal length

Zoom range   The ***zoom range***, also called zoom ratio, refers to how close a view you can achieve when zooming in from the farthest wide-angle position to the closest narrow-angle position. The higher the first number of the ratio, the closer you can get to the object from the farthest wide-angle position. A 20:1 zoom lens lets you narrow the field of view (your vista) 20 times when zooming in from the farthest wide-angle position to the closest narrow-angle position. In practical terms you can move in to a pretty good close-up from a wide-angle shot. The 20:1 zoom ratio can also be indicated as 20×. **SEE 4.6**

Small camcorder lenses rarely go above an optical zoom ratio of 20:1. Most studio lenses have a zoom ratio of between 15:1 and 30:1. A 30× zoom gets you a good close-up without moving the camera in even a large studio. Field cameras, however, need much greater zoom ranges. Covering sports or other outdoor events demands lenses with zoom ratios of 40:1 or even 60:1. With such a lens, you can zoom in from a wide shot of the entire football field to a close-up of the quarterback's face. The large zoom range is necessary because these cameras are usually relatively far from the event. Instead of moving the camera closer to the event, as is possible with a camcorder, the zoom lens must bring the event closer to the camera that might be positioned on top of the sports stadium. Unfortunately, the higher the zoom ratio, the larger the lens gets. A 60:1 field lens is quite a bit larger and certainly heavier than the camera to which it is attached.

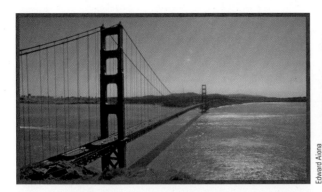
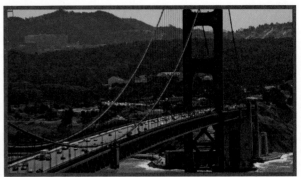

Edward Aiona

Edward Aiona

4.6 MAXIMUM WIDE-ANGLE AND NARROW-ANGLE POSITIONS OF A 10:1 ZOOM LENS
A 10× zoom lens can narrow the angle of view by 10 times. It appears to bring a portion of the scene closer to the camera.

The focal length of a lens influences not only the field of view (how close or far away an object seems) but also how far apart objects appear to be. (You will learn more about these and other aspects of framing and perception in chapters 5 and 6.)

Digital zoom   There is a great difference between an optical zoom and a digital zoom. In an optical zoom, the elements inside the lens change its focal length. In a digital zoom, the center of the digital image is gradually magnified; we perceive this gradual magnification as the image coming closer. The problem with digital zooms is that the enlarged image becomes progressively less sharp and eventually displays oversized pixels that look like tiles of a mosaic. Inevitably, a digital zoom-in to a fairly tight shot produces a slightly fuzzy image. An optical zoom does not influence the sharpness of the picture, which is why optical zooms are preferred.

Lens speed   This term refers to how much light can pass through a lens to the imaging device. A **_fast lens_** can let a relatively great amount of light pass through; a **_slow lens_** is more limited in how much light it can transmit. In practice a fast lens allows you to produce acceptable pictures in a darker environment than does a slow lens. Fast lenses are therefore more useful than slow ones, but they are also larger and more expensive.

You can tell whether a lens is fast or slow by looking at its lowest f-stop number, such as $f/1.4$ or $f/2$ (see figure 4.7). The lower the number, the faster the lens. A lens that can open up to $f2$ is pretty fast; one that can't go below $f4.5$ is quite slow.

Lens iris and aperture   Like the pupil of your eye, all lenses have an **_iris_** that controls the amount of light transmitted. In a bright environment, your iris contracts to a smaller opening, restricting the amount of light passing through; in a dim environment, it expands to a larger opening, admitting more light.

The lens iris, or lens diaphragm, operates in the same way. Like your pupil, the center of the iris has an adjustable hole, called the **_aperture,_** that can be made large or small. The size of the aperture controls how much light the lens transmits. When there is little light on a scene, you can make the aperture bigger and let more light through. This is called "opening the lens" or "opening the iris." When the scene is

4.7 IRIS CONTROL RING

The *f*-stop calibration is printed on a ring that controls the iris opening, or aperture, of the lens. The *C* on the control ring of this lens refers to *cap,* which means the iris is totally closed, letting no light pass through the lens, thus acting like a physical lens cap.

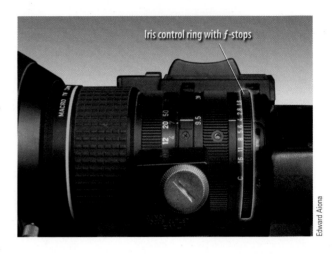

Iris control ring with *f*-stops

Edward Aiona

well illuminated, you can make the aperture smaller, or "close down" the lens, to restrict the light going through. You can thus control the exposure of the picture so that it looks neither too dark (not enough light) nor too washed out (too much light).

Now you can explain a fast or slow lens in more technical terms: a fast lens transmits more light at its maximum aperture than does a slow one. **ZVL3** CAMERA→ Exposure control→ aperture

f-stop   We measure how much light is transmitted through the lens with the help of the ***f-stop***. Normally, lenses have a ring at their base with a series of *f*-stop numbers (such as 1.4, 2.8, 4, 5.6, 8, 11, 16, and 22) printed on it that controls the iris opening. **SEE 4.7** You won't find such numbers on many studio camera lenses, however. Studio lenses are encased in a protective cover, so you couldn't see the markings even if they were on the lens. Camcorders usually display the *f*-stop numbers in the viewfinder menu.

When you turn the ring so that *f*/1.4 lines up with the indicator, you have "opened" the lens to its maximum aperture; it now transmits as much light as it possibly can. When you turn the ring to *f*/22, the lens is "stopped down" to its minimum aperture, letting very little light pass through. Notice that the *f*-stop numbers mean just the opposite of what you would expect: The lower the *f*-stop number, the larger the aperture and the more light is transmitted. The higher the *f*-stop number, the smaller the aperture and the less light is transmitted. **SEE 4.8** **ZVL4** CAMERA→ Exposure control→ *f*-stop

Auto-iris   Most camcorders enable you to choose between the manual iris control and an automatic iris feature. The auto-iris adjusts the aperture electronically to its optimal setting. The camera reads the light level of the scene and tells the auto-iris to open up or close down until the resulting picture is neither too dark nor too light. Such an automated feature is not without drawbacks, however. The problem is that the camera does not know which part of the picture you want properly exposed. If you are video-recording a brief field interview, with the reporter and her guest standing in front of a white sunlit building, the auto-iris will adjust the aperture to bring down the glare of the white building while ignoring the two people standing in front

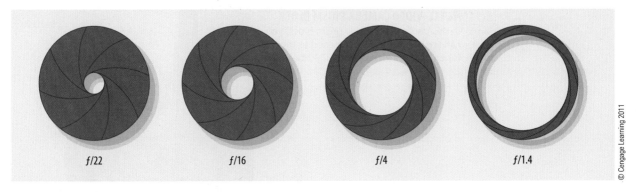

f/22   f/16   f/4   f/1.4

© Cengage Learning 2011

4.8 f-STOP SETTINGS
The higher the f-stop number, the smaller the aperture and the less light is transmitted by the lens. The lower the f-stop number, the larger the aperture and the more light is transmitted by the lens.

of it. The result will be a perfectly exposed background but woefully underexposed people in the foreground. A similar problem can occur in reverse when you try to frame a scene with dark tree branches in the foreground and a bright, snowcapped mountain in the far background. The automatic iris will dutifully lighten up the dark foreground objects (the tree branches), thereby overexposing the mountain in the background. You will end up with nicely detailed branches in the foreground that frame a uniformly bright background. Most likely, you will have lost the mountain.

Beam Splitter and Imaging Device

A second main system within the camera comprises the beam splitter and the imaging device, usually called the sensor, which transduces light into electric energy. **ZVL5** CAMERA→ Camera introduction

Beam splitter The ***beam splitter*** consists of a series of prisms and filters locked into a prism block. **SEE 4.9** Its function is to separate the ordinary white light of the lens-projected image into the three primary light colors—red, green, and blue (RGB)—and

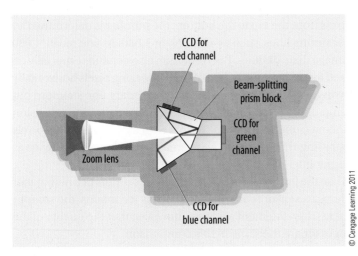

CCD for
red channel

Beam-splitting
prism block

CCD for
green
channel

Zoom lens

CCD for
blue channel

© Cengage Learning 2011

4.9 BEAM-SPLITTING PRISM BLOCK
The prism block contains prisms and filters that split the incoming white light into its three basic light colors—red, green, and blue—and direct these beams to their corresponding CCDs.

4.10 VIDEO CAMERA PRISM BLOCK

In this photo of an actual prism block, you can see the three CCDs attached to the port (opening), one for each RGB light beam.

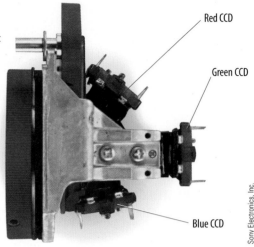

Red CCD

Green CCD

Blue CCD

Sony Electronics, Inc.

to direct these light beams at their corresponding sensors. Most larger camcorders use three sensors: one for the red beam, one for the green beam, and one for the blue beam. Each of the three sensors is solidly attached to the prism block. **SEE 4.10**

Sensor   The *sensor*, also called a chip, is an imaging device that transduces light into an electrical charge, which, after processing, makes up the video signal. The most common sensor in video cameras is the **CCD** (charge-coupled device). Higher-end cameras or camcorders use the more refined **CMOS** chips. You will find them exclusively in DSLR (digital single-lens reflex) cameras and digital cinema cameras. One of the great operational advantages of a CMOS sensor over a CCD is that the CMOS uses less battery power.

Both types of sensors basically consist of a solid-state silicon chip containing thousands or even millions of light-sensing pixels that are arranged in horizontal rows (representing each scanning line) and vertical stacks (representing the number of scanning lines). This is quite an accomplishment considering that most chips in video cameras are no larger than your thumbnail. Each pixel can translate the light energy it receives into a corresponding electric charge.

When counting pixels from the top to the bottom, the number is determined by the number of visible scanning lines, such as 480, 720, or 1,080. As you recall, 1,080 lines produce a better image than 480 lines. But resolution also depends especially on how many pixels are used for each scanning line. When squeezing pixels horizontally onto a scanning line, you are no longer bound by the customary line standard but simply by technical limitations. As you recall, high-end high-definition television (HDTV) and digital cinema cameras may use sensors with as many as 4,000 pixels per line ("4K" in industry lingo). The 8K digital cinema cameras may have twice as many horizontal pixels per line. **SEE 4.11**

All pixels function like the individual tiles in a mosaic or the dots in a newspaper photo. Generally, the larger a sensor is and the more pixels it contains, the sharper the image will be. **SEE 4.12** This statement assumes, however, that the quality of the lens and the signal processor are the same in this comparison.

> **KEY CONCEPT**
>
> The CCD converts the light variations of an image into electric energy—the video signal.

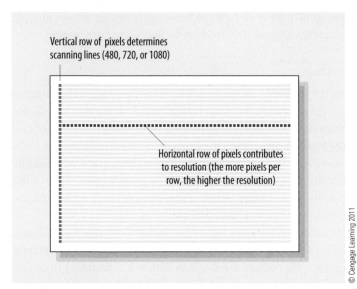

Vertical row of pixels determines
scanning lines (480, 720, or 1080)

Horizontal row of pixels contributes
to resolution (the more pixels per
row, the higher the resolution)

© Cengage Learning 2011

4.11 PIXEL ARRANGEMENT ON A SENSOR
The sensor contains thousands or millions of pixels that are arranged in a vertical stack of horizontal scanning lines. The number of pixels in the vertical stack is defined by the scanning system (480p, 720p, or 1080i). The number of pixels per horizontal line greatly influences the overall picture resolution.

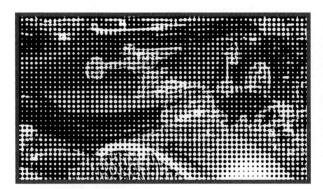
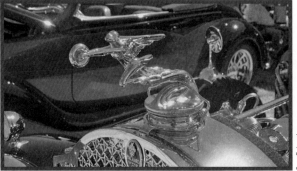

Gary Palmatier

4.12 PICTURE RESOLUTION
The picture on the right is composed of more pixels than the one on the left. It has a higher resolution and looks sharper. The more pixels a CCD contains, the higher the resolution of the video image.

High-quality cameras usually contain three CCDs—one for each of the RGB light beams as delivered by the beam splitter. Many smaller camcorders and, paradoxically, the very high-end digital cinema cameras, however, have just a single chip. In this case the incoming white light is divided by an RGB-striped filter into the three primary colors, which are then processed as individual signals by the single CCD or CMOS. Although single-chip camcorders can produce as sharp a picture as three-chip cameras, their color fidelity is generally inferior. The big advantage of a single-chip camcorder is that it is small, lightweight, and relatively inexpensive—important considerations when aiming at a large consumer or prosumer market.

The single chip in DSLR and digital cinema cameras is quite large and, as just mentioned, contains a vast number of horizontal and vertical pixels; but such sensors are neither practical nor necessary for standard camcorders, whose output will probably not be projected on giant movie screens.

Note that the video signal leaving all types of imaging devices is always analog. This analog signal is then immediately digitized for further signal processing.

Video Signal Processing

Signal processing—how the RGB signals are amplified when they leave the imaging device and how they combine to match the colors of the scene—is another significant factor in producing optimal picture quality. Basically, color signals consist of two channels: a **luminance channel**, also called the luma, or Y, channel (*lumen* is Latin for "light"), which produces the black-and-white image of the scene and is mainly responsible for the picture's sharpness; and a **chrominance channel**, also called the color, or C, channel. In high-quality video, these channels are kept separate throughout signal processing, recording, and transport.

In the old analog standard television, for transmission both the Y and C signals must be combined into a composite analog signal, called the NTSC signal or, simply, NTSC. (*NTSC* stands for *National Television System Committee.*) In digital transmission, the Y and C channels are kept separate and no such translation into an analog composite signal is necessary, unless you are using a converter box for viewing digital television signals on an old analog TV set.

Viewfinder and Monitor

The **viewfinder** is a movable tubelike device attached to the camera. It shows a black-and-white or color image of what the camera sees. The flat-panel LCD display, which is attached to the camera or can be folded out, is called the monitor. Because the small eyepiece viewfinder often produces a sharper picture than the standard foldout monitor and does not wash out in sunlight, most camcorder operators prefer the viewfinder over the foldout monitor. **SEE 4.13**

4.13 LARGE-EYEPIECE VIEWFINDER AND FOLDOUT LCD MONITOR
This camera has a relatively large viewfinder and an LCD foldout monitor that give the operator great flexibility in camera handling. Such flat-panel displays can wash out in bright surroundings.

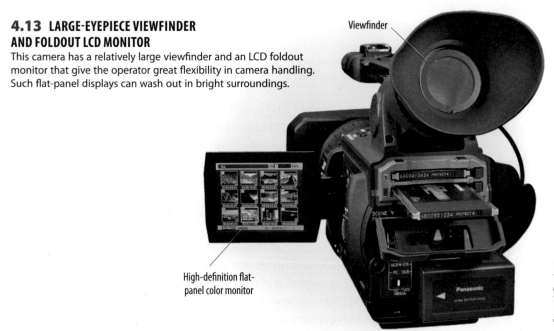

Viewfinder

High-definition flat-panel color monitor

Panasonic Broadcast

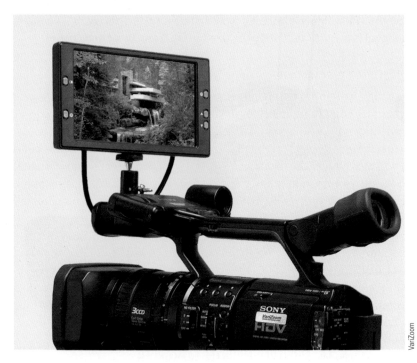

VariZoom

4.14 LCD MONITOR ATTACHED TO CAMCORDER
To optimize the handling of a large camcorder, you can attach a flat-panel monitor to the camcorder handle. This way you can frame a shot while carrying the camera close to the ground.

Some large camcorders have high-resolution color viewfinders but no foldout flat-panel monitor. If used in electronic field production, many camera operators opt to connect the camera's video output to a larger, independent, high-resolution monitor panel. **SEE 4.14** This detachable flat-panel display is mounted on a flexible arm, or "hot shoe," which lets you see the camera output even while taking the camcorder off your shoulder for certain shots. Note that all flat-panel monitors tend to drain the camera battery significantly faster than the built-in viewfinder, and they are worthless if the sun shines on them.

TYPES OF CAMERAS

Although their functions often overlap, we can distinguish among six types of video cameras: shoulder-mounted (large) and handheld (small) camcorders, ENG/EFP (electronic news gathering/electronic field production) cameras, studio cameras, DSLR cameras, digital cinema cameras, and 3D camcorders.

Camcorders

As pointed out before, a ***camcorder*** (for *cam*era and re*corder*) is a portable video camera with its recording device attached to it or built-in. The large ones are usually called shoulder-mounted camcorders, and the small ones are called handheld camcorders. Of course this classification should not prevent you from carrying your large camcorder in your hand or carrying one of your larger handheld ones on your shoulder. The very small point-and-shoot camcorders, which fit into a shirt pocket, can under good conditions produce excellent video and audio. **SEE 4.15–4.17**

KEY CONCEPT

A camcorder has its video recorder built-in.

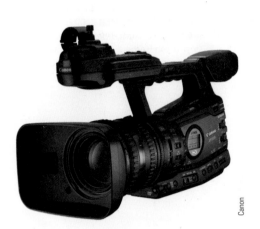

Canon

4.15 HIGH-END HANDHELD CAMCORDER
This small high-end HDTV camcorder has three
CMOS sensors, an 18× optical zoom lens, and
two professional (XLR) microphone inputs. It
records in all HDTV standards, with a variable
frame rate on CF (compact flash) memory cards.

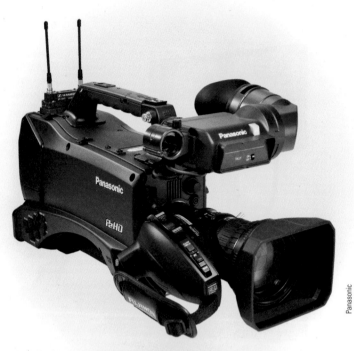

Panasonic

4.16 SHOULDER-MOUNTED CAMCORDER
This large camcorder has three high-density MOS (metal-oxide semiconductor) sensors (an improved CMOS-type sensor), a 17× zoom lens,
and four separate audio channels. It can hold two P2 memory cards for
continuous variable-frame-rate HDTV recording.

The recording device in a camcorder is either some kind of tapeless device, such
as a memory card, a hard drive, or an optical disc, or, in older models, a videotape
recorder (VTR). The tapeless recording devices are described in more detail in
chapter 11.

Except for the pocket-sized models, all other camcorders—shoulder-mounted
and handheld—have at least two audio inputs: one is normally used for the camera
mic, and the other is for an additional, external microphone. In small camcorders
the camera mic is built-in. Larger models have two jacks (inputs) that let you plug in
specific mics (see chapter 7). Many high-end camcorders have provisions for plugging in a wireless microphone receiver, which makes the use of an external receiver
expandable when wireless mics are used.

Most camcorders also have a camera light for illuminating small areas during
ENG or to provide additional illumination. Note that if you run the camera light off
the camcorder's battery, the battery will run down considerably faster; it's best to
use a separate battery pack for the light.

Some high-end camcorder models have provisions to send their video and
audio signals to a satellite.

Quality difference When you compare the pictures your friend took with his
digital camcorder to a similar scene shot with an expensive and much larger and
heavier camcorder, you will probably not see much difference in how the pictures

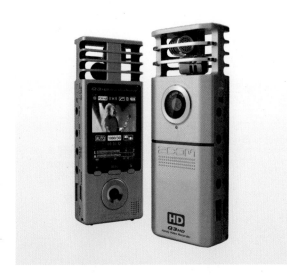

4.17 POINT-AND-SHOOT CAMCORDER

This pocket camcorder can record 720p or 1080p HD video and superior stereo audio, all on an SD (Secure Digital format) memory card. It displays audio-recording levels on the monitor and has additional input and output jacks for a variety of external devices.

look. Why, then, do you still see professional ENG shooters lugging around heavy camcorders on their shoulders? One of the main reasons is that television stations are reluctant to dump a perfectly fine camera that they purchased for a hefty price not too long ago. But there are also some technical advantages to using the larger camcorder for critical shoots.

The single-most important difference between large and standard small camcorders is that the small cameras have a built-in zoom lens that cannot be exchanged. When using a large camcorder or a DSLR camera, however, you can choose the lens that best suits your purpose. For example, you can use a very-wide-angle lens when shooting in confined quarters, such as the inside of an automobile, or a lens that lets you get a close-up view from far away. Additionally, the lens of a large ENG/EFP camcorder has better optics (high-quality lens elements) and a smoother zoom mechanism. Large camcorders also have more manual video and audio controls for overriding the automatic ones, robust recording devices, and usually a better processing system with better color sampling that ensures faithful colors even when shooting in low-light conditions.

But don't worry: even if you don't have a shoulder-mounted ENG/EFP camcorder, you can still produce professional-looking video footage. You will find that shooting good video depends more on what shots you select and how you frame them than on the technical specifications of the camcorder. (The discussion in chapter 6 about looking through the viewfinder will help you achieve maximally effective shots.)

ENG/EFP Cameras

The basic difference between an ENG/EFP camera and a camcorder is that the ENG/EFP camera does not have a built-in video recorder (VR) but must feed its output via cable to a stand-alone VR. Like a camcorder, the ***ENG/EFP camera*** is self-contained, but it can be, and often is, connected with a camera cable to a remote control unit (RCU) and an external recording device. Why use an RCU when the camera is basically self-contained and has automatic controls?

4.18 **ENG/EFP CAMERA CONNECTED TO RCU AND EXTERNAL VIDEO RECORDER**
This high-end ENG/EFP camera has no built-in video recorder but is connected to a remote control unit and from there to a high-capacity hard drive or studio VTR for high-quality recording.

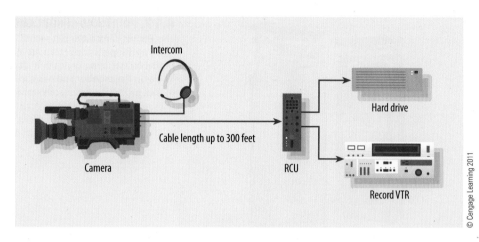

First, although an ENG/EFP camera is capable of running on batteries, it is often better to power it with an external source. External power frees you from worrying about battery life during a long shoot or a live pickup. Second, in situations where optimal pictures are critical, the RCU allows the video operator (VO) to override the camera's automatic circuits and tweak the settings for optimal performance under a variety of shooting conditions. This way the camera operator can pay full attention to composing effective shots. **SEE 4.18** Third, because the director can see on a monitor what the camera operators see in their viewfinders, he or she can give them the necessary instructions over the intercom headsets while the multicamera event is in progress. All of these production advantages considerably outweigh the slight disadvantage of having the cameras tethered to a remote truck or a temporary video control. The ENG/EFP camera is now operating much like a highly portable studio camera.

Studio conversion of ENG/EFP camera   Because ENG/EFP cameras are considerably cheaper and easier to handle, they are often used in place of studio cameras, even if they can't quite match the quality. To adapt an ENG/EFP camera to studio conditions, you replace the small viewfinder with a larger one, attach a faster lens (lower maximum f-stop number) that has a zoom range more appropriate for studio dimensions (15× or 20×), affix cables for focus and zoom controls, and install a frame and mounting devices for a tripod or studio pedestal. Unless the PL (private line or phone line) is wireless, an intercom connection box must be attached to the mounting frame. **SEE 4.19**

Studio Cameras

The large HDTV cameras you normally find in television studios are, appropriately enough, called studio cameras. They are built to produce exceptionally good pictures under a variety of conditions. They usually contain a high-quality (fast) zoom lens, three high-density CCDs or CMOS chips as sensors, extensive signal-processing equipment, and a large, high-definition viewfinder.

Studio cameras are usually bulky and too heavy to be maneuvered without the aid of a pedestal or some other kind of camera mount. What makes the equipment

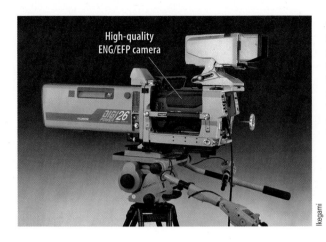

4.19 STUDIO CONVERSION OF ENG/EFP CAMERA
Converting a high-quality ENG/EFP camera for studio use usually requires adding a large viewfinder, a faster lens with a zoom range appropriate for the studio size, cables that allow zooming and focusing from the operator's position, and a frame and mounting devices for a tripod or studio pedestal.

so heavy is not necessarily the camera itself but the large zoom lens and, typically, the teleprompter attached to it. **SEE 4.20** Studio cameras are used for such programs as news, interviews, game shows, music and dance spectaculars, and of course soap operas. These cameras are also taken on big remotes, such as football games and parades. For this function they are equipped with higher-ratio zoom lenses (40× or even 60×) and mounted on field dollies or heavy-duty tripods (see chapter 5).

Wherever studio cameras may be located, they are always connected by cable to their CCUs (camera control units) and to other essential equipment, such as the sync generator and the power supply. These three elements constitute what is called the camera chain.

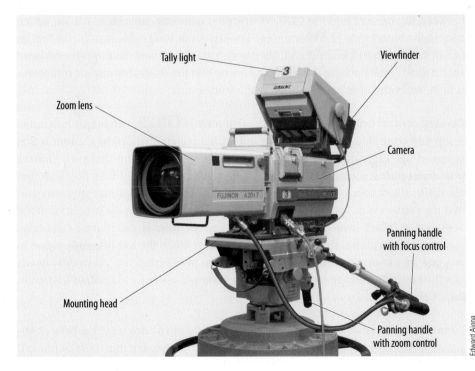

4.20 STUDIO CAMERA
Studio cameras normally use three high-density CCDs or CMOS chips and a variety of picture-enhancing electronic circuits. This studio camera uses a high-quality 25× zoom lens and a large 9-inch high-definition viewfinder. Most studio cameras also have a teleprompter attached, which makes the whole camera head considerably heavier than an ENG/EFP camera or camcorder.

4.21 STANDARD CAMERA CHAIN

The standard camera chain consists of the camera head (the actual camera), the power supply, the sync generator, and the CCU.

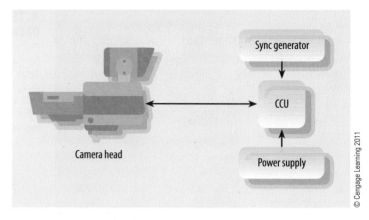

© Cengage Learning 2011

Camera chain   The standard ***camera chain*** consists of four parts: the camera itself, the power supply, the sync generator, and the camera control unit. **SEE 4.21**

As the front part of the camera chain, the camera itself is called the camera head. It cannot function by itself without the other parts of the chain. The power supply feeds the electricity to the camera head through the camera cable. Unlike ENG/EFP cameras or camcorders, studio cameras cannot be powered by batteries.

The sync generator produces the uniform electrical pulse that is necessary to synchronize the scanning of the video pictures in all cameras used in a multicamera telecast. This pulse also keeps in step the scanning of a variety of other equipment, such as viewfinders, video monitors, and video recorders.

Camera cable   The camera cable carries the power to the camera and transports the picture signal, the intercommunication signal, and other technical information between the camera and the CCU. Most studio cameras use triaxial cables, which can reach about 1 mile (1.6 kilometers). For extremely long cable runs (up to 2 miles or a little more than 3 kilometers), fiber-optic cables are used. Studio cameras need such a great reach because they are used not only in the studio but also on remotes—scheduled events that happen outside the studio.

Camera control unit   The ***camera control unit (CCU)*** has two major functions: setup and control. Setup refers to the adjustments made when the camera is first powered up. The video operator, who is in charge of ensuring that each camera produces optimal pictures during recording, makes sure even before the show that the colors the camera delivers are true, that the iris is at its optimal aperture, and that the camera is adjusted for the brightest spot (white-level adjustment) and the darkest spot (black-level or pedestal adjustment) in the scene so that we can see all the major steps within this contrast range. Fortunately, the VO is greatly aided in this task by a computerized setup panel. During production the VO usually needs to adjust only the lens aperture, by moving a remote iris control knob or a lever on the CCU. **SEE 4.22**

Connectors   Is a discussion of connectors necessary in a book on video basics? Absolutely. Whenever you work with several pieces of equipment that must be hooked

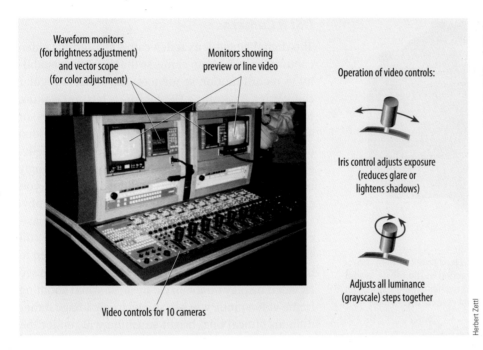

Waveform monitors
(for brightness adjustment)
and vector scope
(for color adjustment)

Monitors showing
preview or line video

Operation of video controls:

Iris control adjusts exposure
(reduces glare or
lightens shadows)

Adjusts all luminance
(grayscale) steps together

Video controls for 10 cameras

Herbert Zettl

4.22 CAMERA CONTROL UNIT

The CCU has a variety of controls with which the video operator can continuously monitor and adjust picture quality. The remote version of a CCU is called an RCU.

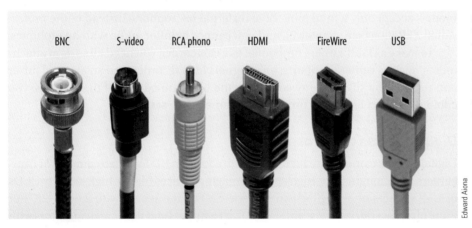

BNC   S-video   RCA phono   HDMI   FireWire   USB

Edward Aiona

4.23 STANDARD VIDEO CONNECTORS

The standard video connectors are the BNC, S-video, RCA phono (also used for audio), HDMI, FireWire, and USB 2.0 or 3.0 connectors. Adapters enable you to interconnect all of them in various configurations.

together to form a video or audio system, you need the appropriate cables and especially the right connectors; and despite careful preproduction, many productions have been delayed or even canceled because the connectors for camera or audio cables did not fit. Though you may hear production people call all connectors "plugs," regardless of whether they represent the male or female part of the connector, it is more precise to call the male part of the connector a plug and the female part a jack.

The most widely used video connectors are the BNC, S-video, RCA phono, HDMI, and FireWire (IEEE 1394). Some systems allow you to use a USB 2.0 or USB 3.0 cable to transfer video. **SEE 4.23** (The standard audio connectors are shown in figure 7.26.) A variety of adapters let you change from one plug to another, such as from a BNC to an RCA phono, but don't rely on them. An adapter is strictly a makeshift solution and always presents a potential trouble spot.

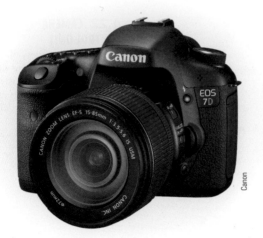

Canon

4.24 DSLR CAMERA

This still-photography digital single-lens reflex camera can be used for video recording when switched to the movie mode. Because of the superior sensor and exchangeable lenses, DSLR cameras are also adopted for digital cinema production.

DSLR Cameras

The digital single-lens reflex cameras used for video capture are still-photo cameras that have the capability to record motion sequences, much like a regular camcorder. Basically, a DSLR camera lets you capture motion at the traditional 24 frames per second (fps) or at 30 fps. The advantages of DSLR cameras for video capture are their very large CMOS sensor, which delivers superior HD footage, great color, and surprisingly brilliant pictures in low-light conditions. Best of all, you can use all of the lenses available for still photography.

The disadvantage is that DSLR cameras are basically designed for normal photographic work of still shots. Unless you use an external monitor, you need to have the camera right in front of you so that you can see its video display on the back. Because when shooting in the video mode you see an electronic image rather than an optical one, bright sunshine will render the DSLR monitor pretty much useless. The duration of a shot is also quite limited, as is the total recording time. One of the most serious disadvantages is in audio. Most models accept only a mini plug for an external microphone instead of the professional XLR plug (see chapter 7), and you cannot monitor audio with headphones.

To make a DSLR camera functional as a camcorder, you need all sorts of attachments, such as camera supports, an external video recorder, and an external mixer and recorder for high-quality sound. By the time you add all of these extras, you could get an excellent camcorder for the same price. **SEE 4.24**

Digital Cinema Cameras

Digital cinema cameras are highly specialized super-HDTV video cameras or camcorders that contain ultra-high-quality imaging devices (either high-density CCDs or CMOS chips or a single custom-made CMOS-like sensor with 2,000 ["2K"] or more pixels per horizontal scanning line), viewfinders and flat-screen monitors with high-resolution images, and various attachments that are adapted from standard film cameras. One of the most useful electronic features for filmmaking with the digital cinema camera is its variable frame rate, which permits a change from 24 fps scanning (modeled after the standard film frame rate) to a slower rate for fast-motion effects, called undercranking, or a higher rate for slow-motion effects, called overcranking. Though it seems paradoxical, you need fewer frames per second than the normal speed to accelerate the screen action and more frames to slow it down.[1] **SEE 4.25**

Although far from being ideal for motion picture production, the small DSLR cameras have caught the fancy of some filmmakers. One reason is because these

---

1. See Herbert Zettl, *Sight Sound Motion: Applied Media Aesthetics,* 6th ed. (Boston: Wadsworth, 2011, pp. 265–68.

cameras produce dazzling images. The more expensive ones have a large CMOS sensor and let you mount any type of high-quality lens.

The small size of a DSLR camera should be a great advantage because you can point the camera in any direction. This is true so long as you don't have to see the viewfinder in the back. In most cases, however, you must always hold the camera in front of your nose, usually with partially outstretched arms. This is as awkward as is it tiring, especially for longer takes. The various camera mounting devices will not make it easier to get unusual angles unless you twist and bend your body to keep the viewfinder in sight. The small size is also a problem when trying to use the camera for long, smooth dolly and tracking shots. Other problems lie in the audio area. The built-in mics and the jacks for external mics are simply not sufficient for high-quality audio recording. Nevertheless, when used for standard photographic work, these cameras can deliver stunning still images and bursts of several still images, which cannot be matched by even a good-quality camcorder.

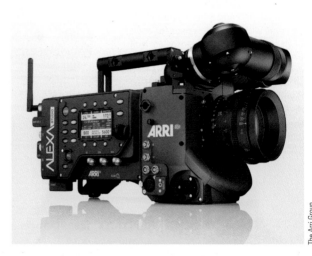

4.25 **DIGITAL CINEMA CAMERA**
This super-high-definition electronic cinema camera contains a large 2K+ sensor and records video and audio on high-capacity memory cards. It offers a 4 × 3 or 16 × 9 aspect ratio and a variety of frame rates, including the digital movie favorite of 24 fps.

Fortunately, you don't need such cameras to produce your documentary or short movie. Many documentaries and even feature films have been shot with so-called consumer camcorders and successfully shown in motion picture theaters. It is, after all, your creativity and aesthetic judgment that make for a good film rather than high-end equipment. Yes, you knew that all along, but it is worth repeating from time to time, especially if you feel that you would rather upgrade your equipment than rewrite your script.

3D Camcorders

Pushed by equipment manufacturers and 3D movies, three-dimensional video is trying to find its way into independent video productions. The current problem is that the equipment has clearly outrun its proper use. The basic principle of 3D image projection is based on the fact that our two eyes see a scene from slightly different angles. When superimposed by our brain, the two offset images result in a stereo image that reinforces all the other 3D cues we get even when looking at it with only one eye. Wouldn't we then need two cameras as substitutes for our two eyes for 3D vision? Yes, indeed.

To capture 3D video, you can use two small identical camcorders mounted next to each other on a 3D rig, or a single camcorder housing with a twin lens. Each lens sends its image to its own camera recording device, such as a high-capacity SD (Secure Digital format) card. **SEE 4.26** Just like the stereo audio left and right channels, which are mixed by our brain into a single, multidimensional sound image, the 3D video camera records simultaneously a left-eye channel and a right-eye channel.

4.26 3D CAMCORDER

This small 3D camcorder has two cameras with a CMOS sensor for each. Both cameras and twin lenses are built into a single housing. Both the left-eye camera and the right-eye camera record HDTV signals (1080 and 720) on their own large-capacity internal memory device or on twin SD cards. You can view the 3D images on the foldout monitor without glasses.

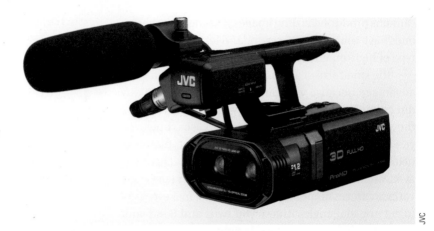

The two video channels are then mixed by our brain into a single 3D stereoscopic visual image.

In some camera setups, both lenses are pointed straight ahead so that what they see will always be slightly offset. Other types of 3D camera rigs allow the lenses of the two cameras to be toed-in to a certain degree, which means that they can be panned slightly toward each other so that their divergent views will at one point converge and perfectly overlap. All 3D camera setups have provisions to change the distance between their lenses. We discuss the perception of 3D images further in chapter 6.

MAIN POINTS

▶ **Basic Camera Elements**

These are the lens, the beam splitter and imaging device, and the viewfinder and monitor.

▶ **Lenses**

Lenses are classified by the focal length (short and long), angle of view (wide and narrow), and speed (largest aperture expressed in the lowest f-stop). The zoom lens has a variable focal length. The zoom range is stated as a ratio, such as 20:1 or 20×. A 20:1 lens can show the angle of view 20 times narrower than the extreme-wide-angle position with the background magnified.

▶ **Lens Iris and Aperture**

One quality factor of the lens is determined by its speed, that is, the maximum aperture, or iris opening. A fast lens lets a relatively large amount of light pass through; a slow lens, relatively little. A fast lens is better than a slow one. The specific aperture is indicated in f-stops. The lower the f-stop number, the larger the aperture and the more light is transmitted. A fast lens has a low minimum f-stop number (such as $f/1.4$). The higher the f-stop number, the smaller the aperture and the less light is transmitted. A slow lens has a relatively high minimum f-stop number (such as $f/4.5$).

▶ **Beam Splitter and Imaging Device**

These devices change the light of the optical image as produced by the lens into electric charges of various strengths. The beam splitter divides the light that comes through the lens into red, green, and blue (RGB) light beams. The imaging device, usually called a sensor, is attached to the beam splitter and transduces the colored light beams into electric charges, which are then further processed into the video signal.

▶ ***Types of Cameras***

Camera types include small handheld and large shoulder-mounted camcorders—portable cameras with the recording device attached or built-in; ENG/EFP cameras, which are high-end, shoulder-mounted field cameras; high-definition television (HDTV) studio cameras, which with a different lens are also used in the field; DSLR (digital single-lens reflex) cameras; super high-definition digital cinema cameras, and 3D camcorders.

▶ ***Camera Chain***

The studio camera chain consists of the camera head (the actual camera), the power supply, the sync generator, and the camera control unit (CCU). A camcorder contains the entire camera chain plus the recording device.

▶ ***Connectors***

The most widely used video connectors are the BNC, S-video, RCA phono, HDMI, FireWire (IEEE 1394), and USB 2.0 and 3.0.

▶ ***DSLR and Digital Cinema Cameras***

DSLR cameras are designed for still photography. Because of their large HD sensors, which produce superior images, DSLR cameras are occasionally used for filmmaking. Digital cinema cameras are highly specialized super-HDTV cameras or camcorders that produce extremely high-resolution pictures. All have large sensors and are also equipped with high-resolution viewfinders and other attachments carried over from film.

▶ ***3D Camcorders***

To produce three-dimensional footage, you need to capture the event with either two identical camcorders mounted side-by-side, or a camera with twin lenses, which records what one lens sees on a left-eye channel and what the other lens sees on a right-eye channel.

Z E T T L ' S   V I D E O L A B

 For your reference or to track your work, the *Zettl's VideoLab* program cues in this chapter are listed here with their corresponding page numbers.

KEY TERMS

arc To move the camera in a slightly curved dolly or truck.

calibrate the zoom lens To preset a zoom lens to stay in focus throughout the zoom.

cant To tilt the camera sideways.

crane To move the boom of the camera crane up or down. Also called *boom*.

dolly To move the camera toward (dolly in) or away from (dolly out) the object.

jib arm A small camera crane that can be operated by the cameraperson.

mounting head A device that connects the camera to its support. Also called *pan-and-tilt head*.

pan To turn the camera horizontally.

pedestal To move the camera up or down using a studio pedestal.

shutter speed A camera control that reduces the blurring of bright, fast-moving objects. The higher the shutter speed, the less blurring occurs but the more light is needed.

studio pedestal A heavy camera dolly that permits raising and lowering the camera while on the air.

tilt To point the camera up or down.

tongue To move the boom with the camera from left to right or from right to left.

tripod A three-legged camera mount. Also called *sticks*.

truck To move the camera laterally by means of a mobile camera mount. Also called *track*.

white-balance To adjust the color circuits in the camera to produce white color in lighting of various color temperatures (relative reddishness or bluishness of white light).

zoom To change the focal length of the lens through the use of a zoom control while the camera remains stationary.

Operating the Camera

Let's watch a tourist who is itching for something interesting to shoot with his brand-new camcorder. He quickly takes aim at one of the towers of the Golden Gate Bridge, tilts his camera up to the top, zooms in, zooms out again, tilts down to the bay just as a freighter passes below, zooms in on the containers, zooms out again, tilts up to the rail where some seagulls have perched, zooms in on one of the more aggressive birds that refuses to stay in the frame, and finally zooms out to catch a passing jogger, who waves at him.

Although such camera handling may be good exercise for the arm and the zoom mechanism, it rarely results in satisfactory footage. Such unmotivated camera motion produces images that seem restless and unsettling for anyone except, perhaps, the person who shot them. The tourist would have done much better had his camera been mounted on a tripod.

When operating a handheld camcorder, you are virtually unrestrained in moving the camera. But when the camera is mounted on a tripod, its movements become much more restricted. Initially, you will probably feel that a tripod constrains your artistry and that it is much better to handhold the camera so long as it is not too heavy. After some experience with camera operation, however, you will discover that it is actually easier to operate the camera and control picture composition when the camera is mounted on some kind of support. In fact, the art of operating a camera is not as dependent on its electronic design or basic operational controls as it is on its size and especially on how it is mounted.

This chapter explores basic camera movements and operation and how they can be accomplished.

▶ **BASIC CAMERA MOVEMENTS**
   Pan, tilt, cant, pedestal, dolly, truck, arc, crane, tongue, and zoom

▶ **CAMERA MOUNTS AND HOW TO USE THEM**
   Handheld and shoulder-mounted cameras, tripods, special camera mounts, and the studio pedestal

▶ **OPERATIONAL FEATURES**
   Focusing, adjusting shutter speed, zooming, and white-balancing

▶ **GENERAL GUIDELINES**
   Checklists for camcorders, ENG/EFP cameras, and studio cameras

■ BASIC CAMERA MOVEMENTS

The various camera mounts are designed to steady the camera and help you move it as smoothly and easily as possible. To understand the features and the functions of camera mounting equipment, you should first learn about the major camera movements. The terms are the same regardless of whether the camera is carried on your shoulder or mounted on a tripod, a studio pedestal, or some other camera support.

There are nine basic camera movements: pan, tilt, cant, pedestal, dolly, truck, arc, crane, and tongue. Sometimes zoom is included in the major camera movements, although the camera itself does not normally move during a zoom. **SEE 5.1**

Pan   To *pan* is to turn the camera horizontally, from left to right or from right to left. To pan right means to swivel or move the camera clockwise so that the lens points more to the right; to pan left means to swivel or move the camera counterclockwise so that the lens points more to the left.

Tilt   To *tilt* is to make the camera point up or down. A tilt up means to point the camera gradually up. A tilt down means to point the camera gradually down.

Cant   To *cant* is to tilt the camera sideways. You can cant the camera either left or right. When you cant right, the horizon line will be slanted uphill; its low point will be screen-left, its high point screen-right. Canting left will produce the opposite effect. Canting is easy with the handheld or shoulder-mounted camera, but you cannot cant a camera supported by a standard camera mount.

Pedestal   To *pedestal* is to elevate or lower the camera on the center column of a tripod or studio pedestal. To pedestal up you crank or pull up the center column, thereby raising the camera. To pedestal down you crank or pull down the center column, lowering the camera. This motion puts the camera into different vertical positions, which means that the camera sees the scene as though you were looking at it from the top of a ladder or while kneeling on the floor. You can "pedestal" a handheld camera by simply raising it slowly above your head or lowering it to the ground.

Dolly   To *dolly* is to move the camera toward or away from an object in more or less a straight line by means of a mobile camera mount. When you dolly in, you move the camera closer to the object; when you dolly out or dolly back, you move the camera farther away. With the handheld or shoulder-mounted camera, you simply walk the camera toward or away from the scene. Some directors call this "dollying" in or out, even though the camera is not mounted on a dolly; others simply ask you to get closer or back up.

5.1 MAJOR CAMERA MOVEMENTS
The major camera movements are pan, tilt, cant, pedestal, dolly, truck or track, arc, crane or boom, and tongue.

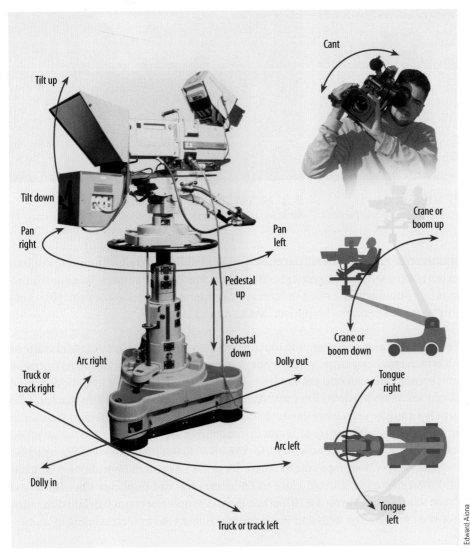

Cant

Tilt up

Tilt down

Pan right

Pan left

Crane or boom up

Pedestal up

Pedestal down

Dolly out

Crane or boom down

Arc right

Truck or track right

Tongue right

Dolly in

Arc left

Truck or track left

Tongue left

Edward Aiona

Truck   To **truck**, or **track**, is to move the camera laterally by means of a mobile camera mount. When you truck right or truck left, you move the camera mount to the right or left with the camera lens pointing at a right angle to the direction of travel. If you want to follow somebody walking on a sidewalk, you would truck with the camera alongside on the street, with the lens pointing at the person. Tracking often means the same as trucking. Sometimes tracking refers simply to a moving camera's keeping up with a moving object. With a handheld or shoulder-mounted camera, you walk parallel to the moving object while keeping the camera pointed at it.

Arc   To **arc** is to move the camera in a slightly curved dolly or truck movement. To arc left means that you dolly in or out in a camera-left curve, or you truck left in a curve around the object. To arc right means that you dolly in or out in a camera-right curve, or you truck right in a curve around the object. With the handheld or

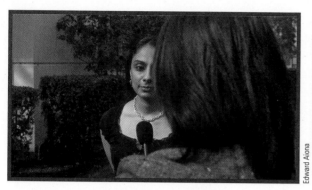

5.2 CAMERA-FAR PERSON PARTIALLY BLOCKED
In this over-the-shoulder shot, the camera-near person partially blocks the camera-far person.

5.3 ARC CORRECTS BLOCKED SHOT
By arcing left you can properly frame the camera-far person.

shoulder-mounted camera, you simply walk in a slight arc while pointing the lens at the scene. Arcing is often required to reveal more of the camera-far person in an over-the-shoulder shot when the camera-near person is blocking or nearly blocking our view of the camera-far person. **SEE 5.2 AND 5.3**

Crane   To *crane*, or *boom*, is to move the camera up or down on a camera crane or jib arm. A crane is a large and bulky device that can lift the camera and its operator, and sometimes a second person (usually the director), up to 30 feet aboveground in one impressive sweep. The crane itself is moved by a driver and an assistant. A jib arm is a simpler crane that can be handled by a single camera operator (as shown in figure 5.21). To crane up or boom up means to raise the boom with the attached camera; to crane down or boom down means to lower the boom and the attached camera. Simply holding a small camcorder or DSLR camera high above your head and then swooping it down close to floor level will not duplicate the feeling of a crane motion; unless you are 10 feet tall, there is simply not enough height difference between the extreme high and low camera positions to simulate a crane motion.

Tongue   To *tongue* is to move the whole camera from left to right or from right to left with the boom of a camera crane or jib arm. When you tongue left or right, the camera usually points in the same general direction, with only the boom swinging left or right. Tonguing creates an effect similar to a truck except that the horizontal arc of the boom with the camera is usually much wider and can be much faster. Tonguing is often combined with a boom-up or boom-down movement.

The crane and tongue movements are somewhat of a special effect. Even if you have access to a crane, use such extreme camera movements sparingly and only if they contribute to the shot's intensity.

Zoom   To *zoom* is to change the focal length of a lens through the use of a zoom control while the camera remains stationary. To zoom in means to change the lens gradually to a narrow-angle position, thereby making the scene appear to move closer to the viewer; to zoom out means to change the lens gradually to a wide-angle position, thereby making the scene appear to move farther away from the viewer.

Although the effect of a zoom is the object's moving toward or away from the screen rather than the camera's moving into or out of the scene, the zoom is usually classified as one of the camera "movements." **ZVL1** CAMERA→ Camera moves→ dolly | zoom | truck | pan | tilt | pedestal | try it

■ CAMERA MOUNTS AND HOW TO USE THEM

You can support a camera in four ways: by carrying it with your hands or on your shoulder, with a tripod, with special camera mounting devices, and with a studio pedestal. They all influence greatly, if not dictate, how you operate the camera.

Handheld and Shoulder-Mounted Camera

We have already mentioned that the small, handheld camcorder invites excessive camera motion. You can point it easily in any direction and move it effortlessly, especially if it has a foldout monitor. Although such high mobility can be an asset, it is also a liability. Too much camera movement draws attention to itself and away from the scene you want to show. Unless the camera has a built-in image stabilizer to absorb minor camera wiggles, you will find it difficult to avoid some wobbling during a long uninterrupted shot. When zoomed in all the way (with the lens in the narrow-angle, or telephoto, position), it is almost impossible to avoid some shaking and unsteadiness in the handheld shot.

To keep the handheld camera as steady as possible, support the camera in the palm of one hand and use the other hand to support the camera arm or the camera itself. **SEE 5.4**

With a foldout monitor, press your elbows against your body and use your arms as shock absorbers. Avoid operating the camera with your arms outstretched, which invites annoyingly quick pans and tilts. Inhale and hold your breath during the shot. The lack of oxygen will obviously limit the length of the shot, and that is probably a good thing. Shorter shots that show a variety of viewpoints are much more interesting than a long one with constant panning and zooming. Handheld camera mounts can reduce the wobbles of small camcorders (see figure 5.18). When using your arms as a camera mount, bend your knees slightly when shooting or, better, lean against a sturdy support, such as a building, wall, parked car, or lamppost, to increase the camera's stability. **SEE 5.5**

If you or the event moves, keep the lens in the wide-angle position (zoomed out) to minimize camera wiggles. When using a DSLR camera with a wide-angle lens, watch that your fingers are not in front of the lens, blocking part of the shot. If you need to get closer to the scene, stop the video recording, walk closer to get the tighter shot, and start to record again. If you need to zoom, work the zoom controls gently during the shot. For a relatively long take without a tripod, try to find something stable on which to place the camera, such as a table, park bench, or the roof or hood of a car.

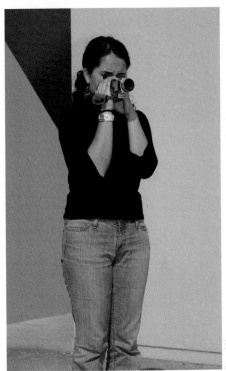

Edward Aiona

5.4 HOLDING THE SMALL CAMCORDER
Hold the camcorder with both hands, with the elbows pressed against the body.

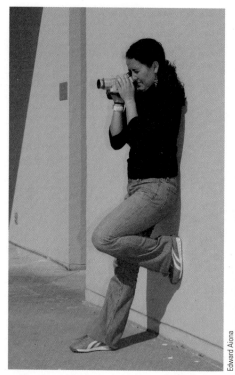

5.5 STEADYING THE CAMERA OPERATOR
Leaning against a support will steady both camera operator and camera.

5.6 PANNING THE CAMCORDER
Before panning, point your knees toward the end of the pan, then uncoil your upper body during the pan.

When moving the camera, do it smoothly. To pan the camera, move it with your whole body rather than just your arms. Point your knees as much as possible to where you want to end the pan, while keeping your shoulders in the starting position. During the pan your upper body will uncoil naturally in the direction of your knees and will carry the camera smoothly with it. **SEE 5.6** If you do not preset your knees, you will have to coil your body rather than uncoil it when panning, which is much harder to do and usually results in jerky camera motion.

When tilting the camera (pointing it up or down), try to bend forward or backward at the waist as much as possible while keeping your elbows against your body. As with a pan, your body motion makes the tilt look smoother than if you simply moved your wrists to point the camera up or down.

When walking with the camera, walk backward rather than forward whenever possible. **SEE 5.7** While walking backward you will lift your heels and walk on the balls of your feet. Your feet rather than your legs will act as shock absorbers. Your body, and with it the camera, will tend to glide along rather than bounce up and down.

For unconventional shots you can tilt the camera sideways, raise it above your head, and shoot over the people or other obstacles in front of you, or you can lower it close to the ground to get some low-angle views. Most regular viewfinders can be adjusted (at least tilted up and down) so that you can see what you are shooting

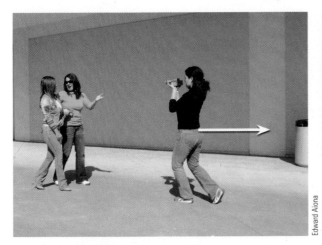

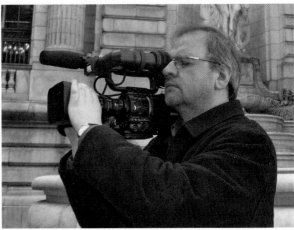

5.7 WALKING BACKWARD
Walking backward rather than forward makes it easier to keep the camera steady.

5.8 SHOULDER-MOUNTED CAMCORDER
When carrying the camcorder on the shoulder, one hand slips through a strap attached to the lens, leaving the fingers free to operate the zoom control. The other hand steadies the camera and operates the focus ring.

during such maneuvers. The foldout monitor offers a great advantage in such situations, especially if you find that the only way to get a good shot is to hold the camera high above your head and aim the lens more or less in the direction of the event. The foldout monitor still enables you to see the shot the camera is getting.

One of the problems when using a DSLR camera is that you need to keep it in front of your eyes to see what you are shooting. You can keep track of your shot only if you connect the camera to an external monitor. In normal lighting conditions, the foldout monitor of a small camcorder displays crisp color images; in bright light, however, you can see nothing or, at best, only a very dim image. In such situations, you may find that you might get usable shots by simply pointing the camera in the general direction of the event without ever looking at the monitor.

Larger camcorders that are too heavy to be handheld for long are best supported by the shoulder. Although the shoulder-mounted camera is slightly more restrictive than the handheld camcorder, the basic moves are much the same. **SEE 5.8** When carrying the camcorder on your shoulder, you need to adjust the viewfinder to fit your prominent (usually right) eye. Some camera operators keep the left eye open to see where they are going; others prefer to close it and concentrate on the viewfinder image. Most viewfinders of large camcorders can be flipped over for the left eye, and there are lenses with straps and zoom operating controls for the left hand.

Tripod-Supported Camera

Unless you are running after a breaking news story, the best way to keep the camcorder or ENG/EFP camera steady and the movements as smooth as possible is to support it on a ***tripod***, called "sticks" in production lingo. A good tripod, or some other similar mount, should be lightweight but sturdy enough to support the camera during pans and tilts. Its collapsible legs must lock securely in place at any extension

5.9 TRIPOD WITH SPREADER

The tripod has three adjustable legs that are sometimes secured by a spreader.

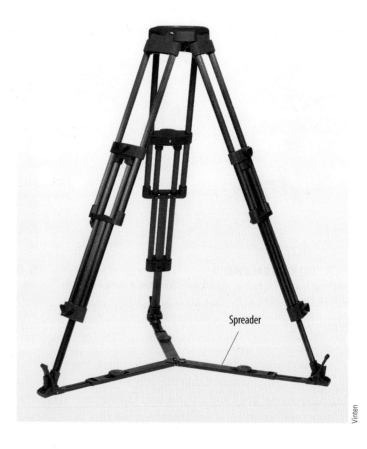

Spreader

Vinten

point and should have rubber cups and spikes at the tips. The rubber cups prevent the tripod from slipping on smooth surfaces, as do the spikes on rough surfaces.

Most professional tripods come with a spreader, a triangular base mount that locks the tips in place and prevents the legs from spreading no matter how much weight is put on them. Some spreaders come as part of the tripod. **SEE 5.9**

Some tripods have a center column that enables you to elevate and lower a small camcorder without having to adjust the tripod legs. Unless the camcorder is very small, such columns may not be sturdy enough for smooth shots, especially when the column is fully extended. All good tripods have a leveling bubble at or near the top ring so that you can ensure that the tripod is level.

Camera mounting head   One of the most important parts of a tripod is its camera ***mounting head***. This device, also called the pan-and-tilt head, permits smooth pans and tilts. It also lets you attach the camera and remove it from the tripod quickly. Many mounting heads have an additional leveling bubble so that you can easily adjust the head even if the tripod is on uneven ground.

Most big tripod mounting heads have a load limit of 30 to 45 pounds—ample to hold even a large camcorder and a teleprompter. These days the problem is not whether the mounting head can support a heavy camera but whether it can function smoothly with a small, lightweight camcorder. Even with a midsized camcorder, use a mounting head with a rating of 10 pounds or below. If the weight rating of the

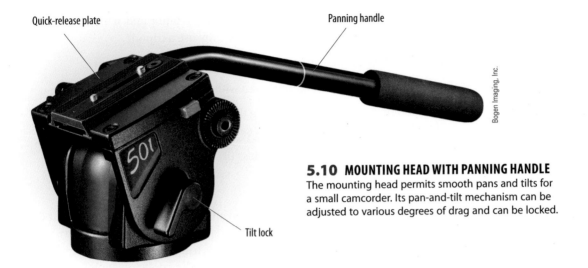

Quick-release plate

Panning handle

Bogen Imaging, Inc.

Tilt lock

5.10 MOUNTING HEAD WITH PANNING HANDLE
The mounting head permits smooth pans and tilts for
a small camcorder. Its pan-and-tilt mechanism can be
adjusted to various degrees of drag and can be locked.

mounting head is much higher than the actual weight of the camera, even the lowest
drag position will be too tight for smooth pans and tilts.

All mounting heads have similar basic controls. You move the mounting head
(and with it the camera) with the attached panning handle. **SEE 5.10** Lifting the handle
makes the camera tilt down; pushing it down makes the camera tilt up. Moving the
panning handle to the left pans the camera to the right; moving the handle to the
right pans the camera to the left. *Right* and *left* always refer to where the camera lens
is supposed to point, not to movement of the panning handle.

To prevent jerky, uneven movements, a mounting head must provide a certain
degree of drag, or resistance, to panning and tilting. The pan and tilt drags can
be adjusted to fit the weight of the camera and your personal preference. A small
camcorder needs a lighter drag adjustment than does a large camcorder. Now you
know why the weight rating for cameras is important: the heads for large camcorders have a much higher minimum drag than is necessary or even desirable for
small camcorders.

The mounting head also has pan and tilt lock mechanisms that prevent the camera from moving horizontally or flopping forward or backward when unattended.
Lock the mounting head every time you leave the camera unattended, no matter
how briefly. Never use the drag mechanism to lock the camera.

> **KEY CONCEPT**
>
> Lock the mounting head
> every time you leave the
> camera unattended. Don't
> use the drag mechanism
> to lock the camera.

Quick-release plate   This mechanism consists of a small rectangular plate that attaches to the bottom of the camera. The quick-release plate makes it easy to attach
a camcorder in a balanced position. This feature is especially useful when you want
to take the camera off the tripod to run after a new shot and then reattach it quickly
when returning to the tripod position. You simply slide the camcorder into the plate
receptacle on the mounting head, and it is locked in place and ready to go without
your having to rebalance its weight (see figure 5.10).

When switching from a handheld to a tripod-supported camera, you will initially
find that the tripod severely restricts your use of the camera. You can no longer run
with the camera, lift it above your head, shoot from close to ground level, cant it, or

swing it through the air. You are limited to panning and tilting and, if there is a center column, a rather modest camera elevation. So why use a tripod?

- The tripod steadies the camera, whether you are zoomed in or out.

- Pans and tilts are much smoother than with a handheld camera.

- The tripod prevents you from moving the camera excessively—a positive rather than a negative factor in good camera work.

- Mounting the camera on a tripod is less tiring than carrying it on your shoulder or in your hand.

Tripod dolly   To dolly or truck with a tripod-mounted camera, you must put the tripod on a three-caster dolly, which is simply a spreader with wheels. **SEE 5.11** With the casters in a freewheeling position, you can dolly, truck, and arc. Most professional dollies let you lock the casters in position for straight-line dollying. Be sure to check that the floor is smooth enough for an "on-air" move while the camera is "hot," or operating. When moving the tripod dolly, you usually push, pull, and steer with your left hand while guiding the panning handle and the camera with your right hand.

When a camera or camcorder is connected to a camera cable, you must adjust the cable guards so that the cable does not get wedged under the dolly casters. It is also a good idea to tie the cable to one of the tripod legs so that it is not pulled by its connector. **SEE 5.12**

Field dolly   When dollying on a rough surface, such as gravel or grass, you need to mount the tripod on a field dolly—a platform supported by four wheels with pneumatic tires. The steering mechanism works like the one you may remember

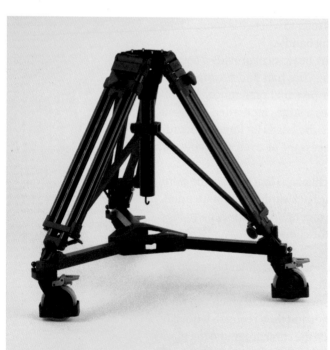

Vinten, Inc.

5.11 TRIPOD DOLLY
The tripod can be mounted on a three-wheel dolly, which permits quick repositioning of the camera.

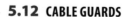
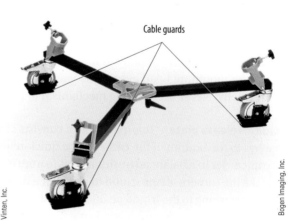

Cable guards

Bogen Imaging, Inc.

5.12 CABLE GUARDS
Cable guards prevent the dolly wheels from running over the camera cable. They must be close enough to the studio floor to push the cable aside.

from your red Radio Flyer wagon: a large handle turns the front wheels in the desired direction and lets you pull or push the entire platform. **SEE 5.13**

To operate the camera, you can stand on the dolly or walk alongside while the dolly operator pushes or pulls it along the dolly path. When the surface is especially rough, you can underinflate the tires to make the trip smoother. Many dollies are homemade and constructed from parts readily available in hardware stores.

Special Camera Mounts

Special camera mounts range from beanbags, skateboards, and wheelchairs to heavy Steadicam mounts. This is an area in which you can put your imagination and creativity to work.

Homemade devices   A simple beanbag, made from a pillowcase filled with foam packing peanuts, can serve as a reasonably good device for mounting a camcorder on the hood of a car or on bicycle handlebars. Professional "beanbags" are filled with a very flexible synthetic material that adjusts to the shape of the camera yet remains highly shock absorbent. **SEE 5.14**

Mounting a small camcorder on a skateboard and pulling it along a smooth surface can give you an interesting low-angle dolly shot. And a wheelchair or shopping cart is a cheap but effective device for transporting camera operator and camcorder for a long tracking shot. If the floor is smooth, such tracking shots can rival the ones done with a much more expensive studio pedestal.

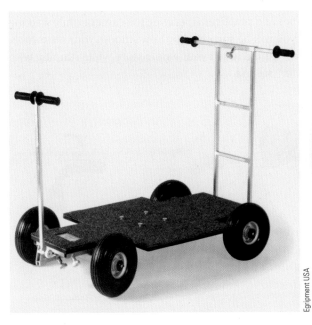

Egripment USA

5.13 FIELD DOLLY
The field dolly has a platform with four pneumatic tires that supports the tripod-mounted camera and the camera operator.

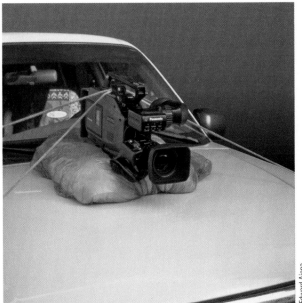

Edward Aiona

5.14 BEANBAG AS CAMERA MOUNT
A pillowcase filled with foam packing peanuts cradles the camera and prevents minor wiggles. Professional beanbags are filled with a flexible synthetic material.

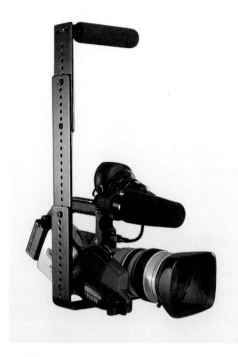

Glidecam

5.15 STUNT BAR

This extendable bar lets you lower the camcorder close to the ground for low-angle shots or raise it above your head for high-angle shots. Note that it does not absorb camera wobbles.

Handheld camera mounts   A variety of handheld stabilizers allow you to carry a small camcorder with one or both hands and keep the shot relatively steady so long as you don't jump up or down.

A simple yet highly effective handheld camera mount consists of an extendable bar to which you can attach the camera. This bar allows you to lower the camera close to the ground for from-below-eye-level shots or to raise it above your head while walking, running, or sitting in a shopping cart for low-angle tracking shots. You keep track of what the camera sees by looking at the foldout monitor. Note, however, that such a device will not absorb any camera wobbles. **SEE 5.15**

When using a DSLR camera for still shots, you can easily support it in the palm of one hand while adjusting focus and activating the shutter release with the other. When recording video, however, you need some kind of support to keep the camera steady during the shot. One useful device is the monopod, which is simply an extendable pole onto which the camera is mounted. Other useful supports for a small camera are the single- or double-handled plate and the lightweight brace that rests on your shoulder. **SEE 5.16** For a pocket camcorder, you can use a miniature tripod with flexible legs, or you can mount it on a flexible arm that can be attached with a suction cup to smooth surfaces. **SEE 5.17**

If you want the shots to appear wobble-free while you are running with the camera, you need a stabilizer. Once you have used one a few times and practiced operating the camera while walking or running, you will be surprised by how smooth your shots look. But don't be tempted to tell your whole story while running with the camcorder! **SEE 5.18**

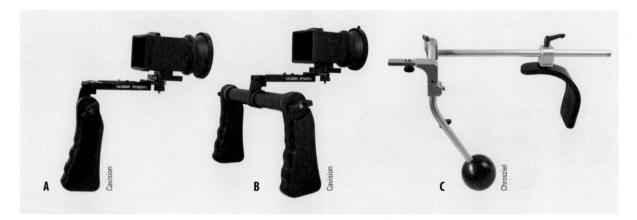

A Cavision   B Cavision   C Chrosziel

5.16 DSLR SUPPORTS

A The single handgrip facilitates the movement and the operation of a DSLR camera.

B The dual handlebar facilitates moving the camera during a shot.

C Shoulder camera mounts are especially designed to keep the DSLR camera steady during longer takes.

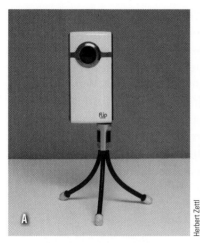

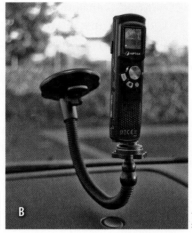

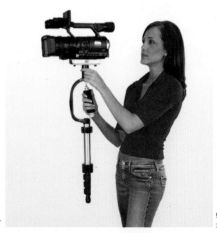

5.17 POCKET CAMCORDER SUPPORTS

A This tiny tripod has flexible legs to support a pocket camcorder on various surfaces.

B The suction cup on this flexible cable can be attached to any smooth surface to support a pocket camcorder.

5.18 HANDHELD STABILIZER

This handheld stabilizer is built for small camcorders. If you're strong enough, you can carry it with one hand. The foldout monitor helps you get the right shots.

Body-mounted stabilizers   A more elaborate but more comfortable way to operate a camera relatively wobble-free is by wearing a stabilizer harness. **SEE 5.19** For large camcorders, the operator wears a harness that is similar to the one for small camcorders except that the stabilizing system of gimbals and springs is built for the heavier camera. Despite the relative comfort of the vest, you will find that wearing such a device and operating the camcorder for even a relatively short period of time can be, at least initially, a challenge for even a strong person. **SEE 5.20**

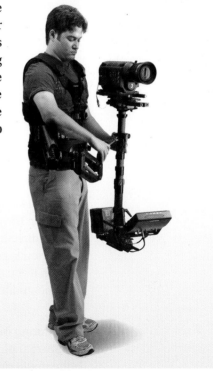

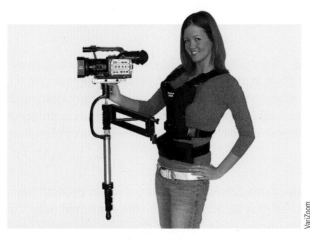

5.19 BODY-MOUNTED STABILIZER FOR SMALL CAMCORDERS

Wearing a camera support vest facilitates camera operation and is certainly less tiring than using a handheld stabilizer. The harness has a spring-loaded mechanism that lets you walk and even run with the camera, using the foldout monitor as your primary viewfinder.

5.20 BODY-MOUNTED STABILIZER FOR LARGE CAMCORDERS

This sturdy harness is designed to support a large camcorder or an ENG/EFP camera. The mechanism of gimbals and springs allows you to walk, run, and jump, with the camera remaining steady. Part of the counterweight is a large monitor.

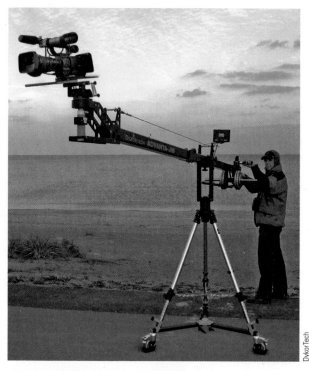

5.21 JIB ARM

This camera support operates like a big camera crane except that one person can operate both the jib and the camera. You can use it in the studio or in the field, and you can disassemble it for easy transport in a van to a remote location.

Jib arm   The *jib arm* operates just like a crane except that it is lighter, easier to operate, and less expensive. Jib arms are designed for shooting on-location and in studios. You can operate the jib arm and the attached camera or camcorder all by yourself. With the remote controls on the jib arm handles, you can lower the camera close to the ground or studio floor, elevate it to at least 10 feet, and pan, tilt, zoom, and focus the camera at the same time. Some long jib arms have an 18-foot reach but can be easily dismantled and transported in a small van. **SEE 5.21**

Studio Pedestal

Studio cameras, or ENG/EFP cameras converted for studio use, are usually mounted on studio pedestals. A **studio pedestal** is a relatively expensive camera mount that supports even the heaviest camera and additional equipment, such as a big zoom lens and a teleprompter. The studio pedestal lets you pan, tilt, truck, arc, and pedestal while the camera is on the air. By turning the steering ring, you can move the camera in any direction; by pulling it up or pushing it down, you can change the camera height. The telescoping center column is pneumatically counterbalanced so that the camera stays put at any height, even if you let go of the steering ring. If the camera begins to creep up or down by itself, the center column must be rebalanced. Instead of the three cable guards of the tripod dolly, the studio pedestal has a skirt, or housing, on the pedestal base to prevent the cable from getting caught in the casters. **SEE 5.22**

Parallel and tricycle steering   The studio pedestal has two different steering positions. In the parallel, or crab, position, the steering ring points all the casters in the same direction. **SEE 5.23A** Parallel steering is used for all normal camera moves. In the tricycle position, only one wheel is steerable. **SEE 5.23B** You use this steering position if you need to rotate the pedestal itself to move it closer to a piece of scenery or the studio wall.

Mounting head   Like the tripod, the center column of the studio pedestal has a camera mounting head attached to it. To accommodate the combined weight of the studio camera, its heavy lens, and the teleprompter, the customary tripod head has been replaced by a sturdier and more elaborate camera mount. Its operational controls are similar to those of the mounting heads for lightweight cameras: pan and tilt drags, locking devices, and panning handles. Some studio cameras have a wedge mount attached to the underside, which fits a receptacle on the top of the mounting

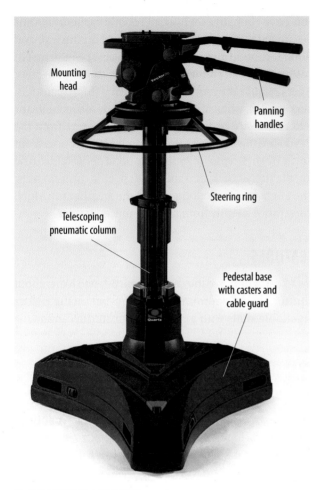

Mounting head

Panning handles

Steering ring

Telescoping pneumatic column

Pedestal base with casters and cable guard

5.22 STUDIO PEDESTAL

The studio pedestal permits you to pan, tilt, truck, arc, and pedestal while the camera is on the air. If the pedestal is equipped with a telescoping column, you can move the camera from about 2 feet to about 5 feet above the studio floor.

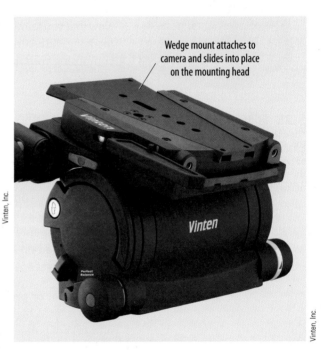

© Cengage Learning 2011

5.23 PARALLEL AND TRICYCLE STEERING

A In the parallel steering position, the three casters point in the same direction.

B In the tricycle steering position, only one wheel is steerable.

Wedge mount attaches to camera and slides into place on the mounting head

Vinten, Inc.

5.24 STUDIO CAMERA MOUNTING HEAD

This mounting head is designed especially for heavy studio cameras. The counterbalance and tilt-and-drag systems allow extremely smooth tilts and pans. The wedge mount ensures proper camera balance each time the camera is put back on the pedestal.

head. Once the camera is balanced, the wedge mount ensures proper balance every time the camera is put back on the pedestal. SEE 5.24

The mounting head has two panning handles that allow you to pan and tilt smoothly while simultaneously operating the attached zoom and focus controls. Before operating the studio camera, always unlock the mounting head and adjust the pan and tilt drags. When leaving the camera unattended, even for a short time, you should lock the mounting head—but never use the drag controls to do it. You should also cap the lens by putting the metal or plastic cap over the front of it or, when operating a studio camera, by asking the video operator to close the iris electronically so that no light will go through the lens.

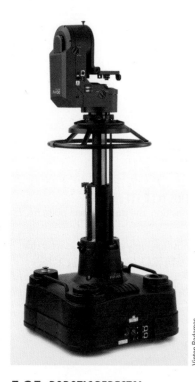

5.25 ROBOTIC PEDESTAL

The robotic pedestal can pan, tilt, pedestal, dolly, truck, and zoom according to computer instructions instead of those of a camera operator. It is used mainly for news presentations.

Vinten Radamec

Robotic pedestal   You have probably seen small robotic camera mounts for little cameras in lecture halls. They are usually mounted on the wall and aimed at the lectern. Similar robotic mounting heads can also be attached to simple tripods or pedestals for small camcorders. Robotic studio pedestals, however, are much larger because they must support heavy studio cameras. You can see them in news studios, where a single robotic-pedestal technician/camera operator/director runs two or three large studio cameras from the control room. In fact, if you are the floor manager in such a studio, watch out that you don't get run over by such a moving robot. Robotic pedestals can be preprogrammed to pan, tilt, dolly, truck, and zoom for specific camera shots, such as a two-shot of the anchors or a medium shot of the weather set. Much like in a sci-fi movie, they move silently from place to place. **SEE 5.25**

▇ OPERATIONAL FEATURES

Now that you know how to carry or move the camera, you need to learn about focusing, adjusting shutter speed, zooming, and white-balancing before composing your unforgettable shots with a camcorder or studio camera.

Focusing

Normally, we want all pictures on-screen to appear in focus (sharp and clear). You can achieve focus by manual or automatic controls.

Manual focus   To ensure sharp, clear pictures, you should focus manually rather than rely on the automatic focus. The manual focus control of all non-studio lenses is on a ring at the front of the lens that you can turn clockwise or counterclockwise. **SEE 5.26** **ZVL2** CAMERA→ Focusing→ focus ring | try it

When operating a studio camera, you stay in focus by turning a twist grip mounted on the left panning handle and connected to the zoom lens by a cable. **SEE 5.27**

Calibration, or presetting the zoom lens   Assume that you are to video-record a local high-school fund-raising event. The principal is auctioning off works of pottery made by students in the ceramic shop. She stands about 10 feet in front of the display tables along the back wall of the gym. During the video recording, you are asked to zoom from a medium shot of the principal to a fairly tight close-up of a ceramic pot, but during the zoom the shot gets progressively out of focus. When you reach the desired close-up, you can hardly make out the shape of the pot. What happened? You neglected to calibrate, or preset, the lens before zooming in for the close-up.

To *calibrate the zoom lens* means to adjust it so that it will maintain focus during the entire zoom. You must first zoom in to the desired close-up of the farthest target object—the pot—and bring it into focus by turning the focus ring at the front of the lens (or the twist grip on the studio panning handle). When you then zoom back to the medium shot of the principal, she will be in focus (although you may have to adjust the focus a little). When you zoom in again to another piece of pottery next to the previous pot, you will stay in

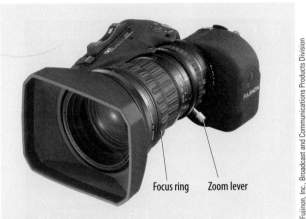

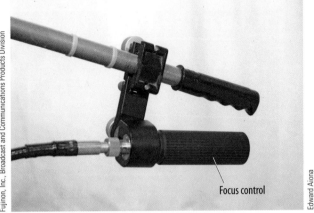

5.26 MANUAL FOCUS ON CAMCORDERS AND ENG/EFP CAMERAS
The manual focus control on camcorders and ENG/EFP cameras is a ring at the front of the lens that can be turned by hand.

5.27 MANUAL FOCUS CONTROL ON STUDIO CAMERAS
The focus control on a studio camera is a twist grip attached to the left panning handle. To focus you turn it either clockwise or counterclockwise.

focus and the close-up of the new pot will be sharp and clear. As soon as you reposition the camera, however, or if the principal moves toward or away from the display tables, you will need to recalibrate the lens. This means zooming in on the farthest pot again, focusing, zooming back to include the principal, and seeing whether you have to tweak the focus a little to keep her sharp and clear in subsequent zooms.

Now let's move into the studio, where your camera is assigned to cover a famous jazz pianist from the side so that you can zoom in from a medium shot to a tight close-up of the keyboard and the pianist's hands. How do you preset the zoom lens for this? You zoom in for a tight close-up of the keyboard and bring the lens into focus by turning the twist grip on the left panning handle. But exactly where on the keyboard should you focus? Probably the far end because you can then zoom in and out and stay in reasonably sharp focus regardless of whether the pianist displays his virtuosity at the near or far end of the keyboard.

Auto-focus Most handheld camcorders and some large cameras are equipped with an automatic focusing system, called the auto-focus. Through some electronic wizardry (reading the angle of a little radar beam or measuring the contrast), the camera focuses on a scene all by itself. Most of the time, these systems work well, but there are times when the camera cannot accommodate very bright or low-contrast scenes, leaving you with a blurred image. Or it may not detect exactly which object in the picture to bring into focus. You may not want to focus on the obvious foreground object but instead on the middleground. Unable to infer your artistic intent, the auto-focus will focus on the most prominent object closest to the camera. To achieve such a selective focus (see Lenses and Depth of Field in chapter 6), you need to switch from auto-focus to manual. The auto-focus can also have trouble keeping up with fast zooms. **ZVL3** CAMERA→ Focusing→ auto-focus

When working with a high-definition video camera, you may have trouble focusing. Because everything looks so much sharper than with standard television, you may not see in the relatively small viewfinder when your shots are slightly out

> **KEY CONCEPT**
>
> To calibrate a zoom lens, zoom in as close as possible on the farthest target object and bring it into focus. All subsequent zooms will be in focus so long as the camera-to-subject distance remains the same.

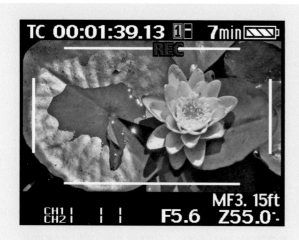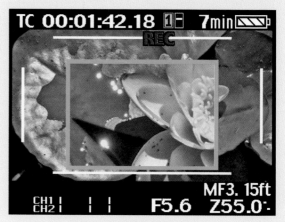

Gary Palmatier

5.28 FOCUS-ASSIST
The focus-assist feature enlarges the center of the image. Once you bring this section into focus, the whole image will be in focus.

of focus. The increased sharpness of the high-definition image also lures you into perceiving a much greater depth of field than you actually have—foreground and background seem to be in focus. When watching your shots on a high-quality monitor or a flat-panel display, however, you may discover that not only is the background out of focus but the foreground is as well. Switching to manual focus and racking in and out of focus will help you determine where the optimal focus lies. If you have a choice, always focus by looking at the black-and-white viewfinder and not the foldout color monitor; usually, the black-and-white image has a higher resolution.

Focus-assist   The difficulty of focusing high-definition pictures, especially on a color viewfinder, led to the development of a focus-assist feature. In most applications the center of the viewfinder shows an enlarged section of the image that lets you readily see whether it is in focus. If this center section is in focus, the whole image is in focus. **SEE 5.28**

Adjusting Shutter Speed

Like on a still camera, the camcorder has a variable ***shutter speed*** control to avoid image blur when shooting a fast-moving object. Although the way the shutter speed is controlled in both types of cameras is quite different, the effect is the same. If, for example, a cyclist with a bright yellow jersey is racing from one side of the screen to the other, you need to set a higher shutter speed than if the cyclist were pedaling along casually. When setting a fairly high electronic shutter speed (such as ½,₀₀₀ second), you will notice that the yellow jersey looks considerably darker than with lower shutter speeds. All of this translates into a simple formula, which is similar to still photography: the higher the shutter speed, the more light you need.

> **KEY CONCEPT**
> The higher the shutter speed, the less blurring occurs but the more light you need.

Zooming

All camcorders have a rocker switch on the lens that activates the zoom mechanism. By pressing the front of the switch, usually labeled *T* for *telephoto* or *tight,* you trigger a motor that rearranges elements in the zoom lens for the zoom-in effect.

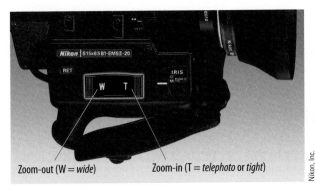

Zoom-out (W = *wide*)   Zoom-in (T = *telephoto* or *tight*)

Nikon, Inc.

5.29 CAMCORDER ZOOM CONTROL
Camcorders have a rocker switch near the lens that controls the zoom-in and zoom-out motion.

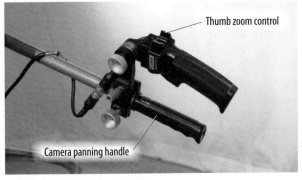

Thumb zoom control

Camera panning handle

Edward Aiona

5.30 STUDIO ZOOM CONTROL
The zoom control of the studio camera is a rocker switch on the right panning handle that is activated by the thumb of your right hand.

By pressing the back of the switch, labeled *W* for *wide,* you zoom out. This motorized servo-zoom mechanism, which is activated by the rocker switch, keeps the zooming smooth and steady. **SEE 5.29**

Some cameras offer a choice between a slow and a fast zoom speed. You may also find on some shoulder-mounted-camcorder lenses an additional manual zoom control that allows you to override the motorized mechanism by turning the zoom lever on the lens barrel for extremely fast zooms (see figure 5.26).

Studio cameras have a rocker switch mounted on the right panning handle. This thumb-operated switch is connected by cable to the servo-zoom mechanism of the studio lens. By pressing the *T* side of the switch, you zoom in; by pressing the *W* side, you zoom out. **SEE 5.30**

Because the servo-zoom mechanism makes zooming relatively easy, you may be tempted to zoom in and out unnecessarily. Keep zooming to a minimum; frequent and unmotivated zooming reveals the inexperience of the camera operator as readily as excessive camera movement. **ZVL4** CAMERA→ Zoom lens→ focal length | zoom control

> KEY CONCEPT
> Keep zooming to a minimum.

White-Balancing

To **white-balance** means to adjust the camera so that a sheet of white paper looks white on the television screen regardless of whether the light that illuminates the page is reddish, such as candlelight, or bluish, such as outdoor daylight. Most handheld camcorders do this automatically, although some have you set the white-balance switch to the proper setting, such as outdoors or indoors.

High-end handheld and shoulder-mounted camcorders, as well as all ENG/ EFP cameras, have a semiautomatic white balance, which means that you have to activate a white-balance switch. (See chapter 8 for a more detailed explanation of white-balancing.) **ZVL5** LIGHTS→ Color temperature→ white balance

> KEY CONCEPT
> Unless the camera has a fully automatic white-balance system, you need to white-balance every time you enter a new lighting environment.

■ GENERAL GUIDELINES

Whether you are operating a small camcorder or a large studio camera, treat it with extreme care as with all electronic equipment. Always be mindful of safety—yours and others'. Do not risk your neck and the equipment to get an especially spectacular shot that merely embellishes, rather than tells, the story. Do not abandon standard operational procedures for the sake of expediency. Whatever you do, use common sense. Like bicycling, you learn to operate a camera only by doing it. The following guidelines can make learning easier and also serve as useful checklists.

CHECKLIST: CAMCORDERS AND ENG/EFP CAMERAS

☑ **Don't expose the camera to the elements** Never leave the camera unprotected in the sun or in a hot car. Also watch that the viewfinder is not pointed into the sun; the magnifying glass in the viewfinder can collect the sun's rays and melt the viewfinder housing and electronics. Use plastic camera covers, called "raincoats," or a large umbrella when shooting in the rain or extreme cold. In case of emergency, a plastic grocery bag will do.

☑ **Leave the camera with care** Lock the mounting head on the tripod whenever you leave the camera unattended. When putting the camera down, place it upright. Laying it on its side may damage the viewfinder or attached microphone.

☑ **Use the lens cap** Even if a camera can be "capped" internally to prevent light from reaching the imaging device, always put the plastic or metal cap over the front of the zoom lens. This lens cap protects the delicate surface of the expensive lens.

☑ **Use fully charged batteries** Always see to it that the battery is fully charged. Normally, batteries must first be "trained" to avoid memory. When first using a new battery, run it until it is totally discharged, then charge it again. From now on it should fully charge regardless of how much charge was left before the charging. Do not drop batteries or expose them to extreme heat.

☑ **Verify the recording media** Make sure that the recording media fits the camera model. Even though different makes of cassettes, memory cards, and optical discs look similar to the eye, they may not fit a particular camera.

☑ **Examine all connections** Check all connectors, regardless of what they connect, to see whether they fit their designated jacks (see figure 4.23). Use adapters only in an emergency; an adapter is by design a stopgap and, as such, a potential trouble spot. Small camcorders normally use RCA phono connectors; larger camcorders have three-pin (XLR) audio connectors. (See chapter 7 for further information about audio connectors.)

☑ **Test the camera** Even when in a hurry, always do a brief test recording to verify that the camcorder records video as well as audio. Bring headphones along to check the audio. Use the same power supply and connectors that you intend to use during the actual video recording. Check the full range of the zoom lens and the focus. In extremely cold or damp conditions, zoom lenses sometimes stick or give up altogether.

☑ **Set the switches** Have all the switches—such as auto-focus or manual focus, auto-iris, zoom speed, and shutter speed—in the desired positions. The faster the action in front of the camera, the higher the shutter speed must be to prevent the moving object from blurring. Remember that higher shutter speeds require higher light levels. This presetting of major functions is especially important when working in the field, where the sun can render the camcorder monitor useless.

☑ **Perform a white balance** White-balance the camera before beginning the video recording, unless the system is fully automatic. White-balance under the light that actually illuminates the event.

☑ **Always capture audio** Make it a habit to turn on the camera microphone and record ambient sound with the pictures. This sound will help you identify the event location and will aid shot continuity during postproduction editing.

☑ **Heed the warning signs** Take note of caution signals in the viewfinder display and try to address the problem immediately. You may be able to dismiss the "low light level" warning on the camera if you are not concerned with picture quality, but you cannot ignore a "low battery" warning.

CHECKLIST: STUDIO CAMERAS

☑ **Get in touch and in control** Put on your headset to establish contact with the control room and the video operator. Unlock the mounting head and adjust the pan and tilt drags. Pedestal up and down to get a feel for the pedestal range and motion. A properly balanced pedestal should prevent the camera from creeping up or down when left in a vertical position.

☑ **Tame the cables** Position the cable guards close enough to the floor to prevent the pedestal from rolling over the camera cable. Uncoil the cable and check its reach. To avoid the inevitable tug of the cable during a dolly, tie it to the pedestal but leave enough slack so that you can freely pan, tilt, and pedestal.

☑ **Test-zoom and focus** Ask the video operator to uncap the camera so that you can rack through the zoom and focus ranges and, if necessary, adjust the viewfinder. Practice calibrating the zoom lens so that the scene remains in focus during subsequent zooms.

☑ **Practice your moves** Use masking tape on the studio floor to mark the critical camera positions. Write down all on-air camera moves so that you can set the zoom lens in the wide-angle position before the required move.

☑ **Move carefully** Ask a floor person to help you steer the camera during an especially tricky move. If the cable gets tangled up during a dolly, don't drag the whole mess along. Signal the floor person to untangle it for you. When dollying or trucking, start slowly to overcome the inertia of the heavy pedestal and slow down just before the end of the dolly. When raising or lowering the camera, brake the pedestal column before it reaches its maximum or minimum height; otherwise the camera and the picture might receive a hefty jolt.

☑ **Don't jump the red light** Wait for the tally light (the red light inside the viewfinder and on top of the camera) to go out before moving the camera into a new position or presetting the zoom lens. The tally light tells the camera operator, talent, and studio production crew which camera is hot. During special effects the tally light may remain on even if you think your shot is finished. Normally, the ENG/EFP camera or camcorder has only a viewfinder tally light, which tells only the camera operator when the camera is operating.

☑ **Avoid nervous camera movements** Keep your eyes on the viewfinder and correct slowly for minor compositional defects. If a subject bounces back and forth on a close-up, don't try to keep it in the frame at all costs. It is better to let it move out of the frame from time to time than to play catch-up by rapid panning.

☑ **Let the director direct** Always follow the director's instructions even if you think he or she is wrong. Do not try to outdirect the director from your position—but do alert the director if you are asked to do such impossible things as dollying or trucking on the air with your lens in the narrow-angle (zoomed-in) position.

☑ **Be observant and attentive** Be aware of the activity around you. Pay particular attention to where the other cameras are and where they are asked to move. By listening to the director's instructions, you will be able to stay out of the way of the other cameras. When moving a camera, especially backward, watch for obstacles that may be in your path. Ask a floor person to guide you. Avoid unnecessary chatter on the intercom.

☑ **Anticipate your next shot** Try to line up the next shot before the director calls for it, even if you work without a shot sheet that lists the nature and the sequence of your shots. For example, if you hear on the intercom that the other camera is on the air with a close-up, pull out to a medium shot or get a different angle to provide the director with another field of view. Do not duplicate the shot of another camera.

☑ **Put all tools away properly** At the end of the show, wait for the "all clear" signal before preparing your camera for shutdown. Ask the video operator to cap the camera. As soon as the viewfinder goes dark, release the pan and tilt drags, lock the mounting head, and cap the lens. Park the camera in its usual place and coil the cable in the customary figure-eight loops. If your dolly has a parking brake, activate it.

MAIN POINTS

▶ ***Camera Movements***

The movements include pan, tilt, cant, pedestal, dolly, truck or track, arc, crane or boom, and tongue. The zoom is also included, although the camera does not move.

▶ ***Camera Mounts***

There is a wide variety of basic tripods and mounts for handheld camcorders, DSLR cameras, and pocket camcorders. Larger field productions require special mounts such as the jib arm and the Steadicam. Studio productions require studio pedestals. Whenever possible, put the camcorder or ENG/EFP camera on a tripod. Keep the handheld or shoulder-mounted camera as steady as possible and zoomed out when moving.

▶ ***Camera Mounting Head***

This mechanism connects the camera to the tripod or the studio pedestal. It facilitates pans and tilts. Always lock the mounting head when leaving the camera unattended.

▶ ***Focus and Shutter Speed***

Normally, we want all pictures on-screen sharp and clear. You can achieve focus by manual or automatic controls. A high shutter speed reduces the blurring of bright, fast-moving objects. The higher the shutter speed, the less blurring occurs but the more light is needed.

▶ ***Calibrating the Zoom Lens***

To preset a zoom, the lens must be zoomed in on the farthest target object and brought into focus. All subsequent wide-angle zoom positions will be in focus so long as the camera-to-subject distance remains the same.

▶ ***White-Balancing***

This procedure ensures that white and all other colors look the same under different lights. It needs to be done every time the camera operates under new lighting conditions, unless the camera has a fully automatic white-balance mechanism.

ZETTL'S VIDEOLAB

 For your reference or to track your work, the *Zettl's VideoLab* program cues in this chapter are listed here with their corresponding page numbers.

KEY TERMS

aspect ratio The ratio of the width of the television screen to its height. In STV (standard television), it is 4 × 3 (4 units wide by 3 units high); for HDTV (high-definition television), it is 16 × 9 (16 units wide by 9 units high). Mobile media devices have various aspect ratios, including vertical ones.

close-up (CU) Object or any part of it seen at close range and framed tightly. The close-up can be extreme (extreme or big close-up) or rather loose (medium close-up).

cross-shot (X/S) Similar to the over-the-shoulder shot except that the camera-near person is completely out of the shot.

depth of field The area in which all objects, located at different distances from the camera, appear in focus. Depends primarily on the focal length of the lens, its ƒ-stop, and the distance from the camera to the object.

field of view The portion of a scene visible through a particular lens; its vista. Expressed in symbols, such as CU for close-up.

headroom The space between the top of the head and the upper screen edge.

leadroom The space in front of a laterally moving object or person.

long shot (LS) Object seen from far away or framed very loosely. The extreme long shot shows the object from a great distance. Also called *establishing shot*.

medium shot (MS) Object seen from a medium distance. Covers any framing between a long shot and a close-up.

noseroom The space in front of a person looking or pointing toward the edge of the screen.

over-the-shoulder shot (O/S) Camera looks over the camera-near person's shoulder (shoulder and back of head included in shot) at the other person.

point of convergence (POC) The point where z-axis vectors of the right and left 3D lenses meet, resulting in a perfect overlap of the right-eye and left-eye images.

psychological closure Mentally filling in missing visual information that will lead to a complete and stable configuration. Also called *closure*.

vector A directional screen force. There are graphic, index, and motion vectors.

z-axis Indicates screen depth. In standard two-dimensional video space, it extends from the screen (camera lens) to the background (horizon). In three-dimensional video space, it also extends from the screen to the viewer.

Looking through the Viewfinder

ffective camera operation depends not only on how to use certain buttons and levers but especially on how to frame impressive shots. In fact, good camera operation requires first and foremost a keen and sensitive eye and a basic knowledge of picture *aesthetics*—what makes one shot composition superior to another. Despite all the automated features, the camera cannot make aesthetic decisions for you. You must therefore also learn the basic compositional principles so that you can produce pictures that have impact and convey meaning.

Framing a good shot has lately become more difficult because you must account for different aspect ratios (shapes of a frame), various screens sizes, and 3D (three-dimensional) video. For example, the large home theater–type display and digital movie screens can show small details quite well even without close-ups. For the tiny cell-phone display, however, close-ups are essential; the relatively small screen and the limited presentation time make it impractical to introduce a scene by moving from an overall view to a close-up. Rather, you need to select only the most significant event details and show them as a series of close points of view. In this way you not only reveal the features necessary to tell the story but also establish the energy of an event that might otherwise get lost on the small screen.

Because video viewing is done mostly at home, however, such a close-up technique is also effective when composing shots for the large high-definition television (HDTV) screen. Even motion pictures intended for theater viewing have finally learned from television the high-energy impact of telling a story primarily in a series of close-ups. When dealing with 3D, however, the close-up is generally considered a problem. Having the nose stick out of the frame, with the ears relegated to the background does not make for a pleasing portrait.

This chapter takes a closer look at the aesthetics of picture composition. Note that in video you are working mostly with moving images, so some of the traditional compositional principles for still photography must be modified to fit a shot series rather than a single picture. Such considerations are especially important when editing the various shots—called clips—to tell a story. (We discuss such principles in chapter 13.)

▶ **FRAMING A SHOT**
Aspect ratio, field of view, vectors, composition, and psychological closure

▶ **MANIPULATING PICTURE DEPTH**
Defining the z-axis and the 3D z-axes, 3D lens separation and convergence, lenses and perceived z-axis length, lenses and depth of field, and lenses and perceived z-axis speed

▶ **CONTROLLING CAMERA AND OBJECT MOTION**
Camera movement and zooms, and shooting moving objects

▪ FRAMING A SHOT

The most basic considerations in framing a shot are how much territory you include in the shot, how close an object appears to the viewer, where to place the object relative to the screen edges, and how to make viewers perceive a complete object when only parts of it are visible on-screen. In the terminology of photographic arts, including video, these factors are known as aspect ratio, field of view, vectors and composition, and psychological closure.

Aspect Ratio

Your framing of a shot depends to a great extent on the kind of frame you have available—the relationship of the width of the screen to its height, or ***aspect ratio***. In video you will most often work with two aspect ratios: the 4 × 3 aspect ratio of standard television (STV) and the 16 × 9 aspect ratio of high-definition television. A 4 × 3 aspect ratio means that the screen is 4 units wide by 3 units high; a 16 × 9 screen is 16 units wide by 9 units high. When working in digital television (DTV), many cameras allow you to switch between the standard 4 × 3 ratio and the wide-screen 16 × 9 ratio of HDTV.

You will find that on the small screen your compositions will not differ significantly between the two aspect ratios. **SEE 6.1 AND 6.2**

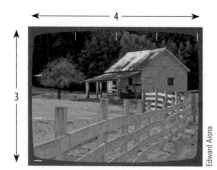

6.1 4 × 3 ASPECT RATIO
The aspect ratio of STV is 4 units wide by 3 units high.

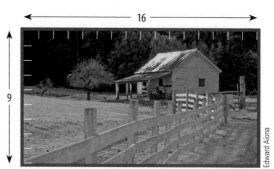

6.2 16 × 9 ASPECT RATIO
The HDTV aspect ratio is 16 units wide by 9 units high. Most DTV cameras permit switching between the standard 4 × 3 ratio and the wide-screen 16 × 9 ratio.

On a large video display or when video is projected onto a movie screen, however, the difference between the two aspect ratios is prominent. A close-up of a face is much simpler to compose in the 4 × 3 ratio than on the HDTV screen. On the other hand, the 16 × 9 ratio allows you to frame wide vistas without losing too much event impact. The wider aspect ratio not only preserves but emphasizes the landscape character of a horizontal vista. **SEE 6.3** It also makes it easier to frame a profile shot of two people talking to each other.

Letterbox and pillarbox   When using an STV screen or monitor with a 4 × 3 aspect ratio, you may have to show a movie or HDTV program that was originally shot in a 16 × 9 or slightly wider aspect ratio. Making the entire frame of a wide-screen movie fit into the 4 × 3 aspect ratio of STV results in empty (black) space at the top and the bottom of the screen. The resulting horizontal aspect ratio is called a letterbox. **SEE 6.4** When showing a standard 4 × 3 television image on the 16 × 9 screen, there are empty dead zones, or side bars, on both sides of the screen. The resulting vertical aspect ratio is called a pillarbox. **SEE 6.5** Because of such manipulations of aspect ratios, good directors try to restrict the major action as much as possible to the center of the screen.

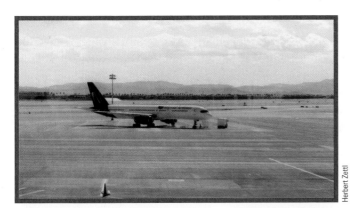

Herbert Zettl

6.3 WIDE VISTA EMPHASIZED
The wide 16 × 9 aspect ratio accentuates the horizontal stretch of this airfield.

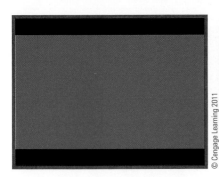

© Cengage Learning 2011

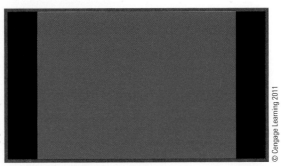

© Cengage Learning 2011

6.4 LETTERBOX
Making the entire frame of a 16 × 9 or movie aspect ratio fit into a 4 × 3 frame will leave empty space at the top and the bottom of the screen. The resulting horizontal aspect ratio is called a letterbox.

6.5 PILLARBOX
Using the total height of a 16 × 9 frame for showing a 4 × 3 aspect ratio will leave dead zones on both sides of the screen. The resulting vertical aspect ratio is called a pillarbox.

Effects   You will find that on a large screen, the 16 × 9 aspect ratio can make certain special effects much more obvious if not overbearing. The reverse happens on the small mobile media display: most special effects lose their impact. To help you get used to framing for the wider screen, in this book we display all the camera framings in the 16 × 9 aspect ratio. **ZVL1** CAMERA→ Screen forces→ aspect ratio

Field of View

Field of view refers to how close the object seems to the viewer, or how much of the "field," or scenery, in front of you is in the shot. When organized by how close we see the object, there are five field-of-view designations: extreme long shot (ELS or XLS), *long shot (LS)*, *medium shot (MS)*, *close-up (CU)*, and extreme close-up (ECU or XCU). **SEE 6.6**

When categorized by how much of a person we see, the shots are called: bust shot, which frames the upper part of a person; knee shot, which shows the person approximately from the knees up; two-shot, which shows two people or objects in the frame; three-shot, which shows three people or objects in the frame; *over-the-shoulder shot (O/S)*, which shows the camera looking at someone over the shoulder of another person closer to the camera; and *cross-shot (X/S)*, which looks alternately at one or the other person, with the camera-near person completely out of the shot. **SEE 6.7**

The field of view is relative, which means that what you consider a close-up someone else may think of as a medium shot. As mentioned, the relatively small size of the standard video screen made the close-up the most frequently used field of view in video production. These field-of-view designations hold true regardless of whether you shoot for a small screen or a large screen or for a 4 × 3 or a 16 × 9 aspect ratio.

You can change the field of view either by moving the camera closer to the event or farther away from it or by changing the focal length of the lens by zooming in or out. As you learned in chapter 4, zooming in puts the lens in the narrow-angle (telephoto) position and brings the subject closer to the camera for a close-up view. When you zoom out, the lens gradually assumes a wide-angle position and shows

6.6 FIELD-OF-VIEW DISTANCE STEPS
The field-of-view distance steps are relative and depend on how a long shot or close-up is visualized.

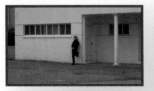

Extreme long shot (ELS),
or establishing shot

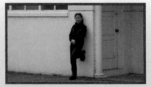

Long shot (LS), or full shot

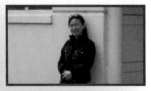

Medium shot (MS),
or waist shot

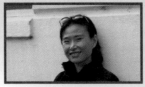

Close-up (CU)

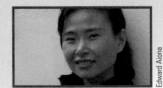

Extreme close-up (ECU)

Edward Aiona

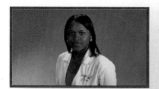
Bust shot

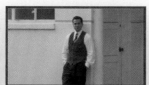
Knee shot

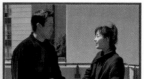
Two-shot (two persons or objects in frame)

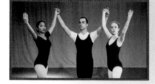
Three-shot (three persons or objects in frame)

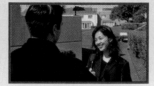
Over-the-shoulder shot (O/S)

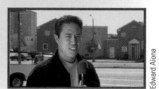
Cross-shot (X/S)

Edward Aiona

6.7 OTHER SHOT DESIGNATIONS

Other shot designations tell where the subject is cut off by the upper or lower part of the frame, how many subjects are in the frame, or how they are arranged.

more territory farther away. There are important visual differences between moving the camera closer or farther away from the subject and zooming in and out. (We discuss these differences in the context of controlling camera and object motion later in this chapter.) **ZVL2** CAMERA→ Composition→ field of view

> **KEY CONCEPT**
> Video is a close-up medium.

Vectors

A ***vector*** is a directional screen force with varying strengths. This concept will help you understand and control the specific screen forces generated by someone looking, pointing, or moving in a particular direction or even by the horizontal and vertical lines of a room, desk, or door. A thorough understanding of vectors will aid you in blocking—designing effective positions and movements of talent and cameras.

> **KEY CONCEPT**
> Vectors are directional screen forces that influence composition and the blocking of talent and cameras.

Graphic vectors These vectors are created by lines or an arrangement of stationary objects that lead the eye in a general direction. Look around you. You are surrounded by graphic vectors, such as the horizontal and vertical lines that are formed by this book, the window and door frames in the room, or the line where the walls meet the ceiling. The lines of a skyscraper form a series of graphic vectors. **SEE 6.8**

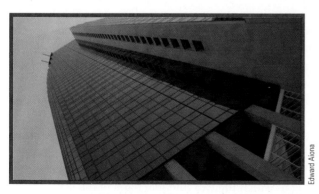

Edward Aiona

6.8 GRAPHIC VECTORS

Graphic vectors are created by lines or an arrangement of stationary objects that leads the eye in a certain direction.

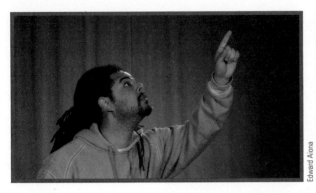

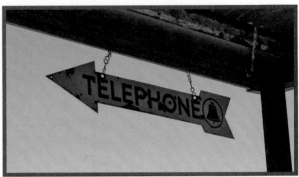

6.9 INDEX VECTORS
Index vectors are created by someone or something that points unquestionably in a particular direction.

Index vectors   These are created by something that points unquestionably in a specific direction, such as an arrow, a one-way-street sign, or somebody looking or pointing. **SEE 6.9** The difference between graphic and index vectors is that index vectors are much more definite as to direction. Going against the index vector of a one-way sign may jolt your sense of good composition as well as your body.

Motion vectors   A motion vector is created by an object that is actually moving, or is perceived to be moving, on-screen. People walking, a car speeding along the highway, a bird in flight—all form motion vectors. For an illustration of motion vectors, look around you where things are moving or turn on your TV set (motion vectors obviously cannot be illustrated by a still picture). **ZVL3** CAMERA→ Screen forces→ vectors

Composition

Our perceptual faculties are always striving to stabilize the chaotic world around us. Good picture composition helps us in this task. In fact, professional videographers apply effective compositional principles even when shooting under extreme pressure, such as while covering a storm or a war. Some of the most basic compositional factors involve subject placement, headroom and leadroom, and the horizon line.

Subject placement   The most stable and prominent picture area is screen-center. If you want to draw attention to a single subject, place it there. **SEE 6.10** The same goes for framing a person who is addressing viewers directly, such as a newscaster or a company president. **SEE 6.11**

If the newscaster has to share screen space with a visual, such as the secondary frame—the box—over her shoulder, you obviously need to move her to one side, not only to make room for the visual but also to balance the two picture elements within the frame. **SEE 6.12**

Sometimes when you frame large vistas that contain a distinct single vertical element, such as a telephone pole, tree, or skyscraper, you can place the single vertical element off-center, at about the one-third or two-thirds mark of screen width. Such nonsymmetrical framing in which the two unequal parts of the screen con-

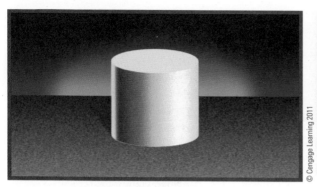

6.10 SCREEN-CENTER PLACEMENT
The most stable screen position is screen-center. All screen forces are neutralized at this point.

6.11 SCREEN-CENTER PLACEMENT OF NEWSCASTER
A single newscaster should be placed screen-center. This position draws undivided attention to the newscaster and what she is saying.

tain different visual elements is often called the rule of thirds. You may have heard of framing according to the golden section. In this case, the horizontal division is placed at the two-fifths or three-fifths mark. Either division makes the picture look more dynamic and the horizon less divided than if you placed the vertical object at exactly midpoint. **SEE 6.13**

The rule of thirds also applies to placing objects within the frame, such as having a person stand at the one-third mark of the screen width. Some directors and DPs (directors of photography) use the rule of thirds as a guide for close-ups, placing the eyes of a person in the upper third of the screen. Such a placement, however, depends on how big the close-up is, whether the subject wears a hat, and whether you need adequate headroom. If, for example, you would tilt down a bit to place the eyes of the man in figure 6.15 in the upper third of the frame, you would severely cramp the necessary headroom. But why do we need headroom anyway?

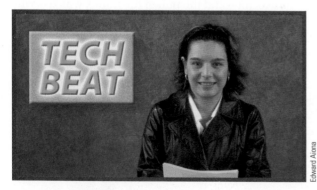
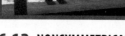
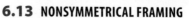

6.12 PICTURE BALANCE
When the newscaster has to share the screen space with other visuals, the elements must be placed in opposite screen halves so that they balance each other.

6.13 NONSYMMETRICAL FRAMING
A prominent horizontal line can best be divided by a vertical object located at about two-fifths (for the STV aspect ratio) or one-third (for the HDTV aspect ratio) the distance from either the left or the right screen edge. In this way the screen is not divided visually into two equal halves, which makes for a more dynamic and interesting composition.

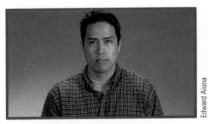

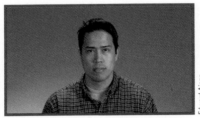

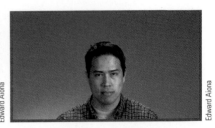

6.14 NO HEADROOM
Without headroom the person seems glued to the top edge of the screen.

6.15 PROPER HEADROOM
Correct headroom neutralizes the magnetic pull of the upper edge and makes the person look comfortable within the frame.

6.16 TOO MUCH HEADROOM
Too much headroom tends to dwarf the person and push the image against the lower half of the screen.

Headroom, noseroom, and leadroom   Somehow the edges of the video screen seem to act like magnets and attract objects close to them. This pull is especially strong at the top and bottom edges of the screen. For example, if you frame a man so that his head touches the upper screen edge, his head seems to be pulled up, or even attached, to the frame. **SEE 6.14** To counteract this pull, you must leave adequate space, called *headroom*. **SEE 6.15**

If you leave too much headroom, however, the bottom edge exerts its force and seems to pull the man downward. **SEE 6.16** Because you may lose some picture space when transmitting via cable or an on-the-air channel or because of a slightly mis-aligned TV receiver, you should leave just a little more headroom than what seems appropriate; this way the viewer will see framing with exactly the right headroom. **SEE 6.17** **ZVL4** CAMERA→ Composition→ headroom

The sides of the frame are similar graphical "magnets" that seem to pull persons or objects toward them, especially when they are oriented toward one or the other side of the screen. Take a look at the next figure. **SEE 6.18** Do you feel that this is a good composition? Of course not. The person seems to push his nose into the right screen edge. Correct framing requires some breathing room to reduce the force of his glance—his screen-right index vector—and the pull of the frame, which is why

Picture loss

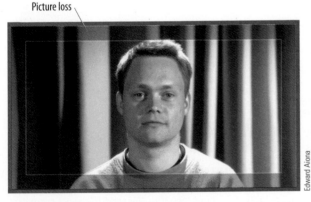

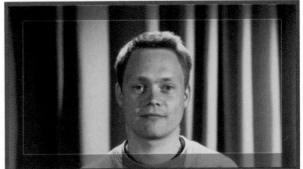

6.17 HEADROOM FOR TRANSMISSION
The framing on the left is correct for the viewfinder display, but the inevitable picture loss during transmission or video recording requires more initial headroom. The framing on the right is therefore more appropriate.

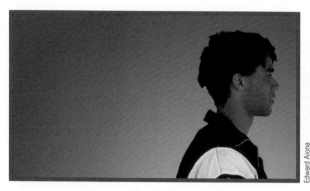

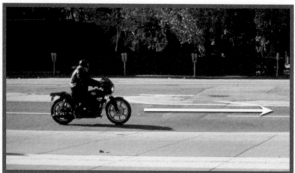

6.18 NO NOSEROOM
Without any space between the nose and the screen edge, the person seems to be glued to the frame or crashing into it.

6.19 PROPER NOSEROOM
This noseroom is sufficient to counter the pull of the screen edge and the force of the glance.

this type of framing is called *noseroom*. **SEE 6.19** Note that the rule of thirds also applies to noseroom: as you can see, the center of the person's head is approximately in the left third of the frame.

The same "breathing room" principle applies when you frame someone moving laterally. **SEE 6.20** You must leave some room in the direction of movement to show where the person is going and to absorb some of the directional energy of the motion vector. Because the camera must be somewhat ahead of the subject's motion and should lead the action rather than follow it, this is called *leadroom*. It is not always easy to keep proper leadroom for a moving person or object, especially if the subject moves quickly. **SEE 6.21** **ZVL5** CAMERA→ Composition→ leadroom

Now that you have learned all about the rule of thirds, a word of caution is in order: if you always apply this rule in a mathematical fashion, your pictures will look mechanical, as though you consistently edited them to a musical beat. In certain circumstances you need to break this rule and frame the subject unconventionally to give your pictures an additional edge. For example, if you want to emphasize the beautiful colors of the evening sky, you should ignore the rule of thirds and tilt the

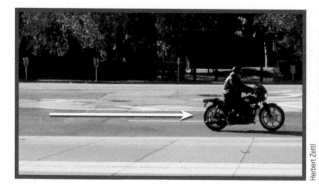

6.20 NO LEADROOM
Without proper leadroom the laterally moving subject or object seems oddly impeded by the screen edge.

6.21 PROPER LEADROOM
With proper leadroom the laterally moving subject or object seems able to move freely in the given direction.

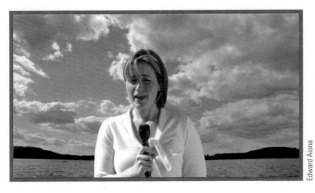

6.22 LEVEL HORIZON LINE

When framing a person standing in front of a prominent horizon line, make sure that it is level.

6.23 TILTING THE HORIZON LINE

A tilted horizon line increases the dynamic tension of the event.

camera up to lower the horizon line as much as possible. Or you may want to place a person right next to the screen edge to intensify his claustrophobia. As you can see, you can—and should—bend the compositional rules if it intensifies the message. But before you can bend a rule, you must understand it.

Horizon line   Normally, we expect buildings and people to stand upright on level ground. This principle is especially important when you shoot outdoors and where there are distinct vertical and horizontal graphic vectors. For instance, when video recording a weathercaster reporting from the shores of a lake, make sure that the background lines (graphic vectors) of the lake are parallel to the upper and lower screen edges. **SEE 6.22** A slight tilt of the handheld camcorder may not readily show up on the weathercaster in the foreground but is easily detectable by the tilted horizon line in the background.

If you intend to upset a stable environment by deliberately canting the camera, however, a tilted horizon line can make the picture more dynamic and increase its aesthetic energy. Of course, the subject matter must lend itself to such aesthetic manipulation. **SEE 6.23** Canting the camera on a dull speaker will not improve his speech; it will simply alert the viewer to sloppy camera work.

Psychological Closure

Our minds try to make sense of the bombardment of impressions we receive every second and to stabilize the world around us as much as possible. Our perceptual

6.24 PSYCHOLOGICAL CLOSURE

We perceive these three angle brackets as a triangle by mentally filling in the missing parts.

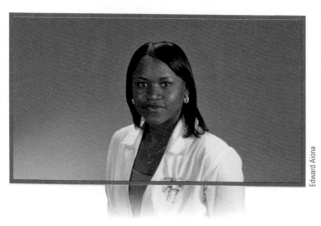

6.25 FRAMING A CLOSE-UP
A properly framed close-up leads our eyes into off-screen space to complete the figure.

Edward Aiona

mechanism does this by ignoring most sense impressions that are not immediately relevant and by combining visual cues or filling in missing visual information to arrive at complete and stable configurations. This process is called *psychological closure*, or closure for short.

Take a look at the arrangement of angle brackets on the facing page. **SEE 6.24** Although we actually see three separate brackets, we perceive a single triangle. Through psychological closure we automatically fill in the missing lines. In fact, you will probably have a hard time seeing them as three isolated angles without covering two of the three.

Now look at the close-up above. **SEE 6.25** Again you mentally fill in the rest of the subject's body although you actually see only her head and shoulders on-screen.

The graphic vectors of the shoulders that led your eye outside the frame helped you to apply closure to fill in the missing parts. One of the most important principles in framing a close-up in which only part of the subject is shown is to provide sufficient visual clues (in this case, graphic vectors) that enable the viewer to mentally complete the figure in off-screen space. Below are two different ECUs of the same person. Which one do you prefer? **SEE 6.26**

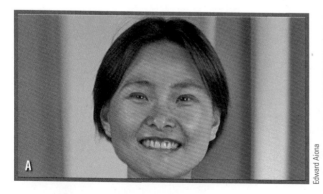

A

Edward Aiona

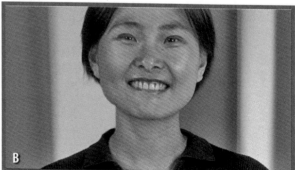

B

Edward Aiona

6.26 CHOOSING THE PROPER FRAMING
Here are two extreme close-ups. Which one looks better to you?

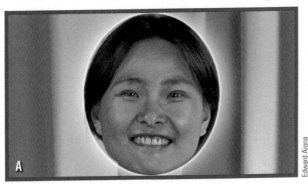

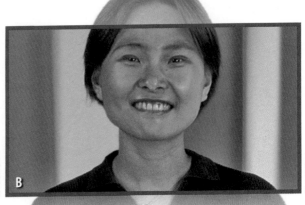

Edward Aiona

Edward Aiona

6.27 IMPROPER AND PROPER FRAMING

A This extreme close-up is improperly framed because it invites us to apply closure within the frame (an oval) without extending into off-screen space.

B This framing properly extends into off-screen space and allows us to apply closure to the whole figure.

Most likely, you chose the photo on the right (figure 6.26b) as the better ECU. But why? Because, as you can see in figure 6.27b, the close-up on the right has sufficient clues (graphic vectors) to tell us that the subject is continuing in off-screen space. In contrast, the framing on the left gives practically no visual clues that would lead us into off-screen space (see 6.27a). In fact, our perceptual mechanism is happy with having found a stable configuration within the frame: the head forms an oval. **SEE 6.27**

The disagreement between our experience, which tells us that there must be a body attached to the head, and our automated perception, which is perfectly happy with the circlelike configuration, is the principal reason why we feel uncomfortable with such a composition. **ZVL6** CAMERA→ Composition→ close-ups | try it

The need for psychological closure can also produce visual paradoxes and bad compositions by combining parts of the foreground and the background into a single configuration. Examples are the rubber plant on the set that seems to grow out of the guest's head as well as the tree or street sign that extends out of the person standing in front of it. **SEE 6.28** Although we know that such elements are in the background, our perceptual need for stable figures makes us perceive such visual paradoxes as a single unit.

6.28 UNDESIRABLE CLOSURE

Because of our tendency to stabilize the environment, we perceive this background object as part of the main figure.

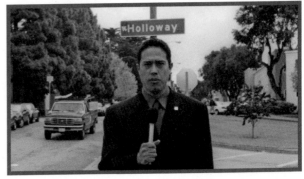

Herbert Zettl

When looking through the viewfinder, you must learn to see not only the foreground (target) object but also what is *behind* it. By looking behind the target object or scene, you will readily discover potential closure problems, such as the street sign that the reporter seems to balance on his head. Looking behind may also reveal other visual hazards, such as billboards that compete with your sponsor, or garbage cans, camera or mic cables, or light stands in the shot. **ZVL7** CAMERA→ Composition→ background

■ MANIPULATING PICTURE DEPTH

So far we have been concerned mainly with organizing the two-dimensional area of the video screen.[1] This section explores the depth dimension. Whereas the width and the height of the video screen have definite limits, the depth dimension extends from the camera lens to the horizon. Although illusory, the screen depth, or z-axis (a term borrowed from geometry), is the most flexible screen dimension. The *z-axis* is an imaginary line that stretches from camera lens to horizon, regardless of where the lens is pointing. You can place many more objects along this depth axis than across the width of the screen. You can also have objects move toward and away from the camera at any speed without having to worry about losing them in the viewfinder or providing adequate leadroom. **ZVL8** CAMERA→ Picture depth→ z-axis

Defining the Z-Axis

If you point a camera at the cloudless sky, you have just about as long a z-axis as you can get—but it does not show its depth. To show screen depth, you need to define the z-axis by placing objects or people along it. The traditional way of creating the illusion of depth is to place objects in a distinct foreground, middleground, and background. **SEE 6.29** Even on a relatively small set, a prominent foreground piece or person will help define the z-axis and suggest screen depth. **SEE 6.30**

---

1. For more information about picture composition, see Herbert Zettl, *Sight Sound Motion: Applied Media Aesthetics,* 6th ed. (Boston: Wadsworth, 2011), pp. 103–14.

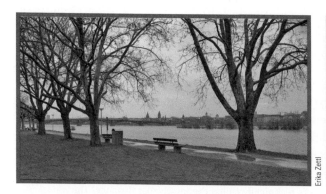

Erika Zettl

6.29 FOREGROUND, MIDDLEGROUND, AND BACKGROUND
A distinct division of the z-axis into foreground (trees and benches), middleground (river), and background (skyline) creates the illusion of depth.

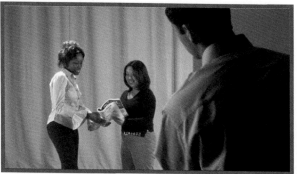

Edward Aiona

6.30 FOREGROUND PERSON TO CREATE DEPTH
The person standing in the foreground increases the illusion of screen depth.

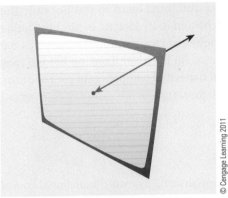

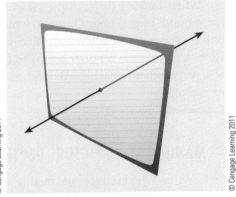

© Cengage Learning 2011

© Cengage Learning 2011

6.31 **2D Z-AXIS VECTOR**
In a two-dimensional monocular projection, the z-axis stretches from the screen (camera lens) to the background (horizon).

6.32 **3D Z-AXIS VECTORS**
In a three-dimensional projection, the z-axis extends from the screen to the horizon but also through the screen to the viewer. In effect, you have a z-axis in front of the screen that extends to the viewer and another one in back of the screen that extends to the horizon.

Defining the 3D Z-Axes

The crucial perceptual difference between a two-dimensional and a three-dimensional stereo projection is that in the standard 2D projection the z-axis extends only from the screen (camera lens) to the background (horizon). In 3D stereo projection, however, you have two z-axes: one goes from the screen to the background, and the other goes from the screen to the viewer. Depending on the projected motion, the z-axis can go from the background *through* the screen toward the viewer. **SEE 6.31 AND 6.32** This screen penetration by the z-axis that extends toward the viewer is one of the unique perceptual components of z-axis projection.

3D Lens Separation and Convergence

As you recall from chapter 4, your left eye sees an object from a slightly different angle than your right eye, but your brain fuses the two images, giving you an added and fairly accurate binocular clue of how far the object is from you. When duplicating this sensation in photography, including video and film, we use two cameras whose lenses substitute for our eyes.

Lens separation   Contrary to our eyes, which are at a fixed distance of about 2.5 inches (6.35 centimeters) from each other, the 3D camera rig or 3D software allows you to adjust the spread between the two lenses.[2] **SEE 6.33** The farther the lens-eyes are apart, the greater the difference of how each lens sees the same object or scene and therefore the more exaggerated the stereo effect becomes. The stereo image

2. The distance between the eyes is technically called the interocular distance. The interocular distance between lenses can be adjusted by either physically moving the cameras or through a mirror/prism system.

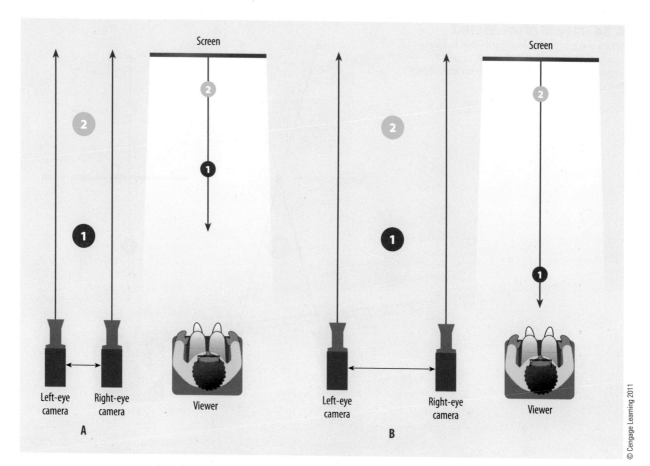

6.33 LENS SEPARATION AND STEREO EFFECT

A When the lenses of both the left-eye camera and the right-eye camera are parallel, the resulting stereo effect shows objects positioned on their z-axis (1 and 2) on the z-axis from screen to viewer. The objects seem to float in front of the screen.

B When you increase the distance between the cameras, the z-axis in front of the screen stretches. It also increases the perceived distance between objects 1 and 2, with object 1 now appearing to be much closer to the viewer.

produces a highly exaggerated z-axis that stretches from the screen to the viewer. Perceptually, the objects closest to the lenses seem to float right in front of your nose.

This is a great special effect if you want to invade the viewer's personal space or make something shoot out of the screen, causing the audience to duck from the oncoming object. But such maneuvers are also likely to give the viewer a severe headache because the brain is working overtime to fuse the two disparate images into a single stereo one.

Convergence   The lenses can either sit side-by-side pointing straight ahead to create parallel z-axes from cameras to the horizon or be swiveled toward each other to a certain degree. By having the lenses not only closer or farther away from each other but also slightly pigeon-toed to various degrees, their z-axes intersect at a predeter-mined point. This intersection is the ***point of convergence (POC)***, or convergence

6.34 **3D POINT OF CONVERGENCE**
When the point of convergence lies behind object 1, but in front of object 2, object 1 appears to be in front of the screen and object 2 in the screen background.

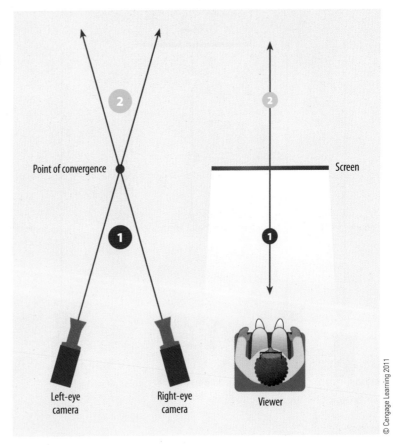

© Cengage Learning 2011

point: the location at which the pictures of the left-eye camera and the right-eye camera overlap perfectly, nullifying any stereo effect.

In stereo video or film, the POC generally marks the screen position—the reference plane of what is perceived to be behind and in front of the screen. Whatever is positioned in front of the POC appears to float in front of the screen, and whatever is behind the POC appears to lie behind the screen. **SEE 6.34**

But what if both lenses are fixed in a parallel position, preventing their z-axes from converging? Everything they see appears to float in front of the screen. In this case, the point of convergence must then be set in postproduction. You should realize that good 3D is not just having something pop out of the screen (along the z-axis from screen to viewer) but also, if not especially, giving more air between objects behind the screen (along the z-axis from screen to horizon). In fact, a good 3D director tries to keep most of the action behind the screen and away from the screen edges; otherwise you may end up with partial close-ups bleeding out of the side of the screen, a problem known as a window violation.

Going any further with explaining the pitfalls of 3D video and film would prove counterproductive at this point because many of the standard 2D production aspects yet to be learned differ considerably from what is currently being explored in 3D video. So, for now, we'll return to the 2D world.

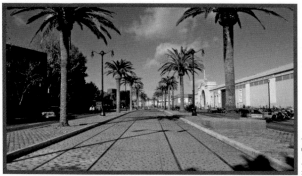

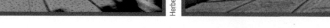

6.35 WIDE-ANGLE Z-AXIS

The wide-angle lens stretches the z-axis and increases the perceived distance between objects (palm trees).

6.36 NARROW-ANGLE Z-AXIS

The narrow-angle (telephoto) lens shrinks the z-axis, compresses the distance between objects (palm trees), and enlarges the background (building).

Lenses and 2D Z-Axis Length

In standard two-dimensional video, the focal length of a lens has a great influence on our perception of z-axis length and the distance between objects placed along the z-axis.

Wide-angle position   When zoomed all the way out (wide-angle position), the z-axis appears elongated and the objects placed along it seem to be farther apart than they really are. **SEE 6.35**

Narrow-angle position   When zoomed all the way in (narrow-angle, or telephoto, position), the z-axis seems to be shorter than it really is and the distance between the objects placed along it seems reduced. The z-axis and its objects seem compressed. **SEE 6.36**

Lenses and Depth of Field

You have probably noticed when zoomed all the way in (with the lens in the telephoto position) that you have more trouble keeping in focus an object traveling along the z-axis than when zoomed all the way out to a wide-angle position. When zoomed in, the z-axis area that is in focus is considerably shallower than when zoomed out. We call this area in which objects are in focus ***depth of field***. **SEE 6.37**

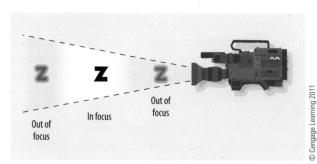

6.37 DEPTH OF FIELD

The area along the z-axis in which objects appear in focus is called depth of field.

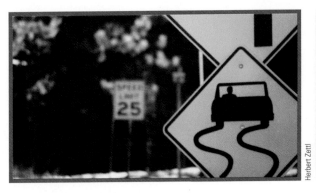

Herbert Zettl

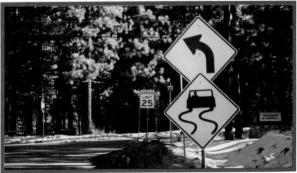

Herbert Zettl

6.38 SHALLOW DEPTH OF FIELD

Narrow-angle (telephoto) lenses have a shallow depth of field. When zoomed in, the depth of field is shallow.

6.39 GREAT DEPTH OF FIELD

Wide-angle lenses have a great depth of field. When zoomed out, the depth of field is great.

In the narrow-angle position, lenses have a shallow depth of field. This means that if you are focused on a foreground object, objects in the middleground and the background are out of focus. If you shift your focus to an object in the middleground, the foreground and background objects are out of focus. If you focus on the background, the middleground and foreground objects are out of focus. Note that with a shallow depth of field, an object can move only a short distance along the z-axis before it goes out of focus. **SEE 6.38** `ZVL9` CAMERA→ Focusing→ depth of field | shallow

A wide-angle position creates a great depth of field: objects that are widely scattered along the z-axis are all in focus. For example, when you focus on the foreground object in a large depth of field, the middleground and background objects remain in focus as well, and an object can travel a great distance along the z-axis and still be in focus. **SEE 6.39**

In practice this means that when zoomed out to a wide-angle position, you don't have to worry much about staying in focus. But when zoomed in to a narrow-angle position, you need to adjust the focus constantly whenever the camera or the object moves along the z-axis.

Depth of field is also influenced by object-to-camera distance and the size of the lens aperture. The closer the camera is to the object, the shallower the depth of field becomes; the farther away you are, the greater the depth of field. A large aperture reduces the depth of field; a small one increases it. (See chapter 4 for a discussion of lens apertures.) `ZVL10` CAMERA→ Focusing→ depth of field | great depth

You will find that a great depth of field is desirable for most routine productions. Especially when running after a news story, you want to show as much of the event as clearly as possible without having to worry about keeping the picture in focus. This is why you should zoom out and keep the lens in the wide-angle position. When you need a closer shot, you simply move the camera closer to the event. With the wide-angle lens position, the depth of field remains great enough to stay in focus even when you or the object moves.

For a more deliberate production, there are many instances in which a shallow depth of field is preferred. By focusing on the target object while keeping everything

KEY CONCEPT

With the zoom lens in a narrow-angle position (zoomed all the way in), depth of field is shallow and keeping focus is difficult. With the zoom lens in a wide-angle position (zoomed all the way out), depth of field is great and keeping focus is relatively easy.

KEY CONCEPT

Depth of field is dependent on the focal length of the lens, the distance from camera to object, and the lens aperture.

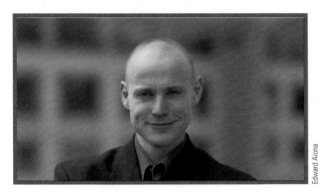

Edward Aiona

6.40 SHALLOW DEPTH OF FIELD IN CLOSE-UPS
Regardless of the focal length of the lens, close-ups have a shallower depth of field than long shots. The clue is the out-of-focus background.

else out of focus, you can emphasize the target without eliminating the environment. Another favorite technique is to shift emphasis from person to person by alternately focusing on one person, with the other person out of focus, and then switching. Realize, however, that this rack-focus effect is so popular that it has become a cliché.

If you move the camera extremely close to the object, the depth of field will shrink even if the lens is zoomed out to the wide-angle position. Because the camera-to-object distance influences the depth of field, as does the focal length of the lens, we can say that, in general, tight close-ups have a shallow depth of field. SEE 6.40 `ZVL11` CAMERA→ Focusing→ depth of field

Lenses and Z-axis Speed

Because a narrow-angle lens position compresses the z-axis, the movement of objects along the z-axis is equally compressed. When the lens is zoomed all the way in, cars seem to be much more crowded and moving more slowly than they actually are. With the lens zoomed all the way out, they seem to be farther apart and moving much faster than they actually are. By simply putting the zoom lens in a narrow-angle or wide-angle position, you can manipulate the viewer's perception of the distance between objects and how fast they move along the z-axis. `ZVL12` CAMERA→ Picture depth→ lens choice | perspective and distortion `ZVL13` CAMERA→ Screen motion→ z-axis

> **KEY CONCEPT**
>
> A narrow-angle lens position compresses the z-axis and slows down z-axis motion. A wide-angle lens position stretches the z-axis and speeds up z-axis motion.

CONTROLLING CAMERA AND OBJECT MOTION

Here we cover a few of the main aesthetic principles of camera and object motion. These include the most obvious do's and don'ts of moving the camera, zooming, and blocking object movement. (Additional information about controlling camera and object motion is presented in subsequent chapters.)

Controlling Camera Movement and Zooms

If there is a single indication of an inexperienced camera operator, it is excessive camera movement and zooms. The wildly roaming camera reminds us more of a firefighter's nozzle than photographic artistry, and the fast out-of-focus zooms produce more eyestrain than dramatic impact.

Moving camera   For some reason most beginners think that it is the camera that has to do the moving rather than the object in front of it, especially when there is not much object motion. If nothing moves, so be it. Aesthetic energy does not come from unmotivated camera movement but from the event itself, regardless of whether it is in motion. If there are any hard-and-fast aesthetic rules in camera operation, this is one of them: always try to keep the camera as steady as possible and have the people and the objects in front of the camera do the moving. The problem with an incessantly moving camera is that it draws too much attention to itself. It is, after all, the event you want to show, not your virtuosity of zooming and camera handling.

For variety and to provide viewers with different points of view, you can shift camera angles or change the camera-to-object distance. Even if there is absolutely no movement in the event, different angles and fields of view will provide enough change to hold viewers' interest and give them more information about the event. To keep camera movement to a minimum, use a tripod or other camera mount whenever possible, even if the camera is small.

KEY CONCEPT
Whenever possible, keep the camera still and let the event do the moving.

Fast zooms   Fast, unmotivated zooms are as annoying as a needlessly roving camera. The major problem is that the zoom—even more than camera motion—is a highly visible technique that draws attention to itself. One of the worst things you can do is follow a fast zoom-in or zoom-out with an equally fast zoom in the opposite direction. Rest on the target object for a while before switching to another angle and point of view. Constant zooming in and out makes viewers feel cheated: you bring the event to them through zooming in only to take it away by immediately zooming out. In the worst case, it may make viewers slightly nauseated. Unless you are planning a highly dramatic effect, a zoom should remain largely unnoticed by the viewer. If you must zoom, do it slowly.

In general, zooming in to a close-up increases tension; zooming out releases it. You will find that it is easier to start with a close-up view of an object and then zoom out than the other way around. When zooming out from a close-up, it is also easier to stay in focus than when zooming in, especially if you have not had time to calibrate the zoom lens (see chapter 5). Even with an automatic focus, fast zooms cause problems because the auto-focus mechanism may not be able to keep up with the speed of the image change. Consequently, the picture will pop in and out of focus during the zoom.

KEY CONCEPT
Avoid fast and constant zooming in and out.

Zoom versus dolly   There is an important aesthetic difference between a zoom and a dolly. When you zoom in or out, the event seems to move toward or away from the viewer; when you dolly in or out, the viewer seems to move toward or away from the event.

If, for example, you want to show that the ringing telephone bears an important message, you zoom in on the phone rather than dolly in. The fast zoom virtually catapults the phone toward the screen and the viewer. But when you want to have the viewer identify with a student who is late for class, you dolly the camera toward the only empty chair rather than zoom in on it. The dolly will accompany the student—and the viewer—to the empty chair. A zoom would bring the chair to the student (and the viewer), and that rarely happens, even in a friendly classroom atmosphere. The

KEY CONCEPT
A zoom-in brings the object to the viewer; a dolly-in takes the viewer to the object.

reason for this aesthetic difference is that the camera remains stationary during the zoom, whereas during a dolly it actually moves into the scene. `ZVL14` CAMERA→ Camera moves→ dolly | zoom

Controlling Object Motion

Despite all the theory about providing leadroom for an object moving laterally from one screen edge to the other, it is hard to keep it properly framed on the traditional 4×3 STV screen. Sometimes even experienced camera operators have trouble following an object that moves laterally in a tight shot. Just try following somebody moving sideways fairly close to the camera—you will be glad just to keep the person in the viewfinder! Framing lateral motion—that is, motion along the x-axis—is somewhat easier with a wide-angle lens position or when shooting for the 16×9 aspect ratio. In any case, when the subject moves in a straight line along the z-axis—toward or away from the camera—you will have much less trouble keeping the person in the shot and properly framed, even if he or she walks briskly. Blocking people along the z-axis rather than the x-axis not only is easier on the camera operator but also produces shots with greater impact.

Z-axis blocking refers to placing people behind rather than next to one another. **SEE 6.41** This arrangement makes it relatively easy to keep several people in a single shot and to capture their movements without excess camera motion. With the lens in the wide-angle position, z-axis movement can look dramatic and spectacular. Also, as you have just learned, the wide-angle lens provides a large enough depth of field so that you need to do little, if any, focusing.

Even when you have no control over the event and cannot influence the blocking, as is the case in most electronic news gathering, you can still conform the object motion to the aesthetic requirements of the small screen and the stable camera: simply position the camera in such a way that most of the object movement occurs along the z-axis. For example, if you cover a parade, don't stand on the sidewalk and try to capture the various bands and floats as they move past you; instead step onto the street and shoot against the oncoming parade traffic. With a zoom lens in the wide-angle position, you will have little trouble covering the event in long shots and close-ups while staying in focus. `ZVL15` CAMERA→ Picture depth→ z-axis

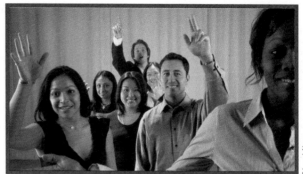

Edward Aiona

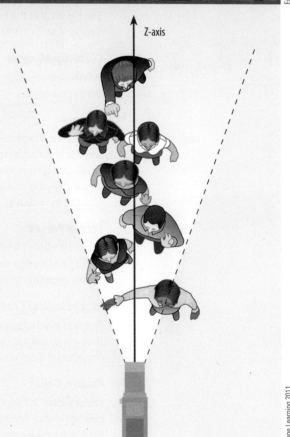

© Cengage Learning 2011

6.41 Z-AXIS BLOCKING
Blocking along the z-axis suits the small video screen.

> **KEY CONCEPT**
>
> Z-axis blocking looks dramatic and requires little camera movement. It is essential for framing several people and capturing motion on the small mobile media display.

M A I N   P O I N T S

▶ *Aspect Ratio*

The standard television (STV) aspect ratio is 4×3. The high-definition television (HDTV) aspect ratio is 16×9.

▶ *Field of View*

The field of view is usually expressed in five shots, ranging from extreme long shot (ELS or XLS) to extreme close-up (ECU or XCU). Other shot designations refer to how much of a person we see (such as bust shot or knee shot) or how many people we see (two-shot or three-shot). In an over-the-shoulder shot (O/S), we see the shoulder and the back of the head of the camera-near person while looking at the camera-far person. A cross-shot (X/S) is closer, with the camera-near person out of the shot.

▶ *Close-Up Medium*

Video is a close-up medium. Select those event details that tell the real story with clarity and impact.

▶ *Vectors*

Vectors are directional screen forces of varying strengths that influence composition and the blocking of talent and cameras. There are graphic vectors, which suggest a direction through lines or objects that form a line; index vectors, which point unquestionably in a specific direction; and motion vectors, which show the actual event or its screen image in motion.

▶ *Screen Forces*

The most stable picture area is screen-center. Headroom neutralizes the pull of the upper screen edge. Noseroom and leadroom neutralize the index and motion vector forces, respectively, and the pull of the frame.

▶ *Psychological Closure*

Through psychological closure we are able to perceive a complete figure even if it is shown only partially in a close-up. Close-ups that show only part of the object must provide sufficient visual clues for closure in off-screen space.

▶ *Picture Depth*

The standard 2D depth dimension depends on defining the z-axis into foreground, middleground, and background. Wide-angle zoom lens positions (zoomed out) make the z-axis look longer; objects seem farther apart, and their z-axis movement appears faster than it actually is. Narrow-angle zoom lens positions (zoomed in) make the z-axis look shorter; objects seem more compressed, and their z-axis movement appears slower. Wide-angle lens positions show a great depth of field; narrow-angle lens positions show a shallow one. In 2D video space, the z-axis extends from the screen (camera lens) to the background (horizon). In 3D video space, it also extends from screen to viewer.

▶ *Motion*

Whenever possible, keep the camera still and let the event do the moving. A zoom-in brings the object to the viewer; a dolly-in takes the viewer to the object. Z-axis movement is well suited to the relatively small TV screen of both aspect ratios. It is essential for the mobile media display.

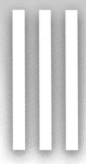

PART

Image Creation: Sound, Light, Graphics, and Effects

CHAPTER 7

Audio and
Sound Control

CHAPTER 8

Light, Color,
and Lighting

CHAPTER 9

Graphics and
Effects

When you review your latest video recordings a little more critically, you can see that your composition has improved considerably. You left proper headroom and leadroom, and your horizon lines are level. But now you are discovering other problems that went unnoticed before. What is most annoying are the hollow sounds you got when you interviewed people in their living room and the crackling of wind and traffic noise when the interview took place on a street corner. Apparently, you forgot to listen to the environment while composing your impressive shots. Despite the good composition, some shots looks grossly overexposed; others hide all the detail in dense shadows. Some of the indoor shots have a strange green tint, and the white wedding gown of your friend's bride looks light blue in your outdoor shots.

Part III introduces you to basic audio and lighting techniques that will help you avoid such problems—and also gives you some pointers on effective graphics and visual effects.

KEY TERMS

cardioid Heart-shaped pickup pattern of a unidirectional microphone.

condenser microphone A high-quality, sensitive microphone for critical sound pickup.

dynamic microphone A relatively rugged microphone. Good for outdoor use.

fader A volume control that works by sliding a button horizontally along a scale. Identical in function to a pot. Also called *slide fader.*

hypercardioid Very narrow unidirectional pickup pattern with a long reach. The mic is also sensitive to sounds coming directly from the back.

jack A socket or receptacle for a connector.

lavalier A small microphone that is clipped to clothing. Also called *lav.*

mini plug Small audio connector.

omnidirectional Pickup pattern of a microphone that can hear equally well from all directions.

pickup pattern The territory around the microphone within which the mic can hear well.

polar pattern The two-dimensional representation of the microphone pickup pattern.

pop filter A wire-mesh screen attached to the front of a mic that reduces breath pops and sudden air blasts.

RCA phono plug Connector for video and audio equipment.

ribbon microphone A high-quality, highly sensitive microphone for critical sound pickup in the studio, usually for recording string instruments.

sweetening The postproduction manipulation of recorded sound.

unidirectional Pickup pattern of a microphone that can hear best from the front.

volume-unit (VU) meter Measures volume units, the relative loudness of amplified sound.

waveform Graphic representation of a sound that occurs over a period of time.

windscreen Acoustic foam rubber that is put over the entire microphone to cut down wind noise.

windsock A moplike cloth cover that is put over the windscreen to further reduce wind noise in outdoor use. Also called *wind jammer.*

XLR connector Professional three-wire connector for audio cables.

Audio and Sound Control

Television is primarily a visual medium, right? Wrong. Video programs rely on the sound portion even more than films do. The audio portion not only conveys information but adds aesthetic energy and structure to the video sequences. You have also no doubt heard that the worst sin you can commit in video production is showing "talking heads"—a criticism that is a total misconception. You will find that there is nothing wrong with talking heads so long as they talk well.

In fact, much of the information in video programs is conveyed by somebody talking. You can do a simple experiment to prove this point: Turn off the video portion of the program and try to follow what is going on; then turn on the video again but turn off the audio. You will probably have little trouble following the story by only hearing the sound track, but in most cases you will have difficulty knowing what is going on by only seeing the pictures. Even if you can follow the story by watching the pictures, the lack of sound leaves the message strangely incomplete. Just turn off the sound for a moment while watching a football game. Without the crowd noise, the play seems to have lost most of its excitement.

Much amateur video is characterized not just by the madly moving camera and the fast zooms but also by the bad audio. Even professional video productions tend to suffer more from poor sound than bad pictures. Why? At first glance the production of sound seems much easier to achieve than the corresponding video. When working a camcorder, you are probably concentrating so hard on getting good pictures that you don't pay much attention to the sounds and assume that the built-in microphone will do the job when set to the automatic volume control. Many times this may be sufficient. For good sound, however, simply turning on the camera mic, or sticking a mic into a scene at the last minute, is not the way to go.

Not all microphones sound the same, nor do they sound the same in different environments. When outdoors there is the additional hazard of wind noise and other unwanted environmental sounds. Unless you do a routine show, you need to consider the audio requirements as an essential part of the production process. The better the original audio pickup, the more time you will save in postproduction. `ZVL1` AUDIO→ Audio introduction

This chapter examines the various tools and techniques of producing good audio for video.

▶ **SOUND PICKUP PRINCIPLE**

How microphones change sound waves into sound signals

▶ **MICROPHONES**

How well they hear, how they are made, and how they are used

▶ **SOUND CONTROL**

Working the audio mixer and the audio console

▶ **SOUND RECORDING**

Digital recording equipment and other audio-recording devices

▶ **AUDIO POSTPRODUCTION**

Audio postproduction room, sound waveform, and automated dialogue replacement

▶ **SYNTHESIZED SOUND**

Computer-generated sounds

▶ **SOUND AESTHETICS**

Context, figure/ground, sound perspective, continuity, and energy and mood

▪ SOUND PICKUP PRINCIPLE

Like the translation process in video, in which the lens image of the object is converted into the video signal, in audio the sounds the microphone hears are *transduced* (transformed) into electric energy—the audio signal. This signal is made audible again through the loudspeaker. The basic sound pickup tool is the microphone, or mic (pronounced "mike").

You can also create sounds synthetically, by electronically generating and recording certain frequencies, a process similar to creating computer-generated video images. We focus first on microphone-generated sounds, then turn briefly to synthesized sounds

▪ MICROPHONES

Although all microphones fulfill the same basic function of transducing sounds into audio signals, they do so in different ways and for different purposes. Good audio requires that you know how to choose the right mic for a specific sound pickup—not an easy task when faced with the myriad mics available. Despite all the brand names and numbers, you can make sense of the different microphones by classifying them by how well they hear, how they are made, and how they are generally used.

How Well Mics Hear: Sound Pickup

Not all microphones hear sounds in the same way. Some are built to hear sounds from all directions equally well; others favor sounds that come from a specific direction. The directional characteristic—the zone within which a microphone can hear well—is specified by its ***pickup pattern***. Its two-dimensional representation is called the ***polar pattern***.

In general, you will find that most microphones used in video production are omnidirectional or unidirectional. The ***omnidirectional*** mic hears equally well from all directions. Visualize the omnidirectional mic at the center of a sphere. The sphere itself represents the pickup pattern. **SEE 7.1**

The ***unidirectional*** mic is designed to hear especially well from one direction—the front. Because the pickup pattern of a unidirectional mic is roughly heart-shaped, it is also called ***cardioid***. **SEE 7.2**

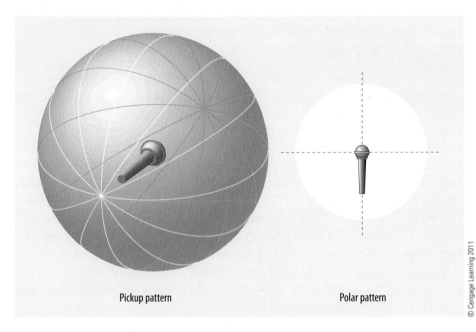

Pickup pattern   Polar pattern

© Cengage Learning 2011

7.1 OMNIDIRECTIONAL MICROPHONE PATTERNS
The omnidirectional microphone hears equally well from all directions.

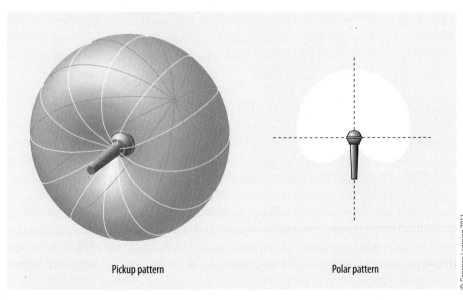

Pickup pattern   Polar pattern

© Cengage Learning 2011

7.2 CARDIOID MICROPHONE PATTERNS
The unidirectional microphone favors sounds that are in front of it. Its pickup pattern is heart-shaped, hence the term *cardioid*.

7.3 HYPERCARDIOID MICROPHONE PATTERNS

The hypercardioid pickup pattern is narrower than the cardioid and has a longer reach. Hypercardioid mics can also hear sounds coming from behind the mic.

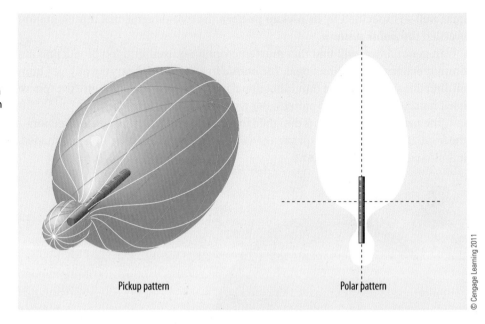

Pickup pattern   Polar pattern

© Cengage Learning 2011

When this pickup pattern gets progressively narrower, the mics are supercardioid, hypercardioid, or ultracardioid. The "heart" of the cardioid pickup pattern has now been stretched to the shape of a thin watermelon. **SEE 7.3** The ***hypercardioid*** and ultracardioid mics have a long reach, which means you can produce sounds that seem to come from fairly close by although they may actually be quite far away. Hyper- and supercardioid mics are also somewhat sensitive to sounds that come directly from behind. Because these microphones are usually fairly long and are aimed in the direction of the sound source, they are commonly called shotgun mics. **ZVL2** AUDIO→ Microphones→ pickup patterns

How Mics Are Made

When selecting a mic for a particular audio task, you need to consider both its specific pickup pattern and its basic mechanics—its sound-generating element. When classifying microphones by how they are made, there are three types used in video production: dynamic, condenser, and ribbon.

The dynamic mic uses a small coil that moves within a magnetic field when activated by sound. The movement of the coil produces the sound signal. The condenser mic has a movable plate—a diaphragm—that oscillates against a fixed plate to produce the sound signal. The ribbon mic has a tiny ribbon, rather than a coil, that moves in a magnetic field. But don't worry too much about exactly how these sound elements work; it is more important to know how these mics differ in their use.

Dynamic   The ***dynamic microphone*** is the most rugged. You can take it outside in all kinds of weather, and it can even withstand occasional rough handling. You can work with the mic close to extremely loud sounds without damaging it or distorting the sound too much. Many dynamic microphones have a built-in ***pop filter***, which

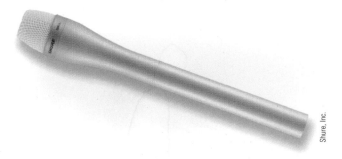

7.4 DYNAMIC MICROPHONE WITH POP FILTER

Dynamic microphones are the most rugged. They can withstand rough handling and extreme temperatures. The built-in pop filter reduces breath pops. This omnidirectional mic is ideally suited for field interviews.

Shure, Inc.

eliminates the breath pops that occur when someone speaks into the mic at very close range. **SEE 7.4** **ZVL3** AUDIO→ Microphones→ transducer→ dynamic mic

Condenser   These microphones are much more sensitive to physical shock and temperature than are dynamic mics, but they produce higher-quality sounds. ***Condenser microphones*** are generally used for critical sound pickup indoors, but they are also used in the field. They are especially prominent in music recording. Unlike dynamic mics, condenser microphones need a power supply to activate the sound-generating device inside the mic and to amplify the electrical signal before it leaves the mic. Some have a battery in the microphone housing. **SEE 7.5** Others get their power supply through the cable from the audio console, mixer, or camcorder (usually called phantom power). If you use a battery, see to it that it is inserted properly (with the + and – poles as indicated in the housing) and that the battery is not rundown. Always have a spare battery handy when using a condenser mic. **ZVL4** AUDIO→ Microphones→ transducer→ condenser mic

When using a condenser shotgun mic (or any shotgun mic) outdoors, you need to protect the entire microphone from wind noise by covering it with a ***windscreen***. **SEE 7.6** Windscreens are made of acoustic foam rubber or other synthetic material, which lets normal sound frequencies enter the mic but keeps most of the lower wind rumbles out. For ENG/EFP (electronic news gathering/electronic field production)

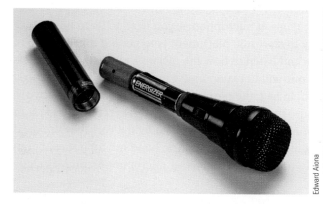

Edward Aiona

7.5 BATTERY POWER SUPPLY FOR CONDENSER MIC

Most condenser mics use a battery to charge the condenser plates. When fed to the microphone from the audio console, the power is called phantom power.

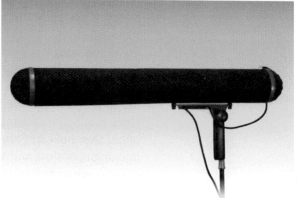

AKG Acoustics, Inc.

7.6 WINDSCREEN ON SHOTGUN MICROPHONE

The windscreen, made of porous material, protects the mic from excessive wind noise.

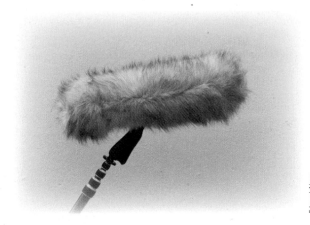

Edward Aiona

7.7 WINDSOCK PULLED OVER WINDSCREEN
The windsock is used on top of the windscreen to further reduce wind noise.

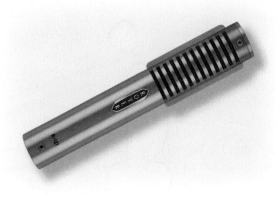

Royer Labs

7.8 RIBBON MICROPHONE FOR HIGH-QUALITY SOUND PICKUP
This ribbon mic is amazingly rugged without sacrificing its warm sound quality. It is an ideal microphone for recording voice-over narration, piano, and a variety of brass, woodwind, and string instruments.

microphones that are used primarily outdoors, you may want to add a ***windsock***, also called a wind jammer—a fuzzy cloth resembling a mop that can be pulled over the windscreen. **SEE 7.7**

Ribbon   You may still find ***ribbon microphones*** in some audio-recording studios or for critical music pickup for television. These highly sensitive mics are normally used for recording acoustic string instruments. **SEE 7.8** For normal video work, however, ribbon mics are just too sensitive. A loud sound burst close to the mic can put it out of commission. **ZVL5** AUDIO→ Microphones→ transducer→ ribbon mic

How Mics Are Used

Now that you know the basic types of microphones, you need to learn how to use them effectively. A good way to start mic placement is to get the mic as close to the sound source as possible and listen to how the pickup sounds. Even the most sophisticated and expensive mic will not guarantee good sound unless it is placed in an optimal pickup position. In fact, the proper positioning of the mic relative to the sound source is often more important than its sound-generating element. In video production, microphones are therefore identified by the way they are used rather than how they are made: lavalier microphones; hand microphones; boom microphones; desk and stand microphones; headset microphones; and wireless, or radio, microphones.

Lavalier microphones   The ***lavalier*** mic, or lav for short, is a very small, rugged, usually omnidirectional microphone (dynamic or condenser) that is used principally for voice pickup. The quality of even the smallest lav, which is about the size of a fingernail, is amazingly good. The combination of small size, ruggedness, and high quality has made the lavalier indispensable in video production. It is usually clipped to clothing, such as the lapel of a jacket or the front of a shirt, 6 to 8 inches below the chin. **SEE 7.9**

Although it is primarily intended for voice pickup, you can also use the lavalier for music. Sound technicians have used the lav successfully taped to violins and string basses. Don't be overly influenced by the normal use of such mics: try them out in a variety of ways and listen to the sound they deliver. If it sounds good to you, you've got the right mic.

The obvious advantage of the lavalier is that the talent has both hands free when wearing it, but there are numerous other advantages to using a lavalier mic, as well:

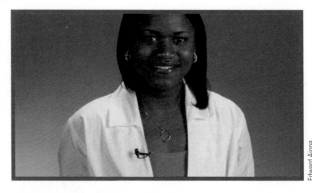

7.9 LAVALIER MICROPHONE
The small lavalier mic is usually clipped to the performer's clothing. It is used primarily for voice pickup.

- Because the distance from mic to sound source does not change once the mic is properly attached, you do not have to ride gain (adjust the volume) once you adjust the volume at the beginning of the shoot.

- Unlike lighting for the boom mic, which must be done in such a way that the boom shadows are hidden from camera view, the lavalier needs no special lighting considerations.

- Although the talent's action radius is somewhat limited by the mic cable, the lavalier lets him or her move more quickly than with a boom mic or even a hand mic. For greater mobility you can plug the talent's lavalier into a small body-pack transmitter and use it as a wireless mic.

There are also some disadvantages to using a lavalier mic:

- If the environment is very noisy, you cannot move the mic closer to the talent's mouth. Consequently, the surrounding (ambient) noise is easily picked up.

- You need a separate mic for each sound source. In a two-person interview, for example, you need separate lavaliers for the host and the guest. In a five-person panel show, you obviously need five lavs.

- Because it is attached to clothing, the lavalier may pick up rubbing noises, especially if the talent moves around a great deal. You may also get occasional popping noises from static electricity.

- If the mic must be concealed under clothing, the sound often takes on a muffled character and the danger of rubbing noises is greatly increased.

- One of the advantages we listed can also be a disadvantage: because the distance from the mic to the mouth does not change, the sounds do not seem to come from a closer distance on a close-up or from farther away on a long shot. Therefore you cannot achieve a desirable sound perspective. (We discuss sound perspective later in this chapter.)

Here are some points to consider when using a lavalier microphone:

■ Once the mic is attached to the mic cable but not yet to the talent, watch that you do not pull the mic off a table or chair and drop it on the floor. Although the lavalier is fairly rugged, it does not tolerate mistreatment. If you accidentally drop the mic during the setup or strike (the clearing of the production space), test it immediately to check that it still functions properly. Ask the talent to avoid hitting it with his or her hand or some object that might be demonstrated on-camera.

■ Be sure to put the mic on. As obvious as this sounds, on the opening cue many a performer has been found sitting on the mic rather than wearing it.

■ To put on the microphone, bring it up underneath the talent's shirt or jacket and attach it securely on the outside. Do not put the mic next to jewelry or buttons. If you have to conceal the mic, don't bury it under layers of clothing; try to keep the top of the mic as exposed as possible. Tuck the cable into the talent's belt or clothing so that it cannot pull the mic sideways or, worse, completely off. To further avoid pops and rumbles, put a small loop in the cable just below the mic clip, or try putting a loose knot in the mic cable where it leaves the mic. Wedging a small piece of foam rubber between mic and clothing will further reduce rubbing noises.

■ When outdoors, attach the little windscreen that slips over the top of the mic.

■ When using a wireless lav, tell the talent to switch the body-pack transmitter to the *off* position during each break. This keeps the battery from running down prematurely and also prevents the transmission of sounds that might be embarrassing to the talent.

■ After the show watch that the talent does not get up and walk off the set without first removing the microphone. `ZVL6` AUDIO→ Microphones→ mic types→ lav mic

Hand microphones   As the name implies, hand microphones are handled by the talent. You select a hand mic for situations in which the talent needs to exercise some control over the sound pickup.

A reporter can move a hand mic closer to his or her mouth when working in noisy surroundings, thereby eliminating much distracting ambience; the reporter can also point it toward the person he or she is interviewing. Because the talent can point the mic toward whoever is doing the talking, you need only a single microphone for an interview with one or even several guests. Performers who do audience participation shows like the hand mic because it allows them to approach people and talk to them spontaneously without an elaborate multiple-microphone setup.

A singer can control the intimacy of the sound (its presence) by holding the unidirectional hand mic very close to his or her mouth during an especially soft passage and pulling it farther away when the song gets louder and more external. Experienced singers use the hand mic as an important visual element; they work the mic during a song by switching it from one hand to the other to signal—visually—a transition or change of pace or simply to supply additional visual interest. **SEE 7.10**

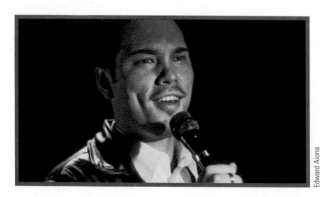

Edward Aiona

7.10 USE OF DIRECTIONAL MICROPHONE BY SINGER
To emphasize the richness of his voice, the singer holds the directional hand mic close to his mouth.

When the hand mic is used outdoors for numerous production tasks and under a great variety of weather conditions, you need a rugged mic that tolerates rough handling and extreme conditions. Dynamic hand mics with built-in pop filters are popular for such productions. Singers, on the other hand, often demand more sound quality than a field reporter and prefer high-quality condenser hand mics.

The control of the mic by the talent can also be a disadvantage. Inexperienced talent often block their own and their guests' faces; this no-no becomes especially apparent when the mic has a large, colored pop filter attached to it. Also, in the excitement of the interview, an inexperienced reporter may aim the microphone toward the guest when asking the question and toward himself or herself when listening to the answer. As humorous as this unintentional comedy routine may seem to the viewer, it is not funny to the production people who see their professional efforts undermined by such a mistake.

Other disadvantages of using a hand mic are that the talent's hands are not free to do other things, such as demonstrate a product. And, unless it is a wireless hand mic, pulling the cable while working a hand mic is not always easy to do.

Here are some hints for working with a hand microphone:

- During rehearsal, check the action radius of the mic cable. Also see that the cable has free travel and will not catch on furniture or scenery. Checking the reach of the cable is especially important when the mic is connected to a camcorder.

- Test the microphone before the video recording or live transmission. Say a few of the opening lines so that the audio engineer or camcorder operator can adjust the volume of the audio signal. When there are several mics in the immediate vicinity and you need to find out which one is turned on, do not blow or whistle into it—or, worse, whack it; rather, lightly scratch the pop filter. This scratching noise will enable the audio technician to identify your microphone and separate it from the others.

- When using a hand mic in the field under normal conditions (the environment is not excessively loud, and there is little or no wind), hold the microphone at chest level and speak *across* rather than into it. **SEE 7.11** In noisy and windy conditions, hold the mic closer to your mouth. **SEE 7.12**

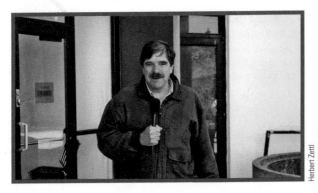

7.11 NORMAL POSITION OF HAND MICROPHONE
In a fairly quiet environment, the hand mic should be held at chest height. The performer speaks across the mic rather than into it.

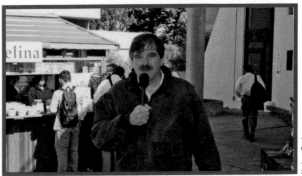

7.12 POSITION OF HAND MICROPHONE IN NOISY SURROUNDINGS
In environments with a lot of ambient noise, the performer holds the mic closer to the mouth and speaks into the mic rather than across it.

- When using a directional hand microphone, hold it close to your mouth and speak or sing directly into it, as shown in figure 7.10.

- When using a hand mic to interview a child, do not remain standing; squat down so that you are at the child's level. In this way you establish personal contact with the child, and the camera can get a good two-shot. **SEE 7.13**

- If the mic cable gets tangled during a take, do not panic and yank on it. Stop where you are and continue your performance while trying to get the attention of the floor manager or somebody else who can untangle it for you.

- If you need to use both hands while holding a hand mic, tuck it temporarily under your arm so that it can still pick up your voice.

- When the hand mic is connected directly to a camcorder, the camera operator should also turn on the camera mic (built-in or attached). The camera mic will supply a second audio track with the ambient sounds without interfering with the hand mic, which is supplying the primary audio. In fact, you should always turn on the camera mic, even if you don't intend to use the ambience. Most likely, these sounds will come in handy during postproduction editing. **ZVL7** AUDIO→ Microphones→ mic types→ camera mic

7.13 INTERVIEWING A CHILD
When interviewing a child, squat down and hold the mic toward the child. The child is now more aware of you than the mic, and the camera operator can include both faces in the shot.

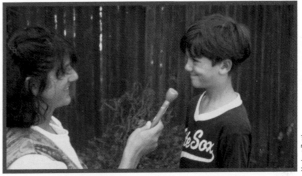

Boom microphones   Whenever the microphone is to be kept out of the picture, it is usually suspended from a fishpole or big boom. Whatever microphone is suspended from such a device is called a boom mic, regardless of its pickup pattern or sound-generating element. But because the boom mic is usually farther away from its sound source than a lavalier or hand mic, hypercardioid or supercardioid shotgun mics are used. As you recall, such highly directional microphones can pick up sounds over a fairly great distance and make them seem to come from close by. You can aim the mic toward the principal sound source while eliminating or greatly reducing all other sounds that lie outside its narrow pickup pattern. Note, however, that it is equally efficient at picking up extraneous noise that lies in its pickup path.

Fishpole   A fishpole is a sturdy, lightweight metal pole that can be extended. The shotgun mic is attached to the pole with a shock mount, which absorbs the vibrations of the pole and the rubbing noises of the mic cable. Always test the microphone before each take to see if the shock mount is transferring the handling noise or pole vibrations. Even the best shotgun mic is rendered useless by a noisy pole or shock mount.

If a scene is shot fairly tightly (with tight medium shots and close-ups), you can use a short fishpole, which is much easier to handle than a long one. You can position it to pick up the sound from either above or below the source. If the sound pickup is from above, hold the boom in your outstretched arms and dip it into the scene as needed. **SEE 7.14** If the sound pickup is from below the source, turn the pole so that the mic is pointing up toward the person speaking. **SEE 7.15**

When the shots are wider and you need to be farther away from the scene, you must use a long fishpole. Because the long fishpole is heavier and more difficult to handle, you should anchor it in a belt and raise and lower it as you would an actual fishing pole. The long fishpole is usually held above the sound source. **SEE 7.16**

Pencil microphone   When picking up dialogue in the studio, some audio engineers prefer to use a pencil mic on a short fishpole. This is a short condenser mic with a cardioid pickup pattern that is often also used for music pickup. The advantage of a pencil mic is that it is very

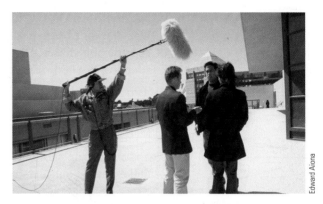

7.14 SHORT FISHPOLE USED FROM ABOVE
The short fishpole is normally held high and dipped into the scene as needed.

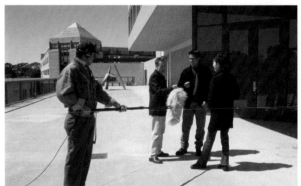

7.15 SHORT FISHPOLE USED FROM BELOW
The short fishpole can also be held low with the mic pointed up for good sound pickup.

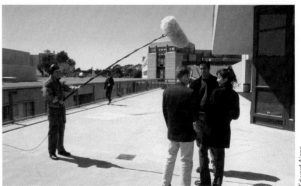

7.16 LONG FISHPOLE
The long fishpole can be anchored in a belt and raised and lowered much like an actual fishing pole. It is usually held above the sound source.

lightweight and has a wider pickup pattern than a shotgun. But isn't a shotgun the ideal mic for a boom because it is highly directional and can pick up sounds over a considerable distance? Yes, it is, especially if you are relatively far from the sound source or in a fairly noisy environment. But if you are to studio-record dialogue between two or more people in a scene that permits you to get close with the fishpole, the pencil mic's slightly wider pickup pattern is an advantage. Because the pickup pattern is a little wider than a shotgun's, you do not always have to point the mic from one person to the other during an exchange of dialogue but can often find an optimal pickup spot between the two speakers. As a side benefit, the lighter mic makes the fishpole operation considerably less tiring.

Here are some additional hints for operating a shotgun mic or pencil mic mounted on a fishpole:

- Always wear headphones so that you can hear what the mic is picking up (including unwanted sounds, such as the drone of an airplane during a Civil War scene). Listen especially for the low rumble of wind, which is easy to miss when concentrating on dialogue.

- With a fishpole it is especially important that you check the reach of the mic cable. Because you must concentrate on the position of the mic during the pickup, you will not be able to monitor the cable.

- Check that the cable is properly fastened to the pole and that it does not tug on the microphone.

- If the performers walk while speaking, you need to walk with them, holding the mic in front of them. If the camera shoots straight on (along the z-axis), you need to walk slightly ahead and to the side of the talent, holding the mic in front of them. If the blocking is lateral (along the x-axis), you need to stay in front, walking backward, while keeping your eyes on the talent and the mic; be careful not to bump into obstacles. Rehearse the walk a few times before the actual take. If possible, have a floor person guide you during the take.

- Watch for shadows that the boom may cast on persons or objects in camera range. **ZVL8** AUDIO→ Microphones→ mic types→ boom mic

Handholding a shotgun mic is as simple as it is effective. You become the boom— and a very flexible one at that. The advantage of holding the shotgun mic is that you can walk up to the scene as close as the camera allows, aiming the mic quickly and easily in various directions. **SEE 7.17**

Some audio people insist on covering the handheld shotgun with a windsock even when shooting indoors, but it is a must when shooting outdoors. As you have learned, the windsock reduces and often eliminates wind noise. Hold the microphone only by its shock mount—never directly. This minimizes handling noise and also prevents covering up the microphone ports—the openings in the mic barrel that make the mic directional.

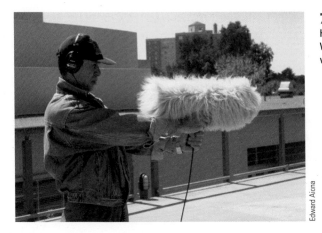

7.17 HANDHELD SHOTGUN MICROPHONE
Hold the shotgun mic only by its shock mount. When it's used outdoors, the windscreen and windsock are a must.

Big boom When used for an elaborate studio production, such as the video recording of a soap opera or sitcom, shotgun mics are suspended from a big boom, more accurately called a studio boom or perambulator boom. A boom operator, who stands or sits on the boom platform, can extend or retract the boom, tilt it up and down, pan it sideways, rotate the mic toward the sound source, and even have the whole boom assembly moved. This is all to have the microphone as close to the sound source as possible while keeping it out of the camera's view.

A studio boom is quite large and takes up a lot of operating space. In some cases it takes two operators: one to work the microphone boom and the other to reposition the boom during an especially tricky scene. You will discover that operating a boom is at least as difficult as running a camera.

Desk and stand microphones Desk microphones are hand mics mounted on a tabletop stand. You use them for panel shows, public hearings, speeches, and news conferences. Because the people using them are usually more concerned with what they are saying than with the quality of the audio, they frequently (albeit unintentionally) bang on the table or kick it while moving in their chairs, and sometimes even turn away from the microphone while speaking. Considering all these hazards, which microphones would you suggest for a desk mic? If you recommend an omnidirectional dynamic mic, you are right. This type of microphone is best suited to abuse. If you need even more precise sound separation, use a unidirectional dynamic mic.

When placing the microphones, you can use a single mic for each speaker or to serve two people simultaneously. Because microphones can cancel each other's frequencies when positioned too closely together—known as multiple-microphone interference—you should place the individual mics at least three times as far apart as any mic is from its user. **SEE 7.18**

Despite your careful placement of the multiple desk mics, inexperienced—and even experienced—users are sometimes compelled to grab the mic and pull it toward them as soon as they are seated. To save your nerves and optimize sound pickup, simply tape the mic stands to the table.

7.18 SETUP FOR MULTIPLE DESK MICROPHONES

To avoid multiple-microphone interference when using several desk mics for a panel show, place them at least three times as far apart as any mic is from its user.

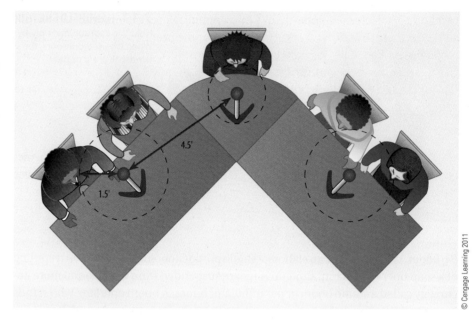

4.5'

1.5'

© Cengage Learning 2011

Stand mics are hand microphones that are clipped to a sturdy floor stand. They are used for singers, speakers, musical instruments, and any other sound source that has a fixed position. The quality of mics used on stands ranges from rugged dynamic mics for news conferences to high-quality condenser mics for singers and instrumental pickups.

For some performers, such as rock singers, the microphone stand is an important prop. They tilt it back and forth, hold themselves up by it, and even swing it through the air like a sword (not recommended, by the way, especially if the microphone is still attached).

Headset microphones   Sportscasters and other performers who are announcing an event often use a headset microphone. **SEE 7.19** This type of mic combines an

7.19 HEADSET MICROPHONE

The headset mic comprises a good-quality microphone and earphones that carry a split audio feed: one carries the program sound and the other carries instructions from the production team.

Mic

Sennheiser Electronic Corporation

earphone headset with a good-quality microphone. The earphones can carry a split audio feed, which means that the talent can hear the program sound (including his or her own voice) in one ear and instructions from production people in the other. Use headset microphones for sportscasters and talent who announce live events in the field. They have their hands free to handle scripts or event lists, can listen to the program audio and the producer's or director's instructions, and speak into a high-quality microphone.

Wireless, or radio, microphones   Wireless microphones are also called radio mics because they broadcast the audio signal from a microphone transmitter to a receiver, which in turn is connected to the camcorder, mixer, or audio console.

The most popular wireless microphones are hand mics used by singers. These high-quality mics have a transmitter and an antenna built into their housing. The performer is totally unrestricted and can move about unimpeded by a mic cable. The receiver is connected by cable to the audio console for sound control and mixing. Because each wireless mic has its own frequency, you can use several simultaneously without signal interference.

Another popular radio mic is the wireless lavalier, which is often used in news and interviews, in electronic field production, and occasionally in sports. If, for example, you are asked to pick up the breathing of a bicyclist during a race or of a climber on a summit bid, a wireless lav is the obvious choice. They are sometimes used for dramatic studio productions instead of boom mics.

The wireless lavalier is plugged into a small transmitter that is worn by the talent. You put the transmitter in the performer's pocket or tape it to the body and string the short antenna wire along the pants, skirt, or shirtsleeve or around the waist. The receiver is similar to that used with wireless hand mics. **SEE 7.20**

Unfortunately, using wireless mics is not without drawbacks. The signal pickup depends on where the talent is relative to the receiver. If the talent walks beyond the transmitter's range, the signal will first become intermittent and then be lost

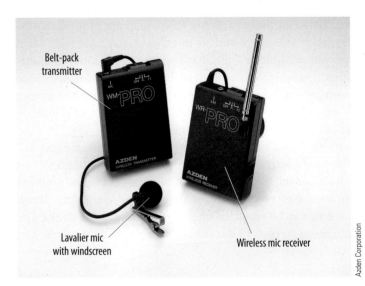

Belt-pack transmitter

Lavalier mic with windscreen

Wireless mic receiver

Azden Corporation

7.20 WIRELESS LAVALIER MICROPHONE AND RECEIVER
Wireless lavaliers are connected to a small transmitter worn by the talent. The receiver picks up the signal and sends it by cable to the audio console.

altogether. For example, if the talent moves behind a tall building or near high-voltage lines or somebody using a cell phone, the audio may become distorted or totally overpowered by the extraneous signals. Concrete walls, X-ray machines, and even the talent's perspiration can affect the transmission and reduce or distort the signal strength. Although wireless equipment has an assigned frequency that is purposely different from police and fire transmissions, you may occasionally pick up a first-responder call instead of the talent's comments. **ZVL9** AUDIO→ Microphones→ mic types→ wireless mic

The table on the facing page gives an overview of some of the more popular microphones. Realize, however, that new mics are developed all the time and that model numbers change accordingly. **SEE 7.21**

■ SOUND CONTROL

When using a small camcorder to record a friend's birthday party, you are probably unconcerned about the various steps of audio control. All you need to do is put a tape or memory card in the camcorder and check that the built-in mic is turned on and in the AGC mode. *AGC* stands for *automatic gain control*—it automatically adjusts the volume of the various sounds to optimal levels, eliminating the need for manual volume control. But because the AGC cannot distinguish between desirable sounds and noise, it amplifies both indiscriminately.

If the audio requirement is more demanding, such as controlling the volume during an outdoor interview or when somebody is playing a musical instrument, you need to switch from AGC to manual control.

Manual Volume Control

As mentioned previously, the better (and more expensive) camcorders have two XLR (balanced) microphone inputs and allow you to switch from AGC to manual volume control for both inputs by using small pots (rotary controls) or the menu on the foldout monitor. Try to do this switchover before you are in the field; the commands are often buried in submenus and are not always easy to activate when you are in a hurry. Also, you will quickly learn that even the best foldout monitors wash out in bright sunlight, making the menus hard if not impossible to see. Once you have switched to manual volume control, you can set a level for each of the two mic inputs before you start recording. You can then monitor the input volume in the viewfinder display.

Although some high-end camcorders have four audio inputs, most camcorders have only two audio channels. Try to use one channel (normally channel 1) for the external mic and the other (channel 2) for recording ambient sound with the camera mic. If there are more than two sound sources, you need to control and mix (combine) them before they can be recorded on one of the two audio tracks. The necessary equipment to do so consists of the audio mixer, the audio console, and the audio cables and patch panel.

7.21 TABLE OF MICROPHONES

	MICROPHONE	TYPE AND PICKUP PATTERN	USE
Sennheiser Electronic Corporation	Sennheiser MKH 70	Condenser Supercardioid	Studio boom, fishpole. Good for EFP and sports.
Sony Electronics, Inc.	Sony ECM 672	Condenser Supercardioid	Fishpole. Excellent for indoors.
Georg Neumann GmbH	Neumann KM-184	Condenser Cardioid	Pencil mic. Used on fishpole for dialogue pickup.
Electro-Voice	Electro-Voice 635A or RE50	Dynamic Omnidirectional	Rugged hand mics. Good for all-weather ENG.
Shure, Inc.	Shure SM63L	Dynamic Omnidirectional	Fairly rugged. Excellent for ENG.
Electro-Voice	Electro-Voice RE16	Dynamic Supercardioid	All-purpose hand mic. Good outdoors (ENG/EFP).
Shure, Inc.	Shure SM58	Dynamic Cardioid	Hand mic for singer. Crisp, lively sound.
beyerdynamic, Inc.	Beyerdynamic M59	Dynamic Hypercardioid	Hand mic. Excellent for ENG.
Sony Electronics, Inc.	Sony ECM 55 or ECM 77	Condenser Omnidirectional	Lavalier. Good voice pickup. Good studio mics that mix well with boom mics.
Sony Electronics, Inc.	Sony ECM 88	Condenser Omnidirectional	Very small lavalier. Excellent quality. Low handling and wind noise.
Sennheiser Electronic Corporation	Sennheiser ME 2	Condenser Omnidirectional	Very small lavalier mic.

7.22 AUDIO FIELD MIXER

The audio mixer allows you to control the volume of a limited number of sound inputs and mix them into a single or stereo output signal. This mixer has three inputs with volume controls and one output with a master fader.

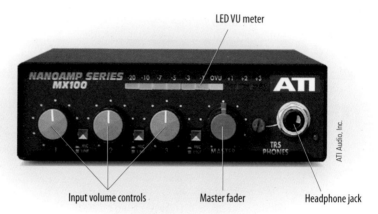

LED VU meter

Input volume controls   Master fader   Headphone jack

ATI Audio, Inc.

Audio Mixer

The audio mixer amplifies the weak signals that come from the microphones and other sound sources and lets you control the sound volume and mix two or more sound inputs. Actually, what you control and mix are not the sounds themselves but the signals, which are then translated back into actual sounds by the loudspeaker. ZVL10 AUDIO→ Systems→ try it

A normal monophonic audio mixer has three or four XLR inputs and one output of the manipulated signal. A stereo mixer has two outputs, one for the left channel and another for the right. Normally, mixers have a rotary pot (for potentiometer) for each input and one master pot or *fader* (two for stereo mixers). They also have a monitor *jack* (outlet) for your earphones so that you can hear the outgoing signal. A **VU meter**, which measures in volume units the relative amplitude (loudness) of the incoming sound signals, helps you visually monitor the volume of each incoming source and the final line-out signal that leaves the mixer. SEE 7.22 ZVL11 AUDIO→ Consoles and mixers→ parts

Mic- and line-level inputs   Normally, professional mixers give you a choice between mic and line inputs, unless they do the switching internally. The difference between the two is that the mic-level input is for weak audio signals, such as those coming from a microphone. The line-level input is for relatively strong audio signals, such as from a video recorder (VR) or CD player. If you plug the output of a CD player into the mic input, a preamplifier will unnecessarily boost the sound; most likely, it will become grossly distorted. If you plug a microphone into the line input, you need to turn the volume control way up to hear anything and in so doing will inevitably cause extensive noise in the audio signal.

If you don't know whether an input source is suited for the mic-level input or the line-level input, do a brief test recording. If the recording sounds much too loud and distorted, you plugged a line-level source into a mic-level input. If you have to crank the volume up all the way just to hear anything, you plugged a mic-level source into a line-level input. If it sounds just about right and responds to the volume control as it should, you plugged the sound source into the correct input. ZVL12 AUDIO→ Consoles and mixers→ signals

Controlling the volume   Controlling sound volume—
or riding gain—is not only to make weak sounds louder
and loud sounds softer but also to keep the sounds at
a level where they do not get distorted. This is especially important when you work with digital audio.
To increase the loudness of a sound, you turn the pot
clockwise or push the horizontal fader up, away from
you. To reduce the sound volume, you turn the pot
counterclockwise or pull the fader down, toward you.
The VU meter reflects the volume (gain) adjustment
by oscillating along a calibrated scale. **SEE 7.23** Some
audio mixers and consoles have VU meters with LED
(light-emitting diode) displays instead of oscillating
needles (see 7.22).

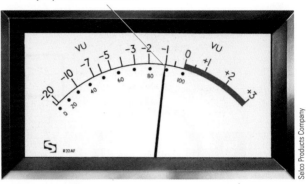

Adjust peak levels to fall near 0

7.23 VU METER
The volume-unit meter indicates the relative loudness of
sound. The scale is given in volume units, ranging from –20
to +3 (upper scale), and percentages, ranging from 0 to 100
(lower scale).

If the volume is very low and the needle of the
standard VU meter barely moves from the extreme
left, or if the LED meter remains at the bottom of the scale, you are riding the audio
"in the mud." When loud sounds make the needle hit the right side of the meter,
you are "bending" or "pinning" the needle and should turn the volume down to
avoid distortion.

When recording analog sound, try to keep the needle between 60 and 100 percent on the lower scale (or between –5 and 0 on the upper scale). Don't worry if the
needle spills occasionally into the red, but keep it from oscillating entirely in this
overload zone. Most LED meters change color when the sound is overmodulated,
that is, when the audio signals are boosted too much. All of these systems indicate
visually whether there is a sound signal in the system and how loud the sound is
relative to a given volume scale.

When working with digital audio, however, you need to keep the volume lower
than with analog audio. Because digital audio does not have any "headroom" that
absorbs occasional bending-the-needle volume levels, keep the master fader at about
–6 decibels (dB) instead of the 0 dB level. Newer machines lower the VU scale so that
you can set the master fader at the accustomed 0 dB as the standard volume level. If
the incoming volume is too high, it will clip the audio signal, which translates into
sound distortion. If volume levels are low, you can always boost them to normal
levels in postproduction without adding too much noise, but you cannot eliminate
the distortion that resulted from recording at too high a volume. Overloading digital
audio not only results in distorted sound but also adds considerable noise to the
recording. **ZVL13** AUDIO→ Consoles and mixers→ control | try it

XLR pad   One way to prevent such high-volume distortion in digital sound is to
use the XLR pad. This volume control looks like an XLR connector, with which you
can join two balanced audio cables (see figure 7.26). By simply plugging the cable
coming from the sound source into one end of the XLR pad, and another cable,
which connects your audio to the camcorder or audio recorder, into the other end,
you have pretty much eliminated the dreaded overload distortion.

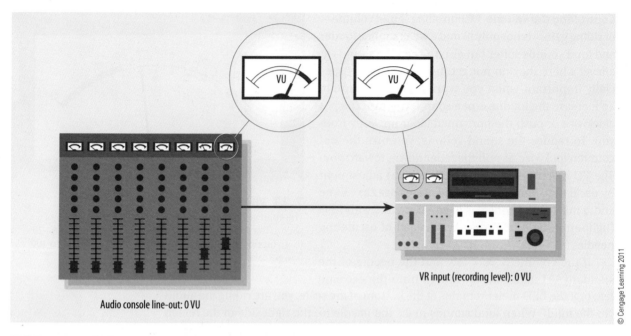

7.24 CALIBRATING AUDIO CONSOLE AND VIDEO RECORDER VOLUME LEVELS
The VU meter on the VR input is adjusted to the 0 VU line-out signal of the console. Once calibrated, both VU meters must read 0 VU (or the designated standard operating level).

Sound calibration   When the sound signals go through a mixer or the console before reaching the camcorder or an audio-recording device, you must adjust the recorder's volume meter so that it reads the identical volume units as on the mixer or console VU meter. This adjustment is called *sound calibration.* Generally, the audio technician feeds a 0 VU tone to the video recorder or other recording system. As mentioned before, some audio technicians suggest calibrating the system at a designated VU setting that is below the standard analog operating level of 0 VU.
SEE 7.24 **ZVL14** ▶ AUDIO→ Consoles and mixers→ calibration

Live field mixing   *Mixing* means combining two or more sounds. You don't need a mixer if you simply interview somebody in the field: you plug the interviewer's hand mic into the appropriate input on the camcorder, turn on the camera mic for ambience, and start recording. But if you have a complicated audio assignment that requires more than two inputs or precise volume control beyond what the AGC or the camcorder volume controls can give you, a small mixer will come in handy.

The following guidelines are intended to assist you with field-mixing tasks, but observe this caveat: if at all possible, try to avoid intricate sound mixing in the field. It is usually easier to achieve a satisfactory mix if you record the various sound sources separately and then do the mixing in postproduction. That said, here are some of the most basic field-mixing guidelines:

■ Even if you have only a few inputs, label each one with what it controls: mic for the host and the guest, ambience mic, and so forth.

- Double-check all inputs from wireless microphone systems. They have a pesky habit of malfunctioning just before the start of an event.

- Always send a test tone at 0 VU (or whatever standard operating level you are working with) from the mixer to the video recorder before the actual recording. Adjust the VU meter on the VR (either the camcorder or a separate unit) so that it also reads 0 VU (or other standard). You have now calibrated the output from the mixer with the input of the recorder.

- Be sure to switch each input to the correct input level (mic or line). Many field productions have been ruined by somebody's not paying attention to the correct input setting.

- When working a mixer, set the master pot to 0 VU (or other standard), then adjust the volume of the various inputs for the proper mix. Watch the VU meter of the master pot (line-out). If it spills into the red zone, readjust the volume of the inputs but leave the master pot at the designated standard operating level.

- For field recording, use an XLR pad to avoid volume overload.

- If you have to do a complicated sound pickup in the field, protect yourself by feeding it not only to the camcorder but also to a separate audio recorder.

- Again, record digital sound at a lower level than analog sound. It is easier to boost a weak sound signal than to get the distortion out of an overmodulated one.

Audio Console

You won't usually need a large audio console for most routine television shows, such as interviews and news, although some productions in high schools and colleges require complex audio setups from time to time. For example, a video recording of a band or an orchestra requires an amazingly elaborate audio setup; a small audio console will no longer suffice. It is always easier to use a larger console for a small audio job than the other way around. This is why fairly large consoles are standard equipment in the audio control rooms and audio postproduction rooms of television stations, large corporate production centers, and major postproduction houses.

Even if a large audio console with its many buttons and levers resembles an exotic control panel in a sci-fi spaceship, there is no reason to be intimidated: the largest audio console operates similarly to a small mixer. Like the mixer, the audio console has inputs, volume meters and controls, mixing circuits, and outputs for the manipulated signal. Unlike the mixer, however, the console has many more inputs and outputs, slide faders instead of rotary pots, and a variety of additional quality controls as well as assignment and on/off switches.

The audio console is relatively large because, instead of the three or four inputs of the small mixer, it may have 24 or even 64. Each input has a separate slide fader and an array of quality controls and switches. Some of the larger consoles have a VU meter for each input channel. The console has additional subgroup faders that control the mix of various inputs before it gets to the two master faders that control the two

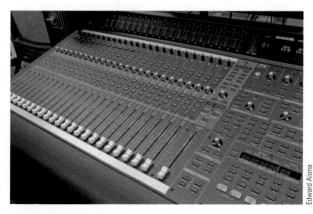

7.25 AUDIO CONSOLE

The audio console has many inputs (24 or more for large video productions), each of which has its own slide fader volume control, a variety of quality controls, various on/off and assignment switches, and a VU meter.

channels of the outgoing stereo signal. Each outgoing channel has its own VU meter. **SEE 7.25** Of course, if you work with 5.1 surround sound, you need six outgoing channels (five for the regular speakers placed in front and back, and one (the .1 subwoofer speaker) that takes care primarily of the very low sounds. A 7.1 system needs eight outputs.

An audio console lets you control the volume of all inputs, mix some or all of the input signals in various ways, and manipulate the sound signals of each input channel for the final mix. For example, with the quality controls you can add reverberation (echo) to the incoming sounds; reduce unwanted frequencies such as a hum or squeal; boost or attenuate (reduce) the high, middle, or low frequencies of each sound; and pan (move) a sound to a specific horizontal position between the two stereo speakers. Some controls allow you to adjust the strength of the signal input before it is amplified or to turn off all other inputs except the one you want to hear. You can also group some inputs into subgroups that can then be further mixed with other inputs or subgroups.

Why so many inputs? Because even a simple six-person panel discussion may use up to 10 inputs: six for the panel's microphones (assuming that each panel member has his or her own mic), one for the moderator's mic, one for the CD that contains the opening and closing theme music, and two more for the two servers (digital VRs) that play back program segments during the discussion.

Considering the many microphones and other sound equipment used in a rock concert, even 24 inputs seem modest. Large professional recording consoles are called in-line, which means that for each input there is a corresponding output. Many digital consoles are computer-controlled, which reduces their physical size despite their increased mixing capabilities. **ZVL15** AUDIO→ Consoles and mixers

Much professional audio postproduction mixing is done with a digital audio workstation (DAW), whose audio software takes care of the signal processing and facilitates volume control and mixing.

Cables and Patch Panel

Audio cables provide an essential link between the sound sources and the audio console or other recording equipment. Because cables have no moving parts or complicated circuitry, we tend to consider them indestructible. Nothing could be further from the truth. An audio cable, especially at the connectors, is vulnerable and must be treated with care. Avoid kinking it, stepping on it, or rolling a camera pedestal over it. Even a perfectly good cable may pick up electrical interference from lighting instruments and produce a hum in the audio—another reason for checking out the audio system before the director calls for a rehearsal.

Another potential problem comes from the various connectors that terminate the cables. All professional microphones and camcorders use three-conductor cables

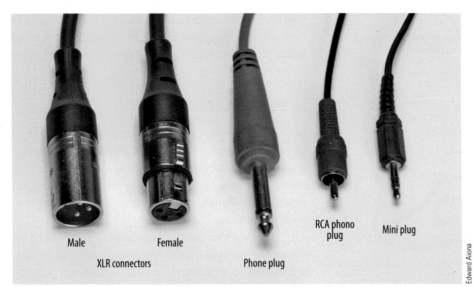

Edward Aiona

Male   Female   RCA phono   Mini plug
                                                     plug

XLR connectors   Phone plug

7.26 AUDIO CONNECTORS
All professional microphones use the three-wire (balanced) cables with XLR connectors. Other audio connectors include the phone plug, the RCA phono plug, and the mini plug.

(called balanced cables) with three-conductor **XLR connectors**. They are relatively immune to outside interference from unwanted frequencies. With an XLR jack in a camcorder, you can use any professional audio cable to connect a high-quality microphone to the camera. Most consumer microphones and small camcorders use the smaller **RCA phono plug** or the **mini plug** for their (unbalanced) cables. Some audio cables terminate with the larger ¼-inch phone plug, which is used for short cable runs to connect musical instruments such as electric guitars. You can, of course, also transport digital audio signals with a USB 2.0 or 3.0, a FireWire (IEEE 1394), or an HDMI (High-Definition Multimedia Interface) cable over short distances. **SEE 7.26** `ZVL16` AUDIO→ Connectors

Adapters make it possible to hook up cables with different connectors. Although you should always have such adapters on hand, avoid using them as much as possible. As with video adapters, an audio adapter is at best a makeshift solution and always a potential trouble spot. `ZVL17` AUDIO→ Connectors→ overview

Using the patch panel will make your life easier by bringing the various sound inputs (microphones, CD players, remote inputs, and the audio tracks of the video recorder) into a desired order on the audio console. For instance, if the various audio sources correspond to widely dispersed faders on the console (such as the lavalier mic of the interviewer at fader 1, the CD player at fader 2, the VR playback at fader 3, and the second lav at fader 4), you may want to move the two lavaliers to adjacent faders, with the VR playback at fader 3 and the CD player at fader 4. Rather than change the cables to different inputs, you simply patch these sound sources so that they appear in the desired order on the console.

Patching can be done in two ways. The old (highly reliable) way is to connect with small cables the incoming signals (called outputs because they are carrying the outgoing audio signals that are to be connected with the audio console) to the various faders on the audio console (called inputs). **SEE 7.27** The most efficient way is to have a computer take over the signal routing, which accomplishes the same

KEY CONCEPT
Always check that the connectors on the cable fit the microphone output and the inputs at the other end (such as camcorder, mixer, or recording device).

KEY CONCEPT
Keep cable connections and adapters to a minimum; each one is a potential trouble spot.

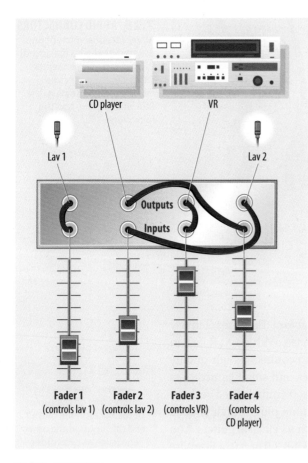

7.27 PATCHING

The four audio sources (lav 1, CD player, VR playback, and lav 2) are rerouted through patching (lav 1, lav 2, VR playback, and CD player).

task faster and without additional cables and connectors. If something goes wrong, however, the computer patch is usually harder to trace than the physical one.

■ SOUND RECORDING

Sound, like video, can be recorded as analog or digital signals. Despite the inherent differences between analog and digital equipment, the old sound-recording rule still applies: careful attention to sound pickup and recording will often save you many frustrating hours of postproduction.

In most video productions, sound is recorded on the audio tracks of the videotape or nonlinear recording device (computer hard drive or memory cards) simultaneously with the video (see chapter 11). Ambitious projects sometimes require that the audio also be recorded on a separate audio recorder. This speeds up audio postproduction, where you may need to replace dialogue or add sound effects and background music to the existing track. Less ambitious audio postproduction, whereby you edit out various unwanted sounds or add a modest amount of sound, such as ambient sound or background music, is normally called *sweetening*. In audio postproduction you can also create an entirely new audio track and add it to the video that has already been shot and edited. Despite the amazing and readily available software for the postproduction of digital sound, you will still be surprised at just how time-consuming even relatively small sweetening jobs can be.

In most video productions, all audio is recorded on the audio tracks of the video recording or on some kind of tapeless recording device.

Digital Audio Recorders

You are certainly familiar with one of the most popular and highly effective small audio recorders: the iPod. With MP3 compression, you can store literally thousands of songs on its tiny hard drive.

Other digital audio recorders are so small you can put them in your pocket, yet they are powerful enough to capture and store hours of high-quality audio. These recorders are especially effective when doing fieldwork. Figure 7.28 shows one of these battery-operated wonder machines. It has two built-in stereo microphones that have an amazing reach, and a standard SD card on which you can store many hours of four-channel audio. **SEE 7.28**

If in a studio production you want to record audio in addition to, or separate from, the video recording, you can use any number of small but highly versatile

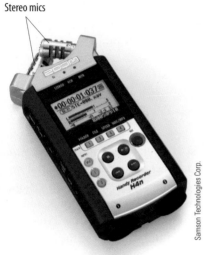

Stereo mics

Samson Technologies Corp.

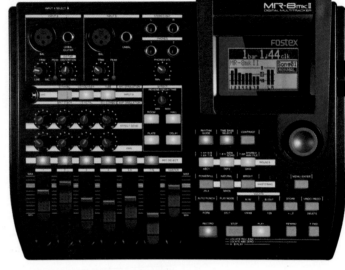

Fostex Company

7.28 **HANDHELD DIGITAL STEREO AUDIO RECORDER**
This high-quality 4-track stereo recorder uses an SD card and accepts balanced XLR inputs. It is lightweight and small enough to fit in your pocket or purse.

7.29 **DIGITAL AUDIO RECORDER**
This digital audio recorder can simultaneously record eight tracks on a memory card. It also offers digital sound effects, has two XLR mic inputs and two headphone outputs, and can be connected to a computer and to CD and DVD players.

audio recorders. The digital recorder in figure 7.29 can record eight audio tracks on a memory card, let you add various sound effects, and finally transfer with a USB cable each pair of stereo tracks to a computer for editing or sweetening. **SEE 7.29** Unless you are specializing in audio recording or working with a DAW, such an audio recorder will most likely suffice for most of your video productions.

Optical Discs: CDs and DVDs

The principal optical audio-recording media used in general video production are the familiar CD (compact disc) and DVD (digital versatile disc). They are called "optical" because they use a laser beam for recording and playback on the 4¾-inch disc. The advantages of these recording media are that they are lightweight and easy to use, transport, and store. Compared with audiotape, both discs reproduce almost noise-free high-definition sound (assuming the recording was relatively noise-free in the first place). The DVD can record a much greater amount of data than the CD. The standard CD and DVD can be used only for a onetime recording of data. The rewritable ones can be used for multiple recordings, much like audio- or videotape, memory cards, and computer hard disks.

Although CDs and DVDs use different systems for writing (recording) and reading (playback) digital information, they are similar in operation.

Operational display A highly accurate LED read-out system, which functions much like a counter, allows you to select a precise starting point regardless of where the segment may be buried on the disc.

7.30 OPERATIONAL DISPLAY FOR OPTICAL DISCS

The typical CD or DVD display consists of seven basic controls: *play, pause, stop, down* button, *up* button, *fast-rewind,* and *fast-forward*. The *down* button jumps to the beginning of the current track and to previous tracks. The *up* button jumps to the end of the current track and to subsequent tracks.

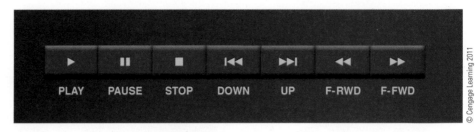

PLAY   PAUSE   STOP   DOWN   UP   F-RWD   F-FWD

© Cengage Learning 2011

The standard CD and DVD displays consist of seven basic controls: *play, pause, stop, down* button, *up* button, *fast-rewind,* and *fast-forward*. Pressing the *down* button takes you to the beginning of the current track; repeated pressing skips to previous tracks. The *up* button takes you to the end of the current track; repeated pressing selects subsequent tracks. *Fast-rewind* moves the laser back until you release the button. *Fast-forward* moves the laser forward until you release the button. You can hear the audio in the fast-rewind and fast-forward modes. **SEE 7.30**

Despite all these spectacular achievements in digital audio recording, don't dismiss analog equipment just yet. It is still—or again—used by audio enthusiasts who are fascinated by the "warmer" quality of analog sound. You may still find analog audiotape and audiocassette recorders in operation in some sound studios; but for all practical purposes, analog audio equipment is no longer used in professional video operation.

▩ AUDIO POSTPRODUCTION

At this point you probably won't be asked to do complicated sound postproduction work, but you should at least know something about it. Although the sound of most routine television shows (news, game shows, and soap operas) is captured during the production, there are just as many productions where the audio track is sweetened, partially reconstructed, made more complex by mixing various sound tracks, or constructed entirely in the postproduction phase. Most of this work is accomplished in an audio postproduction room.

Audio Postproduction Room

There is no specific formula that will tell you just what goes into such a room and where it should be placed. Each sound designer seems to have a slightly different idea of how to produce optimal sound for video. You will find, however, that most such audio postproduction rooms house a large console, a physical patchbay, various digital recorders, at least one digital audio workstation, a keyboard, and a sampler. All of these pieces of equipment are interconnected. **SEE 7.31**

Digital audio workstation   One of the key pieces of equipment in the postproduction room is the digital audio workstation. The typical DAW has a large-capacity hard drive and software that combines a digital audio-recording system with an audio console and editing system. **SEE 7.32** You can call up and operate with the mouse a

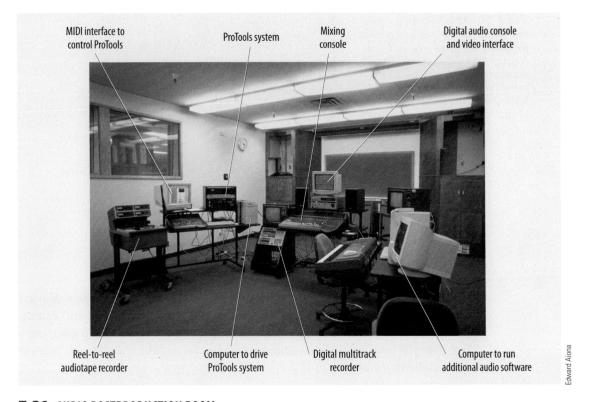

MIDI interface to control ProTools

ProTools system

Mixing console

Digital audio console and video interface

Reel-to-reel audiotape recorder

Computer to drive ProTools system

Digital multitrack recorder

Computer to run additional audio software

Edward Aiona

7.31 AUDIO POSTPRODUCTION ROOM

The audio postproduction room typically contains a digital audio console, audio recorders, a digital audio workstation, various MIDI connections, and a high-fidelity speaker system.

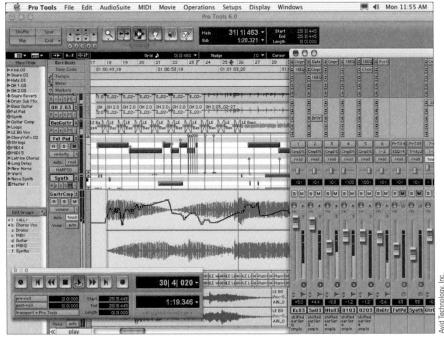

Avid Technology, Inc.

7.32 DIGITAL AUDIO WORKSTATION DISPLAY

Multiple computer interfaces display a variety of audio control and editing functions. They also activate hardware, such as audio consoles and recorders.

7.33 SOUND WAVEFORM

The vertical lines and areas represent the sound amplitude—its loudness. A straight line shows silence. This waveform illustrates various loud bangs (long spikes), a *vroom* sound leading to more and even louder bangs, and two thumps in succession.

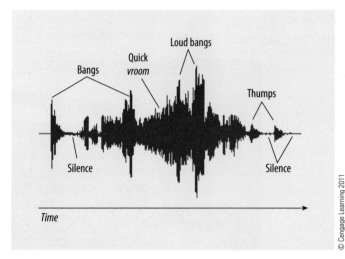

© Cengage Learning 2011

virtual audio console and a great variety of editing controls. The console displays multiple audio tracks as waveforms for accurate sound manipulation and editing. But even relatively inexpensive audio software programs for desktop computers are powerful tools for audio postproduction and for matching audio with video in postproduction editing.

Sound waveform   The purple squiggly lines in the DAW interface in figure 7.32 are waveforms. A ***waveform*** is a graphic representation of a specific sound or combination of sounds that occur over a period of time. (The waveform on the cover of this book represents the words *video basics.*) The standard waveform shows the basic fluctuations of loudness of a sound—the dynamics—but not how high or low the sound is (its frequency).[1] The larger the vertical squiggles are, the louder the sound is. Silence shows up as a horizontal line with no squiggles above or below. Sudden loud sounds have long spikes. **SEE 7.33**

Once you have learned to interpret the sound waveform on the computer screen, you can select certain sound portions with great precision, delete some, or arrange them in any sequence. When editing, the best place to cut is, of course, where you can find a brief silence.

To synchronize the sound track with the video, the computer provides each video frame and the accompanying sound portion with a corresponding address. The most widely used address system is called the SMPTE time code. The displayed time code reads out hours, minutes, seconds, and frames (30 frames per second). (See chapter 12 for a more detailed explanation of the SMPTE time code.)

Automated Dialogue Replacement

Large postproduction rooms, like the ones for digital cinema, have an area specifically for automated dialogue replacement. Although it's sometimes called "automatic

---

1. See Stanley R. Alten, *Audio in Media,* 9th ed. (Boston: Wadsworth, 2011), pp. 421–30.

dialogue replacement," the process is anything but automatic. It requires a fairly large video projection that allows the talent to see the video playback of themselves while repeating their lines in perfect lip sync, perhaps with a dash or two of added emotion—all in the interest of improving the original audio.

SYNTHESIZED SOUND

If we can translate sound into digital information and then manipulate it, could we not use the computer to create digital information that can be translated into actual sound? Yes. The audio synthesizer, commonly called a keyboard, can generate a great variety of complex frequencies that we perceive as sounds produced by musical instruments. A single key can approximate the sound of a piano, an electric or acoustic guitar, a drum, a trumpet, and many more instruments. Such a keyboard, which you can easily carry under your arm, offers more sounds than a rock band and a symphony orchestra combined.

The computer can also be used to grab brief portions of a regular sound, such as a telephone ring, translate it into digital form, store it, and make it available for all sorts of manipulations. With the help of sampling software, you can repeat the telephone ring as often as you want, transform it into a shrill beat, speed it up or slow it down, play it backward, have it overlap, or distort it to the point that you no longer recognize the original sound.

> **KEY CONCEPT**
> Sounds and sound mixes can be entirely computer-generated.

SOUND AESTHETICS

Even the most sophisticated digital sound equipment is of little use if you cannot use your ears—that is, exercise some aesthetic judgment. Sounds can make us feel about pictures in a certain way and add energy to a scene. You can make the same scene appear high-energy or low-energy, happy or sad, simply by putting some happy or sad, or loud or soft, sounds behind it.

The basic aesthetic factors that can help you achieve an effective audio/video relationship are context, figure/ground, sound perspective, continuity, and energy and mood.

Context

In most studio sound-recording sessions, we try to eliminate as much of the ambient sound as possible. In the field, however, the ambient sounds are often as important as the principal ones: they help establish the general context of the event. If you shoot a scene at a busy downtown intersection, the environmental sounds of cars, horns, streetcars, and buses; people talking, laughing, and moving about; the doorman's whistle for a taxi; and the occasional police siren—all are important clues to where you are, even if you don't show the sound sources in the video portion.

> **KEY CONCEPT**
> Sounds can establish the event context.

Think of recording a small orchestra. If you do a studio recording, the coughing of one of the crewmembers or musicians during an especially soft passage would certainly prompt a retake. Not so in the context of a live concert. We have learned to interpret the occasional coughing and other such environmental sounds as proof of the live quality of the event.

As pointed out previously, in normal field recording you should try to use one mic and audio track for the primary sound source, such as a reporter standing on a street corner, and another mic (usually the camera mic) and the second audio track for recording environmental sounds. Separating the sounds on different tracks as much as possible makes it easier to mix the two in the proper proportions in post-production editing.

Figure/Ground

One important perceptual factor is the figure/ground principle. This refers to our tendency to organize our environment into a relatively mobile figure (a person or car) and a relatively stable background (wall, houses, or mountains). If we expand this principle a little, we can say that we single out an event that is important to us and assign it the role of the figure while relegating all other events to the background or, as we just called it, the environment.

For example, if you are waiting for your friend and finally see her in a crowd, she immediately becomes the focus of your attention—the foreground—while the rest of the people become the background. The same happens with sound. We have the ability to perceive, within limits, the sounds we want or need to hear as the figure while pushing all other sounds into the background. For example, if you sit in a busy restaurant and listen to your friend telling you about her new video, you ignore mentally all the other people who are talking at the other tables.

When re-creating such a figure/ground relationship with sound, we usually make the "figure" somewhat louder or give it a distinct quality in relation to the ambient sounds. In the same way, we can easily bring a background sound up in volume to become the figure and relegate the other sounds to the ground. Fading down some sounds to relegate them as background and bringing up the volume of other sounds as foreground has become routine in many documentaries where there is a voice-over narration. In fact, you can get software that automates such figure/ground sound manipulations, a procedure known as "ducking audio."

Sound Perspective

Sound perspective means that close-up pictures are matched with relatively close sounds, and long shots are matched with sounds that seem to come from farther away. Close sounds have more presence than far sounds—a sound quality that makes us feel as though we are near the sound source. Faraway sounds seem to be more distant from us.

As you may recall, this desirable variation of sound presence is virtually eliminated when using lavalier mics. Because the distance between mic and mouth remains the same regardless of whether the performer is seen in a close-up or a long shot, the sound has the same presence. This is why you should use boom mics when controlling sound presence. The boom mic can be moved close to a performer during a close-up and must be somewhat farther away during a long shot to keep out of the picture—a simple solution to a potential audio problem.

Continuity

Sound continuity is especially important in postproduction. You may have noticed the sound quality of a reporter's voice change depending on whether he or she was speaking on- or off-camera. In this case, the reporter used one type of microphone when on-camera and another when off-camera; the reporter also changed environments from on-location to the studio. This change in microphones and locations gives speech a distinctly different quality. Although this difference may not be too noticeable during the actual recording, it becomes readily apparent when the two audio sources are edited together in the final show.

What should you do to avoid such continuity problems? Use identical microphones for the on- and off-camera narration or at least ones that sound alike and, if necessary, mix the off-camera narration with some of the separately recorded ambient sounds. You can feed the ambient sounds to the reporter through earphones while recording the voice-over narration, which will help the reporter re-create the on-site energy.

Sound is also a chief element for establishing visual continuity. A rhythmically precise piece of music can help achieve continuity in a series of pictures that otherwise do not cut together very well. Music and sound are often the critical link among abruptly changing shots and scenes.

Energy and Mood

Unless you want to achieve a special effect through contradiction, you should match the general energy and mood of the pictures with sounds of similar energy and mood. Energy refers to all of the factors in a scene that communicate a certain degree of aesthetic force and power. The major ones are volume and rhythm. High-energy music, for example, is louder and has a more driving beat than low-energy music.

Mood refers to how the music makes us feel: happy, sad, excited, sleepy, uneasy, or frightened. Unless you want to create a conflict between video and audio, high-energy scenes, such as a series of big-screen close-ups of a rock band in action, can stand higher-energy sounds than a more tranquil scene, such as close-ups of lovers sitting by a lakeshore. A sad event is usually accompanied by low-energy music; a happy one with higher-energy music. But what, exactly, is happy and sad music? And what are the correct sound levels for high- and low-energy scenes? There are no clear-cut answers. You simply need to sense them. No musical chart or volume meter can substitute for your aesthetic judgment.

M A I N   P O I N T S

▶ ***Sound Pickup Principle***

Microphones transduce (transform) the sounds we hear into electric energy—the audio signal.

▶ ***Directional Characteristics of Mics***

Omnidirectional mics can hear equally well from all directions; unidirectional, or cardioid, mics can best hear sounds that come from the front. Hyper- and supercardioid mics make faraway sounds that lie in the pickup pattern appear close to the mic.

▶ ***Mechanics of Mics***

Classified by how they are made, there are three types of mics: dynamic (the most rugged), condenser (high-quality but sensitive), and ribbon (high-quality and very sensitive).

▶ ***Use of Mics***

Classified by how they are used, microphones can be divided into six types: small lavalier mics, which are clipped to the clothing of the performer; hand mics, which are carried by the performer; boom mics, which are suspended from a fishpole or a studio boom assembly; desk and stand mics, which are mounted on a tabletop stand or an adjustable floor stand; headset mics, which are worn by the performer and include earphones with a split audio feed; and wireless, or radio, mics, which broadcast the audio signal from a transmitter to a receiver. Treat all mics gently and test them before going on the air.

▶ ***Sound Control***

When using a camcorder, AGC (automatic gain control) must be switched to manual volume control to ensure acceptable sound. Verify that the audio connectors fit their respective jacks. Carry adapters but use them only in an emergency.

▶ ***Audio Mixer and Audio Console***

The mixer amplifies the incoming sound signals, controls the volume of each sound, and mixes (combines and balances) them in specific ways. A field mixer is small and normally has a maximum of four inputs. The audio console is much larger; it has many more inputs, each of which has a volume control and various quality and sound selection controls.

▶ ***Sound Recording***

There are a great variety of digital audio recorders. They record on either hard drives or memory cards. Optical discs include read/write CDs (compact discs), and the higher-capacity DVDs (digital versatile discs).

▶ ***Audio Postproduction***

Audio postproduction consists of sweetening, mixing various sound tracks, and creating new ones. The audio postproduction room contains a variety of sound equipment, most notably a digital audio workstation (DAW).

▶ ***Sound Waveform***

The sound waveform is a graphic representation of the dynamics of various sounds as they progress in time. It facilitates sound editing.

▶ ***Synthesized Sound***

Once sounds are in digital form, you can manipulate them with computer software. Computerized sound equipment, such as the keyboard, can create—synthesize—its own sounds.

▶ ***Sound Aesthetics***

The basic aesthetic factors that can help you achieve an effective audio/video relationship are context, figure/ground, sound perspective, continuity, and energy and mood.

Z E T T L ' S   V I D E O L A B

 For your reference or to track your work, the *Zettl's VideoLab* program cues in this chapter are listed here with their corresponding page numbers.

KEY TERMS

additive primary colors Red, green, and blue. Ordinary white light (sunlight) can be separated into the three primary light colors. When these three colored lights are combined in various proportions, all other colors can be reproduced.

attached shadow Shadow that is on the object itself. It cannot be seen independent of (detached from) the object.

background light Illumination of the set pieces and the backdrop. Also called *set light*.

back light Illumination from behind the subject and opposite the camera; usually a spotlight.

baselight Even, nondirectional (diffused) light necessary for the camera to operate optimally. Refers to the overall light intensity.

cast shadow Shadow that is produced by an object and thrown (cast) onto another surface. It can be seen independent of the object.

color temperature Relative reddishness or bluishness of white light, as measured on the Kelvin (K) scale. The norm for indoor video lighting is 3,200K; for outdoors, 5,600K.

contrast The difference between the brightest and the darkest spots in a video image.

diffused light Light that illuminates a relatively large area and creates soft shadows.

directional light Light that illuminates a relatively small area and creates harsh, clearly defined shadows.

falloff The speed (degree) with which a light picture portion turns into shadow areas. *Fast falloff* means that the light areas turn abruptly into shadow areas and there is a great difference in brightness between light and shadow areas. *Slow falloff* indicates a very gradual change from light to dark and a minimal brightness difference between light and shadow areas.

fill light Additional light on the opposite side of the camera from the key light to illuminate shadow areas and thereby reduce falloff; usually done with floodlights.

floodlight A lighting instrument that produces diffused light.

foot-candle (fc) The unit of measurement of illumination, or the amount of light that falls on an object. One foot-candle is 1 candlepower of light (1 lumen) that falls on a 1-square-foot area located 1 foot away from the light source.

high-key lighting Light background and ample light on the scene. Has nothing to do with the vertical positioning of the key light.

incident light Light that strikes the object directly from its source. To measure incident light, point the light meter at the camera lens or into the lighting instruments.

key light Principal source of illumination; usually a spotlight.

LED lights *LED* stands for *light-emitting diodes*. A solid-state device that changes electric energy into light energy. Most computer screens use LEDs as the light source.

light plot A plan, similar to a floor plan, that shows the type, size (wattage), and location of the lighting instruments relative to the scene to be illuminated and the general direction of the light beams.

low-key lighting Fast-falloff lighting with dark background and selectively illuminated areas. Has nothing to do with the vertical positioning of the key light.

lux European standard unit for measuring light intensity. One lux is 1 lumen (1 candlepower) of light that falls on a surface of 1 square meter located 1 meter away from the light source. 10.75 lux = 1 foot-candle. Most lighting people figure roughly 10 lux = 1 foot-candle.

photographic principle The triangular arrangement of key, back, and fill lights. Also called *triangle*, or *three-point*, *lighting*.

reflected light Light that is bounced off the illuminated object. To measure reflected light, point the light meter close to the object from the direction of the camera.

RGB Stands for *red, green,* and *blue*—the basic colors of television.

spotlight A lighting instrument that produces directional, relatively undiffused light.

triangle lighting The triangular arrangement of key, back, and fill lights. Also called *three-point lighting* and *photographic principle*.

white-balance To adjust the color circuits in the camera to produce white color in lighting of various color temperatures (relative reddishness or bluishness of white light).

Light, Color, and Lighting

A t this point you may ask why you should bother with reading a whole chapter on lighting when your cell-phone camera can practically see in the dark. The answer is easy: if you want to produce professional-looking video, you need to know at least the basic principles of lighting. It is true that the increased light sensitivity of video cameras has encouraged even some well-known video- and filmmakers to shoot scenes in available light without any additional lighting instruments; but, generally, good lighting still calls for deliberate illumination—to determine where and from what angle the light falls, whether the light should be soft or harsh, and what color it should have. Lighting also, if not especially, calls for the careful control of shadows and their relative transparency.

This chapter introduces you to the art of video lighting and the instruments you need to achieve good lighting for a variety of tasks. Once you have learned the basic lighting principles and practiced applying them, you can ignore them in cases where you want to achieve a special effect. **ZVL1** ► LIGHTS → Light introduction

KEY CONCEPT

Lighting is deliberate illumination and shadow control.

► **LIGHT**
Directional and diffused light, light intensity and how to measure it, measuring incident and reflected light, and contrast

► **SHADOWS**
Attached and cast shadows and controlling falloff

► **COLOR**
Additive and subtractive mixing, the color television receiver and generated colors, and color temperature and white-balancing

► **LIGHTING INSTRUMENTS**
Spotlights, floodlights, and instruments for specific tasks

► **LIGHTING TECHNIQUES**
Operation of lights, lighting safety, studio lighting and the photographic principle, the light plot, last-minute lighting techniques, and field lighting

■ LIGHT

Learning about light and shadows seems like a strange assignment, considering that you have been seeing light and shadows all your life. But it makes more sense when you realize that what you see on a video or film screen is nothing but blobs of light and shadows and that lighting is the calculated interplay of these two elements.

Types of Light

No matter how the light is technically generated, you will work with two basic types: directional and diffused.

Directional light has a precise beam that causes harsh shadows. The sun, a flashlight, and the headlights of a car all produce directional light. You can aim directional light at a specific area without much spill into other areas.

Diffused light causes a more general illumination. Its diffused beam spreads out quickly and illuminates a large area. Because diffused light seems to come from all directions (is omnidirectional), it has no clearly defined shadows; they seem soft and transparent. A good example of diffused light occurs on a foggy day, when the fog operates like a huge diffusion filter for the sun. Observe the shadows in bright sunlight and on an overcast or foggy day; they are quite distinct and dense in sunlight but hardly visible in fog. The fluorescent lighting in elevators and supermarkets is a good example of diffused indoor light. It is used to minimize the harsh shadows on a face or an object and to illuminate large areas.

Light Intensity

An important aspect of lighting is controlling light intensity, or how much light falls onto an object. Also called light level, light intensity is measured in American foot-candles or in European lux. A foot-candle is simply a convenient measurement of illumination—the amount of light that falls on an object. One *foot-candle (fc)* is 1 candlepower of light (called a lumen) that falls on a 1-square-foot area located 1 foot away from the light source. The European measure for light intensity is *lux*—1 lumen of light that falls on a surface of 1 square meter that is 1 meter away from the light source (1 meter is a little more than 3 feet).

If you have foot-candles and want to find lux, multiply the foot-candle figure by 10. Twenty foot-candles is approximately 200 lux (20 × 10 = 200). If you have lux and want to find foot-candles, divide the lux number by 10. Two thousand lux is approximately 200 fc (2,000 ÷ 10 = 200). A room that has an overall illumination of 200 fc, or 2,000 lux, has quite a bit of light or, more technically, has a fairly high degree of light intensity. **ZVL2** LIGHTS→ Measurement→ meters

Baselight   Sometimes you may hear the lighting director (LD) or the video operator (VO) complain that there is not enough baselight. *Baselight* refers to general illumination, or the overall light intensity, such as the 200 fc in the room we just talked about. You determine baselight levels by pointing a light meter (which reads foot-candles or lux) from the illuminated object or scene toward the camera. To check the baselight of your living room, you would walk to the different corners of the room and point the light meter toward a real or imaginary camera position (probably in the middle of the room). **ZVL3** LIGHTS→ Measurement→ baselight

Although some camera manufacturers claim that their cameras can see in the dark, you need a certain amount of light to make the cameras see the colors and the shadows that you see when looking at the scene. In technical parlance you need to activate the imaging device and the other electronics in the camera to produce an optimal video signal at a given f-stop. Although newer cameras and lenses are much more sensitive than older ones and need less light, good, crisp video still demands a reasonable amount of illumination. A handheld camcorder may be able to produce recognizable pictures at light levels as low as 1 or 2 lux; but for high-quality pictures, you need more light. Top-of-the-line studio cameras may still require about 1,000 lux (100 fc) at an f-stop of about $f/8$ for optimal picture quality.[1]

Gain   If there is insufficient light even at the maximum aperture (lowest f-stop number), you need to activate the gain circuits of the camera. Most consumer camcorders do this automatically. On camcorders, studio cameras, and ENG/EFP (electronic news gathering/electronic field production) cameras, the gain is activated either via the camera control unit (CCU) or by a switch on the camera. The gain will boost the weak video signal electronically. High-definition cameras can tolerate a relatively high gain before they show picture "noise," that is, artifacts that show up as colored specks. When video quality is of primary concern, it is better to raise the baselight level than to activate the gain switch.

Measuring Illumination

In critical lighting setups, before turning on the cameras you may want to check whether there is enough baselight and whether the contrast between the light and dark areas falls within the acceptable limits (normally 50:1 to 100:1, depending on the camera; see Contrast on the following page). You can check this with a light meter, which simply measures the number of foot-candles or lux emitted by the lighting instruments—the **incident light** (what enters the lens or what comes from a specific instrument) or the **reflected light** (bouncing off the lighted object).

Incident light   An incident-light reading gives you an idea of the baselight level in a given area, which translates into how much light the camera receives from a particular location on the set. To measure incident light, stand next to or in front of the illuminated person or object and point the light meter toward the camera lens. Such a quick reading of incident light is especially helpful when checking the prevailing light levels at a remote location.

If you want a more specific reading of the light intensity from certain instruments, point the light meter *into the lights*. To check the relative evenness of the incident

---

1. An f-stop between $f/5.6$ and $f/8$ produces an optimal depth of field. This is why camera specifications use $f/5.6$ or $f/8$ as the norm for optimal light levels. Some manufacturers use $f/11$ in their specifications, with a higher baselight requirement (such as 200 fc). Of course, with larger apertures you can shoot with less light.

light, point the light meter toward the principal camera positions while walking around the set. If the needle or digital read-out stays at approximately the same intensity level, the lighting is fairly even. If the needle or read-out dips way down, the lighting setup has "holes" (unlighted or underlighted areas).

Reflected light   The reading of reflected light is done primarily to check the contrast between light and dark areas. To measure reflected light, stand close to the lighted object or person and point the light meter at the light and shadow sides from the direction of the camera. Be careful not to block the light whose reflection you are trying to measure. As mentioned before, the difference between the two readings will indicate the lighting contrast. Note that the contrast is determined not only by how much light falls on the object but also by how much light the object reflects back into the camera. The more reflective the object, the higher the reflected-light reading will be. A mirror reflects almost all of the light falling onto it; a black velour cloth reflects only a small portion.

Contrast

Contrast refers to the difference between the brightest and the darkest spots in a video image. Contrary to your eye, which can distinguish subtle brightness steps over a contrast ratio with a wide range, even high-end video cameras may be limited to a lower contrast range. Whereas some equipment salespeople might tell you that high-end video cameras can tolerate a contrast that is close to that of our vision, LDs and VOs say that too high a contrast is one of the most common obstacles to producing optimal video. Believe the people who use the cameras rather than sell them. Video professionals prefer a contrast ratio for studio cameras that does not exceed 100:1. The high number of the 100:1 contrast ratio indicates that the brightest spot in the scene is 100 times more intense than the darkest spot. Small digital camcorders will have trouble producing high-quality video that shows bright highlights as well as transparent shadows if the contrast ratio is higher than 50:1.

Measuring contrast   To measure contrast, point a reflected-light meter close to the bright side of the object, then close to the shadow side. (You will read more about measuring contrast in the next section.) The light meter reads the reflected light, first of the bright side (a high reading) and then of the shadow side (a low reading). If, for example, the light meter reads 800 fc in an especially bright area, such as one side of the reporter's face in direct sunlight, and only 10 fc in the dark background, the contrast ratio is 80:1 (800 ÷ 10 = 80). Even with a fairly good digital camcorder, this contrast may be too high for good pictures. **ZVL4** LIGHTS→ Measurement→ contrast

High-end small camcorders and all professional cameras indicate just which picture areas are overexposed by showing a vibrating zebra-striped pattern over them. Most higher-end camcorders (handheld and shoulder-mounted) let you switch between a 100 percent and a 70 percent zebra setting. In the normal 100 percent mode, all picture areas that show a zebra pattern are overexposed. The 70 percent setting is used primarily to help you achieve correct skin tones. When the zebra stripes appear over the bright areas of the face, the exposure is correct.

As you know, the usual remedy for an overexposed image is to stop down the lens, that is, select a higher *f*-stop. But, while eliminating the white glare, you also compress the shadow areas into a dense, uniform black. So how can you control contrast?

- If you are outdoors, don't place the person in a sunny spot; move him into the shade. If that is not possible, lighten up the harsh shadows (as explained later in this chapter) or activate one of the neutral density (ND) filters that are built into the camcorder. They act like sunglasses, reducing the overall brightness without affecting the colors too much.

- Indoors you can reduce the light intensity by moving the lighting instrument farther away from the object, diffusing the light beam, or using an electronic dimmer to reduce the intensity of the main light source. (How to do all this is explained later in this chapter.)

- Remove overly bright objects from the scene, especially if you are operating with an automatic iris. A pure white object always presents a lighting hazard, no matter how high a contrast the camera can tolerate. The real problem is that even if the camera can manage a high contrast ratio, the average television set cannot always do likewise. **ZVL5** LIGHTS→ Measurement→ try it

SHADOWS

Although we are quite conscious of light and light changes, we are usually unaware of shadows, unless we seek comfort in them on a particularly hot day or if they interfere with what we want to see. Because shadow control is such an important aspect of lighting, let's take a closer look at shadows and how they influence our perception.

Once you are aware of shadows, you will be surprised by the great variety that surround you. Some seem part of the object, such as the shadow on your coffee cup; others seem to fall onto other surfaces, such as the shadow of a telephone pole that is cast onto the street. Some shadows are dark and dense, as though they were brushed on with thick, black paint; others are so light and subtle that they are hard to see. Some change gradually from light to dark; others do so abruptly. Despite the great variety of shadows, there are only two basic types: attached and cast. **ZVL6** LIGHTS→ Light and shadow→ light

Attached Shadows

Attached shadows seem affixed to the object and cannot be seen independent of it. Take your coffee cup and hold it next to a window or table lamp. The shadow opposite the light source (window or lamp) on the cup is the attached shadow. Even if you wiggle the cup or move it up and down, the attached shadow remains part of the cup. **SEE 8.1**

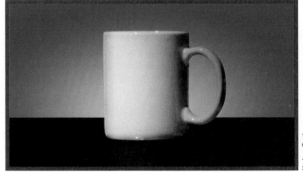

8.1 ATTACHED SHADOW
The attached shadow is always bound to the illuminated object. It cannot be seen separate from the object.

8.2 ATTACHED SHADOWS DEFINE SHAPE
Attached shadows help define the basic shape of the object. Without attached shadows, we perceive a triangle on the left; with attached shadows, we perceive a cone on the right.

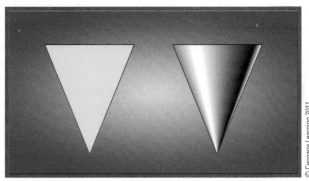

© Cengage Learning 2011

Attached shadows help us perceive the basic form of an object. Without attached shadows the actual shape of an object may remain ambiguous when seen as a picture. In the figure above, the object on the left looks like a triangle; but when you see it with the attached shadows, the triangle becomes a cone. **SEE 8.2**

Attached shadows also contribute to perception of texture. A great amount of prominent attached shadows emphasizes texture; without them things look smoother. Attached shadows on a Styrofoam ball make it look like a moonscape; but when the attached shadows are removed through flat lighting, the ball looks smooth. **SEE 8.3 AND 8.4**

If you had to shoot a commercial for skin cream, you would want to light the model's face in such a way that the attached shadows are so soft that they are hardly noticeable. **SEE 8.5** But if you wanted to emphasize the rich, deep texture of the famous carving of the Aztec Sun Stone (generally known as the Aztec calendar), you would need to light for prominent attached shadows. **SEE 8.6** Highly transparent shadows would make the patterns in the stone hard to see. **SEE 8.7** ZVL7 LIGHTS→ Light and shadow→ attached

Because we normally see the main light source as coming from above (the sun, for example), we are used to seeing attached shadows below protrusions and

> KEY CONCEPT
> Attached shadows reveal form and texture.

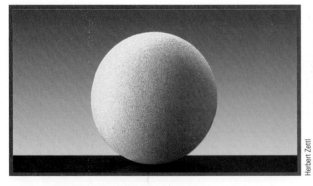

Herbert Zettl

8.3 ROUGH TEXTURE
Prominent attached shadows emphasize texture. The surface of this Styrofoam ball looks rough.

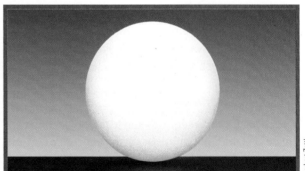

Herbert Zettl

8.4 SMOOTH TEXTURE
Here the attached shadows are almost eliminated, so the surface of the ball looks relatively smooth.

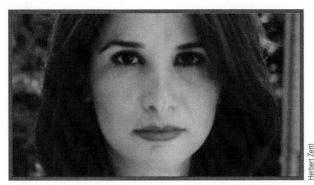

Herbert Zettl

8.5 ATTACHED SHADOWS MINIMIZED
To emphasize the smoothness of the model's face, attached shadows are kept to a minimum.

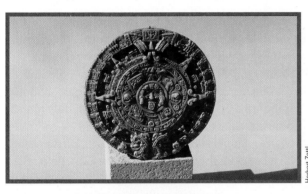

Herbert Zettl

8.6 ATTACHED SHADOWS EMPHASIZED
With the light coming from the side, the attached shadows on this Aztec Sun Stone are more prominent, and the rich, deep texture is properly emphasized.

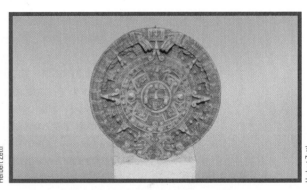

Herbert Zettl

8.7 ATTACHED SHADOWS MINIMIZED
With the light shining directly on the Sun Stone, the lack of attached shadows makes the intricate carvings look relatively flat.

indentations. When you lower the principal light source so that it illuminates an object, such as a face, from below eye level, we experience this departure from the norm as mysterious or spooky. There is probably not a single sci-fi or horror movie that does not use such a shadow-reversal effect at least once. **SEE 8.8** `ZVL8` LIGHTS→ Design→ horror

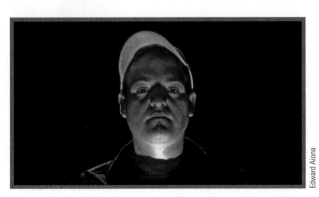

Edward Aiona

8.8 REVERSAL OF ATTACHED SHADOWS
The below-eye-level light source causes the attached shadows to fall opposite their expected positions. We interpret such unusual shadow placement as spooky or mysterious.

8.9 CAST SHADOWS

Cast shadows are usually cast by an object onto some other surface. In this case the cast shadows of the railing fall on the boards of the bridge.

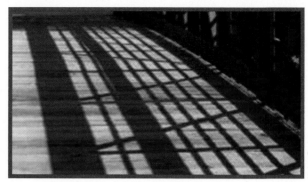

Herbert Zettl

Cast Shadows

Unlike attached shadows, ***cast shadows*** can be seen independent of the object causing them. If you make some shadowgraphs on a wall, for instance, you can focus on the shadows without showing your hand. The shadows of telephone poles, traffic signs, or trees cast onto the street or a nearby wall are all examples of cast shadows. Even if the cast shadows touch the base of the objects causing them, they remain cast shadows and will not become attached ones. **SEE 8.9**

Cast shadows help us see where an object is located relative to its surroundings and often what the object that is causing the shadow looks like. They also help orient us in time, at least to some extent. Take another look at figure 8.9. The cast shadow of the bridge railing gives you more detail of how it is built than looking at the actual railing causing it. **ZVL9** LIGHTS→ Light and shadow→ cast

> **KEY CONCEPT**
>
> Cast shadows help tell us where things are and when events take place.

Falloff

Falloff indicates the degree of change from light to shadow. Specifically, it refers to the relative abruptness—the speed—with which light areas turn into shadow areas, or the brightness contrast between the light and shadow sides of an object. An abrupt change from light to dense shadow illustrates fast falloff; it indicates a sharp edge or corner. **SEE 8.10** Slow falloff shows a more continuous change from light to shadow; the gradual shading indicates a curved object. **SEE 8.11**

Fast falloff can also refer to a high contrast between the light and shadow sides of a face. When the shadow side is only slightly darker than the light side and the shadows are highly transparent, the falloff is slow. If both sides of the face are equally bright, there is no falloff. The perception of texture also depends on falloff. Fast-falloff lighting emphasizes wrinkles in a face; slow-falloff or no-falloff lighting hides them (see figure 8.5). **ZVL10** LIGHTS→ Falloff→ fast | slow | none | try it

> **KEY CONCEPT**
>
> Falloff defines the contrast between light and dark areas and how quickly light turns into shadow.

When generating lighting effects with a computer, the relationship between attached and cast shadows and the rate of falloff have to be carefully calculated. For example, if you simulate a light source striking the object from screen-right, the attached shadows must obviously be on its screen-left side (opposite the light source), and the cast shadows must extend in the screen-left direction. Such careful attention to shadow consistency is also important if you cut a live scene electronically into a photographic background (a process called chroma keying; see chapter 9).

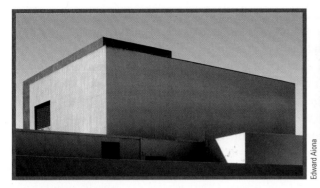

Edward Aiona

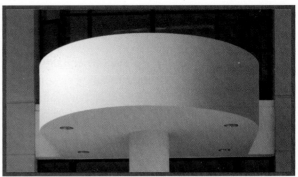

Edward Aiona

8.10 FAST FALLOFF
The change of light to shadow areas on these buildings is very sudden. The falloff is extremely fast, indicating an edge or a corner.

8.11 SLOW FALLOFF
The attached shadow on this balcony gets gradually darker. The falloff is relatively slow, indicating a curved surface.

■ COLOR

In this section we focus on the basic process of color mixing, the color television receiver and generated colors, and color temperature and white-balancing.

Additive and Subtractive Color Mixing

Recall the discussion about the beam splitter that divides the white light transmitted by the lens into the three primary light colors—red, green, and blue *(RGB)*—and how we can produce all video colors by adding the red, green, and blue light in certain proportions. These are called *additive primary colors* because we mix them by adding one colored light beam on top of others.

If you had three identical slide projectors, you could put a red slide into one, a green slide in the second, and a blue slide in the third and aim them at the screen so that their beams overlapped slightly. **SEE 8.12** What you would perceive is similar to the three overlapping circles shown in the figure. The overlapped RGB light primaries

8.12 ADDITIVE COLOR MIXING
When mixing colored light, the additive primaries are red, green, and blue. All other colors can be achieved by mixing certain quantities of red, green, and blue light. For example, the additive mixture of red and green light produces yellow.

Red

Yellow

Magenta

R

White

G

B

Green

Blue

Cyan

© Cengage Learning 2011

show that mixing red and green light adds up to yellow; red and blue mix to a bluish red called magenta; and green and blue combine to make a greenish blue called cyan. Where all three primary light colors overlap, you get white. By dimming all three projectors equally, you get a variety of grays. By turning them all off, you get black. By dimming any one or all projectors independently, you can achieve a wide variety of colors. For example, if the red projector burns at full intensity and the green one at two-thirds intensity with the blue projector turned off, you get a shade of orange. The more you dim the green projector, the more reddish the orange becomes.

You may remember from your finger-painting days that the primary colors were red, blue, and yellow and that mixing red and green paint together did not produce a clean yellow but rather a muddy dark brown. Obviously, paint mixes differently from light. When paint is mixed, its built-in filters subtract certain colors (light frequencies) rather than add them. We call this mixing process subtractive color mixing. Because the video system processes colored light rather than paint, we concentrate here on additive mixing.

Color Television Receiver and Generated Colors

The best way to explain the formation of a color video image is to use an old standard color television set. Instead of the three slide projectors we used for additive color mixing, a CRT (cathode ray tube) color television receiver uses three electron guns in the neck of the picture tube that shoot their beams at myriad red, green, and blue dots—pixels—on the inside of the television screen. As you recall from figure 3.2, one of the three guns hits the red dots, the other the green dots, and the third the blue dots. The harder the guns hit the dots, the more they light up. If the red gun and the green gun hit their dots with full intensity with the blue gun turned off, you get yellow. When all three guns fire at full intensity, you get white; at half intensity, you get gray. All three guns work overtime when you are watching a black-and-white show on a color television set. In the flat-panel displays, the same principle of additive color mixing applies, although the system of activating the pixels is quite different from the CRT one.

Because the video signal consists of electric energy rather than actual colors, couldn't we produce certain colors without a camera simply by stimulating the three types of color pixels with certain voltages? Yes, definitely! In a slightly more complex form, this is how computers generate millions of colors. The various colors in titles and other graphic displays, and the colors on a web page, are all based on the principle of additive color mixing.

Color Temperature and White-Balancing

In chapter 5 you learned that white-balancing is an important operational camera feature. But what exactly is it, and why is it necessary? You need to white-balance a camera because not all light sources produce light of the same degree of whiteness. As mentioned in chapter 5, a candle produces a more reddish light than does the midday sun or a supermarket's fluorescent lights, which give off a more bluish light. Even the same light source does not always produce the same color of light: the beam of a flashlight with a weak battery looks quite reddish, for example, but when fully charged the flashlight throws a more intense, and also whiter, light beam. The same color temperature change happens when you dim lights: the more you dim the lights, the more reddish they get. The camera needs to adjust to these differences to keep colors the same under different lighting conditions, a process called white-balancing.

Color temperature   The standard by which we measure the relative reddishness or bluishness of white light is called *color temperature*. The color differences of white light are measured on the Kelvin (K) scale. The more bluish the white light looks, the higher the color temperature and the higher the K value; the more reddish it is, the lower its color temperature and therefore the lower the K value.

Keep in mind that color temperature has nothing to do with how hot the actual light source gets. You can touch a fluorescent tube even though it burns at a high color temperature; but you wouldn't do the same with the incandescent lamp in a reading light, which burns at a much lower color temperature.

Because outdoor light is much more bluish than normal indoor illumination, two color temperature standards have been developed for lamps in lighting instruments: 5,600K for imitating or compensating outdoor illumination and 3,200K for indoor illumination. This means that when you use a 5,600K lamp in a lighting instrument, the light approximates the bluishness of outdoor light; the 3,200K lamps, on the other hand, emit a warmer, more reddish light. ZVL11 ▶ LIGHTS→ Color temperature→ light sources

Because color temperature is measured by the relative bluishness or reddishness of white light, couldn't you raise the color temperature of an indoor light by putting a slightly blue filter in front of it, or lower the color temperature of an outdoor lamp by using a slightly orange filter? Yes, you can. Such color filters, called gels or color media, are a convenient way of converting outdoor instruments for indoor lighting and vice versa.

Most often, you will have to raise the color temperature of 3,200K indoor lights to match the bluish outdoor light coming through a window. Simply take a piece of light-blue plastic (available in most photo stores) and attach it to the front of the indoor instruments, then white-balance the camera again. Although the color temperatures of the outdoor light (coming through the window) and the indoor light (instruments) may not match exactly, they will be close enough for the camera to achieve a proper white balance. Similar filters are used inside some cameras for rough white-balancing.

White-balancing   Recall that *white balance* refers to adjusting the camera so that it reproduces a white object as white on the screen regardless of whether it is illuminated by a high-color-temperature source (the sun at high noon, fluorescent lamps, and 5,600K instruments) or a low-color-temperature source (candlelight, incandescent lights, and 3,200K instruments). When white-balancing, the camera adjusts the RGB signals electronically so that they mix into white. Most small camcorders have an automatic white-balancing mechanism. The camera measures more or less accurately the color temperature of the prevailing light and adjusts the RGB circuits accordingly.

Large camcorders and ENG/EFP cameras have a semiautomatic white-balance control that is more accurate than a fully automatic one. The disadvantage is that you must white-balance every time you move into a new lighting environment, such as from indoors to outdoors or from the fluorescent lights of a supermarket to

> **KEY CONCEPT**
>
> Color temperature, expressed in K (Kelvin), measures the relative reddishness or bluishness of white light. Reddish white light has a low color temperature; bluish white light has a high color temperature.

the office that is illuminated by a desk lamp. The overriding advantage is that you white-balance a camera in the specific lighting in which you are shooting. When using a fully automatic white balance, you are never quite sure just what the camera considers to be white. As a result, the yellow lemons on the table might look green, and the white tablecloth appears light blue.

Higher-end camcorders allow you to use filters to perform a rough white balance under extremely reddish (low K value) or very bluish (high K value) light. The RGB mix is then fine-tuned with white-balance circuitry. Studio cameras and EFP cameras that are connected to a camera cable are white-balanced from the CCU or the RCU (remote control unit) by the video operator.

Proper white-balancing is very important for color continuity. For example, if you video-record a performer in a white shirt first outdoors and then indoors, his shirt should not look bluish in the outdoor scene or reddish in the indoor scene; it should look equally white in both. **SEE 8.13**

How to white-balance To white-balance a camera with a semiautomatic system, take a screen-filling close-up of a white card, a white shirt, or even a clean tissue and press the white-balance button. Some camera utility bags have a white patch sewn into them, giving you a handy white-balancing standard wherever you go. The viewfinder display (usually a flashing light) will tell you when the camera is seeing true white. Be sure that the white object fills the entire viewfinder and that it is located in the light that actually illuminates the scene you are shooting. For

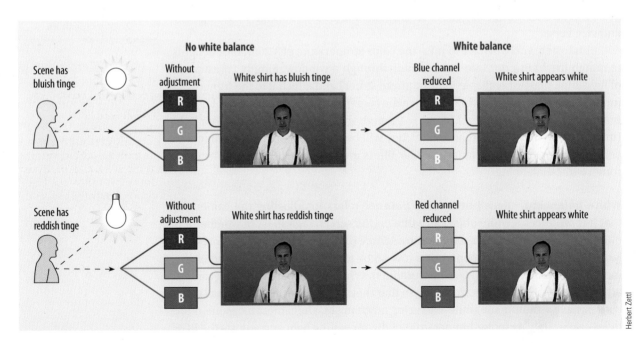

Herbert Zettl

8.13 WHITE BALANCE
To counteract tinting caused by variations in color temperature, you must white-balance the camera. This adjusts the RGB channels to compensate for the unwanted color cast and make white look white.

example, don't white-balance the camera in bright sunlight outside the hotel and then proceed to video-record the fashion show in the hotel lobby. (If you do, you may find that the video colors are quite different from the actual colors the models wore.) You need to white-balance every time you move into a new lighting environment; even if the light seems the same to the naked eye, the camera will detect the difference. **ZVL12** LIGHTS→ Color temperature→ white balance | controlling | try it

◼ LIGHTING INSTRUMENTS

Despite the many lighting instruments available, there are basically only two types: spotlights and floodlights. ***Spotlights*** throw a directional, more or less defined beam that illuminates a specific area; they cause harsh, dense shadows. ***Floodlights*** produce a great amount of nondirectional, diffused light that yields transparent shadows. Some floodlights generate such slow falloff that they seem to be a shadowless light source. Television studio lights are usually suspended from a fixed lighting grid made of heavy steel pipes or from movable counterweighted battens. **SEE 8.14** Portable lights for ENG and EFP are lightweight and more flexible than studio lights but are generally less sturdy and powerful.

Spotlights

Most studio spotlights have a glass lens that helps collect the light rays and focus them into a precise beam. There are also special-purpose spotlights, which differ greatly in size and beam spread.

8.14 STUDIO LIGHTING BATTEN WITH SPOTLIGHTS AND FLOODLIGHT
Lighting battens consist of a large grid of steel pipes that supports the lighting instruments. In this case, the batten can be lowered or raised using a counterweight system.

8.15 FRESNEL SPOTLIGHT

The Fresnel spotlight is the workhorse of studio lighting. Its lens creates a relatively sharp light beam that can be partially blocked by barn doors. This spotlight can be focused, tilted up and down, and panned sideways by turning the knobs with a lighting pole (a wooden pole with a metal hook at the end).

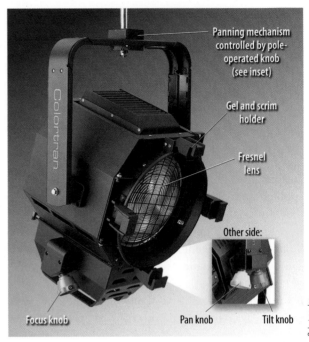

Panning mechanism controlled by pole-operated knob (see inset)

Gel and scrim holder

Fresnel lens

Other side:

Focus knob

Pan knob   Tilt knob

Colortran, Inc.

Fresnel spotlight   The workhorse of studio spotlights is the Fresnel (pronounced "fra-*nel*"). Its thin, steplike lens (developed by Augustin Jean Fresnel of France) directs the light into a distinct beam. **SEE 8.15** It can be equipped with an incandescent TH (tungsten-halogen) quartz lamp or with special metal-halide lamps.

The spread of the beam can be adjusted from a "flood" or "spread" position to a "spot" or "focus" position by turning a knob, ring, or spindle that moves the lamp-reflector unit. To flood the beam in most Fresnel spots, you move the lamp-reflector unit *toward* the lens. The light beam becomes slightly more diffused (less intense), and the shadows are softer than when focused. To focus the beam, you move the lamp-reflector unit *away from* the lens. This increases the sharpness and the intensity of the beam and makes its shadows fairly dense and distinct. **SEE 8.16**

You can further control the light beam with barn doors (see figure 8.14), which are movable metal flaps that swing open and closed like actual barn doors, blocking the beam on the sides or on the top and the bottom. Barn doors slide into a holder in front of the lens. To prevent them from sliding out and dropping, guillotine-like, on somebody, secure all of them to their instruments with safety chains or cables.

The size of Fresnel spotlights is normally given in the wattage of their quartz-halogen lamps. In the studio the most common incandescent Fresnels are the 650-watt (W) and 1K (1 kilowatt = 1,000W) instruments. For older, less sensitive cameras, the 2K (2,000W) Fresnel is still the workhorse. All incandescent studio Fresnel spots burn at the indoor color temperature of 3,200K.

Energy-efficient spotlights   The incandescent quartz Fresnels are being challenged by the more efficient metal-halide spots that can produce an amazing amount of light with lamps in the 100W to 500W range. **SEE 8.17**

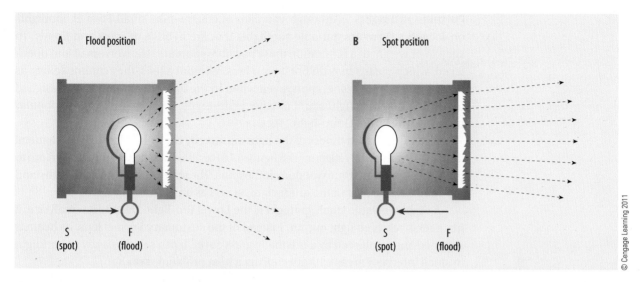

© Cengage Learning 2011

8.16 BEAM CONTROL OF FRESNEL SPOTLIGHT

A To flood (spread) the beam, turn the focus knob, ring, or spindle so that the lamp-reflector unit moves toward the lens.

B To spot (focus) the beam, turn the focus knob, ring, or spindle so that the lamp-reflector unit moves away from the lens.

A metal-halide lamp generates light by sending an electric arc through its high-pressure gas-filled tube. But these highly efficient lighting instruments have serious disadvantages. They operate only with a ballast to get them started, and some of the lamps flicker, which you can't see but the camera can. They still have trouble producing light of exactly the 3,200K indoor and 5,600K outdoor color temperature standards. And, unfortunately, they are usually quite expensive.

The HMI (hydragyrum medium arc-length iodide) instruments have been used for quite some time in the film industry and by large television stations. The HMI instrument emits a 5,600K outdoor light and consumes much less electricity compared with the incandescent equivalents. The reason why you usually don't find them in smaller video operations is that they are still expensive and need more setup time than their incandescent equivalents.

Whatever type of metal-halide instruments you may use, test them out on-camera before using them for a shoot. Some of them may generate a slight tint, such a blue or green. This subtle color shift may not be visible to the naked eye, but, like the flicker, it is certain to show up on-camera even if you have done some careful white-balancing.

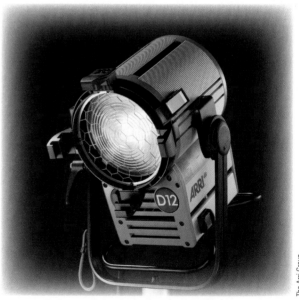

The Arri Group

8.17 METAL HALIDE FRESNEL SPOTLIGHT

This metal-halide Fresnel spot has a built-in ballast. It has a very high light output with relatively low-wattage metal-halide lamps.

> **KEY CONCEPT**
>
> Spotlights produce a sharp, directional light beam and cause fast falloff.

Portable spotlights   Although you can, of course, take small Fresnel spotlights on-location, there are portable spotlights that are hybrids of spots and floods. To keep their weight to a minimum, these portable spots are relatively small and open-faced, which means they do not have a lens. Without a lens, they cannot deliver as precise a beam as Fresnel spots, even when in the focus position. All are designed to be mounted on a light stand or with a clip-on device. One of the more popular models is the Lowel Omni-light. **SEE 8.18**

To reduce the harshness of the light emitted by the quartz lamp, insert a metal diffuser in front of the reflector (see figure 8.18) or attach a piece of spun-glass cloth to the barn doors with some wooden clothespins. The spun glass, which can withstand the considerable heat of the quartz lamps, acts as an efficient diffuser.

A highly versatile small spotlight is the Lowel Pro-light. Despite its small size, it has a relatively high light output. Instead of the customary Fresnel lens, its beam is softened and reinforced by a prismatic glass cover. It can serve as a key or backlight in small interview areas without causing a heat problem. **SEE 8.19**

An old standby is the clip light, with its reflector built into its bulb. The PAR 38 lamp is especially popular for illuminating outdoor walkways and driveways. Clip lights are useful for supplemental illumination of small areas; you can easily clip them onto furniture, scenery, doors, or whatever the clip will fit. Metal housings with barn doors that fit over the clip light are also available. When using fluorescent clip lights, check whether they burn with a high or low color temperature. **SEE 8.20**

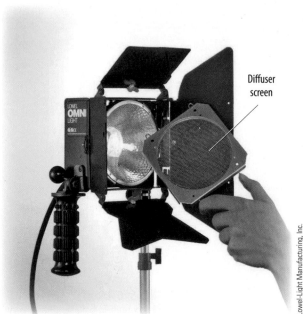

Diffuser screen

Lowel-Light Manufacturing, Inc.

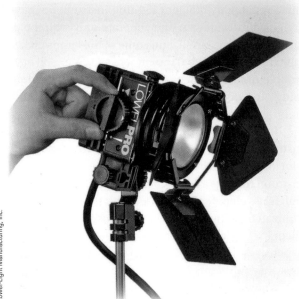

Lowel-Light Manufacturing, Inc.

8.18 LOWEL OMNI-LIGHT
This popular lightweight instrument doubles as a spot and a floodlight and is used mainly in ENG/EFP. You can plug it into any normal household outlet and hold it or fasten it to a light stand or any other convenient mounting device.

8.19 LOWEL PRO-LIGHT
The Pro-light is a small, powerful (250W) ENG/EFP spotlight that can be handheld, clipped to the camera, or mounted on a light stand. With its lenslike prismatic glass, it produces an exceptionally even beam.

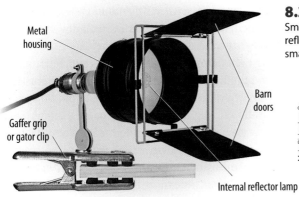

Metal housing

Barn doors

Gaffer grip or gator clip

Internal reflector lamp

Mole-Richardson Co.

8.20 CLIP LIGHT WITH BARN DOORS
Small spotlights, which use ordinary internal reflector lamps, are useful for illuminating small areas during field productions.

Floodlights

Floodlights have been used primarily to control falloff (that is, to fill in dense shadow areas) or to illuminate large areas with an even baselight. With today's lighting techniques, however, they also serve other functions, such as a key light—the principal light source in a standard lighting setup (see the following discussion of lighting techniques).

Floodlights have no lens and use large, relatively low-powered lamps because their purpose is to create highly diffused nondirectional illumination rather than a sharp beam. The diffused light creates soft and highly transparent shadows. When you illuminate an object with a floodlight, the falloff is automatically slower than with a spotlight. The more common studio floods are the scoop, the softlight, the fluorescent bank, and LED light panels.

Scoop   Named after its scooplike reflector, the scoop is an old-fashioned but highly useful floodlight. Scoops can be used as key lights as well as fill lights for dense shadow areas to slow down falloff and make shadows more transparent. They are ideal for lighting large areas with relatively even light. To diffuse the light beam even more, you can attach a spun-glass scrim to the front of the scoop. **SEE 8.21**

Softlight   Softlights are relatively large instruments with long tubelike lamps whose light bounces off a curved, light-diffusing reflector. The opening of the

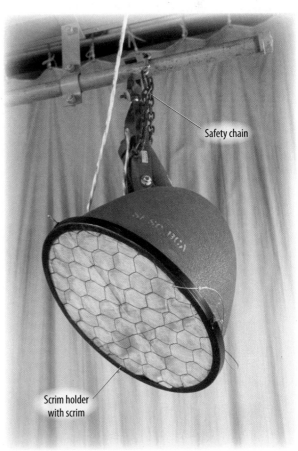

Safety chain

Scrim holder with scrim

Edward Aiona

8.21 SCOOP WITH SCRIM
The scooplike reflector of this floodlight allows you to give its diffused beam some direction, which makes it a good fill light. With a scrim attached to its otherwise open face, it acts more like a broad.

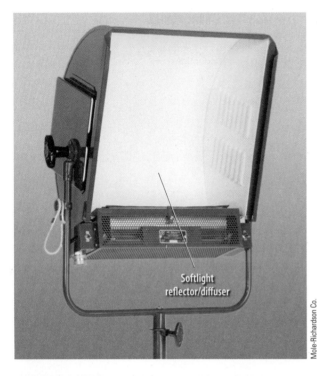

Softlight
reflector/diffuser

Mole-Richardson Co.

8.22 SOFTLIGHT
This floodlight is covered with diffusing material and delivers extremely diffused light. It causes very slow falloff and renders shadows virtually invisible.

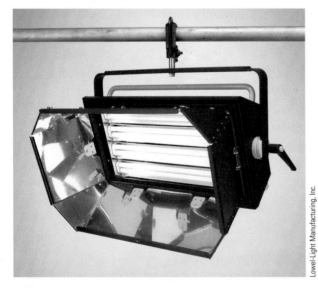

Lowel-Light Manufacturing, Inc.

8.23 FLUORESCENT BANK
The fluorescent bank consists of a series of fluorescent tubes. It produces very soft light with slow falloff.

reflector is covered with a diffusion material that scatters the light so much that it renders shadows virtually invisible. **SEE 8.22**

Softlights come in various sizes and burn at an indoor 3,200K color temperature. Most softlights are quite large and do not fit a cramped production space, but smaller softlights are the mainstay of news sets and interview areas. Some softlights have an attached gridlike contraption, called an egg crate, instead of the customary diffusion cloth. The squares of the egg crate diffuser give you a little more control over the direction of the softlight beam than does the diffusion cloth.

Fluorescent bank   The fluorescent bank, which consists of a row of fluorescent tubes, was one of the main lighting devices in the early days of television. After a hiatus the bank has made a comeback. It is highly efficient, produces extremely diffused light and slow falloff, and does not generate the heat of the other floodlights. You can get fluorescent banks that burn at approximately 5,000K for outdoor light or at 3,000K for indoor light. The manufacturers of fluorescent lights try hard to make the light look similar to that of incandescent floodlights, without the telltale greenish look of the fluorescents. Before you settle on a specific fluorescent bank, try it out: light a white object with the fluorescent bank, white-balance the camera, and video-record it for a minute or two. Then do the same with an incandescent instrument (such as a softlight or a scoop with a scrim). The object should look similarly white in both segments. Besides the color problem, the big disadvantage of all such lights is that the banks are still large and unwieldy, regardless of whether you use them in the studio or in the field. **SEE 8.23** **ZVL13** LIGHTS→ Instruments→ studio

LED light panels   Thanks to the lower light requirements of improved sensors in digital video cameras, new *LED lights* are being manufactured that may eventually replace the incandescent floodlights and probably even the fluorescent instruments in current use. The reason for their rising popularity is that they can now be made large enough to be practical for major studio lighting functions.

LED lights operate on an illumination technology—the *light-emitting diode*—that is similar to the

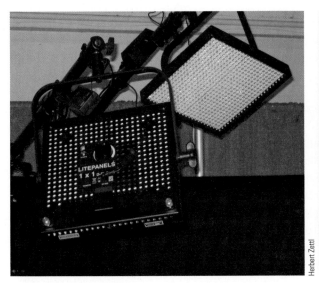

8.24 LED LIGHT PANEL
This 12-by-12-inch LED light panel is dimmable, generates very little heat, draws little power for an amazingly high light output, and burns longer than any kind of incandescent lamp.

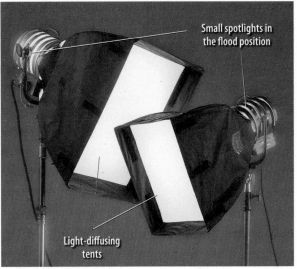

Small spotlights in the flood position

Light-diffusing tents

8.25 DIFFUSION TENT
Small portable lights, including spotlights, can be made into effective softlights by diffusing their beams with light tents.

way a computer screen works. When a computer screen is turned on, it can generate enough light to illuminate an object standing right next to it. If you colorize the screen, you can colorize a nearby white object without having to use color media.

LED panels have been used successfully for some time as camera lights or as floodlights to light small displays. But the larger panels (12-by-12 inches) emit enough light that they can take over most standard lighting functions. **SEE 8.24**

There are multiple advantages of LED lights: they last much longer than incandescent or fluorescent lamps; they use less power; they generate less heat than incandescent lights; they can generate both standard light temperatures (3,200K indoor and 5,600 outdoor); they can be dimmed without affecting the colors or the color temperature; they are flicker-free; and, compared with incandescent instruments, they are quite lightweight and their elements can be made to act more like a spotlight than a floodlight. The big disadvantage is that they are quite expensive.

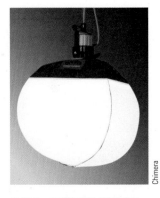

8.26 CHINESE LANTERN
These floodlights produce highly diffused light over a large area.

Portable floodlights When choosing a portable floodlight, look for one that is small, produces a great amount of diffused illumination, has a reflector that keeps the diffused light from spilling all over the area, can be plugged into an ordinary 120-volt (V) household outlet, and is lightweight enough to be supported by a light stand. You can, however, use any type of portable lighting instrument as a floodlight if you diffuse its beam.

When mounted inside an umbrella reflector, a Lowel Omni-light or even a small Fresnel spot can serve as a floodlight. Many portable lights come with light boxes, or light tents, which are tentlike diffusers that you can put over the portable light source to convert it to an efficient softlight. **SEE 8.25** Some diffusers look like Chinese lanterns and totally enclose the lamp. **SEE 8.26** **ZVL14** LIGHTS→ Instruments→ field

Special-Purpose Spotlights and Floodlights

There are numerous spotlights and floodlights that facilitate specific lighting tasks. The most popular are the ellipsoidal spotlight; the strip, or cyc, light; and a variety of small EFP floodlights.

Ellipsoidal spotlight   The ellipsoidal spotlight is used for special effects. It produces an extremely sharp, high-intensity beam that can be made rectangular or triangular with movable metal shutters. **SEE 8.27**

Some ellipsoidals have a slot next to the beam-shaping shutters that can hold a variety of metal sheets with patterned holes. Such metal sheets have acquired a variety of names, depending on the company that produces them or the LD who uses them. You may hear lighting people call them "gobos" (which can also mean the cutouts that are placed in front of a light source or camera) or "cucoloris" ("cookies" for short). Let's settle on *cookies.* When inserted in the slot of the ellipsoidal spot, the cookie pattern can be projected onto a dull-looking surface to make it more interesting. **SEE 8.28**

Strip, or cyc, light   The strip light is used primarily to illuminate cycloramas (the seamless background curtain that stretches along studio or stage walls), drapes,

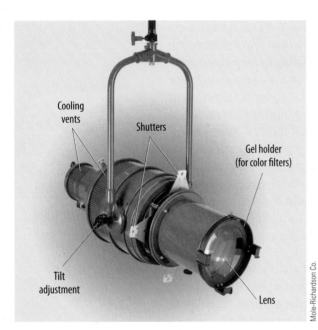

8.27 ELLIPSOIDAL SPOTLIGHT
The ellipsoidal spotlight produces an extremely sharp, bright beam. It is used to illuminate precise areas.

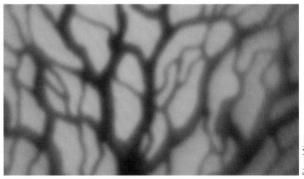

8.28 COOKIE PATTERN
Some ellipsoidal spotlights double as pattern projectors. You can insert a variety of metal cutouts, called cookies, whose patterns are projected by the spotlight onto a wall or other surface.

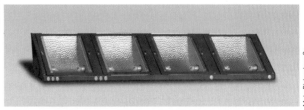

8.29 STRIP, OR CYC, LIGHT
These instruments are used primarily to illuminate cycloramas, drapes, and large scenic areas.

or large areas of scenery. They are similar to theater border lights and consist of rows of four to 12 quartz lamps mounted in long, boxlike reflectors. These strips are usually positioned side-by-side on the studio floor and shined upward onto the background. **SEE 8.29** There are LED strip lights available that can light up a cyc portion with a great many colors without the need for color gels.

Small EFP floodlight The ENG/EFP task of lighting up an interior quickly and efficiently to get sufficient baselight has been greatly aided by small but powerful floodlights run off regular household current. **SEE 8.30** Much like clip lights, you can move them into position quickly and set them up in a matter of minutes. Trying to use a larger, more cumbersome studio light to illuminate the same area would probably take considerably longer. Don't touch the instruments once they are turned on; some of then get very hot and can cause serious burns.

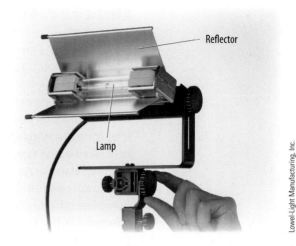

8.30 SMALL EFP FLOODLIGHT
This small EFP floodlight (Lowel V-light) runs off ordinary household current and can be used to illuminate small areas. When mounted inside an umbrella reflector, it serves as a softlight.

◼ LIGHTING TECHNIQUES

Now let's find out what to do with all these instruments. Start your lighting task with an idea of how you would like a person, scene, or display to look on the video screen, then choose the simplest way to achieve that look. Although there is no universal recipe that guarantees good lighting for every situation, there are established techniques that you can easily adapt to the specific task at hand. But do not become a slave to such methods. Although you may often wish you had more instruments, more space, and especially more time to do justice to the lighting, you should realize that the final criterion for video lighting is not how faithfully you imitate nature, or how closely you observe the standards as outlined in a book, but how it looks on the monitor and, especially, whether you get it done on time.

Let's take a look at some of the lighting basics: operation of lights, studio lighting, and field lighting.

Operation of Lights

Lighting presents some obvious hazards. Ordinary household current is powerful enough to kill. As just pointed out, the lamps, barn doors, and sometimes the instruments themselves get so hot that they can cause serious burns. If placed too close to combustible material, lighting instruments can cause fires. The instruments with barn doors are suspended far above studio floor areas and, if not properly secured, can come crashing down. Staring into a bright, high-intensity light beam can cause temporary vision problems. Even so, you don't need to be intimidated and give up lighting before getting started. You can easily eliminate these hazards by observing a few safety rules.

CHECKLIST: LIGHTING SAFETY

☑ **Electricity** Don't ever handle an instrument with wet hands, even if it is un-plugged. Do not "hot-plug" an instrument; switch off the power before connecting or disconnecting the power cables or patch cords. Patch cords connect selected lighting instruments to specific dimmers. Wear gloves. Use fiberglass safety ladders rather than metal ones. Do not touch any metal while working with a power cable. If you need an adapter to connect a power cable or to plug it in, tape the connection with electrician's tape. Use only those instruments that are absolutely necessary. If you can, let the larger instruments warm up through reduced power before bringing the dimmer up full. Turn off the studio lights and use house lights for basic block-ing rehearsals; this will keep the studio cooler and will also extend the life of the expensive bulbs. Do not waste electric energy.

☑ **Heat** The quartz lamps (quartz housing and a TH filament) get extremely hot. They heat up the barn doors and even the housing of the lighting instrument itself. Never touch the barn doors or the instrument with your bare hands once it is turned on. Use gloves or a lighting pole (a long wooden pole with a metal hook at one end) to adjust the barn doors or the instrument.

Keep instruments away from combustible materials, such as curtains, cloth, books, and wood paneling. If you need to place a lighting instrument close to such materials, insulate the materials with aluminum foil. Let lamps cool down before re-placing them. This is the big advantage of fluorescent and LED lights: you won't burn your hand or objects close to the switched-on instrument even during hours of use.

☑ **Fingerprints** Don't ever touch quartz or metal-halide lamps with your fingers. Fingerprints or any other residue clinging to the quartz housing will cause the lamp to overheat at those points and burn out. In extreme cases, the weakened housing can explode because both types of lamps are highly pressurized. Use a tissue or, in case of emergency, your shirttail when exchanging lamps. Be sure the power is shut off before reaching into an instrument.

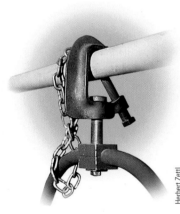

8.31 C-CLAMP
Use the C-clamp to fasten heavy lighting instruments to the lighting battens. Even when tightly fastened to the batten, the C-clamp allows a lighting instrument to be rotated.

☑ **Hanging instruments** Before lowering movable battens, see to it that the stu-dio floor is clear of people, equipment, and scenery. Because the tie-off rails, where the counterweighted battens are locked, are often hidden behind the cyclorama (so you can't see the studio floor), always give a warning before actually lowering the batten, such as "Batten 5C coming down!" Wait for an "all clear" signal before lower-ing the batten, and have someone watch the studio floor while you do so. Tighten all necessary bolts on the C-clamp. **SEE 8.31** Secure the instrument to the batten—and the barn doors to the instrument—with a safety chain or cable. Check the power connections for obviously worn or loose plugs and cables.

Whenever moving a ladder, watch for obstacles above and below. Don't leave a lighting wrench or other tool on top of a ladder. Never take unnecessary chances by leaning way out to reach an instrument. Whenever possible, have somebody steady the ladder for you.

✔ **Eyes** When adjusting an instrument, try not to look directly into the light. Work from behind, rather than in front of, the instrument. This way you look with the beam, rather than into it. If you have to look into the light, do it very briefly and wear dark glasses.

Studio Lighting

Now you are ready to do some actual lighting assignments. Although you may struggle with lighting at remote locations more often than you do in studio work, you will find that learning to light is easier in the studio than in the field. The art of lighting is neither mysterious nor complicated if you keep in mind its functions: to reveal the basic shape of the object or person, to lighten or darken the shadows, to show where the object is relative to the background, to give the object or person some sparkle and the whole scene a specific mood.

Photographic principle, or triangle lighting Still photographers have taught us that all of these functions can be accomplished with three lights: the *key light*, which reveals the basic shape; the *fill light*, which fills in the shadows if they are too dense; and the *back light*, which separates the object from the background and provides some sparkle. The various lighting techniques for video and motion pictures are firmly rooted in this basic principle of still photography, called the *photographic principle*, or *triangle lighting*. Some lighting people have yet another name for the photographic principle: three-point lighting. **SEE 8.32**

Key light In the studio a slightly diffused Fresnel spot is normally used for the key light. A Fresnel lets you aim the beam at the object without too much spill into other set areas. But you can also use other instruments for a key light, such as an Omni-light, a scoop, an LED light panel, or even a light that is reflected off a white card. As you can see, the key light is not defined by the instrument used but by its function: to reveal the basic shape of the object. The key light is usually placed above and to the right or left of the front of the object. **SEE 8.33** Note that when a spotlight is used as a key, it produces fast falloff (a dense attached shadow); when you use a floodlight, the falloff is slower, and the shadows are more transparent. **ZVL15** LIGHTS→ Triangle lighting→ key

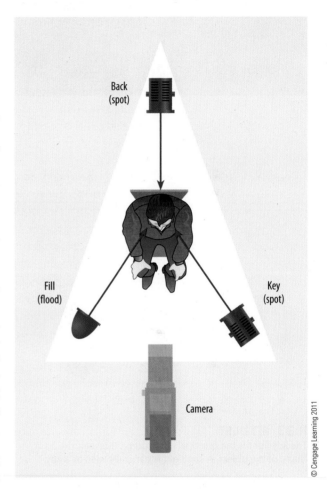

© Cengage Learning 2011

8.32 BASIC PHOTOGRAPHIC PRINCIPLE

The basic photographic principle uses a key light, a fill light, and a back light. They are arranged in a triangle, with the back light at its apex, opposite the camera.

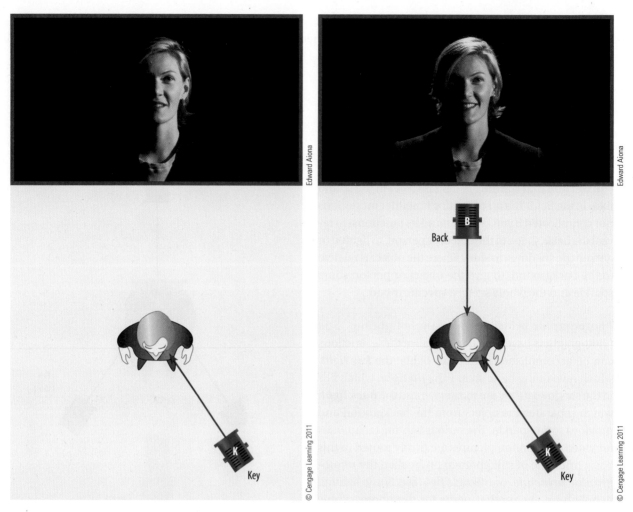

8.33 KEY LIGHT
The key light is the principal light source. It reveals the basic shape of the object. A spotlight is generally used as a key.

8.34 BACK LIGHT ADDED
The back light outlines the subject against the background and provides sparkle. Focused spots are used as back lights.

Back light   To outline the subject more clearly against the background, and especially to give the hair—and with it the whole picture—some sparkle and luster, you need a back light. Some lighting people believe that it is the back light in particular that gives the lighting its professional polish. **SEE 8.34**

As the name suggests, the back light falls on the back of the subject's head. You place it opposite the camera above and directly behind the subject. Because the area to be illuminated by the back light is quite limited, use a Fresnel spot. To keep the back light from shining into the camera or being in the shot, place it fairly high behind the subject.

Some LDs insist on having the back light burn with the same intensity as the key. Such a rule makes little sense because the intensity of the back light depends on the relative reflectance of the object or subject. A blond woman wearing a white blouse certainly needs a less intense beam than a man in a dark suit who has curly black hair. `ZVL16` LIGHTS→ Triangle lighting→ back

Fill light To slow down falloff and thereby render dense shadows more transparent, you need a fill light. A floodlight is generally used, but you can of course also use a Fresnel (or any other spotlight) for fill. Obviously, you place the fill light on the side opposite the key light and aim it toward the shadow area. **SEE 8.35** `ZVL17` LIGHTS→ Triangle lighting→ fill

The more fill light you use, the slower the falloff. If the fill light is as strong as the key light, you have eliminated the attached shadow and, with it, any falloff. Many news and interview sets are deliberately lighted flat with floodlights (such as LED panels), with equally strong softlights for key and fill, to render the close-up faces of the newspeople and the guests relatively wrinkle-free (but, unfortunately, also flat). You still need spot lights for the back lights, however.

Background light Unless you want a dark background, you need additional light to illuminate the background or set. This additional source is called the **background light** or set light. For a small set, you may need only a single Fresnel spot or scoop. **SEE 8.36** A large set may require a few more instruments, each of which illuminates a specific set area. To keep the attached shadows of the background on the same side as the foreground shadows, the background light must be on the same side of the camera as the key light.

You can also use the background light to provide some visual interest to an otherwise dull background: you can produce a "slice" of light, a prominent cast shadow that cuts across the background, or a cookie pattern. To suggest nighttime when lighting an interior set, keep the background generally dark and illuminate only small portions of it. If you want to evoke daylight, illuminate the background evenly. You can colorize a neutral gray or light background simply by putting color gels in front of the background lights. Colored light can save you a lot of painting. `ZVL18` LIGHTS→ Triangle lighting→ background

Adapting the lighting triangle Whenever possible, put up the set where the lights are rather than move the lights to the set location. If, for example, you have to light a simple two-person interview in the studio, look up at the lighting grid and find a key, fill, and backlight triangle and place the chair in the middle of it. Even if you can't find another lighting triangle for the other chair, you are still ahead—half of the

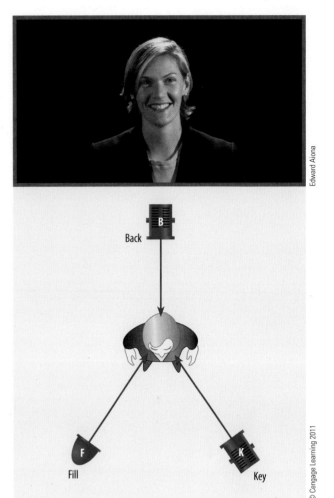

Edward Aiona

© Cengage Learning 2011

8.35 FILL LIGHT ADDED
The fill light slows down falloff and renders shadows more transparent. Floodlights are generally used to fill in dense shadows.

8.36 BACKGROUND LIGHT ADDED

The background, or set, light illuminates the background and various set areas. Spots or floodlights are used on the same side as the key.

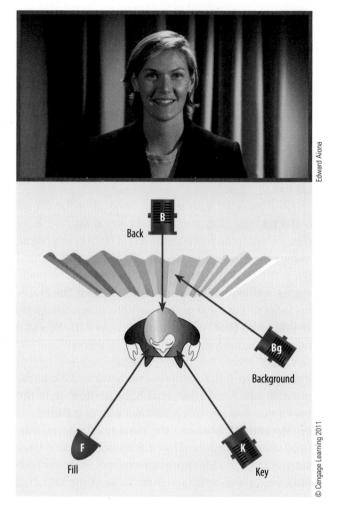

lighting is already done. You will find that you cannot always apply the photographic principle so that the three instruments form the prescribed triangle. This is perfectly normal. Realize that the lighting triangle is a basic principle, not a mandate.

Always try to accomplish a lighting setup with as few instruments as possible. If the falloff from a diffused key light is slow enough (the shadow side is not too dense), you may not need a fill light. Even when doing studio lighting, you may find that a reflector is more effective for filling in shadows than setting up a fill light. (We discuss the use of reflectors in the context of field lighting later in this chapter.) Sometimes the key light will spill over onto the background and eliminate the need for a set light.

In any case, don't be a slave to the photographic principle. Sometimes a single Fresnel aimed at the windshield of a car is all you need to produce a convincing nighttime effect for the car interior; at other times you may need four or five carefully placed instruments to re-create the effect of a single candle. The effectiveness of the lighting is determined not by how faithfully you observe traditional lighting conventions but by how the scene looks on the monitor. Always keep in mind that you light for the camera. **ZVL19** LIGHTS→ Triangle lighting→ try it

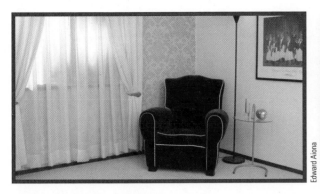

Edward Aiona

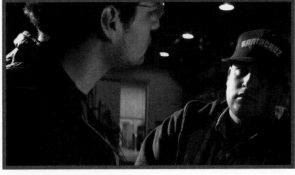

Edward Aiona

8.37 HIGH-KEY LIGHTING
High-key lighting shows a bright scene with an abundance of diffused light. The background is usually light.

8.38 LOW-KEY LIGHTING
Low-key lighting shows dramatic, selective lighting with fast-falloff attached and prominent cast shadows. The background is usually dark.

High-key and low-key lighting   Sometimes you will hear the terms *high-key* and *low-key* lighting. This has nothing to do with the vertical positioning of the key light. Rather, it describes the overall lighting effect and its general feel. A scene with ***high-key lighting*** has an abundance of bright, diffused light, resulting in slow-falloff or flat lighting. The background is usually light and projects a high-energy, upbeat feeling. Game shows and situation comedies are usually lighted high-key. Because of the slow falloff, high-key lighting is also used for commercials that advertise beauty products. **SEE 8.37** `ZVL20` LIGHTS→ Design→ high key

A scene with ***low-key lighting*** is much more dramatic; it uses relatively few spotlights to create selective lighting with fast-falloff attached shadows and prominent cast shadows. The background and, wherever possible, the floor areas are kept dark. Most outdoor night scenes exhibit low-key lighting. It is also frequently used in dramatic scenes in soap operas, in mystery and crime shows, and sometimes in sci-fi movies. **SEE 8.38** `ZVL21` LIGHTS→ Design→ low key

Light Plot

For all but routine shows, you need to prepare a ***light plot***. Some light plots are rough sketches to indicate the approximate positions of lights; arrows indicate the approximate directions of their beams. **SEE 8.39** Others are drawn on a floor plan grid, which shows the background scenery, the major action areas, and the principal camera positions. Detailed light plots show the position, type, and functions of the lighting instruments needed. **SEE 8.40**

Last-Minute Lighting Techniques

When you are called upon to do some eleventh-hour lighting, do not whine about artistic integrity or lack of time. Simply turn on as many floodlights as possible and try to place some back lights to give the scene some sparkle. This is not the time to fret about triangle principles or falloff. Every so often such an emergency technique will result in surprisingly good lighting—but don't rely on it.

8.39 SIMPLE LIGHT PLOT SKETCH FOR TWO-PERSON INTERVIEW

Most light plots are rough sketches that indicate the types of lights used (spots or floods), their approximate positions, and the general direction of their beams.

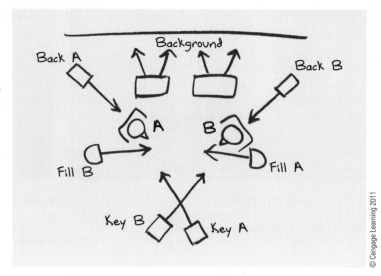

8.40 DETAILED LIGHT PLOT FOR TWO-PERSON INTERVIEW

This light plot shows the type and the position of the lighting instruments used and the approximate directions of their beams. Sometimes light plots even indicate the size (wattage) of the instruments. Note that there are two overlapping lighting triangles—one for person A and the other for person B.

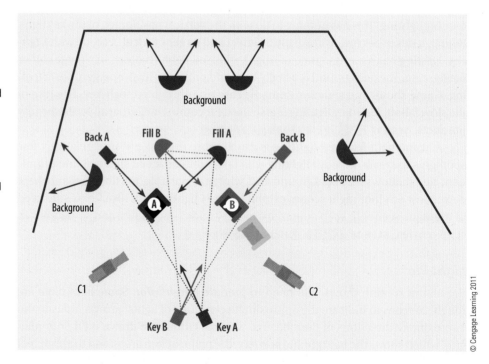

Field Lighting

Whereas studio lighting is done exclusively with various types of instruments, field, or location, lighting often extends to the control or augmentation of available light. When shooting outdoors you are pretty much dependent on available light. Your lighting job is to manipulate sunlight so that it yields, at least to some extent, to the basic lighting principles. When shooting indoors you can apply all studio lighting principles, except on a smaller scale. Windows often present a problem because the light entering from outside is usually brighter than the indoor light and has a much higher color temperature. But light from windows can also be an important illumination source.

Outdoors—overcast and shadow area   A foggy or overcast day is ideal for outdoor shooting. The fog and the clouds act as giant diffusion filters: the giant and brutally bright spotlight of the sun becomes a huge but gentle softlight. The highly diffused light produces slow falloff and transparent shadows. The camera likes such low-contrast lighting and produces crisp and true colors throughout the scene. The scene is basically illuminated by high-intensity baselight. Be sure to white-balance the camera before video-recording; the light on an overcast day has a surprisingly high color temperature (bluish tint).

A large shadow area will provide you with similarly slow-falloff lighting. Whenever possible, put the on-camera people in the shade. Besides the gentle shadows, you will have no contrast problems unless you include part of the sunlit area in the picture. As you can see, this is a quick solution to a potentially difficult lighting situation.

Bright sunlight   When forced to shoot in bright sunlight, you are not so lucky. The bright sun acts like a giant high-intensity spotlight, which renders the falloff appropriately fast; the shadows are very dense, and the contrast between light and shadow sides is extremely high. This extreme contrast can present a formidable exposure problem. If you close down the iris (high f-stop setting for a small aperture) to prevent too much light from overloading the sensors, the shadow areas will turn uniformly dark and dense and will show no detail. If you open up the iris to see some detail in the shadow areas, you will overexpose the bright areas. The automatic aperture in a camcorder is of no help in this situation: it simply adjusts to the brightest spot in the scene and renders all shadow areas equally dark. Even the most sophisticated camera cannot adjust itself to accommodate these conditions.

There are two things you can do. As mentioned earlier, you can first use an ND (neutral density) filter on the camera to reduce the overly bright light without affecting the colors. Second, you can provide enough fill light to slow down the falloff, reduce the contrast, and make the attached shadows more transparent without overexposing the bright areas. But where in the field can you get a fill light strong enough to offset the sun?

In expensive and elaborate productions, high-intensity spotlights (usually HMI lights) that burn at 5,600K are used as outdoor fill lights. Fortunately, you can also use the sun to serve simultaneously as both key and fill lights—all you need is a reflector to bounce some of the sunlight back toward the shadow area. **SEE 8.41** You can use a sheet of white foam core or a white card as a reflector, or use crumpled aluminum foil taped to a stiff backing. You can also use a number of commercially available reflectors that fold up and prove effective over considerable distances. The closer you hold the reflector to the object, the more intense the fill light will be. Some LDs and DPs (directors of photography) use multiple reflectors to reflect light into areas that face away from the light source. In this case the reflector becomes the principal light source. With good reflectors (mirrors), you can even guide sunlight indoors to light up a room or hallway without any lighting instruments.

KEY CONCEPT

Reflectors can replace lighting instruments.

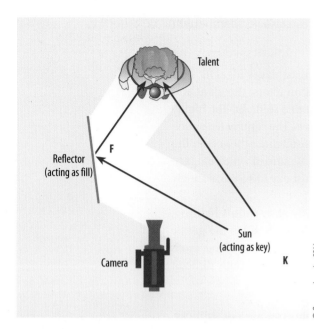

8.41 USE OF A REFLECTOR

The reflector acts like a fill light: it bounces some light back toward the dense shadow areas and slows down falloff.

Avoid shooting against any bright background, such as a sun-drenched white wall, the ocean, or a lake. Anyone standing in front of it will be rendered in silhouette unless you use huge reflectors or high-intensity fill lights. Whenever possible find some shade in which to position the subject. When shooting at a lakeshore or the ocean beach, use a large umbrella to create the necessary shadow area. The umbrella will not only make your lighting job considerably easier but also provide some visual interest. **ZVL22** LIGHTS→ Field→ outdoor | use of reflectors

Indoors without windows   If the room is adequately illuminated, try to shoot with available light and see how it looks on the monitor. We discussed earlier that the high light-sensitivity of camcorders and ENG/EFP cameras enables DPs to shoot much more often in available light than was previously possible. The basic rule still applies for available light: if it looks good to you, there is no need for additional instruments.

Remember to white-balance the camera to the available light before starting to shoot. Most indoor lighting can be easily improved by adding some back lights in the appropriate areas. Potential problems include light stands that show up on-camera or a back light that cannot be positioned high enough to be out of camera range. In this case, place the instrument somewhat to the side, or use some 1 × 2 lumber to create a temporary support for it. Move the back light close enough to the subject to keep it out of camera view.

When lighting a person who remains stationary in a room, as in an interview, you use the same photographic principle as in the studio except that you now have to place portable lights on stands. Try to have the key or fill light double as the background light. To avoid the infamous reddish or white hot spot on the subject and to make the light look generally softer, attach spun-glass scrims to all three instruments. You can use wooden clothespins to attach the scrims to the barn doors. Floodlights, such as LED panels, are ideal instruments for achieving good key and fill lighting. For the backlight use a small spotlight.

If you have only two lights with which to light a person indoors, you can use one as the key, the other as the back, and a reflector to act as the fill. **SEE 8.42** You can also place a softlight for the key (light diffused by a light tent) almost directly opposite the person to avoid a dense shadow side, then use the second light as a back light.

If you have just one lighting instrument, such as an Omni-light, you can use it as a key, with the reflector acting as the fill. In such a setup, you must necessarily sacrifice the back light. If you diffuse the key light and move it closer to the camera than it is in figure 8.42, however, you can light the face almost straight on. Then use the reflector in the back (out of camera range) to provide the all-important back light.

© Cengage Learning 2011

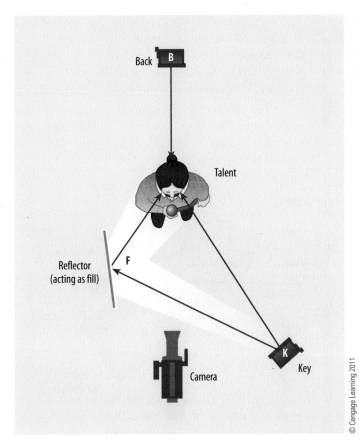

8.42 TWO-POINT INDOOR LIGHTING
To achieve effective triangle lighting with only two lights, use one for the key light and the other for the back light. Fill light is achieved with a reflector.

To light an ordinary-sized room so that you can follow somebody walking through it, use the portable lights in the flood position and reflect them off the ceiling or walls, or diffuse their beams with scrims. If available, use a light-diffusing umbrella. Aim the instrument into the umbrella, with the opening of the umbrella toward the scene, or at reflectors rather than directly toward the action area. You can apply the same technique for lighting a large interior except that you need more or higher-powered instruments. The idea is to get as much baselight (highly diffused overall light) as possible with a minimum of instruments.

Indoors with windows   By now you know that windows can present a formidable lighting problem. Even if you don't shoot against them, they admit a great amount of high-color-temperature light. If you try to augment the bluish 5,600K outdoor light with normal indoor 3,200K lighting instruments, the camera will have trouble finding the correct white balance. The simplest way to match the lower 3,200K indoor color temperature with the prevailing 5,600K outdoor color temperature is to attach a light-blue gel (color media) to the indoor lighting instruments. The blue gel helps raise their color temperature to approximate the 5,600K outdoor light. Even if it is not a perfect match, the camera can be properly white-balanced for both the light coming through the window and the indoor lighting instruments.

KEY CONCEPT

In the field, light for visibility rather than artistic impact.

8.43 WINDOW USED AS BACK LIGHT

In this interview setup, the lighting is done with a single instrument. A diffused Lowel Omni-light with a light-blue gel acts as the key. The back light is provided by the window, which is kept out of camera range.

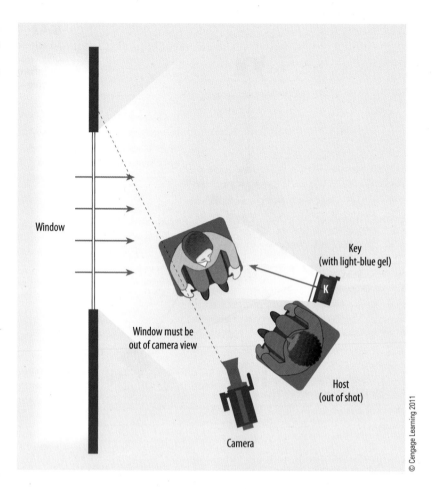

© Cengage Learning 2011

The best way to cope with windows is to avoid them: draw the curtains and use a normal triangle lighting setup. Many times, however, you can use the window light as a back light or even as a key. For example, when using the window as a back light, you need to position the subject in such a way that the light strikes from the side and the back. Then position the key light and the camera. **SEE 8.43** Obviously, the window should be off-camera. By changing the window from a hazard to an asset and with only one lighting instrument in the room, you have achieved a professional lighting setup. What about the fill light? The spill from the window and the diffused key light should be enough to provide for relatively slow falloff. If not, you can always use a reflector to bounce some of the key light back as fill. **ZVL23** LIGHTS→ Field→ indoor | mixed

GUIDELINES: FIELD LIGHTING

☑ **Scout ahead** Check out the location and determine the lighting requirements before the actual shooting date. Establish a contact person and get his or her name, address, and all phone numbers. Check the breaker box and determine the available power, the nature of the outlets, and the extension cords needed. Have adapters available that fit the various outlets.

✅ **Be prepared** Always take with you a few rolls of gaffer's tape, a roll of aluminum foil, gloves, a wrench, some wooden clothespins (plastic ones melt), and a fire extinguisher.

✅ **Don't overload circuits** Once on-location don't overload the circuit. Although a normal 15-amp household outlet will accommodate 1,500 watts of lighting instruments, do not plug more than 1,000 watts into a single circuit. Realize that several outlets may be on the same circuit even if they are in different corners of the room. To test which outlets are on the same circuit, plug a light into various outlets and turn off the breaker. If the light goes out, you are on the designated circuit. If the light stays on, the outlet is connected to another circuit. Keep in mind that even long extension cables can add to the circuit load.

✅ **Don't waste lamp life** Turn on the lights only as needed. The incandescent quartz lamps for portable lighting instruments have a limited life span. Turning off the lights as much as possible will preserve energy, extend the life of the lamps, and reduce the heat in the performance area.

✅ **Secure the light stands** Be especially careful when placing lighting instruments on portable stands. Secure all light stands with sandbags so they won't tip over when somebody brushes against them. Route extension cords out of the main traffic pattern. If you have to lay them across a hallway or threshold, tape them securely in place (here is where the gaffer's tape comes in handy) and put a rug or rubber doormat over them.

✅ **Move cords carefully** Don't pull on an extension cord that is connected to a lighting instrument; light stands tip over easily, especially when fully extended.

✅ **Be time conscious** Don't underestimate the time it takes to set up even simple location lighting.

M A I N   P O I N T S

▶ *Light and Shadow Control*
Lighting is the deliberate illumination of a performance area and the control of attached and cast shadows.

▶ *Types of Light and Light Intensity*
The two basic types of light are directional and diffused. Directional light is focused and causes harsh shadows. Diffused light is spread out and creates soft shadows. Light intensity is measured in foot-candles (fc) or European lux. There is approximately 10 lux per foot-candle.

▶ *Contrast and Measuring Light*
Contrast is the difference between the darkest and the brightest areas in the video image. This contrast is often expressed as a ratio, such as 60:1, which means that the brightest spot is 60 times the intensity of the darkest spot. Many cameras tolerate a

relatively limited contrast ratio, ranging from 50:1 to 100:1. When measuring contrast, the light meter must read reflected light. When measuring baselight levels, the meter reads incident light.

▶ Shadows and Falloff

There are two types of shadows: attached and cast. Attached shadows are affixed to the object; they cannot be seen independent of it. Cast shadows can be seen independent of the objects that cause them. Falloff indicates the change from light to shadow and the contrast between light and shadow areas. Fast falloff means that the light area changes abruptly into dense shadow area; the contrast is high. Slow falloff means that the light turns gradually into the shadow side; the contrast is low.

▶ Colors and Color Temperature

Colors are generated through additive color mixing. All colors are mixed by adding the primary light colors—red, green, and blue (RGB)—in various proportions. Color temperature refers to the relative reddishness or bluishness of white light. White-balancing adjusts the camera to the color temperature of the prevailing illumination so that the camera will reproduce a white object as white on the video screen.

▶ Lighting Instruments

Lights are usually classified into spotlights and floodlights, and studio and portable lights. Spotlights produce a sharp, focused beam; floodlights produce highly diffused, nondirectional illumination. Studio lights are normally suspended from the ceiling. Portable lights are smaller and supported by collapsible light stands.

▶ The Photographic Principle, or Triangle Lighting

Lighting functions can usually be achieved with the basic photographic principle: a key light (principal light source), a fill light (fills in dense shadows), and a back light (separates the subject from the background and gives it sparkle). This is also known as three-point lighting. Reflectors frequently substitute for fill lights. The background light is an additional light used for lighting the background and the set area. In field, or location, lighting, it is often more important to provide sufficient illumination than careful triangle lighting. In the field floodlights are used more often than spotlights.

▶ High-Key and Low-Key Lighting

High-key lighting uses an abundance of bright, diffused light, resulting in slow-falloff or flat lighting; the high-key scene generally has a light background and an upbeat mood. Low-key lighting uses few spotlights to create fast-falloff lighting and prominent cast shadows; it illuminates only selected areas and projects a dramatic mood.

▶ Windows

In EFP lighting, a window can serve as a key or a side-back light, so long as it is off-camera. All indoor incandescent instruments must have light-blue color media attached to match the color temperature of the outdoor light coming through the window.

ZETTL'S VIDEOLAB

 For your reference or to track your work, the *Zettl's VideoLab* program cues in this chapter are listed here with their corresponding page numbers.

KEY TERMS

aspect ratio The ratio of the width of the television screen to its height. In STV (standard television), it is 4 × 3 (4 units wide by 3 units high); for HDTV (high-definition television), it is 16 × 9 (16 units wide by 9 units high). Mobile media devices have various aspect ratios, including vertical ones.

character generator (CG) A computer dedicated to the creation of letters and numbers in various fonts. Its output can be directly integrated into video images.

chroma key Key effect that uses a color (usually blue or green) for the key source backdrop. All blue or green areas are replaced by the base picture during the key.

digital video effects (DVE) Video effects generated by an effects generator in the switcher or by a computer with effects software. The computer system dedicated to DVE is called a *graphics generator*.

electronic still store (ESS) system Stores still video frames in digital form for easy random access.

essential area The section of the television picture that is seen by the home viewer, regardless of minor loss during signal transmission or signal processing by the television receiver. Also called *safe title area*.

key An electronic effect in which the keyed image (figure—usually letters) blocks out portions of the base picture (background) and therefore appears to be layered on top of it.

matte key The key (usually letters) is filled with gray or a color.

super Short for *superimposition*. A double exposure of two images, with the top one letting the bottom one show through.

wipe A transition in which one image seems to "wipe off" (gradually replace) another from the screen.

Graphics and Effects

Because you now know how to give lens-generated images effective composition, you can expand your creative efforts to synthetic video—images that are electronically manipulated or totally computer-generated. These synthetic images can be as simple as electronically generated titles that appear over a background image, or a computer-generated landscape that changes with your point of view. Although the camera still supplies the majority of video images, synthetic images are becoming more a part of video production.

This chapter explains analog and digital image manipulation and the major aspects of synthetic image creation.

▶ **PRINCIPLES OF GRAPHICS**

   Aspect ratio, essential area, readability, color, animated graphics, and style

▶ **STANDARD ELECTRONIC VIDEO EFFECTS**

   Superimposition, key, and wipe

▶ **DIGITAL EFFECTS**

   Digital image manipulation equipment, common digital video effects, and synthetic image creation

The relative ease with which you can change fonts and their appearance with a word-processing program has spilled over into television graphics. You are certainly familiar with the many variations of letters in titles: Some fly onto or dance across the screen. Weather maps not only display the temperatures but have clouds or fog drift over them or rain and snow fall on them. Traffic maps show where accidents occurred and how to bypass a traffic jam. We have become so accustomed to these graphics that we don't consider them special effects, although such effects demand highly sophisticated graphics software and especially skilled computer artists.

Unfortunately, many such dazzling displays do not always contribute to effective communication. Even if you don't intend to become a graphic artist or an art director, you need to understand the basic principles of video graphics and the common video effects. This knowledge will help you integrate appropriate and effective graphics into your productions. Just don't forget that even the most dazzling video effects cannot improve weak content. In many cases they will accentuate it.

■ PRINCIPLES OF GRAPHICS

The basic elements and principles of video graphics include aspect ratio, essential area, readability, color, animated graphics, and style.

Aspect Ratio

As you recall from chapter 6, ***aspect ratio*** describes the basic shape of the television screen—the relationship between screen width and height. The STV (standard television) aspect ratio is 4 × 3, which means its screen is 4 units wide by 3 units high (see figure 6.1). A unit can be any length—inches, feet, or meters. The ratio is also expressed as 1.33:1. This means that for every unit of screen height, there are 1.33 units of screen width. The HDTV (high-definition television) aspect ratio is 16 × 9, or 1.78:1, which means the screen is horizontally stretched, not unlike the screen in a movie theater (see figure 6.2). The screens of mobile media, such as cell phones, have a variety of aspect ratios, including 4 × 3 and 16 × 9 as well as wider and even vertical orientations. Within the overall aspect ratio of the display, you can generate digital picture frames with a variety of horizontal and vertical aspect ratios and even irregularly shaped ones.

The advantage of the HDTV aspect ratio is that you can include horizontally stretched scenes and titles that you would have to crop (cut at the sides) or rearrange in the standard aspect ratio. **SEE 9.1 AND 9.2** It can display wide-screen motion pictures without the need for dead zones (black bars) at the top and the bottom of the screen. Close-ups of faces, however, are more effectively framed in the STV aspect ratio.

Essential Area

Regardless of the aspect ratio, you need to keep all the important information within the ***essential area***. Also known as the safe title area, this is the picture area displayed by the average home receiver regardless of manipulation of picture area

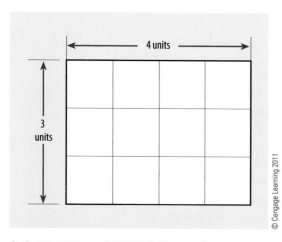

9.1 STANDARD TELEVISION ASPECT RATIO
The STV aspect ratio is 4 units wide by 3 units high,

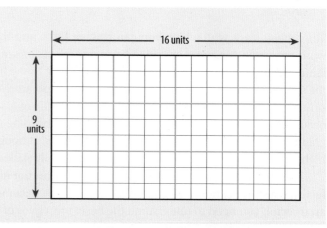

9.2 HIGH-DEFINITION TELEVISION ASPECT RATIO
The HDTV aspect ratio is 16 units wide by 9 units high, or 1.78:1.

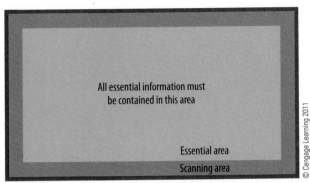

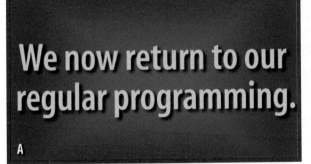

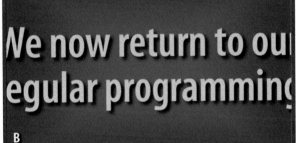

9.3 ESSENTIAL AREA

The essential, or safe title, area is centered within the television screen. All necessary information must be contained in the essential area.

9.4 TITLE OUTSIDE THE ESSENTIAL AREA

A Although we can read the complete title on a well-adjusted monitor...

B ...the information that lies outside the essential area gets lost on the home receiver.

during transmission, slightly inaccurate signal processing or a misaligned display by the TV set, or a shift of aspect ratio from HDTV (16×9) to STV (4×3) or vice versa. **SEE 9.3 AND 9.4** The viewfinders of most studio cameras allow you to switch to a secondary frame that outlines the safe title area.

> **KEY CONCEPT**
>
> All necessary information must be contained within the essential (safe title) area.

Readability

Even if the camera part of your camcorder reproduces exceptionally fine picture detail, its video-recording system and your TV set may not. In practice this means that you need to choose lettering that can be easily read on-screen. Sometimes the titles dance so much or appear for such a short time that only a speed-reader can make sense of them. The following points will assist you in designing effective video graphics:

- Keep all the information within the essential area. If you use the essential area of the 4×3 aspect ratio, your graphics will also show up clearly on a 16×9 screen.

- Use fonts that are big and bold enough to show up even when the picture resolution is less than ideal and when the background is especially cluttered. **SEE 9.5**

9.5 BOLD LETTERS OVER A BUSY BACKGROUND

This title reads well despite the busy background. Its letters are bold and have enough contrast from the background to ensure readability.

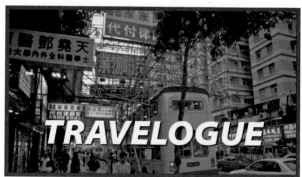

Herbert Zettl

- Limit the amount of information and arrange the lettering in blocks. The information should form distinct patterns rather than be randomly scattered on-screen. This block design is especially important for web pages, where display space is severely limited. **SEE 9.6 AND 9.7**

- Use a block design especially when dividing up the screen area for unrelated information. **SEE 9.8**

Color

You already learned that the video camera and the television receiver produce all colors from the three additive (light) primaries of red, green, and blue (RGB). Now you need to arrange these colors so that they help clarify and intensify the intended message. Without going into complicated color theory, we'll jump directly to a practical way of using colors effectively in graphics and scenic displays: divide them not into their hues—their actual colors—but into high-energy and low-energy categories.

High-energy colors are what we ordinarily call "loud" or "bright," such as bold reds, yellows, and blues. Low-energy colors are the more washed-out pastels, such

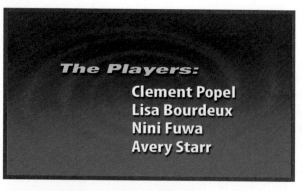

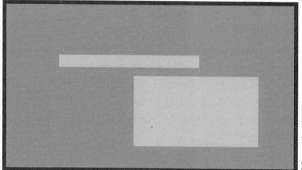

© Cengage Learning 2011

9.6 BLOCK ORGANIZATION OF TITLES

Information is easier to read when the titles are organized in graphic blocks.

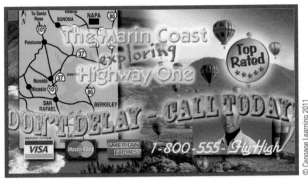

© Cengage Learning 2011

Edward Aiona

9.7 DISORGANIZATION OF TITLES
Visual clutter occurs when the information is not graphically organized. The scattered bits of information are hard to perceive, especially on a video screen.

9.8 MULTISCREEN BLOCKS
When dissimilar pieces of information are graphically organized into blocks or multiple screens, the information is easier to read.

as beige, pink, light blue, and shades of gray. **SEE 9.9 AND 9.10** To draw attention to a title or graphic area, use a high-energy color set off against a low-energy background.

Applying high-energy colors to both the foreground (title) and the background is less effective—both shout with equal intensity and vie for attention. Many web pages suffer from such an indiscriminate use of high-energy colors. As a result, the user is likely to ignore all these areas and surf to a less demanding page. If both foreground and background colors are low-energy, the overall graphic is subdued. Many commercials that are deliberately low-energy are shot in black-and-white. The idea is to give you relief from loud, high-energy messages and stimulate you to mentally supply your own color palette.[1]

KEY CONCEPT

Use high-energy colors for the foreground (titles) and low-energy colors for the background.

1. See Herbert Zettl, *Sight Sound Motion: Applied Media Aesthetics,* 6th ed. (Boston: Wadsworth, 2011), pp. 65–66 and color plate CP21.

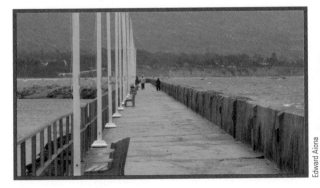

Edward Aiona

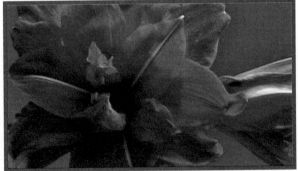

Herbert Zettl

9.9 LOW-ENERGY COLOR
Low-energy colors are desaturated, which means they have little color strength. Most pastel colors are low-energy.

9.10 HIGH-ENERGY COLOR
High-energy colors have high saturation, which makes them bold. They are especially effective when set against a low-energy background.

Animated Graphics

To capture your attention, titles are often animated, that is, made to move in some fashion. Written information crawls sideways across the screen, from one edge to the other. Some titles fly onto the screen or appear gradually from the sides or the top or bottom. Other titles zoom in or out, dancing or flashing on-screen. Although such titles draw immediate attention, they are apt to lose the viewer's attention just as quickly. When using animated titles, ask yourself whether they are appropriate for the content and the overall style of the show.

Style

Style in graphic design means that the visual display shows common elements that are appropriate for the message. The style of the opening titles should convey the nature of the show that follows. Bouncing cartoon letters are obviously the wrong choice for introducing a program that bares human suffering; so are titles that use somber, formal letters to announce a goofy cartoon. To learn more about style, read books on typography and graphics, watch the graphics of established news presentations, or look through some chic fashion magazines.

> **KEY CONCEPT**
>
> Titles must match the style of the program.

■ STANDARD ELECTRONIC VIDEO EFFECTS

The standard electronic effects are achieved with an electronic switcher (see chapter 10) and a special-effects generator (SEG) that normally is built-in or connected to the switcher. Most postproduction editing software contains more special effects than you will ever need. Many special effects have become so commonplace that they are no longer "special" but are part of the normal video vocabulary, such as the superimposition and various types of keys.

Superimposition

The superimposition (or *super* for short) shows a double exposure; it is a simultaneous overlay of two pictures. In a super you can see both complete images at the same time. **SEE 9.11** A super is simply a dissolve at the halfway point. Stopping the dissolve a little before the midpoint gives you a superimposition that favors the image from which you were dissolving; stopping a little after the midpoint favors the image to which you are dissolving. (Chapter 10 explains how to do a superimposition with the switcher.)

Supers are used mainly to show inner events—thoughts and dreams—or to make an image more complex. You are certainly familiar with the slightly worn close-up of a sleeping face over which a dream sequence is superimposed. To reveal the complexity of the movement and the grace of a ballet, you could superimpose a long shot and a close-up of the dancer. This synthetic image now generates its own meaning. As you can see, you are no longer simply photographing a dance but (sometimes to the dismay of the choreographer) helping create it.

> **KEY CONCEPT**
>
> The superimposition is a simultaneous overlay of two pictures.

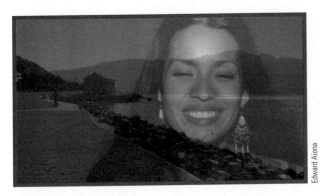

9.11 SUPERIMPOSITION
The superimposition, or super for short, shows two images simultaneously, as in a double exposure.

Key

The **key** is another method of electronically combining two video images. But unlike a super, where you can see the base picture through the superimposed image, the keyed image (figure) blocks out portions of the base picture (ground) and appears to be layered on top of it. Paradoxically, there are also keys that are partially transparent, revealing the background image.

To understand how a key works, consider the white lettering of a name that appears over a scene. The character generator (CG) supplies the white title against a darker background. The background picture is normally supplied by the ESS (electronic still store system, which is a large electronic slide library), a video recording, or a live camera. The title is called the key source, and the background picture of the scene constitutes the base picture, or background. During the key, the key source cuts itself electronically into the base picture. The effect, however, is that the letters appear pasted over the scene. **SEE 9.12**

Of course, you can key any electronic image into a base picture, such as lines that divide the screen into sections, or boxlike screen areas that highlight different images. The box over the news anchor's shoulder is a well-known example of such a key (see figure 9.24).

Because the key effect has numerous technical variations, there are different—and often confusing—names for them. You may hear the terms *key, matte, matte key,* and *chroma key* used interchangeably. We group them here by the way they are commonly used: the normal, or luminance, key; the matte key; and the chroma key.

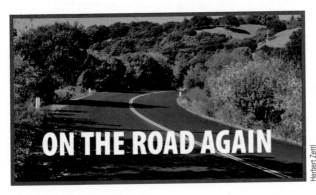

9.12 KEYED TITLE
The keyed letters seem pasted on top of the background image.

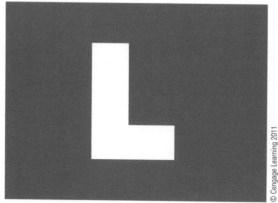

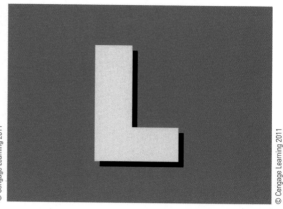

© Cengage Learning 2011

© Cengage Learning 2011

9.13 NORMAL, OR LUMINANCE, KEY
A normal key responds to the dark/light contrast between the background and the letters that cut into the background.

9.14 MATTE KEY IN DROP-SHADOW MODE
A matte key fills the letters with grays or colors. The drop-shadow mode gives the letters a three-dimensional appearance.

Normal, or luminance, key In a normal key, there are only two video sources: the key source and the base picture. The normal key simply replaces the dark areas around the key source, such as a title, making the lighter title appear to be layered on top of the base picture. Because the key process is technically triggered by the light/dark contrast between the title letters and the background (as in figure 9.12), the normal key is also called a luminance (light) key. **SEE 9.13** **ZVL1** SWITCHING→ Effects→ keys

Matte key In this key you add a third video source, which is generated by either the switcher or an external video source. Most often a ***matte key*** refers to the letters of a title that are filled with colors or grays or that have different borders. **SEE 9.14** **ZVL2** SWITCHING→ Effects→ key types

Chroma key When using a ***chroma key***, the subject or object to be keyed is placed in front of a plain colored backdrop, which is usually blue or green, mainly because these colors are notably absent in skin tones. A typical example of chroma keying is the weathercaster who seems to stand in front of a large weather map. She is actually standing in front of a plain chroma green (an even, saturated medium green) backdrop; the weather map is computer-generated. During the key the weather map replaces the green areas, making the weathercaster appear to be standing in front of it. When she turns to point to the map, she actually sees only the green backdrop. To coordinate her gestures with the actual weather map, she must watch a monitor that shows the entire key effect. **SEE 9.15** **ZVL3** SWITCHING→ Effects→ special effects

Assuming that you use blue as the chroma-key color, everything that is blue, even if it is in front of the blue background, will be replaced by the weather map; therefore the weathercaster cannot wear blue. You cannot wear anything that approximates the color of the backdrop. For example, if the weathercaster in figure 9.15 were standing in front of a blue background, her jeans would disappear during the key and be replaced by part of the weather map. We would see only her upper body pointing at the high-pressure area on the map.

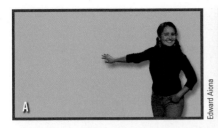
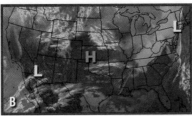
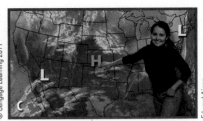

9.15 CHROMA-KEY EFFECT: WEATHERCASTER

A In this chroma key, the weathercaster stands in front of a green backdrop.

B During the key the backdrop is replaced by the computer-enhanced satellite photo.

C The weathercaster seems to stand in front of the photo.

Chroma keying is sometimes used to achieve special effects. If, for example, you cover a dancer's upper body and head with a chroma-key blue material and have her move in front of the blue backdrop, the key will show only her legs dancing.

Chroma keys are often used to simulate backgrounds. You could replace the view of a parking lot from an office window with a spectacular panorama of the skyline by simply putting the desk and the chair in front of a chroma-key backdrop and using a photo of the skyline as the background source. During the chroma key, the person behind the desk would appear to be sitting in front of a high-rise picture window. The advantage of such a key effect is that you would avoid the formidable lighting problem of having the person silhouetted against the bright window (see chapter 8). **ZVL4** SWITCHING→ Effects→ key types

In film production chroma keying is usually called blue-screen technique.

Wipe

Although the wipe is technically a transition because it usually connects two images, it is such an obvious, if not intrusive, device that you should consider it a special effect. In a *wipe* a portion of or a complete video image is gradually replaced by another. Perceptually, one image wipes the other off the screen. Wipes come in a great variety of configurations and are usually displayed as icons on the switcher buttons with which you can preset a particular wipe. **SEE 9.16**

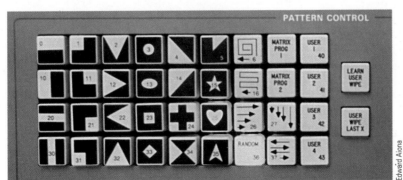

9.16 WIPE PATTERNS

A group of buttons on the switcher shows the various wipe patterns available. Elaborate systems offer up to 100 different patterns.

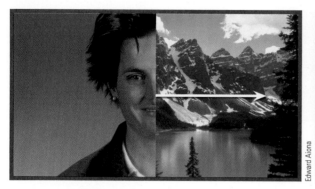

9.17 HORIZONTAL WIPE

In a horizontal wipe, the base picture is gradually replaced by another from the side.

9.18 VERTICAL WIPE

In a vertical wipe, the base picture is gradually replaced by another from the top down or from the bottom up.

Some of the most common wipes are the horizontal and vertical wipes. In a horizontal wipe, the second image gradually replaces the base picture from the side. **SEE 9.17**

A split screen done with a switcher is simply a horizontal wipe that is stopped midway. More often split screens are generated by digital effects, which give more control over the size of the split image than does the analog wipe. In a vertical wipe, the base picture is gradually replaced by the second image from the top down or from the bottom up. **SEE 9.18**

Other popular wipes are corner wipes, whereby the second image originates from one corner of the base image, and diamond wipes, in which the second image originates in the center of the base image and expands as a diamond-shaped cutout. **SEE 9.19 AND 9.20**

In a soft wipe, the demarcation line between the two images is purposely blurred. **SEE 9.21** **ZVL5** SWITCHING→ Transitions→ wipe

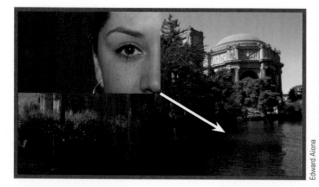

9.19 CORNER WIPE

In a corner wipe, the base picture is gradually replaced by another that starts from a corner of the screen.

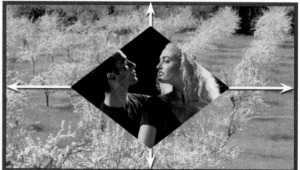

9.20 DIAMOND WIPE

In a diamond wipe, the base picture is gradually replaced by the second image in an expanding diamond-shaped cutout.

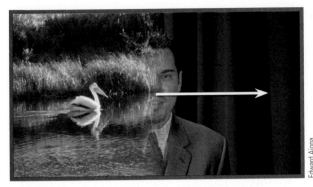

Edward Aiona

9.21 SOFT WIPE
The soft wipe renders the demarcation line between the two images purposely less prominent.

Don't go overboard with wipes simply because they are so easy to do. All wipes are highly visible, especially on a large HDTV screen with the horizontally stretched 16 × 9 aspect ratio. When using a wipe as a transition, you must be careful that it fits the character and the mood of the video material. Using a diamond wipe during a news program to reveal a more detailed shot of a murder scene is highly inappropriate; but it is quite acceptable when transitioning from a beautiful shot of spring blossoms to graceful ballet dancers (see figure 9.20).

DIGITAL EFFECTS

The computer has greatly expanded the range of possibilities for manipulation of the lens-generated image; it can even create still or animated images that rival high-quality lens-generated images in every respect. For example, the equipment for ***digital video effects (DVE)*** can grab a frame from any digital video source (live camera or video recording), store it, manipulate it according to the effects software available, and retrieve the effect on command.

To keep this topic manageable, we focus on three major aspects of digital image manipulation and image creation: digital image manipulation equipment, common digital video effects, and synthetic image creation.

Digital Image Manipulation Equipment

With readily available DVE software, all desktop computers are capable of manipulating video images so long as they have enough RAM and a high processing speed. Four types of systems facilitate image manipulation: an editing system with graphics software, a graphics generator, an electronic still store system, and a frame store synchronizer.

Editing system with graphics software   Most high-end desktop editing systems include so many effects possibilities that you will probably (and ideally should) use only a fraction of them. It may be tempting to try them all simply because they are available and relatively easy to use, but keep effects to a minimum. As pointed out earlier, it is not the effect that makes a program interesting but the program content. Realize that any digital effect is purposely visible, which means it is made to draw attention to itself. Ask yourself whether an effect is appropriate in the context of the show content and whether it is used to intensify, rather than falsify, the message. To add or remove a person digitally from a news story, for example, is certainly possible but definitely unethical.

In case you need even more effects than are included in your editing program, there is DVE software available that would satisfy even the most imaginative director of sci-fi movies.

Graphics generator Most television stations and independent production and postproduction companies use a digital graphics generator for manipulating and creating graphic images. Graphics generators are large-capacity, high-speed dedicated computers that can perform different jobs, depending on the software. Some have peripheral hardware, such as a drawing tablet, which allows you to draw with a light pen. Daily weather and traffic maps are usually created with a graphics generator.

Electronic still store system With an *electronic still store (ESS) system*, you can grab any video frame, digitize it, and store it on a disk. These systems—which can store tens of thousands of frames—perform like a superfast slide projector. You can call up and display any stored image in a fraction of a second. The digital still images can be shrunk, expanded, and used in combination with other images. The familiar box above the newscaster's shoulder is usually a digitized frame that is keyed into the base picture of the news set.

Frame store synchronizer The primary function of the digital frame store synchronizer is to stabilize a picture and synchronize two different video sources so that they don't roll when switching from one to the other, but some can also be used for simple DVE. With the frame store synchronizer, you can freeze a moving image, change it into a mosaic, advance it frame-by-frame at different rates (a process called jogging), or solarize it—mix the positive image with its negative. **SEE 9.22 AND 9.23**

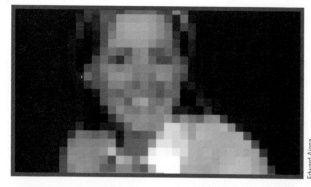

9.22 MOSAIC EFFECT

With the mosaic effect, the image is distilled into equal-sized squares, resembling mosaic tiles. In such an electronic mosaic, the size of the tiles can be manipulated.

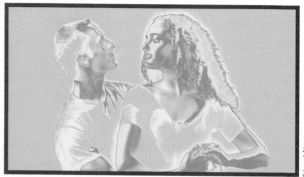

9.23 SOLARIZATION

Solarization is a special effect that is produced by a partial polarity reversal of an image. In a color image, the reversal results in a combination of complementary hues.

Common Digital Video Effects

To understand the analog-to-digital translation process, try to visualize how a photo is transformed into a mosaic, as shown in figure 9.22. The analog video frame shows a continuous change of shape, color, and brightness. In digital form the same image is seen as a series of mosaic tiles, each representing a discrete picture element—a pixel. Because the computer can identify each pixel separately, you can take some out, move them, or replace them with a different color. Once satisfied with the manipulation, you can store the image on disk for later use.

Once again, the box over the news anchor's shoulder is a good example of digital manipulation. It can contain an entire static scene as well as any number of moving scenes that are squeezed digitally to fit inside the box. **SEE 9.24**

Elaborate DVE can change the size of the image (lettering or an actual scene), squeeze or stretch it, paste it on a cube, and have it tumble, flip, spin, bounce, and fly through the screen space. **SEE 9.25–9.27** **ZVL6** SWITCHING→ Effects→ special effects

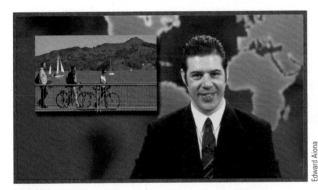

Edward Aiona

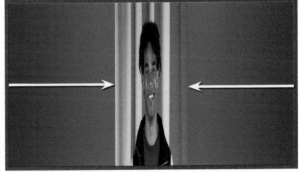

Edward Aiona

9.24 BOX OVER THE NEWS ANCHOR'S SHOULDER
The box over the newscaster's shoulder can take on many shapes and sizes. The digital image inside the box can be stationary or moving.

9.25 SQUEEZING
Squeezing or stretching changes the format of the frame and the image within it.

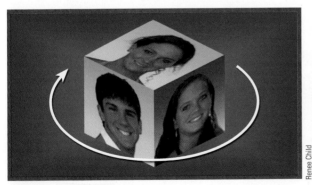

Renee Child

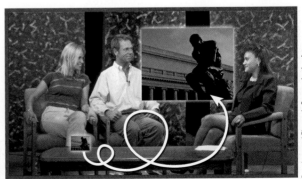

Broadcast and Electronic Communication Arts Department at San Francisco State University

9.26 CUBE EFFECT
In the cube effect, the images seem glued to the sides of a rotating cube.

9.27 FLY EFFECT
In the fly effect, the image zooms from a certain spot to a full image or recedes to another screen position.

Synthetic Image Creation

Synthetic images range from simple lettering of titles to complex 3D motion sequences that rival well-shot and well-edited video-recorded footage.

Character generator   The most common synthetic image creation is the production of various titles. As indicated earlier, the ***character generator (CG)*** is designed to produce letters and numbers of different fonts and colors. A laptop computer can be an efficient CG, assuming you have the appropriate software. More elaborate character generators are designated computers that offer a rich menu from which to select the background and the size, style, and color of the letters and numbers. You then type the copy on the keyboard, colorize the characters, position them on the display screen, insert or delete words, scroll the copy up or down the screen, or have it crawl sideways—all with a few simple commands. The CG renders titles and simple graphics very rapidly and is therefore used extensively for live and live-recorded events. **SEE 9.28** Using the switcher you can key the copy directly into the video of the program in progress or save it to disk for later retrieval.

Graphics generator   As you just learned, a graphics generator with appropriate software lets you create a great variety of images independent of the video camera. Drawing software enables you to create maps, floor plans, light plots, other designs, and even storyboards. **SEE 9.29** Painting software enables you to modify or create digital images that imitate different painting styles and techniques. **SEE 9.30**

You can also simulate three-dimensional images that seem to occupy 3D screen space. These resemble lens-generated images and exhibit the same characteristics: texture, assumed volume, attached and cast shadows, and perspective that shows the object from a specific point of view. With computer programs called fractals, you can even "paint" freeform images, such as trees, mountains, or colorful patterns. **SEE 9.31**

9.28 VIDEO CREATED WITH CHARACTER GENERATOR
The CG is designed to generate titles.

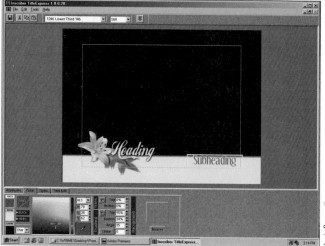

Harris Corporation

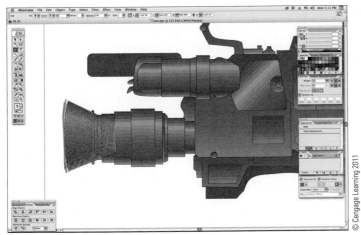

9.29 IMAGE CREATED WITH DRAWING PROGRAM

The drawing program facilitates technical drawings and two-dimensional images.

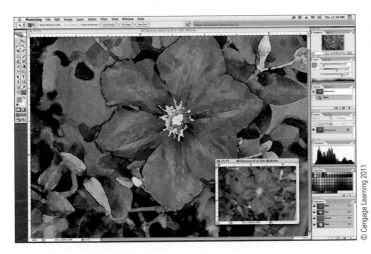

9.30 COMPUTER-MODIFIED PHOTO

This photograph of a flower was given a watercolor quality using the computer.

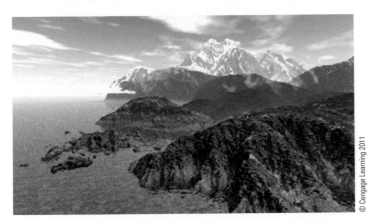

9.31 FRACTAL LANDSCAPE

Some computer programs allow you to "paint" irregular images using mathematical formulas.

Synthetic image creation is becoming more common, even in relatively simple video production processes and interactive video programs. Such computer-generated images and their applications are explored further in chapter 15.

To reinforce our basic caveat: don't get carried away by all the digital wizardry. After all, the content of the package is still more important than its wrapping. Even the best DVE treatment will not change a basically insignificant message into a significant one. On the other hand, properly used effects can clarify and intensify the screen event, supply additional meaning, and, like music, increase its energy.

M A I N   P O I N T S

▶ **Aspect Ratio**

Aspect ratio is the relationship of the width of the television screen to its height. In STV (standard television), it is 4 × 3 (4 units wide by 3 units high); for HDTV (high-definition television), it is 16 × 9 (16 units wide by 9 units high). Mobile media displays have various aspect ratios, including vertical ones.

▶ **Essential Area**

All the important information must be contained in the essential area—the screen area that is reproduced by the home television set even under adverse conditions. It is also called the safe title area.

▶ **Titles**

When using letters against a busy background, make them big and bold enough that they can be read easily on the home receiver. In designing color graphics, try to set off high-energy colors (bright and rich hues) against a low-energy background (washed-out, pastel colors).

▶ **Special Effects**

Standard electronic video effects are achieved with an electronic switcher and a special-effects generator (SEG). They include superimpositions, normal (luminance) keys, matte keys, chroma keys, and wipes. Most chroma keys use either blue or green as the backdrop color. Although wipes function technically as transitions rather than effects, they are so obvious that they are usually considered an electronic effect. Digital video effects (DVE) can be generated by the switcher as well as by computers with DVE software.

▶ **Character Generator**

The character generator (CG) is a computer with software designed to create titles; graphics generators are dedicated computer systems that can create or manipulate 3D still and animated images.

Z E T T L ' S   V I D E O L A B

For your reference or to track your work, the *Zettl's VideoLab* program cues in this chapter are listed here with their corresponding page numbers.

IV

Image Control: Switching, Recording, and Editing

Everything you see on television has been edited in some way—live shows included. In a live show, the editing is done "on the fly." It is more accurately called *instantaneous* editing because the selection and the sequencing is done while the event is unfolding. For example, when you see a quick series of shots—extreme long shot of the stadium, close-up of the coach on the sidelines, extreme close-up of the quarterback—the shots are selected by the director and instantly switched on the air by the technical director by pressing various buttons on a switcher. Many TDs think that there is nothing more exciting than switching a live show or a live recording of one. And if you've ever witnessed such a switching process during a live football game, you will readily concede that this type of instant insanity is indeed exciting. But the benefit of live productions is that the viewers can share the open future of every moment during the actual event.

Although switching, or instantaneous editing, is highly desirable for the live pickup of a unique or especially significant event, such as a major sporting match, it is rarely appropriate for a constructed event, such as the production of a fully scripted play. There is no open future in such a production, unless somebody makes an obvious mistake. What you may gain in spontaneity you lose in production control. In fact, most video productions and motion pictures are carefully constructed through the deliberate selection and sequencing of shots that have been recorded for postproduction editing.

Unfortunately, some directors think that postproduction gives them a convenient means for fixing mistakes and, therefore, a license to be sloppy in the production phase. So, when you hear crewmembers say, "Don't worry, we'll fix it in post," they are merely uttering what has become a rather worn production joke. But then they go back right away and do another take to correct whatever had gone wrong. "Fixing it in post" is not only costly but a misconception of what postproduction is all about.

Part IV covers the basics of image control—deliberate editing that should not be seen as a convenient rescue operation for a haphazard production but as an organic extension of the production process in which the various segments are given form and order.

downstream keyer (DSK) A control that allows a title to be keyed (cut in) over the picture (line-out signal) as it leaves the switcher.

effects bus Row of buttons on the switcher that can select the video sources for a specific effect. Usually the same as a mix bus that has been switched to an effects function.

fader bar A lever on the switcher that activates buses and can produce superimpositions, dissolves, fades, keys, and wipes of different speeds. Also called *T-bar*.

key bus Row of buttons on the switcher used to select the video source to be inserted into the background image.

line-out The line that carries the final video or audio output.

M/E bus Row of buttons on the switcher that can serve mix or effects functions.

mix bus Row of buttons on the switcher that permits the mixing of video sources, as in a dissolve or a super.

preview bus Row of buttons on the switcher that can direct an input to the preview monitor at the same time another video source is on the air. Also called *preset bus*.

program bus Row of buttons on the switcher, with inputs that are directly switched to the line-out.

switcher (1) A panel with rows of buttons that allow the selection and the assembly of multiple video sources through a variety of transition devices as well as the creation of electronic effects. (2) Production person who is doing the switching.

switching A change from one video source to another and the creation of various transitions and effects during production with the aid of a switcher. Also called *instantaneous editing*.

Switcher and Switching

When you first look at a switcher, you may feel slightly puzzled and feel as though it may be easier for you to direct a show than operate the switcher. But once you understand the basic workings—the architecture—of the switcher, you will find that its operation is not as complicated as it initially seemed. Although there are many different models of switchers in studios and remote trucks, you will find that you can adjust to them rather quickly once you understand the basic switcher architecture.

This chapter introduces you to a basic switcher layout, explains what the buttons are for, and covers how to do basic switching. Reading this chapter will not substitute for actual practice on a switcher, but it will certainly accelerate your learning once you have a chance to work with an actual switcher.

▶ **PRODUCTION SWITCHER**

What a switcher does

▶ **BASIC SWITCHER FUNCTIONS**

Selecting, previewing, and mixing video sources and creating effects

▶ **SWITCHER LAYOUT**

Program bus, preview bus, key bus, fader bar and auto-transition, and delegation controls

▶ **SWITCHER OPERATION**

Cuts, dissolves, wipes, keys, working the downstream keyer, chroma keying, and special effects

▶ **AUTOMATED PRODUCTION CONTROL**

The automated, centrally controlled newsroom

PRODUCTION SWITCHER

Switching refers to instantaneous editing using simultaneously available video sources. The term *switcher* can also refer to the person who does the switching, although usually the technical director (TD) fills this production role. You accomplish this type of "editing on the fly" with a switcher, which operates much like a

10.1 PRODUCTION SWITCHER

Large production switchers have many rows with buttons and several levers. The buttons permit the selection of video sources, switching functions, and a variety of transitions and special effects. The levers control the speed of transitions and fades. The joystick positions an image within the screen.

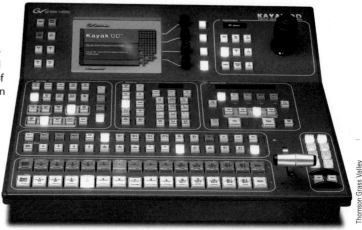

Thomson Grass Valley

pushbutton radio. The pushbutton radio lets you select and instantly switch from one station to another. Similarly, a production *switcher* allows you to punch up video sources, such as the pictures supplied by two or more cameras, a video recorder (VR), a server file, or a character generator (CG), while the production is in progress. Unlike a pushbutton radio, however, the switcher offers transitions, such as cuts, dissolves, and wipes, with which you can join the selected pictures. It also has a number of standard electronic effects built into it (see chapter 9)

The large production switcher is used primarily in multicamera studio productions or in big remotes for instantaneous editing. It is occasionally used in digital cinema when multiple cameras are used simultaneously. **SEE 10.1** **ZVL1** SWITCHING→
Switching introduction

Not surprisingly, the digital age has spawned a great variety of switchers. Some come in compact cases; others display virtual switching buttons and all other functions on a computer screen. **SEE 10.2 AND 10.3**

10.2 SMALL PORTABLE PRODUCTION SWITCHER

Portable production switchers contain an astonishing variety of additional production functions. This Sony Anycast switcher has two M/E buses (program and preview) and a key bus for six video inputs, with a variety of transitions and special effects, an LED panel with a line monitor and various thumbnail previews, six stereo audio channels, and other important features—all in a relatively small suitcase.

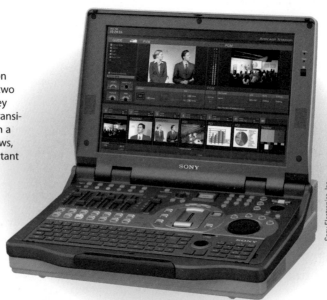

Sony Electronics, Inc.

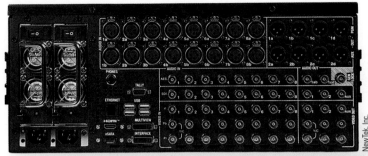

A

10.3 PORTABLE SWITCHER/RECORDER WITH VIRTUAL INTERFACE
A This compact switcher lets you switch among eight camera inputs, select various transitions and effects, create titles and even virtual sets through chroma keying, and mix four channels of digital audio. It can also record and simultaneously broadcast or stream its signals.

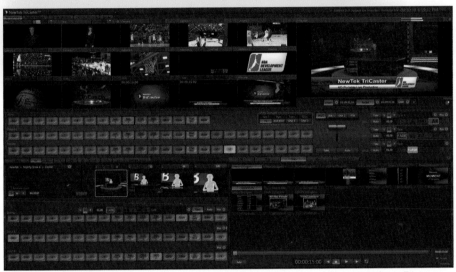

B

B Its software displays all major functions in this computer interface, which you activate with a keyboard and a mouse. It also has a remote keyboard that allows you to switch by pressing real buttons.

On the virtual switchers, the actual switching can be done with the mouse. The problem with switching with a mouse on a virtual display is that it is too slow, especially if you need to switch among more than two or three video sources. Just try to type a word by clicking on the letters of a virtual alphabet display! Even if you were an expert mouse handler, it would take you much too long to write anything. This is why you have a keyboard—and why the virtual switcher in figure 10.3 comes with an actual switching panel as an option.

Regardless of model and appearance, all switchers allow you to make basic transitions between two shots, such as a cut, whereby one shot is instantly replaced by another; a dissolve, in which two images temporarily overlap; and a wipe, in which a portion of an image is gradually replaced—wiped off the screen—by another. They also offer a variety of effects, as you learned in chapter 9.

> **KEY CONCEPT**
> Switchers allow the selection of multiple video inputs and the immediate creation of transitions and effects.

■ BASIC SWITCHER FUNCTIONS

The four basic switcher functions are selecting video sources, previewing upcoming video sources or special effects, mixing video sources, and creating effects. **ZVL2** SWITCHING→ Switching functions→ select | connect | transitions | create effects

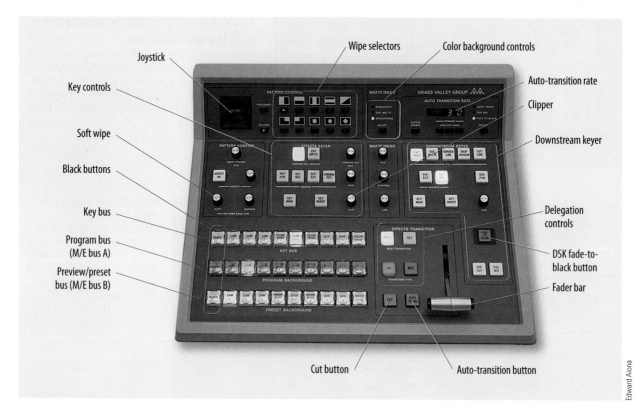

Wipe selectors

Color background controls

Joystick

Key controls

Auto-transition rate

Clipper

Soft wipe

Downstream keyer

Black buttons

Key bus

Delegation controls

Program bus (M/E bus A)

DSK fade-to-black button

Preview/preset bus (M/E bus B)

Fader bar

Edward Aiona

Cut button

Auto-transition button

10.4 BASIC PRODUCTION SWITCHER ARCHITECTURE

This production switcher has only three buses: a pre-view/preset bus, a program bus, and a key bus. You can delegate the preview and program buses an M/E (mix/effects) function.

A row of buttons on a switcher is called a bus. The selection of sources is done with the program bus, and the previewing is done with the preview, or preset, bus. These two buses can also be used as mix buses, which means you can mix two video sources for dissolves and supers. When you want to put titles over a scene, you need still another bus—the key bus.

Let's take a look at how a relatively simple switcher is laid out.[1] **SEE 10.4**

■ SWITCHER LAYOUT

Regardless of whether switchers are analog or digital, they all operate on a similar principle—the switcher architecture. This standardization helps you greatly when you're called upon to operate a variety of switcher models.

Program Bus

To select and connect certain shots, you need several video inputs. If all you had were two cameras and you simply wanted to cut from one camera to the other, you could get by with only two switcher buttons: one that activates camera 1 and another for camera 2. By pressing the *C-1* (camera 1) button, camera 1 would be put "on the air";

---

1. The Grass Valley 100 switcher is used here because its architecture has become the standard for most multifunction production switchers. Even the more state-of-the-art digital high-definition switchers operate in similar ways.

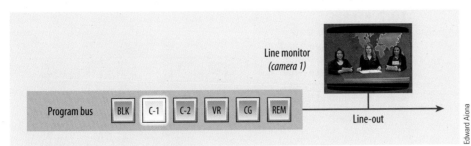

that is, it would go to the ***line-out***—the line that carries the final video output—and from there to the video recorder and/or the transmitter.

Because you would probably want to select from additional video sources, such as a VR, a CG, and a source that is fed from a remote location, you need three additional buttons in the switcher row: *VR, CG,* and *REM,* respectively. To quickly dump the video and "cut to black," you need still another button, called the black *(BLK)* button.

The switcher now has six separate buttons on a single bus. By pressing any one except the *BLK* button, the designated video source will be put on the air; the *BLK* button takes it off the air (actually, *BLK* selects a black video signal). This bus, which sends the chosen video source directly to the line-out, is called the ***program bus.*** **SEE 10.5**

> **KEY CONCEPT**
>
> Whatever is punched up on the program bus goes directly to the line-out.

Preview Bus

Before putting the selected shots on the air, you will undoubtedly want to see whether they cut together properly—whether the sequence fulfills your aesthetic continuity- or complexity-editing requirements (see chapter 13). You may also want to see whether a superimposition has the right mix of the two images or whether you have the correct name for a title key over a guest. To preview the sources, the program bus buttons are simply repeated in an additional bus, appropriately called the ***preview bus.*** **SEE 10.6** Because the preview bus is also used to preset complex effects, you may also hear it called the preset bus.

> **KEY CONCEPT**
>
> The preview bus sends its video to the preview monitor but not to the line-out.

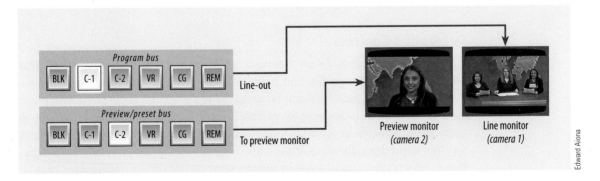

10.6 PREVIEW BUS
The preview bus lets you preview an upcoming source or effect before it is punched up on the air. The preview bus is identical to the program bus except that its output goes to the preview monitor rather than the line-out.

10.7 KEY BUS

The key bus has the same buttons as the program and preview buses. Each button activates a key source—the image you want to key into (over) a background image.

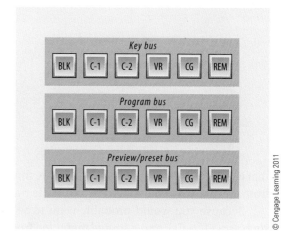

Key Bus

The **key bus** duplicates the video inputs of the program and preview buses but serves as the selector for the key source—what you want to appear over a background picture (supplied by the program bus). For example, if you want a specific title to be keyed over a person or an object (as shown on the preview or line monitor), you need to select the title at the CG and then press the *CG* button on the key bus in preparation for the actual key. **SEE 10.7**

> **KEY CONCEPT**
>
> The key bus selects the key source.

Fader Bar and Auto-Transition

To fade from black or fade to black, to superimpose two images, or to use transitions other than cuts, you need to use a fader bar or an auto-transition (how to do this is described later in this chapter). The **fader bar**, also called T-bar, activates and regulates the speed of fades and dissolves (see figure 10.4). The faster you move the fader bar from one limit of travel to the other, the faster the dissolve or wipe will be. When stopped midway, the dissolve becomes a superimposition, and the wipe yields a split-screen effect.

The full travel of the fader bar can be substituted by the auto-transition button, although you must select the speed of the desired mix or effect before activating the auto-transition (see figure 10.4).

Delegation Controls

The delegation controls assign functions to the program and preview buses. This keeps switchers manageable and prevents them from getting too large. Because the buses of digital switchers can be assigned to perform a great many functions, the switchers often look deceptively small. The program and preview buses of all switchers can also be assigned to function as mix buses, which allows them to work together to produce dissolves, supers, and wipes. They can also be assigned to function as effects buses, in which they usually serve as background images for keys.

These assignments are made possible by the delegation controls on the switcher. The various mix/effects (M/E) functions of the program and preview (preset) buses

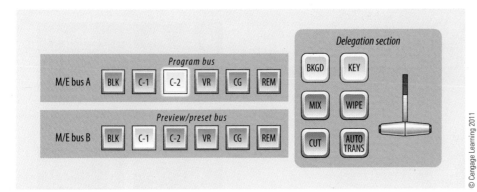

10.8
DELEGATION SECTION
The delegation section of a switcher assigns functions to the program and preview buses and activates the key bus.

are assigned by pressing one or more of the delegation buttons in the effects/transition section of the switcher (see figure 10.4). **SEE 10.8**

For example, by pressing the background *(BKGD)* and *MIX* buttons next to the fader bar, you delegate a mix function to the two **M/E buses** (program and preview). You can now dissolve from the picture punched up on the program bus (M/E bus A) to the one punched up on the preview bus (M/E bus B). By pressing the *WIPE* button next to the *MIX* button, you can now wipe from the program source to the one punched up on the preview bus. The two buses have now become **mix buses**. By pressing the *KEY* button, the program and preview buses become **effects buses**. **ZVL3** SWITCHING→ Architecture→ program bus | preview bus | delegation controls | mix buses | key bus

KEY CONCEPT

The delegation controls can assign the program and preview buses the function of mix and effects buses.

▧ SWITCHER OPERATION

It's time now to press a few buttons and learn how to switch—that is, select video inputs and sequence them through transitions and effects. Yes, you certainly need a switcher, or at least a computer simulation of a switcher, to become proficient in the art of switching. By first studying the basic principles of switching, however, you will make your actual practice much more efficient and rewarding.

When you simply read the instructions on how to achieve a cut or a dissolve, you may be as puzzled as when reading about how to use new computer software. You should therefore pretend that the illustrations are part of a switcher and that you are actually pressing the buttons. If you have *Zettl's VideoLab 4.0* DVD-ROM available, engage in the switching exercises right away to reinforce the text.

Working the Program Bus: Cuts-Only

As you recall, the program bus is basically a selector switch of video sources for the line-out. It has this function assigned to it by simply powering up the switcher. If you want to cut from one video source, let's say C1 (camera 1), to another, C2 (camera 2), you can simply press the *C-2* button, assuming that C1 is already on the air (the *C-1* button has been pressed previously). Camera 1's picture will be instantly replaced by camera 2's picture; you have performed a cut from C1 to C2. **SEE 10.9** Because the

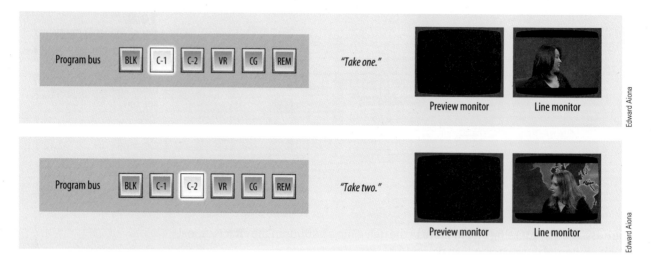

Edward Aiona

10.9 SWITCHING ON THE PROGRAM BUS

When switching on the program bus, the transitions will be cuts-only. With camera 1 on the air, you can cut to camera 2 by pressing the *C-2* button.

program bus sends its signals directly to the line-out, you cannot preview the upcoming image (C2). The preview monitor remains black when you switch exclusively on the program bus. **ZVL4** SWITCHING→ Transitions→ cut

Working the Mix Buses: Cuts

If you want to preview the upcoming video source, or if you want to dissolve to camera 2 (mix) instead of cut to it, you first need to delegate a mix function to both buses. You do this on the Grass Valley 100 switcher (and the ZVL 4.0 switcher) by pressing the *BKGD* and *MIX* buttons. To cut from camera 1 to camera 2, you need to punch up C2 on the preview bus (which is now M/E bus B) and press either the *CUT* button or the *AUTO-TRANS* button next to the preview bus. Camera 2 will instantly appear on the line monitor, and camera 1 will automatically jump to the preview monitor. The *C-2* button will light up full, called high tally, on the program bus, and *C-1* will have low tally (lighted halfway) on the preview bus. If you pressed the *CUT* button again, C1 would switch to the line monitor, and C2 would appear on the preview monitor. **SEE 10.10** **ZVL5** SWITCHING→ Transitions→ try it

Is the benefit of seeing the next shot in the preview monitor worth this rather complicated switching maneuver? No, if you simply want to cut between two obvious sources. Yes, if you switch among various video sources and effects or if you need to use a variety of transitions. Let's see how a dissolve works.

Working the Mix Buses: Dissolves

Because you have delegated both buses to the mix mode, you can also perform a dissolve. To dissolve from camera 1 (punched up on the program bus and therefore on the air) to camera 2, you need to press the *C-2* button on the preview bus and move

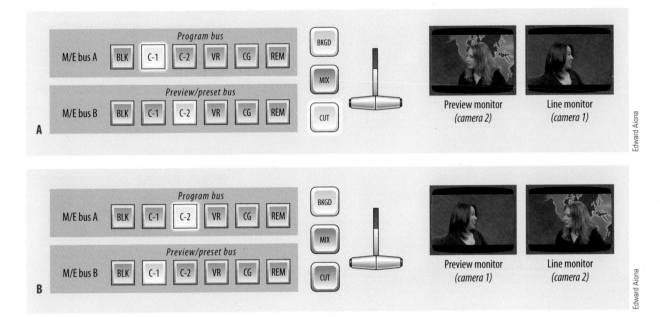

10.10 SWITCHING IN THE MIX MODE
When delegated a background and mix function, the program bus becomes M/E bus A and the preview/preset bus becomes M/E bus B.

A Here camera 1 is punched up on bus A and on the air. Camera 2 is preset to replace camera 1 as soon as you press the *CUT* button.

B When the cut is complete, the program bus shows camera 2 on the air, and the preview/preset bus switches automatically to camera 1's picture.

the fader bar either up or down to the full extent of travel (or press the *AUTO-TRANS* button). On the switcher in figure 10.10, the fader bar is in the down position. You will have to move it all the way up to achieve the dissolve. **SEE 10.11**

Note that when the fader bar reaches the opposite limit of travel (in this case, up), finishing the dissolve from C1 to C2, camera 1 (which was punched up on the program bus) will be replaced by camera 2 on the program bus, with camera 1 appearing on the preview monitor and in low tally on the preview bus. If you now want to dissolve back to C1, you simply move the fader bar to the opposite position or press the *AUTO-TRANS* button again. This will dissolve C2's picture on the line-out monitor back to C1's picture. If, however, you want to dissolve from C2 to another video source, such as C3, you need to press the *C-3* button on the preview bus before moving the fader bar in the opposite direction. **ZVL6** SWITCHING→ Transitions→ mix/dissolve

As you can see, the preview and line monitors reflect which camera is on the air and which is ready to go on the air. Once you have a little more practice, such presetting of shots will become second nature.

With camera 3 on the air, how can you fade to black? You simply press the *BLK* button on the preview bus and move the fader bar in the opposite direction (regardless of whether you move it toward or away from the program bus) or press the

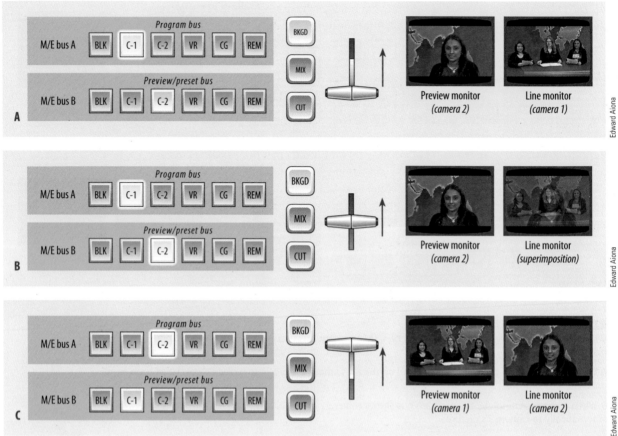

10.11 DISSOLVE

Once you have assigned the mix function through the mix delegation control, you can dissolve from camera 1 to camera 2.

A Assuming that camera 1 is on the air on bus A, you need to preset camera 2 on bus B.

B When the fader bar is stopped midway, you have a super.

C By moving the fader bar to the full limit of travel, you activate the dissolve from camera 1 to camera 2. Once the dissolve is complete, camera 2 will replace camera 1 on the program bus.

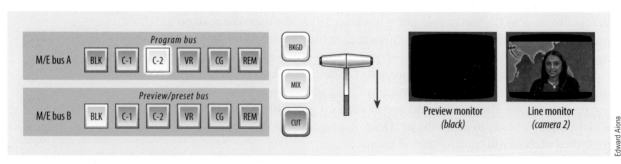

10.12 FADE

When fading to black from camera 2, you need to punch up the *BLK* button on bus B (preview/preset) and dissolve to it by moving the fader bar down to its full limit of travel.

AUTO-TRANS button. As soon as the fader bar reaches the opposite limit of travel (or the auto-transition is at the end of its run), the fade-to-black command is transferred back to the program bus. **SEE 10.12** `ZVL7` SWITCHING→ Transitions→ fade

Working the Effects Bus: Wipes

Wipes, in which the base image is gradually replaced by another in some geometric pattern, are accomplished similarly to a dissolve except that you need to tell the switcher that you want to use wipes instead of a mix. You do this by first pressing the *BKGD* and *WIPE* delegation buttons (instead of *BKGD* and *MIX* in the effects/ transition section). You then need to select a wipe pattern from the wipe selector section. Moving the fader bar activates the wipe and controls its speed, just like in a dissolve. The faster you move the fader bar, the faster the wipe will be. The *AUTO-TRANS* button will also accomplish the wipe in the time you specify. `ZVL8` SWITCHING→ Transitions→ wipe

Working the Key Bus: Keys

Keying is not a transition but a special effect. As you learned in chapter 9, a key allows you to insert (cut electronically) an image (usually a title) into a background picture. Most often you will work with a luminance key, which is used to insert a title over an on-the-air background image. Before you activate a title key while on the air (the background picture is displayed by the line monitor), you should set up the key in preview and then transfer the completed key from the preview bus to the program bus. In this way you can verify that you got the correct title and that it is legible.

Setting up a key is a little more involved than making a transition, and the exact sequence of keying differs from switcher to switcher. Regardless of the specific switcher architecture, you select the key source (usually the CG with the desired title) on the key bus. You then need to work some buttons and/or rotary controls (called the clip control, or clipper) to make sure the key has clean edges and does not tear. (Such an operation may differ from one switcher to another.) Then you press the *KEY* button in the delegation controls. This changes the mix function of the buses to an effects function—in this case the key function. The picture you have on the air already (an image of a dancer from camera 2) can serve as the background for the title you want to key over the dancer ("Palmatier Dance Company"). **SEE 10.13**

The best way to learn keying is to sit down with an actual switcher and perform a variety of switching exercises. You can use *Zettl's VideoLab 4.0* for initial keying

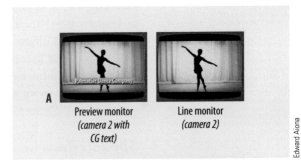

A

Preview monitor
(camera 2 with CG text)

Line monitor
(camera 2)

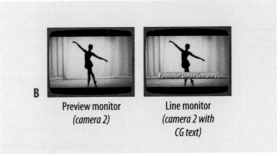

B

Preview monitor
(camera 2)

Line monitor
(camera 2 with CG text)

Edward Aiona

10.13 KEY EFFECT

This key sequence is constructed for the preview monitor before it is transferred to the line-out. Assume that the key bus has been delegated.

A The camera 2 long shot appears on both the line monitor (outgoing signal) and the preview monitor. By pressing the *CG* button on the key bus, the title is selected and appears on the preview monitor.

B Pressing the *CUT* button (or moving the fader bar) transfers the complete key to the line-out monitor.

Keying is an effect, not a transition.

The downstream keyer is independent of the program bus.

practice, but the keying procedures on this switching simulation are greatly simplified. **ZVL9** SWITCHING→ Effects→ keys | key types

Working the Downstream Keyer

To complicate matters further, there is still another—very important—key control. The ***downstream keyer (DSK)*** lets you key yet another title over the complete line-out video image just before it leaves the switcher. In our example the DSK would enable you to add the name of the choreographer ("Robaire") to the original key ("Palmatier Dance Company") without changing the original key. Note that the downstream keyer is independent of the program bus and puts its title on the air even if the program bus is in black. If you have used the downstream keyer, going to black on the program bus will not eliminate the DSK title: you need to use the DSK black button to eliminate this type of key. **ZVL10** SWITCHING→ Effects→ downstream keyer

Chroma Keying

As you recall from chapter 9, chroma keying uses color (not luminance) as the agent that triggers the key effect. It is normally used to key a foreground object (such as a weathercaster) into the background image (the weather map). For a chroma key, the foreground object is placed in front of an evenly illuminated color backdrop (usually blue or green). During the key all the blue or green areas are replaced by the selected background image. The actual setup for a chroma key is more complicated than for a regular luminance key and must be practiced on an actual switcher. **ZVL11** SWITCHING→ Effects→ key types

Special Effects

All switchers can create and store special effects. Digital switchers have a relatively large memory that can hold a great number of complex effects, which are usually recalled by their file name or number.

◼ AUTOMATED PRODUCTION CONTROL

A new kind of video control has evolved through automating most of the presentation techniques of newscasts: the automated production control (APC). In an extreme case, the only live elements left are the news anchors in the studio and the rather overworked APC operator in the control room.

APC Function

The basic function of the APC system is to centralize the production control during a show that has a standard presentation format, such as a newscast or an interview. Assuming that the news presentation rundown—including news stories, commercials, and bumpers (brief independent audio/video transitions between program segments)—has already been preprogrammed for APC, a single operator (sometimes the TD) can switch among live feeds, the anchors and weather- and sportscasters, video and audio servers or VR segments, the electronic still store (ESS) system, and robotic studio cameras while also controlling the audio and calling up a variety of special effects. If you feel that such an assignment is a bit much for one person to carry out and may not necessarily contribute to a more effective production, you are quite right. But this system is primarily designed to minimize production personnel: you can now do a live newscast without a director, audio technician, at least two camera operators, and possibly a floor manager.

Control Panels

This wonder machine is based primarily on a computer with sophisticated software and various devices that shake hands with compatible production switchers, CG and ESS systems, audio and video servers, and the robotic camera controls (pan, tilt, dolly, truck, zoom, and focus). The APC operator works a deceptively simple-looking control panel, which typically has three sections: the audio control for the incoming audio; a rundown control, which is similar to a source-switching section; and a robotic camera control. Basically, the control panel triggers computer functions, which are also displayed on flat-panel touch screens. **SEE 10.14**

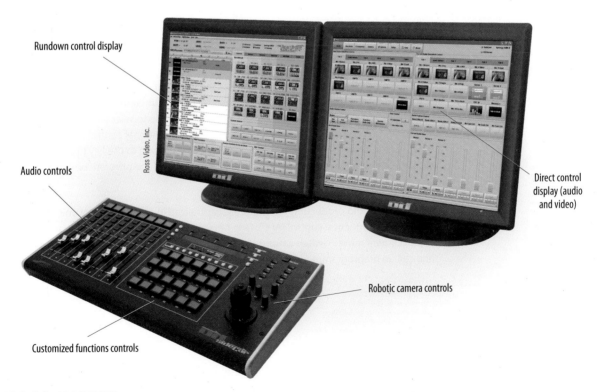

Rundown control display

Ross Video, Inc.

Audio controls

Direct control display (audio and video)

Robotic camera controls

Customized functions controls

10.14 APC SYSTEM

With this system (Ross OverDrive), one operator can activate and control a great variety of production elements, such as the rundown of news stories, commercials, bumpers, video and audio servers, special effects, CG and ESS systems, and robotic cameras.

MAIN POINTS

▶ **Production Switcher**

Switching is a form of instantaneous editing. You can select various video inputs (camera, VR, CG, remote), sequence them with different transitions, and create a number of effects while the show is in progress.

▶ **Basic Switcher Functions**

The four basic switcher functions are selecting various video sources, previewing upcoming video sources or special effects, mixing video sources, and creating effects.

▶ **Switcher Layout**

Whatever is punched up on the program bus goes directly to the line-out. The preview bus sends its video to the preview/preset monitor. The key bus lets you select key sources. The fader bar and the auto-transition facilitate transitions other than cuts.

▶ **Delegation Controls**

The delegation controls can assign the program and preview buses various mix and effects functions. The key bus has its own row of buttons and maintains its function.

▶ **Switcher Operation**

The program bus allows cuts-only switching. The preview bus routes the upcoming picture to the preview monitor. When the program and preview buses are delegated as mix buses, you can create dissolves, superimpositions, wipes, and fades. The fader bar (T-bar) activates and regulates the speed of dissolves, wipes, and fades and even governs the extent of a wipe. The function of the fader bar can be duplicated by the auto-transition button. Like the mix function, the effects function of the switcher must be assigned in the delegation section. This allows you to select the key source on the key bus and activate a key through a variety of additional controls. The downstream keyer (DSK) enables the addition of another title to the key just before the line-out signal leaves the switcher. It is independent of the program bus.

▶ **Automated Production Control**

Most major studio production functions are centralized in a single control unit—the automated production control (APC). One person (the APC operator) can initiate preset camera moves, switch among performance areas and live feeds, control audio, and call up preprogrammed effects. So far APC is used mostly for newscasts.

Z E T T L' S   V I D E O L A B

 For your reference or to track your work, the *Zettl's VideoLab* program cues in this chapter are listed here with their corresponding page numbers.

KEY TERMS

audio track The area of the videotape used for recording the audio information.

composite video A system that combines the Y (luminance, or black-and-white) and C (color—red, green, and blue) video information into a single signal. Also called *NTSC*.

control track The area of the videotape used for recording synchronization information.

DVR Stands for *digital video recorder*.

field log A record of each take during the video recording.

frame store synchronizer Image stabilization and synchronization system that has a memory large enough to store and read out one complete video frame. Used to synchronize signals from a variety of video sources that are not locked to a common sync signal.

luminance The brightness (black-and-white) information of a video signal. Also called *luma* to include the grayscale information.

memory card A read/write solid-state portable storage device that can download, store, and upload a limited amount of digital audio and video information. Also called *flash drive*.

nonlinear recording media Storage of video and audio material in digital form on a hard drive, memory card, or read/write optical disc. Each single frame can be instantly accessed by a computer.

NTSC Stands for *National Television System Committee*. Normally refers to the composite video signal, consisting of the Y signal (luminance, or black-and-white information) and the C signal (red, green, and blue color information).

pocket recorder Small camcorder, such as a cell phone, that fits into a shirt pocket. Records exclusively on memory cards. Also called *mobile media*.

tapeless systems Refers to the recording, storage, and playback of audio and video information via digital storage devices other than videotape.

time base corrector (TBC) An electronic accessory to videotape recorders that helps make videotape playbacks electronically stable. It keeps slightly different scanning cycles in step.

video server A large-capacity hard-drive array that can ingest, store, and play back a great amount of audio and video information. It can be accessed by several users simultaneously.

video track The area of the videotape used for recording the video information.

Y/C component video A system that keeps the Y (luminance, or black-and-white) and C (color—red, green, and blue) signals separate. Y and C are combined again when recorded on a specific media. Also called *Y/C system* and *S-video*.

Y/color difference component video Video-recording system wherein the three signals—the luminance (Y) signal, the blue signal minus its luminance (B–Y; in digital, Pb), and the red signal minus its luminance (R–Y; in digital, Pr)—are kept separate during the transport and recording process.

Video Recording

The relatively slow transition from videotape to an entirely tapeless video operation is complete. All new camcorders record the digital video and audio signals on some kind of tapeless recording device. Videotape is still very much alive in various forms, however. In fact, you may still have a VCR (videocassette recorder) and a number of ½-inch videocassettes stacked somewhere that contain the recordings of important events in your life. But even if you had the good sense and the heart to discard your still-functioning analog video equipment, as a video professional you will inevitably be asked from time to time to work with some form of tape-based video. At least for the time being, you cannot ignore videotape entirely and need to know how the videotape-recording process actually works. You will find that many video-recording procedures overlap regardless of whether you use a tapeless recording system or a videotape recorder (VTR).

This chapter explores the major tapeless and tape-based recording systems and processes.

▶ **TAPELESS VIDEO-RECORDING SYSTEMS**
  Tapeless systems, recording media, and digital video recorders

▶ **TAPE-BASED VIDEO-RECORDING SYSTEMS**
  How VTRs work and basic videotape tracks

▶ **SIGNAL TRANSPORT AND VIDEO STABILIZATION**
  Composite and component signal transport, and video stabilization with a frame store synchronizer

▶ **VIDEO-RECORDING PROCESS**
  The necessary checklists: before, during, and after

All video-recording systems operate on the same general principle: the digital or analog video and audio signals are recorded on some kind of electronic device and can be played back in a specific order on demand. The systems vary greatly, however, in how the signals are recorded and stored.

The two video-recording categories are tapeless or nontape systems and tape-based systems.

■ TAPELESS VIDEO-RECORDING SYSTEMS

Tapeless systems record only digital information. A tapeless system cannot record analog signals unless they are first converted into a digital format. Just how the digital information is recorded and stored differs greatly among the various tapeless systems. The tendency is to cram more and more information onto smaller and smaller media (recording devices), which is greatly aided by improved codecs (compression/decompression systems) such as MPEG-4. Recall from chapter 3 the discussion about lossless and lossy compression. Lossless compression simply repacks the video information; lossy compression eliminates nonessential and redundant information. Tapeless systems could not exist without such codecs.

Tapeless systems are also called nonlinear media because they allow random access of all recorded material. With ***nonlinear recording media,*** you can call up any frame, regardless of the sequence in which it was captured. Shot 27 is as readily accessible as shot 1. In contrast, all videotape recordings are linear. We explain the difference later in the chapter.

Recording Media

The nontape digital recording media range from small memory cards for camcorders to large-capacity servers for handling the daily program fare of television stations. Let's take a look at some of the current media.

Memory cards   ***Memory cards*** are solid-state recording devices, also known as flash drives. They operate much like the thumb drive you may be carrying in your pocket except that they hold much more information. Depending on the codec used, a tiny 32-gigabyte SD (Secure Digital) memory card can record almost three hours of high-definition television (HDTV) footage. Their great advantages are their ease of use, their fast data transfer speed, and, best of all, that they have no moving parts. They are quite rugged and can be used over and over again without having to worry about some mechanism eventually breaking down. **SEE 11.1**

Some videographers may still feel that the recording time for HDTV video is somewhat limited, but you will find that the high-capacity SD memory cards have enough storage space even for extensive field recording. You can always bring along several cards for more ambitious electronic field productions (EFPs). The only problem is cost. Some large-capacity memory cards can be quite expensive, which may prevent you from using them for archiving your footage until after you have edited it. You therefore need to transfer their content to the hard drive of your nonlinear editing (NLE) system or a server right after the production to free up the cards for further use in the camcorder.

Read/write optical discs   These laser-operated optical discs let you read (play back) previously recorded material and write (record) new material, just like with a hard drive. You are certainly familiar with the various types of DVDs that have all but replaced VHS tapes as the favorite movie playback device.

In camcorders these optical discs are encased in cartridges, which protect the delicate laser mechanism enough to make the laser media relatively rugged and

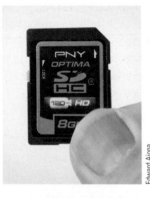

Edward Aiona

11.1 SD MEMORY CARD
This solid-state device can record and store an amazing amount of video and audio information. Because it has no moving parts, it is relatively immune to breakdown.

immune to heat, moisture, and rough camera handling. Again, the maximum recording time depends on whether you record your scenes in 1080i HDTV or a lower-scan digital format. In any case, you can always bring along a spare disc if you think you may need more recording time. The disadvantages of optical discs are that they can be accidentally scratched and they have moving parts that may break down from time to time.

Hard drives Some camcorders use hard drives as their video recorder (VR). In concert with data compression, even small hard drives can record a relatively large amount of video and audio. Even if a hard drive is encased in a cassette, however, it is susceptible to shock and extreme weather conditions. This is why you will find that memory cards are the preferred nontape recording media for camcorders and portable VRs.

Digital Video Recorders

In the videotape age, video recorders were complex machines that differed greatly in quality, from simple home recorders to top-of-the-line professional models. In the tapeless era, you can use even your iPhone or iPod to capture high-definition pictures and sound. Assuming that you have the appropriate software, your laptop computer can serve as a high-quality recording device, as can an external hard drive. Why then bother with a digital video recorder? Because **DVRs** provide you with features that are not readily available on a laptop and that speed up your workflow, from video capture to editing your footage on an NLE system such as your laptop.

Portable DVRs To extend the recording capacity of a camcorder, you can connect it to a portable DVR. When doing extensive fieldwork, you will find such small direct-to-edit (DTE) recorders invaluable for additional signal storage and as backup for your camcorder footage. Figure 11.2 shows a battery-operated DTE unit that records in a variety of HDTV formats on removable memory cards. Only slightly larger than an iPhone, such a **pocket recorder** lets you view thumbnail clips of your video, add logging (identification) information about your shots, transfer your video and audio files directly to your NLE system via USB 2.0 or FireWire, and send your footage to your home computer over the Internet. **SEE 11.2**

Studio DVRs Studio DVRs are used to record in-house productions and large EFPs. They are often the primary recording unit, with the larger servers providing the recording backup. Much like smaller DVRs, they vary in recording capacity, storage media, codecs, and file formats. Although some DVRs use solid-state devices as recording media, most DVRs use high-capacity hard drives. The DVR in figure 11.3 uses removable hard-drive

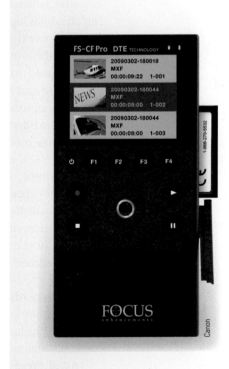

11.2 PORTABLE DVR
This small field DVR records video files that can be used directly for editing, minimizing the workflow.

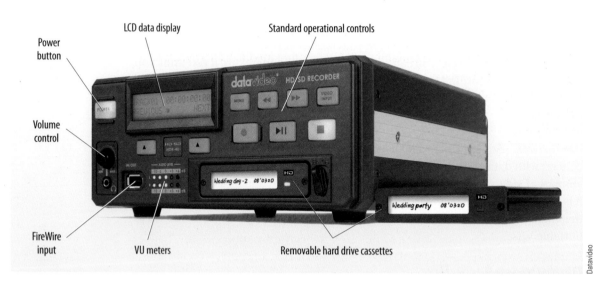

Power button

LCD data display

Standard operational controls

Volume control

FireWire input

VU meters

Removable hard drive cassettes

Datavideo

11.3 STUDIO DVR

This studio DVR can record STV (standard-definition television) and all HDTV formats on a removable hard-drive cassette. You can connect this recorder to your NLE system for file transfer or eject the hard drive cassette and use it independently for content capture by the NLE system. This DVR has the normal operational controls, including LED volume meters.

cassettes, which can record a minimum of about 20 hours of video footage, depending on which high-definition format (1080i or 720p) and bit rate (how much data to be processed per second) you select. The higher the definition and the faster the capture (the more megabytes per second), the more disk space you need. The removable hard drive is a great feature, as you can connect it directly to your computer for capture and editing—even after you eject it from the DVR. As you can see, the operating controls are pretty much the same as on a VTR, with *play, record, pause, fast-forward, fast-rewind,* and *stop.* You can monitor the stereo audio input on two LED volume meters. **SEE 11.3**

Video servers   A ***video server*** is a highly reliable hard-drive system with a large, superhigh-capacity (in the multi-terabyte range) disk array. Such disk arrays not only facilitate the simultaneous recording of various sources but also accommodate multiple users during playback; when the source material is stored on the server, several editors can work on different projects simultaneously. All video servers can be programmed for automated playback of specific program sequences.

Regardless of what nontape device you use for video recording, this simple rule applies: the more lines per frame and the more frames per second you choose for your recording, the larger the files get and, consequently, the less video you can store on a specific media.

All of these nonlinear recording systems are intended for video and audio acquisition during production or in preparation for postproduction editing. Once your edited masterpiece is on your computer hard drive, you can export it and burn it to a DVD-R or, if you have a Blu-ray burner, on the higher-capacity Blu-ray disc.

TAPE-BASED VIDEO-RECORDING SYSTEMS

All tape-based systems use videotape as their recording media. VTR systems have been the mainstay of video production for decades. The first VTRs used large, 2-inch-wide tape reels for all professional recordings, which over time shrank to ¼-inch tape cassettes even for high-end color digital video recordings. Digital? Yes, contrary to nonlinear recording media, which can record only digital signals, videotape can record both analog and digital video and audio. A single cassette can record and store an amazing amount of video and audio signals, which makes it a relatively inexpensive recording media. Why, then, are we so eager to replace videotape with nontape media? Because compared with nontape systems, tape-based systems have serious drawbacks. Here are some of them:

- All videotape systems are linear. This means that a videotape recording does not allow random access to shots or frames. Access to content is serial: you need to roll through the first 26 shots, for example, to reach shot 27. This seems like a minor problem until you are trying to find the best shots for a news story scheduled to be aired in less than an hour. Locating a shot that is buried somewhere on a 30-minute videotape can try your patience, even if the VTR has fast shuttle (forward and rewind) speeds.

- Tape quality can differ considerably. A low-quality tape will not only introduce video noise (artifacts that reduce picture quality) but generate even more noise after each reuse. It can also gum up the record/playback heads.

- Contrary to nonlinear media, whose picture and sound quality remains pretty much the same no matter how often you make a copy of the previous one, even a high-quality videotape recording deteriorates markedly from one generation to the next. This is especially noticeable when building complex special effects though multiple rerecordings.

- All VTRs, regardless of whether they are large studio recorders or small ones in camcorders, have complicated mechanisms that are apt to wear down after extended use or use in extreme weather conditions.

- Not all VTRs run at exactly the same speed. To synchronize the play VTR with the source VTR, you need additional stabilizing equipment, such as a time base corrector.

How VTRs Work

All VTRs use record/playback heads with which to write video and audio signals on the videotape and also to read the signals already recorded.

To avoid superfast tape travel when recording the high-frequency video signal and to squeeze the maximum amount of information onto the videotape, all recorders—analog and digital—move the tape as well as the record heads. In this way the tape moves in a loop around a head drum, which contains the spinning record heads. The record heads in digital systems spin at very high speeds. **SEE 11.4**

11.4 BASIC VIDEOTAPE RECORDING PROCESS

The videotape moves past the spinning heads inside the drum at an angle, creating a slanted video track.

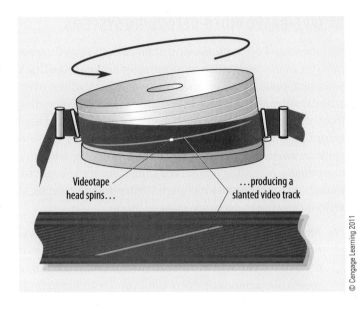

Videotape head spins...

...producing a slanted video track

© Cengage Learning 2011

Basic Videotape Tracks

There is a great difference between analog and digital videotape tracks. Most analog VTRs put at least four tracks onto a videotape: the ***video track*** containing the picture information, two ***audio tracks*** containing the sound information, and a ***control track*** that synchronizes the frames.   **SEE 11.5**   **ZVL1** EDITING→ Postproduction guidelines→ tape basics

The two most popular digital systems, DVCAM (Sony) and DVCPRO (Panasonic), split each track into video, audio, and code information. Contrary to analog tape, which records a complete field on each track and takes only two tracks for a complete frame, most digital systems use several tracks for a complete frame. The DVCPRO50 system, for example, needs 20 tracks to complete a single frame. High-quality recording systems may use even more tracks for each frame.   **SEE 11.6**

11.5 BASIC ANALOG VIDEOTAPE TRACK SYSTEM

The basic analog track system of a videotape consists of a slanted video track, two or more audio tracks, and a control track.

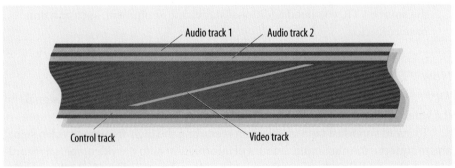

Audio track 1   Audio track 2

Control track   Video track

© Cengage Learning 2011

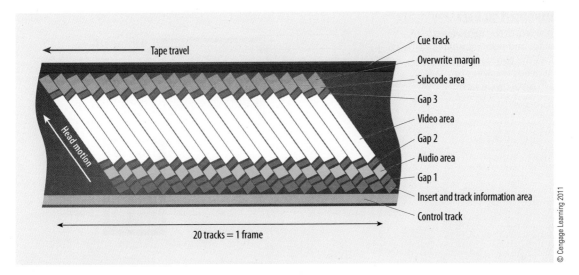

11.6 DVCPRO50 TRACKS
This digital system uses 20 tracks for a single frame. Each track has video, audio, and code information.

SIGNAL TRANSPORT AND VIDEO STABILIZATION

Signal transport refers to how a color video signal is transported within a VR and finally recorded while maintaining an optimal video quality. Video stabilization is necessary to prevent picture breakup because of weak signals or signals that are slightly out of sync.

Signal Transport

From time to time, you may hear engineers refer to composite or component signals. To enable you to at least nod knowingly, you need to learn about the basic difference between the two.

Composite signal   The composite (*NTSC*) system is the standard for analog video and broadcast. *Composite video* combines the *luminance* (black-and-white, or Y) and color (C) information in a single signal. It needs only one wire to transport the combined analog signal, which is recorded as a combined signal on a single videotape track. The cable that might transport such a composite NTSC signal from recorder to TV screen usually has a yellow plug and jack. *NTSC* stands for *National Television System Committee.* **SEE 11.7**

The disadvantage of NTSC composite video has always been the crossover of the Y and C signals. This means that the two signals occasionally get into each

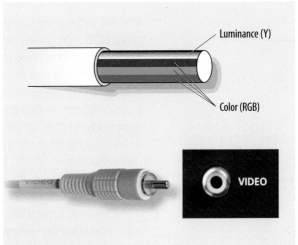

11.7 COMPOSITE SIGNAL
Composite video, also called NTSC, combines the luminance and color video information into a single signal. It needs a single wire—normally coded yellow—to be transported and recorded on videotape as a single signal.

11.8 Y/C COMPONENT SIGNAL

Y/C component video, or S-video, separates the luminance and color information but combines the two signals on the videotape. It needs two wires to transport the two separate signals.

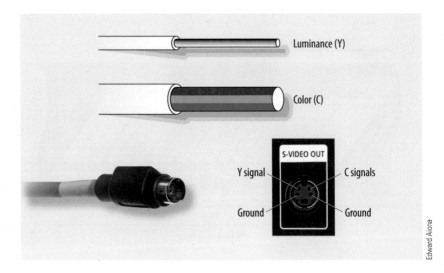

Luminance (Y)

Color (C)

S-VIDEO OUT

Y signal   C signals

Ground   Ground

Edward Aiona

other's way, causing video noise. Such video interference is multiplied with each tape generation, so the video quality of subsequent dubs deteriorates rather quickly.

Y/C component signal   To counteract the detrimental "cross-talk" between Y and C, these major signal components are kept separate as much as possible. In ***Y/C component video***, commonly called S-video, the Y and C signals are kept separate during transport but are combined as a single track on the videotape. The S-video cable has two wires to transport the Y and C signals plus a ground wire for each. Be careful when using this cable; do not force its fragile plug it into the jack because the pins bend, or even break off, quite easily. **SEE 11.8**

Y/color difference component signal   The ideal situation would be to keep all three RGB (red, green, and blue) channels separate during transport and recording. In fact, this is done in very high-end VTRs. But you probably guessed that this would take too much time and bandwidth for the massive signals to be transported, recorded, and especially transmitted. ***Y/color difference component video*** is such a good alternative that it is even used in digital video. It separates the Y (luminance) channel from the C (color) channels but then reduces the color channels as well by using only the blue and red signals without the luminance: B–Y and R–Y. This color difference signal has the rather clumsy name YPbPr for the analog one and YCbCr for its digital cousin. The RCA phono connectors for this system are normally green for the Y channel, red for R–Y channel, and blue for the B–Y channel. **SEE 11.9**

If you are somewhat confused by all of these systems, you may simply want to remember that the system that mixes luminance (brightness) and color information into one signal is *composite*. The other two systems, which separate luminance from color, are *component*. The Y/color difference system produces the best-quality video.

Video Stabilization with a Frame Store Synchronizer

When you watch a live television program that originates from a remote location, you sometimes see the picture break up into different parts and even freeze for a

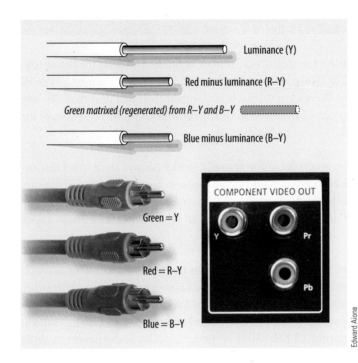

11.9 Y/COLOR DIFFERENCE COMPONENT SIGNAL
Y/color difference component video needs three wires to transport the three component signals: the Y (luminance) signal, the R–Y (red minus luminance) signal, and the B–Y (blue minus luminance) signal.

moment until it shows the normal action again. But how can the action temporarily freeze when the telecast is live? The reason is that even if a program is broadcast live, each frame is temporarily recorded and, if necessary, corrected before it is sent on its way to your television receiver. The ***frame store synchronizer*** is pressed into service to synchronize and stabilize the scanning of different video sources so that there is no breakup during switching from one to the other. Its memory is large enough to store and read out one complete video frame.

As mentioned in chapter 9, the digital frame store synchronizer is an advanced version of the ***time base corrector (TBC)***, which was developed primarily to make videotape playbacks, dubs, and edits electronically stable and to synchronize the scanning cycles of various video sources during switching.

VIDEO-RECORDING PROCESS

The relative ease with which you can operate any type of video recorder may cause you to put mastering video recording at the bottom of your production priority list. Such an attitude often leads to serious problems and headaches. Bringing the wrong recording media on an EFP shoot is as serious a problem as forgetting the camcorder. As with any other major production activity, video recording requires careful preparation and meticulous attention to detail in the preproduction, production, and postproduction phases.

Similar to a pilot who must go through a checklist before every flight, you should establish your own "before, during, and after" recording checklists. Such checklists are especially helpful when doing field productions. Note that *VR* in these checklists refers to videotape recorders as well as to digital video recorders.

THE "BEFORE" CHECKLIST

☑ **Schedule** Is the video-recording equipment actually available for the studio or field production? Most likely, your operation will have more than one type of video recorder available. Be reasonable in your request. You will find that VRs are usually available for the actual production or the remote shoot but not always for your playback demands.

☑ **VR status** Does the video recorder actually work? Always do a brief test recording and play it back before the actual video capture. Sometimes one of the tiny switches on the VR may be in the wrong position, preventing you from recording either video or audio. If using tape, you may need an adapter to play MiniDV tapes in a digital studio VTR.

☑ **Power supply** When you use a camcorder in the field, do you have enough batteries for the entire shoot? Are they fully charged? Electronic image stabilization, which corrects minor camera wobbles, and using the foldout monitor and the camera light also drain the battery rapidly. If you use household current for power, you will need the appropriate adapter. Check whether the connectors of the power cable fit the jacks of the power supply and the camera. Don't try to make a connector fit a jack for which it isn't designed; even if you can force it in, you may blow more than a fuse.

☑ **Recording media** Does the media fit the camcorder? Although your camcorder may use a memory card for recording, not all memory cards are alike. Some memory cards may look the same but won't fit the slot in the camcorder. The same goes for tape-based camcorders. Make sure that the videotape you take along actually fits the camcorder. Don't rely simply on the label on the box. Open it and see whether it contains the correct media. Do you have enough media for the proposed production? Experienced videographers always bring along an external hard drive in case the memory cards are not sufficient. Are the media in the record mode? All memory cards and videotape cassettes have a tab that can be moved to prevent accidental erasure. When this tab is in the open position, you cannot record on the card or cassette. **SEE 11.10**

11.10 RECORD PROTECTION
All memory cards, digital ¼-inch videocassettes, and MiniDV cassettes have a movable tab that prevents accidental erasure. When in the open position, the cassette will play back but not record video and audio content.

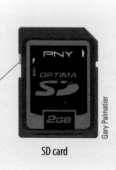

Movable record-protect tab

SD card

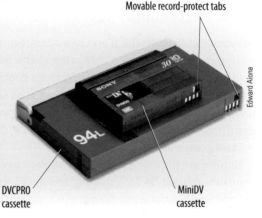

Movable record-protect tabs

DVCPRO cassette

MiniDV cassette

To enable recording on the media, move the tab into the closed (record) position. Routinely check the status of the tab before using any media for video recording. All media will play back with or without record-protect devices in place.

☑ **Cables** Do the cables work? The problem with defective cables is that ordinarily you can't see the damage. If you don't have time to test the cables beforehand, take some spares along. Do the cable plugs fit the jacks of the camcorder or VR? As you recall, most professional recorders and camcorders use XLR jacks for audio inputs, but some may have RCA phono jacks. Video cables have BNC, S-video, or RCA phono connectors (see figures 4.23 and 7.26). Keep a supply of adapters on hand, but always try to have cables with the correct plugs; each adapter is a potential trouble spot.

☑ **Monitor** Most portable monitors can be powered by battery or household current. When using such a monitor on an EFP, bring a long extension cord as well as two fully charged batteries. You can feed the camera output directly into the monitor via a coaxial cable with a BNC or an RCA phono connector at both ends.

If you have the appropriate editing software installed on your laptop, you can use it as a field monitor by feeding the camcorder footage to the laptop via FireWire or some other interface. Note, however, that such a hookup does not work with a live feed from the camcorder.

THE "DURING" CHECKLIST

☑ **Video leader** Whenever possible, start each video recording with a video leader, which consists of a 30- to 60-second recording of color bars and a 0 VU test tone, an identification slate, black or leader numbers (from 10 to 2) that flash on-screen every second for 8 seconds, and 2 seconds of black before the first frame of the program video. **SEE 11.11**

	Blank leader	Color bars (30 to 60 seconds)	Slate visual (15 seconds)	Black or leader numbers 10–3 (8 seconds)	Black (2 seconds)	Program video
Video track	Blank leader	Color bars (30 to 60 seconds)	Slate visual (15 seconds)	Black or leader numbers 10–3 (8 seconds)	Black (2 seconds)	Program video
Audio track	Silence	0 VU test tone	Silence	8 audio beeps (optional)	Silence	Program audio

Gary Palmatier

11.11 VIDEO LEADER
The video leader helps identify content and adjust the playback machine to the video and audio values of the record machine.

The color bars can be generated by the camcorder you actually use or, in a studio production, from the camera control unit. The 0 VU test tone can come from the camcorder, a portable mixer, or the studio console.

During playback you can use the color bars and the test tone as references to match the colors of the playback monitor and the audio volume of the playback VR with those of the video recording. Unfortunately, most consumer camcorders cannot generate color bars. Do not copy the video leader from another recording—you would be adjusting your playback equipment to the wrong standard.

The video slate shows vital production information, such as the show title; the scene and take numbers; the date, time, and location of the recording; and frequently the name of the director and the producer. At a minimum the slate should indicate the name of the show and the take number. The slate is usually done with a character generator (CG) or the camcorder's built-in lettering function. **SEE 11.12**

In field productions this information is normally hand-lettered on a clapboard or simply read into a microphone by the floor manager, the VR operator, or even the talent. Each time you do another take, you need to update the take number on the slate.

When using a clapboard for slating takes, snap down the movable clapstick to make a sound. This generates a sound mark with the frame that shows the clapstick in the down position—both of which mark the first frame of the clip. A holdover from filmmaking, the first frame and the sound mark of the clapstick help synchronize video and audio and especially the clips from multiple camcorders that you might have recorded simultaneously for a particular scene. **SEE 11.13**

The countdown numbers of the video leader are also produced by the CG, unless the clapboard also shows a running time code. These countdown numbers, which were originally developed for film cueing, are used for cueing the playback. This is especially important if you are using videotape for your playback. You can cue the tape at leader number 4, which gives you a 4-second preroll before the first frame of program video appears. These numbers are normally accompanied by corresponding audio beeps. Note that the last two seconds are usually in black and silent. Some leader numbers flash down to 2, with only the last second (1) kept in black. The leader

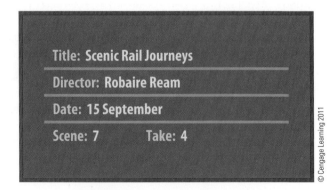

11.12 CHARACTER-GENERATED SLATE
The slate gives vital production information and is recorded at the beginning of each take.

11.13 CLAPBOARD
The clapboard is used for each take and contains the necessary information for locating clips in postproduction. The movable clapstick is snapped closed to synchronize the video and the audio of each take.

numbers are especially helpful when you need to cue a videotape without the aid of time code. Otherwise, the SMPTE/EBU time code or other address system lets you cue up the video recording even more precisely. (Address systems and how they work are covered in chapter 12.) **ZVL2** EDITING→ Postproduction guidelines→ leader

☑ **Recording time readout** Most VRs stamp each frame automatically with some kind of time code or address, which is shown on the digital time readout or tape counter of the VR. This enables you to quickly locate the approximate starting point when asked for a playback. Most professional VRs show hours, minutes, seconds, and elapsed frames. Chapter 12 explores time code in detail.

☑ **Preroll** Contrary to a DVR, which can record as soon as you press the *record* button, a VTR needs a certain amount of preroll time to give the tape transport a chance to stabilize. Most VTRs indicate with a light when they have reached operating speed. To alert the director that the VTR is ready to record, give a "speed," "locked," or "in-record" cue. If you start to record before the VTR has reached proper speed, the recording will most likely suffer from picture and sound breakup. For playback most high-end VTRs reach operating speed within a fraction of a second; they deliver a stable picture even when you shift directly to *play* from the pause mode that displays a freeze-frame.

☑ **Recording levels** Watch carefully the recording levels of the video and especially the audio. You may get so carried away with the exciting visuals of a scene that minor—or even major—audio problems escape your attention. Many camcorders indicate these levels in the viewfinder display or on VU meters on the video recorder. Note that the volume standard for digital audio is considerably lower than that of analog. In any case, the digital audio signal should never peak above 0 dB, or you will end up with irreparable sound distortion.

☑ **Recording for postproduction** When recording for postproduction editing, record enough of each segment so that the action overlaps the preceding and following scenes. Such trim handles (also called pads and edit margins) greatly facilitate editing. If you have enough media, record the camera rehearsals. Sometimes you will get a better performance during rehearsal than during the actual take. Record a few seconds of black after each take before stopping the recorder. This run-out signal acts as a pad during editing or, if you do a live recording, as a safety cushion during playback.

☑ **Retakes** As the VR operator, tell the director right away if you feel that another take is necessary for some reason. It is far less expensive to repeat a take than to try to "fix it in post." When using a VTR, be ready to rewind the tape to the beginning of the flawed take without delay. You can do this quite easily if you keep an accurate field log.

☑ **Recordkeeping** Keep accurate records of each take during the recording. A carefully kept field log can save you considerable time in finding takes during the field production and especially when preparing a more accurate VR log in the postproduction phase. The *field log* should include the production title, the names of the producer and the director, the recording date and location, the media number, the scene and take numbers and their sequence, whether the takes are good, and the VR counter or time code number. You may also list such pertinent production details as mistakes made by the talent or especially serious audio problems. **SEE 11.14**

KEY CONCEPT

Keep an accurate field log during the recording session and carefully label all media.

THE "AFTER" CHECKLIST

☑ **Recording check** Before moving on to the next scene or striking the studio set or remote location, verify that you have actually recorded the scene as planned. Go to the beginning shot, then fast-forward two or three times to spot-check the entire recording. Pay attention to the sound. Sometimes you may think that the audio distortion is in the playback equipment, but more likely than not the problem was caused during the production by connecting the incoming sound signal to the wrong mixer input (line instead of mic and vice versa) or by overloading the incoming digital audio.

☑ **Labeling** Label each recording media with the title of the production, the recording date, the media number, and its content. Label the box with the identical information. As obvious as such labeling seems, countless precious hours of postproduction time have been lost because someone labeled the media boxes but not their content. Watch that the media labels match the information on the corresponding field log.

MEDIA NUMBER	SCENE	TAKE	OK or NO GOOD	TIME CODE		EVENT / REMARKS
				IN	**OUT**	

PRODUCTION TITLE: "impressions"   **PRODUCER/DIRECTOR:** Hamid Khani

RECORDING DATE: 4/15   **LOCATION:** BECA Newsroom

MEDIA NUMBER	SCENE	TAKE	OK or NO GOOD	IN	OUT	EVENT / REMARKS
C-005	2	1	NG	01:57:25	02:07:24	student looks into Camera CU - Z-axis
		(2)	OK	02:09:04	02:14:27	Monitor + L news anchor MS getting ready
		(3)	OK	02:18:28	02:34:22	Pan R to reveal anchor in news set
		4	NG	02:36:22	02:45:18	Rack focus from Floor Mgr to L anchor · OUT OF FOCUS
		5	NG	02:48:05	02:55:12	Rack focus Both out of focus
		6	NG	02:58:13	03:05:11	Rack OK LOST Audio
		(7)	OK	03:12:02	03:46:24	Hurrah! Rack OK
	3	(1)	OK	04:16:03	04:28:11	MS Floor Mgr + Camera op from behind
		2	NG	04:35:13	04:49:05	CU of R anchor Lost audio
		(3)	OK	05:50:00	06:01:24	CU of R anchor
		4	NG	06:03:10	06:30:17	CU of L anchor audio problem
		5	NG	06:40:07	07:04:08	LS of both anchor Floor Mgr walks through shot
		(6)	OK	07:07:15	07:28:05	Good! Floor Mgr silhouette against set
		(7)	OK	07:30:29	07:45:12	slow pullout
C-006	4	(1)	OK	49:48:28	51:12:08	MCU Marty talks to anchors
		2	NG	51:35:17	51:42:01	Lav comes off R anchor

11.14 FIELD LOG
The field log is kept by the VR operator during the production. It normally indicates the production title, names of producer and director, recording date and location, media number, scene and take numbers and their sequence, whether the takes are good, VR counter or time code number, and what the take was all about. It greatly facilitates locating the various media and shots during postproduction previewing.

☑ **Protection copies** As soon as possible, import the raw footage into your NLE system so that you have a backup copy. If using videotape, you can also make window dubs—lower-quality (VCR) recordings that have the time code inserted over each frame. You can then proceed to prepare a VR log (see chapter 12). Don't ever erase your original recordings until you are all done with the editing.

KEY CONCEPT

Keep all recorded material until you are finished with the project.

M A I N   P O I N T S

▶ ***Tapeless Video-Recording Systems***

Tapeless systems can record only digital information. They are also called nonlinear because they allow random access of all recorded content. The nontape recording media for camcorders include a variety of solid-state memory cards of different recording capacities, read/write optical discs, and removable hard-drive cassettes. There are a great many stand-alone digital video recorders (DVRs) available that store either video data streams or video files. Direct-to-edit (DTE) pocket recorders record video files that can be used immediately for editing. All large studio DVRs use multiple disk arrays. Video servers have large-capacity disk arrays that can record a great number of different video sources and can export content to different users simultaneously.

▶ ***Tape-Based Video-Recording Systems***

Tape-based recording systems use a variety of videotape cassettes. They can record either analog or digital signals in various track formats. The major drawbacks when compared with nontape systems are that tape is linear and does not allow random access, tape is subject to deterioration after repeated use, and VTRs have complex mechanisms that need constant maintenance to stay reliable. Although there are differences in how the video and audio signals are processed, all VTRs move the videotape past spinning record/playback heads.

▶ ***Signal Transport and Video Stabilization***

Composite (NTSC) video combines the luminance (Y) information and the color (C) information in a single signal. Y/C component video keeps the Y and C signals separate to avoid interference. Y/color difference component video is used for analog and digital transport. Stabilization is the purview of the frame store synchronizer and the time base corrector (TBC). Both synchronize the scanning of various incoming video sources and help prevent picture breakup.

▶ ***Video-Recording Process***

To make the video-recording process as efficient as possible, you need to follow certain before, during, and after checklists. Whereas some of the recording processes differ when using tapeless media instead of videotape, many of the procedural steps are similar if not identical.

Z E T T L ' S   V I D E O L A B

 For your reference or to track your work, the *Zettl's VideoLab* program cues in this chapter are listed here with their corresponding page numbers.

KEY TERMS

assemble editing In linear editing, adding shots on videotape in consecutive order without first recording a control track on the edit master tape.

capture Moving video and audio from the recording media to the hard drive of a computer with a nonlinear editing program. Analog video signals must be converted to digital before they can be imported by a computer.

digitize Necessary step with analog source material whereby the analog signals are converted to digital signals prior to capture.

edit controller A machine that assists in various linear editing functions, such as marking edit-in and edit-out points, rolling source and record VTRs, and integrating effects. It can be a desktop computer with editing software. Also called *editing control unit*.

edit decision list (EDL) Consists of edit-in and edit-out points, expressed in time code numbers, and the nature of transitions between shots.

edit master The videotape or disc that contains the final version of an edited program. Subsequent copies are struck from the edit master.

insert editing Produces highly stable edits for linear editing. Requires the prior laying of a continuous control track by recording black on the edit master tape.

linear editing system Uses videotape as the editing medium. It does not allow random access of shots.

nonlinear editing (NLE) system Allows random access of shots. The video and audio information is stored in digital form on computer disks. Usually has two external monitors, small loudspeakers, and an audio mixer.

off-line editing In linear editing it produces an edit decision list or a rough-cut not intended for broadcast. In nonlinear editing the selected shots are captured in low resolution to save computer storage space.

on-line editing In linear editing it produces the final high-quality edit master for broadcast or program duplication. In nonlinear editing the shots listed on the edit decision list are recaptured at a higher resolution.

pulse-count system An address code that counts the control track pulses and translates that count into time and frame numbers. It is not frame-accurate. Also called *control track system*.

rough-cut A preliminary edit.

SMPTE time code A specially generated address code that marks each video frame with a specific number (hour, minute, second, and frame). Named for the Society of Motion Picture and Television Engineers, this time code is officially called *SMPTE/EBU* (for *European Broadcasting Union*).

VR log A record of each take on the source media. Also called *editing log*. When the recording media is videotape, the shot record is also called *VTR log*.

window dub A dub of the source tapes to a lower-quality tape format with the address code keyed into each frame.

Nonlinear and Linear Editing

Postproduction editing is the third and final stage of the production process, in which the various video and audio segments are given structure and meaning. Editing enables you to build a show from the recorded shots and clips, gives you a chance to correct mistakes, and offers the final chance to clarify and intensify the intended message. Assuming that the preproduction and production phases went according to plan, you can now use your grasp of the program objective and your creativity to compose a program that has clarity and impact.

Most editors feel that postproduction editing is among the most creative aspects of video production. Very much like writing, editing is an exacting and painstaking activity. To tell the story effectively, you must not only understand the program objective, the angle the director has in mind, and the general feel of the program but also master a complex technical procedure. **ZVL1** EDITING→ Editing introduction

High-capacity hard drives even in laptop computers and the ready availability of editing software have firmly established nonlinear editing techniques. A basic knowledge of linear editing is still important, however, not only because much of linear editing served as a model for the nonlinear procedures but also because you may well be called upon to do linear videotape editing. **ZVL2** EDITING→ Functions

▶ **NONLINEAR EDITING**
   Nonlinear editing system and nonlinear editing phases: capture, editing, and export

▶ **LINEAR EDITING**
   Single-source linear system, multiple-source linear system, pulse-count and address code, assemble editing, and insert editing

▶ **PRODUCTION TIPS FOR POSTPRODUCTION**
   Shooting for continuity, slating each take, leaving edit margins, recording background sounds and cutaways, and keeping a field log

▶ **POSTPRODUCTION PREPARATIONS**
   Making protection copies, adding time code, making a window dub, reviewing and logging the source footage, and transcribing the audio text

▶ **PRE-EDIT DECISION-MAKING**
  Selecting and sequencing clips: paper-and-pencil editing

▶ **OFF-LINE AND ON-LINE EDITING**
  Linear off-line and on-line editing, nonlinear off-line and on-line editing, and on-line editing procedures

▨ NONLINEAR EDITING

The foundation of all nonlinear editing (NLE) systems is a computer with a high-capacity hard drive and a fast processor. The main function of this computer is to facilitate your selection of clips (shots or shot sequences), put them in a specific order, and recall this order during playback. Although there are several high-end editing systems on the market that combine specialized computer hardware and editing software, a laptop computer and a basic editing program will do just fine for even a relatively demanding editing job.

Contrary to linear editing, where you copy a selected clip from one tape to another, the basic principle of nonlinear editing is digital file management. Each file contains a single frame or, for all practical purposes, a series of frames that make up a clip (shot). You probably now see why this system is called "nonlinear": you can access any one of the files (frames or clips) instantly in any order regardless of where the information is located on the NLE hard drive. The computer then flags the selected clips so that they play back in the sequence you specify. Note that the video files themselves are not moved from where they are stored on the hard drive; your editing simply tells the computer the order in which to play back the clips. **ZVL3** EDITING→ Nonlinear editing→ system

> **KEY CONCEPT**
>
> The basic principle of nonlinear editing is file management.

Nonlinear Editing System

If you were to equip an editing suite, opt for a high-end desktop computer with a high-capacity hard drive and a high-speed processor. The typical ***nonlinear editing (NLE) system*** must also include two fairly large external monitors—one for the computer output and the other to show your edited sequences—or a large monitor display that is divided into two screens. Because high-fidelity video needs high-fidelity sound, you will also need two good loudspeakers or high-quality headphones. If you intend to control the volume of additional sound sources, or premix some of them before importing them to the NLE system, you will need a small audio mixer as well. **SEE 12.1**

A computer used for editing must have the necessary software to accomplish the three phases of nonlinear editing—capture, the actual editing, and export—as well as additional special-effects software for creating transitions, graphics, and titles.

Assuming the editing software can read the codec of your recording, you can import—capture—the recorded video and audio data directly from the video recorder (VR) inside the camcorder or from the memory card to the NLE computer. Once the information is on the hard drive, you can select clips and specify their order of play. You can also add new information, such as clips or audio segments from another shoot or source, to heighten the impact of your creation. Special-effects

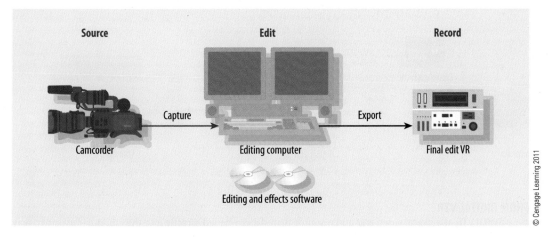

12.1 NONLINEAR EDITING SYSTEM
The major parts of a nonlinear editing system are playback devices for the source clips (normally camcorder VTRs, optical discs, or memory cards), an editing computer and software, and a video recorder for capturing the final edit master recording.

software enables myriad transitions and title possibilities. This is the actual editing phase. Unless you play your masterpiece only on the NLE system, you need to dub—export—the final edited version onto a disc, video server, or edit master tape.

Let's take a closer look at these phases.

Nonlinear Editing Phase 1: Capture

Before you can do any nonlinear editing, you need to transfer the content of the source media to the hard drive of the NLE computer. This represents the *capture* phase. The source media can be hard drives, memory cards, optical discs, or videotape.

Digital source media   If the digital camcorder uses discs, memory cards, or hard drives, you can transfer the source data directly to the hard drive of the NLE system. Connect the tapeless camcorder to the NLE system via RCA phono, HDMI, FireWire, or USB interface. If you use a compatible memory card, insert the cards directly into the slot of the NLE system or a card reader that is connected to the NLE computer.

Digital source tapes   You can transfer digital videotapes directly from the camcorder to the NLE hard drive. If, however, you intend to select shots from the source tapes to save space on the NLE hard drive, you should use a stand-alone videotape recorder (VTR) for the capture. This is where your field log comes in handy. Don't bother capturing shots that you marked as definitely no good, such as the one in which the talent showed the wrong book during an interview with the author. (We discuss the review and logging of source tapes later in this chapter.)

Selecting shots always requires extensive tape shuttle, including repeated fast-forwarding and rewinding, which can be very hard on the camcorder VTR. In this

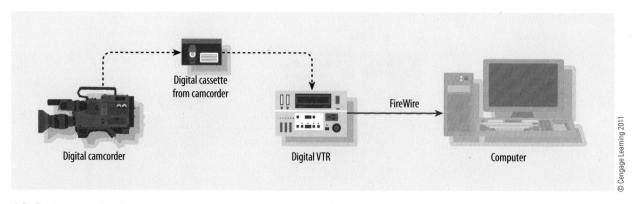

12.2 CAPTURE FROM DIGITAL VTR

When played back on a digital VTR, the digital video and audio source material can be fed directly into the computer via a two-way interface, such as a FireWire.

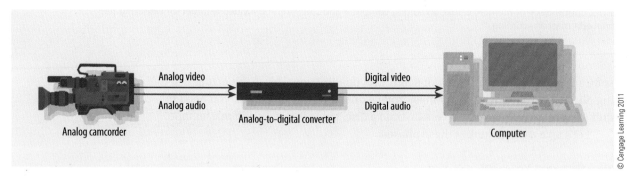

12.3 CAPTURE FROM ANALOG SOURCE TAPES

Analog source tapes must be digitized by a converter box or the NLE system software.

case, you should extract the tape cassette from the camcorder and use it in a sturdier stand-alone VTR for this selection/capture procedure. The stand-alone digital VTR is well suited for the job; extensive shuttles are part of its intended use. You will also find your desired shots much more quickly than with the camcorder VTR.

Once you have inserted the source tape in the sturdier VTR, you can connect it to the NLE system with RCA phono or S-video cables or, better yet, a FireWire (IEEE 1394) cable. **SEE 12.2**

Analog source tapes   If you want to edit some of your old analog tapes, you first need to *digitize* them before capture by the NLE system. To do this you can use RCA phono or S-video cables to connect the analog camcorder to a converter box, which changes the analog content into digital data. A FireWire cable lets you connect the box with the hard drive of the NLE system. **SEE 12.3**

Nonlinear Editing Phase 2: Editing

This phase includes the major steps of editing the imported video: file identification, shot selection, sequencing, transitions, and effects. It also involves building the

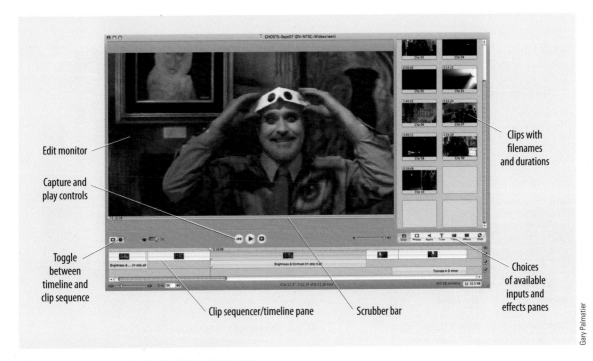

Edit monitor

Capture and
play controls

Clips with
filenames
and durations

Toggle
between
timeline and
clip sequence

Choices
of available
inputs and
effects panes

Clip sequencer/timeline pane   Scrubber bar

Gary Palmatier

12.4 SIMPLE NONLINEAR EDITING INTERFACE

In this editing interface, modeled after iMovie HD, the clips are arranged on a "shelf" as slides. You can order and view the clips in the viewer space or sequence them on the timeline. The timeline below the large editing monitor consists of scrubber bar, the timeline pane, and two audio tracks.

audio track: selecting the acceptable sound portions, importing new sound, mixing sound, and synchronizing it with the video.

Even relatively simple editing software offers so many features that you probably don't need anything more complicated for many of your projects. **SEE 12.4** Sophisticated software can transform even a laptop computer into a powerful professional NLE system.

All NLE programs show in their interface—the window that displays the editing tools—a similar arrangement of the operational features shown in figure 12.5. **SEE 12.5**

All editing software is capable of displaying multiple frames and sequences so that you can preview an edit and see how well the clips cut together. The computer will also display a timeline, which contains all video and audio tracks of a clip. (This NLE timeline has nothing to do with the production time line, which shows a breakdown of all activities on a specific production day.)

Before we get into the editing process, a word of advice: Although a laptop computer can certainly function as a first-class NLE system and will do just fine for the import phase, you will need additional equipment for serious editing. Instead of squinting at the small computer screen, try to get a large, high-quality flat-panel monitor for the editing interface. The larger image prevents eye fatigue and also gives you a better idea of how the pictures will cut together. Also get a second monitor for full-screen video playback or a screen large enough to be divided into two displays. This will cause less confusion about whether you are watching the source

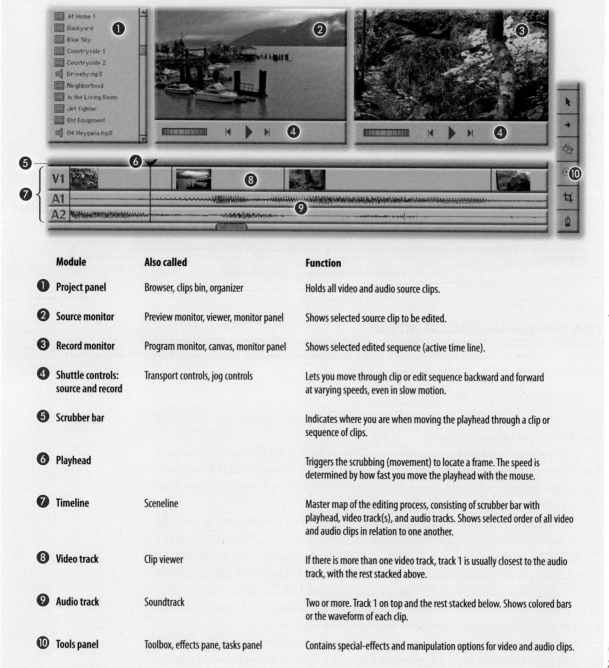

Module	Also called	Function
❶ Project panel	Browser, clips bin, organizer	Holds all video and audio source clips.
❷ Source monitor	Preview monitor, viewer, monitor panel	Shows selected source clip to be edited.
❸ Record monitor	Program monitor, canvas, monitor panel	Shows selected edited sequence (active time line).
❹ Shuttle controls: source and record	Transport controls, jog controls	Lets you move through clip or edit sequence backward and forward at varying speeds, even in slow motion.
❺ Scrubber bar		Indicates where you are when moving the playhead through a clip or sequence of clips.
❻ Playhead		Triggers the scrubbing (movement) to locate a frame. The speed is determined by how fast you move the playhead with the mouse.
❼ Timeline	Sceneline	Master map of the editing process, consisting of scrubber bar with playhead, video track(s), and audio tracks. Shows selected order of all video and audio clips in relation to one another.
❽ Video track	Clip viewer	If there is more than one video track, track 1 is usually closest to the audio track, with the rest stacked above.
❾ Audio track	Soundtrack	Two or more. Track 1 on top and the rest stacked below. Shows colored bars or the waveform of each clip.
❿ Tools panel	Toolbox, effects pane, tasks panel	Contains special-effects and manipulation options for video and audio clips.

Gary Palmatier

12.5 NONLINEAR EDITING INTERFACE

This generic interface shows the basic components of an NLE system. It does not show the menus, which offer a vast array of choices of nonlinear editing functions.

clips or a partially edited sequence, and it will prove especially valuable when scrutinizing effects.

Unless your audio requirements are relatively simple, you will also need an audio mixer and high-quality speakers for monitoring audio. Don't rely on the little speakers of the laptop computer unless you intend to wear headphones. Good speakers or headphones will reveal audio problems right away and tell you whether some audio sweetening is required.

Labeling the imported source material   The computer part of the NLE system now functions as a huge slide library from which you can select specific clips, which in effect are brief slide series. The computer screen can display a selection of shots. But which ones? It should come as no surprise that finding the right clips presupposes that they are labeled properly. The best library in the world is useless if the books are not indexed accurately for quick retrieval. The same is true for files—you need to give all imported clips a unique filename or number. All editing programs have a space for the filename of the imported clips as well as for additional information, similar to a field log. In fact, you should use the names listed on the field log files for the captured clips. (We address labeling and creating an editing log later in this chapter.)

Shot selection and sequencing   The specific techniques of shot selection, shot sequencing, and creating transitions and effects depend to a large extent on the software you are using. All professional NLE systems come with comprehensive user manuals and require dedication, patience, and lots of practice before you feel comfortable using them.

Remember that nonlinear editing is file management. You basically select clips and determine their sequence. The computer follows your instructions and tells every frame how to line up for playback. The random access of clips gives you extraordinary flexibility not only in selecting shots but also in rearranging them.

You will discover that once you have mastered the actual editing techniques, the biggest challenge will always be selecting the most effective shots and sequencing them to convey your message in a clear and concise way. (The checklist on postproduction preparations later in this chapter gives some tips on making the selection process more efficient and less stressful, and chapter 13 is devoted entirely to the basic aesthetic principles of postproduction editing.)

Nonlinear Editing Phase 3: Export to Disc or Videotape

Once you have finished selecting the clips and joining them in the desired sequence through transitions, it's time to get your masterpiece out of the computer and onto disc or videotape. Essentially, you need to export your file sequence to a recording media that you will use as the ***edit master*** for playback and distribution of the finished project. Once recorded on the edit master media, your program is finally and actually edited.

Because software programs vary, you need to check on the export requirements of your NLE system, such as its specific codec (type and degree of compression).

If you intend to distribute your program on DVD or for Internet streaming, you need to encode it in a compression standard that can be decoded (read) by the equipment of the intended user. **ZVL4** EDITING→ Nonlinear editing→ exporting

◼ LINEAR EDITING

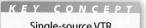

The principle of linear editing is copying selected shots from the source tape to another one, called edit master tape, in a specific sequence, regardless of whether the signals on the videotapes are analog or digital. The edit master tape is the videotape that contains the final version of an edited program and from which subsequent copies are struck. As pointed out in chapter 11, it is called "linear" because you cannot access the source material randomly but must roll through all shots that come before the one you want to access. **ZVL5** EDITING→ Linear editing→ system

Single-Source Linear System

The simplest **linear editing system** consists of a source VTR and a record VTR. You use the source VTR to select the shots and the record VTR to copy them and join them through cuts. The record VTR performs the actual video and audio edits.

Both the source and record VTRs have their own monitors. In a single-source system, the source VTR monitor displays the source material to be edited, and the record VTR monitor displays the edited video portion of the edit master tape. Because there is only one source VTR, the single-source editing system is usually limited to cuts-only transitions. **SEE 12.6**

Edit controller　The **edit controller**, also called the editing control unit, acts like an able and superefficient editing assistant. It is really a forerunner of computerized editing because many of the edit controller's functions are digitally controlled. It can mark and remember frame locations on the source and record tapes, preroll and synchronize the VTRs, allow you to record the audio with the video or separately, and tell the record VTR when to switch to record mode (thereby performing the edit). **SEE 12.7**

The diagram in the following figure shows how the edit controller fits into the single-source editing system. **SEE 12.8** Note that this single-source system integrates an audio mixer and that the output from the mixer goes directly to the record VTR, bypassing the edit controller.

Multiple-Source Linear System

If you want to go beyond cuts-only transitions and use a dissolve or wipe instead, you need a second VTR. When the second signal is fed into a switcher, you can then dissolve from VTR A, which holds source video A (the A-roll), to VTR B, which holds source video B (the B-roll). **SEE 12.9**

AB-roll editing　This editing technique requires two source VTRs: VTR A holds the source footage of the A-roll (long shots), and VTR B holds the B-roll, close-ups to

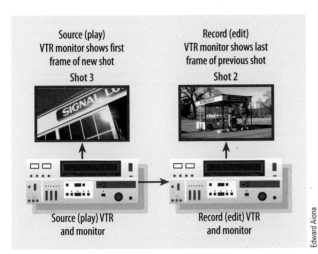

12.6 BASIC SINGLE-SOURCE SYSTEM
The source VTR supplies the selected shots from the original video and feeds them to the record VTR. The record VTR joins them through cuts. The source VTR and the record VTR have their own monitors.

Source (play)
VTR monitor shows first frame of new shot
Shot 3

Record (edit)
VTR monitor shows last frame of previous shot
Shot 2

Source (play) VTR and monitor

Record (edit) VTR and monitor

Edward Aiona

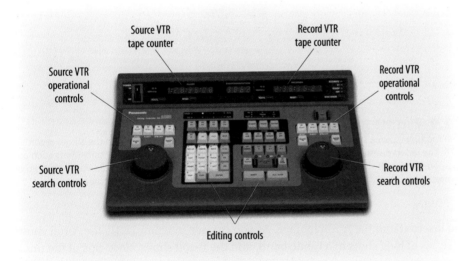

12.7 EDIT CONTROLLER
The edit controller has separate operational controls for the source VTR and the record VTR, such as search and shuttle controls. The controls in the center activate the preroll and editing functions.

Source VTR tape counter

Record VTR tape counter

Source VTR operational controls

Record VTR operational controls

Source VTR search controls

Record VTR search controls

Editing controls

Panasonic

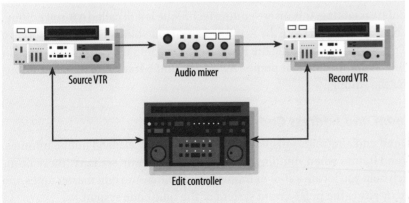

12.8 EDIT CONTROLLER IN SINGLE-SOURCE SYSTEM
The edit controller in a single-source system starts and synchronizes the source and record VTRs and locates the edit in- and out-points for both.

Source VTR

Audio mixer

Record VTR

Edit controller

© Cengage Learning 2011

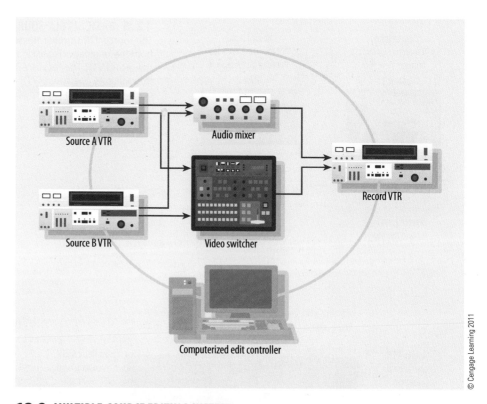

12.9 MULTIPLE-SOURCE EDITING SYSTEM

In a multiple-source system, two VTRs (A and B) supply the source material to the single record VTR. The video output of both source VTRs is routed through the switcher for transitions such as dissolves and wipes. The audio output of both source VTRs is routed through an audio console or a mixer. Multiple-source systems are usually managed by a computer-driven edit controller.

be inserted into the A-roll footage. As you can see in figure 12.10, the A-roll shows a series of long shots of a Celtic band, and the B-roll shows close-ups of the musicians. **SEE 12.10** With the record VTR in the insert mode, you "drop in" (insert-edit) the close-ups from the B-roll into the A-roll at the appropriate edit points. All of this is guided by the continuous audio track of the A-roll.

In nonlinear editing, this insert-editing technique is still called AB-roll editing. Using an NLE system, you store the A-roll footage in one bin and the B-roll footage in another. Then you simply drag the B-roll close-ups onto the A-roll video track in the timeline at the specific edit points. Again, the audio track remains continuous and guides the editing.

KEY CONCEPT

Dissolves, wipes, and other special-effects transitions are possible with a multiple-source linear editing system.

Pulse Count and Address Code

All VTRs and edit controllers display numbers that show elapsed hours, minutes, seconds, and frames when shuttling the tape back and forth **SEE 12.11** These numbers, which help you locate a shot or frame on the source and edit master tapes, are generated by either the pulse-count system or the time code system.

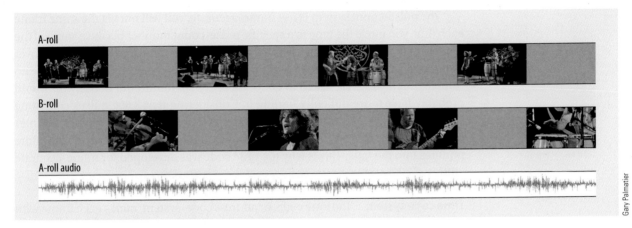

Gary Palmatier

12.10 AB-ROLL EDITING TO COMMON SOUND TRACK

In this AB-roll editing example, the A-roll consists of long and medium shots of the band; the B-roll contains CUs of the individual musicians. Because both source VTRs are synchronized, you can use the A-roll sound track to insert the B-roll video.

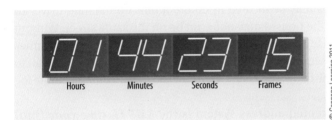

© Cengage Learning 2011

12.11 PULSE-COUNT AND ADDRESS CODE DISPLAY

The pulse-count and address code displays show elapsed hours, minutes, seconds, and frames. The frames roll over (to seconds) after 29, the seconds to minutes and the minutes to hours after 59, and the hours to 0 after 24.

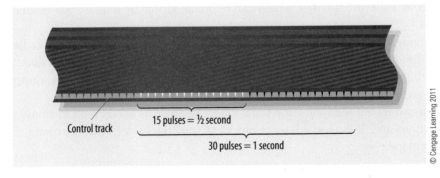

© Cengage Learning 2011

12.12 PULSE-COUNT SYSTEM

The pulse-count, or control track, system counts the control track pulses to find a specific spot on the videotape. Thirty pulses make up one second of elapsed tape time.

Pulse-count system   The *pulse-count system*, also called the control track system, uses the control track pulses of the videotape to count the frames. **SEE 12.12** Each pulse on the control track designates a video frame, so you can locate a specific spot on the tape by counting the pulses on the control track. Thirty frames make up one second on the display, so each new second rolls over after the twenty-ninth frame. Each additional minute is generated by the sixtieth second, as is the hour after the sixtieth minute.

The pulse-count system is not frame-accurate: you will not get the same frame each time you move the tape to a specific pulse-count number because some of the pulses are skipped in the high-speed tape shuttle, or the tape may stretch a little over time. For example, if you had to find the tenth house on a street, you would have no trouble. But if you were asked to go to the thirty-six-hundredth house, you would probably have more difficulty finding it. Considering that 3,600 pulses constitute only two minutes of a videotape recording, you can understand why the counter may be off a few frames when you're trying to find a specific spot some 20 or more minutes into the tape. This is why the time code was developed for frame-accurate editing. **ZVL6** EDITING→ Postproduction guidelines→ tape basics

Time code system   The time code, or address code, system, marks each frame with a unique number. With time code the edit controller guides you precisely to the tenth or thirty-six-hundredth house. To get to the tenth house, the edit controller does not have to start counting from 1 to 10 but simply looks for house number 10. It finds the thirty-six-hundredth house just as easily by looking at its house number: 3600.

In nonlinear editing, the time code is essential for identifying frames because the various clips or frames may be located in different bins on the hard drive. To use our house metaphor, the houses may not even be on the same street. Without a time code (accurate house numbers), the computer could not identify the frames and establish a playback sequence (the letter carrier could not deliver the mail to the right address). The time code also enables you to establish a frame-accurate log of the source footage.

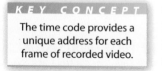

The most widely accepted address system is the ***SMPTE time code*** (pronounced "semp-ty"); its full name is SMPTE/EBU time code (for Society of Motion Picture and Television Engineers/European Broadcasting Union). It marks each frame with a specific number, which can be made visible by a time code reader. **SEE 12.13** **ZVL7** EDITING→ Postproduction guidelines→ time code

Although there are similar time code systems, they are not compatible with the SMPTE time code. You must select a specific time code system and use it throughout the editing process. You cannot synchronize various video- and audiotapes whose frames are marked with different time code systems.

You can record the time code while videotaping or, as is common in smaller productions and EFPs, add it later to one of the cue tracks or free audio tracks of the videotape.

KEY CONCEPT

The time code provides a unique address for each frame of recorded video.

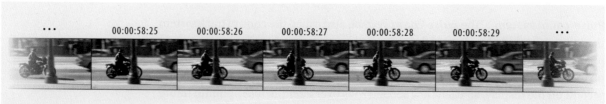

00:00:58:25   00:00:58:26   00:00:58:27   00:00:58:28   00:00:58:29

Herbert Zettl

12.13 TIME CODE ADDRESS SYSTEM
The time code system marks each frame with a unique address.

All linear editing systems give you the choice between assemble and insert mode. Which should you choose? Let's find out.

Assemble Editing

In **assemble editing** the record VTR erases everything (video, audio, control, and time code tracks) on the edit master tape to have a clean slate before copying the video and audio material supplied by the source VTR. During the transfer everything that is recorded on the selected portion of the source tape is copied to the edit master—the tape in the record VTR onto which you copy the selected shots from the source VTR.

Generally, assemble editing is faster than insert editing but less electronically stable at the edit points. This problem occurs when the sync pulses of the new shot coming from the source VTR do not align properly with the sync pulses on the edit master tape. Such a slight misalignment causes a brief sync roll at the edit point—a glitch or diagonal band moving up or down the screen. Another major drawback is that assemble editing does not allow you to edit video and audio independently (called a split edit). This is why most linear editing is done in the insert mode.

Insert Editing

Insert editing produces highly stable edits and lets you do split edits—edit video and audio tracks separately. You will find that in all but the simplest editing jobs, you need to separate audio from video and edit pictures and sound separately. For example, many news and documentary editors prefer to edit the audio track first and then "drop in" (match) the video so that it is synchronized with the sound.

Insert editing does, however, require that you first record a continuous control track on the edit master tape so that the sync pulses remain evenly spaced at all of the edit points. When inserting a new shot, its sync pulses are not transferred with the picture. Instead it simply uses the sync pulses of the edit master tape. **SEE 12.14**

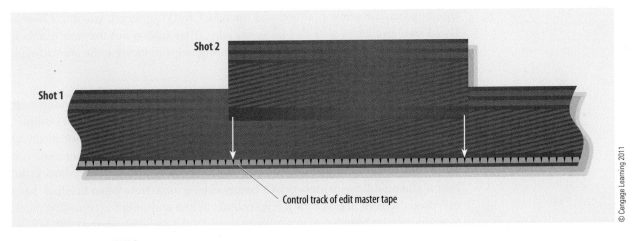

Shot 2

Shot 1

Control track of edit master tape

© Cengage Learning 2011

12.14 INSERT EDITING
The source material is transferred to the edit master tape without its control track and is placed according to the prerecorded control track on the edit master.

KEY CONCEPT

The edit master tape must be prepared for insert editing by first recording black on it.

The most common way to record a continuous control track is to record black on the master edit tape, which will provide the continuous control track without putting any pictures on it. Note that the recording of black happens in real time, which means you must run the blank edit master tape for 30 minutes to lay a 30-minute control track. Only then do you have a truly continuous guide for the edit points.

If you have the feeling that things got a bit more complicated than what you expected from a discussion of video "basics," you are right. This is why nonlinear editing has virtually replaced all linear multiple-source editing.

PRODUCTION TIPS FOR POSTPRODUCTION

Recall from chapter 1 that efficient postproduction starts in the production phase and, to some extent, even in preproduction. The following checklist of production steps will help you save time and prevent headaches during postproduction editing, regardless of whether your original footage was analog or digital and captured on videotape or other recording media. Some of these points were made in earlier discussions, but because they can greatly facilitate postproduction editing we reiterate them here.

✅ *Shoot for continuity* Good directors and camera operators not only are able to visualize each shot and give it composition and meaning but they also think ahead about how those shots will cut together and look in sequence. In complicated productions such as dramas, commercials, and carefully constructed EFPs, sequencing is determined by a storyboard, which shows key visualizations and the major sequencing of shots. **SEE 12.15**

✅ **Slate each take** Identify each take with a visual or at least a verbal slate. In the studio this is usually done with the character generator (CG). In the field you should have a handheld slate or a clapboard that shows the date of the shoot, the tape number, the scene number, and the take (shot) number. If you don't have a visual slate available, slate the takes verbally. After calling out the take number, count backward from five to zero. This counting helps in locating the approximate beginning of a shot after the slate.

✅ **Leave margins for editing** When video-recording, do not stop the camcorder exactly at the end of a shot; record a few more seconds before stopping. For instance, if the software company president has finished describing the latest nonlinear editing system, have her remain silent and in place for a few seconds, or have her move out of the shot, before cutting the action and stopping the recording. When starting the next segment, roll the camera briefly before calling for action; when finished, have everybody remain in place for a few seconds before stopping the recording. Such margins, or trim handles, give you more flexibility in deciding on the exact edit-in and edit-out points.

✅ **Record background sounds** Even if you plan to reconstruct the audio track in postproduction, always record a few minutes of ambient sound (room tone,

shot 1

ACTION: LONG SHOT -- DRAMATIC

The SUN rises behind a picturesque WINDMILL.

shot 2

ACTION:

The light gleams through the windmill blades.

We hear: DISTANT JINGLING.

shot 3

ACTION:

MATCH CUT TO:

shot 3 continued

ACTION: CLOSE ON A SILVER HARNESS-BELL

Slightly tarnished. It JINGLES from the motion of the horse. The sun gleams on its surface, the cross-cut of the bell's face reminiscent of the blades of the windmill.

shot 4

ACTION: WIDE -- DRAMATIC

DON QUIXOTE and SANCHO PANZA ride "screen left," the bell on Don Quixote's harness JINGLING as his makeshift armor CLATTERS.

shot 5

ACTION:

D.Q. reacts dramatically to the windmill ahead.

DON QUIXOTE
Lo! The enemy is sighted!

Bob and Sharon Forward

12.15 STORYBOARD

The storyboard shows key visualizations and the major sequencing of shots, with action and audio information given below. It can be hand-drawn on preprinted storyboard paper or computer-generated.

traffic noise, or the sounds of silence in the mountains) before changing locations or finishing the recording. This environmental sound will help mask silent periods during an edit or within a shot. You may even decide to use the sounds after all to reinforce the location.

☑ **Record cutaway shots** Get some cutaways for each scene. A cutaway is a brief shot that will help improve or establish visual continuity between two shots; it is usually related to the event, such as a bystander watching a parade or a reporter's camera during a hearing. Make the cutaways long enough—at least 15 to 20 seconds. Cutaways that are too short can be as frustrating to an editor as no cutaways at all. Always let the camera run for a few more seconds than you think necessary; if the cutaway is too short, it will look more like a mistake than a continuity link. ZVL8 EDITING→ Production guidelines→ cutaways

☑ **Keep a field log** Keep an accurate field log of what you record. Label all recording media and boxes with the media number and the production title. The field log will aid you greatly in locating the video-recorded material for the first screening.

POSTPRODUCTION PREPARATIONS

As with all other production activities, editing requires diligent preparation. The only editing for which preparations are kept to a minimum is in news. There is no way to predict the amount and the nature of news footage you may have to edit on a given day, and you always have precious little time to make deliberate editing decisions. All you can do is try to select the most telling shots and sequence them into a credible, responsible news story.

☑ **Make protection copies** Your production efforts are wasted if you lose the source media or damage them in some way. Experienced production people always make protection copies of all source footage as soon as possible after the recording. The best way to do this is to import the clips right way into the NLE system, although this requires a high-capacity hard drive and a high transfer speed. If this is not possible or desirable, back up your source footage with an external video recorder. As you know, there is no quality loss in copying digital media; the copies will be as good as the original source footage. If your source clips are recorded on analog videotape, you need to use an external digitizer (a very small peripheral with RCA phono input and output jacks) before importing then into the computer. Most digital editing systems, however, can do this signal translation automatically. **ZVL9** EDITING→ Production guidelines→ housekeeping

> **KEY CONCEPT**
>
> Always make protection copies of the original source clips.

☑ **Add time code** Unless the camcorder supplied the desired time code during the recording, you need to add it to all source footage at this point. You do this by "laying in" the time code signals from a time code generator on the appropriate time code track of the recording media.

☑ **Make a window dub** When laying in the time code, you can simultaneously make a *window dub*—a lower-quality videotape or low-resolution copy of all the original clips that have the time code "burned in," or keyed over each frame. Each single frame of each clip displays a box, called a window, which shows its time code address. **SEE 12.16**

Even if you have labeled some takes on your field log as no good, it is usually easier to window-dub all clips, regardless of whether you intend to use them in the final edit. Every once in a while, the video from an initially NG (no good) take proves invaluable as a cutaway or a substitute shot. You can still eliminate the really bad clips later when doing the actual editing.

The window dub will serve you in the accurate logging of all recorded clips; in preparing an *edit decision list (EDL)*, which lists the in- and out-points of each edit; and even when performing a rough-cut—a preliminary version of the desired sequencing of your clips.

☑ **Review and log the source footage** It is now time to make a list of all of the source clips, regardless of whether the take was properly field slated as usable. This list—called a *VR log* or an editing log—is a written document based on the window dub of the source clips. This log helps you locate specific shots and their principal screen directions without having to preview the source material over and over again. **SEE 12.17** Most editing software enables you to log each shot with its specific name

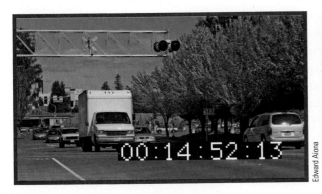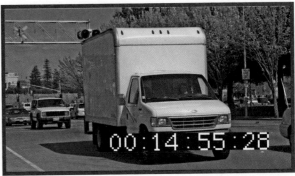

Edward Aiona

12.16 SMPTE TIME CODE WINDOW DUB
The time code can be keyed directly into a copy of the source tape. Each frame displays its own unique time code address.

PRODUCTION TITLE: Traffic Safety					PRODUCTION NO: 114		OFF-LINE DATE: 07/15

PRODUCER: Hamid Khani		DIRECTOR: Elan Frank					ON-LINE DATE: 07/21

MEDIA NO.	SCENE/SHOT	TAKE NO.	IN	OUT	OK/NG	SOUND	REMARKS	VECTORS
4	2	1	04 44 21 14	04 44 23 12	NG		mic problem	m ←
		②	04 44 42 06	04 47 41 29	OK	car sound	car A moving through stop sign	m ←
		③	04 48 01 29	04 50 49 17	OK	brakes	car B putting on brakes (toward camera)	⊙ m
		④	04 51 02 13	04 51 42 08	OK	reaction	pedestrian reaction	→ i
5	5	1	05 03 49 18	05 04 02 07	NG	car brakes ped. yelling	ball not in front of car	⊙ m ←m ball
		2	05 05 02 29	05 06 51 11	NG	"	Again, ball problem	⊙ m ←m ball
		③	05 07 40 02	05 09 12 13	OK	car brakes ped. yelling	car swerves to avoid ball	⊙ m ←m ball
	6	①	05 12 03 28	05 14 12 01	OK	ped. yelling	kid running into street	→ i ←m child
		②	05 17 08 16	05 21 11 19	OK	car	cutaways car moving	⊙ ∙ m ↓ ↙
		3	05 22 15 03	05 26 28 00	NG	street	lines of sidewalk	↔ g

© Cengage Learning 2011

12.17 VR LOG
The VR log, or editing log, contains the necessary specifications about all video and audio information recorded on the source media. Notice the notations in the vectors column: *g, i,* and *m* refer to graphic, index, and motion vectors. The arrows show the principal directions of the index and motion vectors. Z-axis index and motion vectors are labeled with ⊙ (toward the camera) or ● (away from the camera).

and time code. Note that some postproduction people use the term *VTR log* even if the shots were recorded on tapeless media.

Although logging may initially seem like a waste of time, an accurate and carefully prepared VR log will save you time, money, and ultimately nerves during the actual editing. Besides the usual data, such as the production title, the name of the director, and the production number and date, the VR log should contain the following information:

- Media (memory card, disc, tape) number

- Scene number

- Take number

- Time code in- and out-numbers of each shot

- Whether the shot is OK or NG (if you don't have a designated OK/NG column, you can simply circle the good takes in the third column)

- Important audio information

- Remarks (brief description of the scene or event)

- Vector type and direction

You will probably not find a vectors column in commercially available editing log forms or computer displays, but vectors provide extremely important logging information. As discussed in chapter 6, they depict lines and something pointing or moving in a particular direction. (We elaborate on vectors further in chapter 13.) The advantage of a vector designation is that you can identify a particular screen direction quickly and easily without having to play the source clips again.

If, for example, you need a shot that has objects moving in the opposite direction from the previous shot, all you need to do is glance down the vectors column and look for shots whose *m* symbol (indicating a motion vector) has arrows pointing in an opposing direction. As you can see in figure 12.17, the vector notations use arrows for the main direction of *g* (graphic), *i* (index), and *m* (motion) vectors. **ZVL10** EDITING→ Postproduction guidelines→ VTR log

KEY CONCEPT

The vector notations on the VR log facilitate locating shots that point in specific directions.

A circled dot ⊙ indicates somebody looking at or moving toward the camera; a single dot • indicates somebody looking or moving away from the camera. Don't worry too much about the vectors column right now, but after you have read chapter 13 you should revisit figure 12.17 and study the vectors column once more. See whether it helps you visualize the shot sequence listed on this editing log.

Most editing software allows you to enter specific log information and, in some cases, even actual pictures of the first and last frames of each clip. The thumbnail frames help greatly in locating clips. If using thumbnail frames, you can skip the vectors column because you can clearly see the principal vectors of each clip's first and last frames.

The advantage of a computerized log is that you can quickly find a particular scene by entering either the filename or the time code number. You can then automatically transfer it to the EDL, which will guide the final sequencing of the edit master recording.

☑ **Transcribe the audio text** Transcribing all speech to typed pages is another time-consuming but important pre-editing chore. Once it is done, it definitely speeds up the editing phase. If, for example, you need to edit a long interview or cut a speech so that it fits an allotted time slot, reading the printed page gives you a much quicker overview than repeatedly listening to the audio on the video recording. Because scanning a page is much faster than listening to the track word for word, you can jump around in the text with great speed. Of course, in most news coverage you have no time for such transcriptions; all you can usually do is run the source clips and take notes about which ones best tell the story. `ZVL11` EDITING→ Postproduction guidelines→ audio transcript

▣ PRE-EDIT DECISION-MAKING

We are jumping the gun a little because even the most basic editing decision-making presupposes a basic knowledge of selection criteria—why you choose one clip over another. These criteria are the subject of chapter 13. For now, you need to know the initial procedural steps because they will influence, at least to some extent, your selection of clips in the decision-making phase.

Clips Selection

Unless you are editing news footage that gets into your hands just 30 minutes before the newscast, think again about what it is you want to tell the viewer. This means going back to the basic program objective (communication intent) and the angle that you originally stated. After all, how can you select and assemble event essences if you don't know what the story is all about? The actual video-recorded clips may suggest a slight variation or a restatement of the original objective, but don't let spectacular shots negate the original approach.

Visualize as best as you can the most relevant clips. If you can't remember a specific sequence, rerun the clip. One of the great advantages of nonlinear editing over linear editing is that you can call up any clip for review in a fraction of a second, no matter where it may be located on the NLE hard drive. Such a review will inevitably suggest a tentative sequence and, more importantly, will give you a chance to identify the takes you are pretty sure you won't use (but don't throw them away just yet—you may decide to use them after all).

Clips Sequencing: Paper-and-Pencil Editing

A simple way to create the first tentative edit decision list is by paper-and-pencil editing, or paper editing for short. This is how it works:

1. Watch, once again, the source clips that you would like to use and see which shots strike you as especially relevant and effective. Such a review will suggest, however indirectly, a tentative sequence.

2. When done with this review, think more seriously about sequencing. While keeping the program objective and the available footage in mind, prepare a rough storyboard (see figure 12.15). This is the time to take a good look at the

MEDIA NO.	SCENE/ SHOT	TAKE NO.	IN	OUT	TRANSITION	SOUND	REMARKS
1	2	2	01 46 13 14	01 46 15 02	CUT	car	
		3	01 51 10 29	01 51 11 21	CUT	car	
	3	4	02 05 55 17	02 05 56 02	CUT	ped. yelling—brakes	
		5	02 07 43 17	02 08 46 01	CUT	brakes	
		6	02 51 40 02	02 51 41 07	CUT	ped. yelling—brakes	

PRODUCTION TITLE: Traffic Safety   PRODUCTION NO: 114   OFF-LINE DATE: 07/15

PRODUCER: Hamid Khani   DIRECTOR: Elan Frank   ON-LINE DATE: 07/21

© Cengage Learning 2011

12.18 HANDWRITTEN EDIT DECISION LIST
The EDL is the road map for on-line editing. It lists the media number, the scene and take numbers, the in- and out-numbers for each selected shot, and major audio information. This handwritten EDL contains information for the first, tentative edit.

VR log and locate the key clips. If several clips would be equally effective for a particular scene, list them all.

> KEY CONCEPT
>
> Paper-and-pencil editing is a good way to create a preliminary editing guide.

3. Identify the selected clips with the time code in- and out-numbers and add them to your handwritten EDL. Sometimes it is the audio that dictates the sequence rather than the video portion of the clip. Indicate such places by making notes in the sound and remarks column. **SEE 12.18** ZVL12 EDITING→ Linear editing→ paper edit

■ OFF-LINE AND ON-LINE EDITING

Regardless of whether you are engaged in linear or nonlinear editing, *off-line editing* usually refers to a preliminary, low-quality edited version intended for critical review. *On-line editing*, on the other hand, always results in the final edited version for broadcast or other forms of distribution. The way you do off- and on-line editing, however, is quite different for linear and nonlinear approaches. In any case, you are now ready to sit down and do some actual editing.

If you have done a good job with your paper-and-pencil editing, you can try to edit the first tentative sequence of clips as indicated on your handwritten EDL. This will give you a rough idea of how the clip sequence looks and feels—appropriately called a *rough-cut*. The process of producing a rough-cut is called "off-line" because its result is not intended for distribution. On-line editing produces the edit master for final release. Even if the off- and on-line processes don't differ much in intent—to first produce a rough-cut and then a final edit master—they differ considerably in editing procedure.

Linear Off-Line and On-Line Editing

In linear editing, the rough-cut is usually made using lower-quality equipment. This first tentative edit is done with cuts-only and normally shows the clip sequences without any special transitions, effects, or audio sweetening. At this point don't worry too much about edit glitches or frame-accurate audio. You can do the fine-tuning in the on-line phase. All you want to do at this point is see whether the selected clips tell the story.

Once you and the client are satisfied, you redo the off-line edit with the best equipment available, using your off-line EDL or rough-cut as a guide. This then becomes your final on-line edit, which results in the edit master recording. **ZVL13** EDITING→ Linear editing→ on-line edit

Nonlinear Off-Line and On-Line Editing

In nonlinear editing, off-line means that the selected source clips are first captured in low-resolution video for the preliminary edit, or rough-cut. This saves storage space on the NLE computer. Because you capture the clips in low resolution, you usually have enough room on the hard drive to import several different takes of the selected clips so that you can try out a few to find the one that optimizes the desired sequence. Thanks to the relative ease with which you can manipulate the clips and change their sequence, you can produce several versions and pick the one that meets your and your client's expectations. You can now use this rough-cut to generate the computerized EDL, which will then tell you which clips to render in high resolution for the final on-line edit. **SEE 12.19** Note that at this point you still need to add all of the transitions and effects as well as mix the sound track. Once this is done, you can export the final on-line version to the edit master disc or tape. **ZVL14** EDITING→ Nonlinear editing→ off-line and on-line

On-Line Editing Procedures

Regardless of whether you use a linear or a nonlinear editing system, on-line editing will produce the final edit master recording. In a way, on-line editing is easier than off-line editing because the editing decisions have already been made in the off-line process and listed on the EDL. From this point on, the EDL usually guides the on-line edit. **ZVL15** EDITING→ Linear editing→ on-line edit

In linear editing, the edit controller will read the in- and out-numbers and help you set up the source and record VTRs for the final edits. In nonlinear editing, the EDL will tell you or the computer which files to play in which order and which transitions and effects to use during sequencing.

Although it is still possible to make last-minute changes at this point, try to avoid them. More often than not, such eleventh-hour decisions make the edit less effective than the previous version.

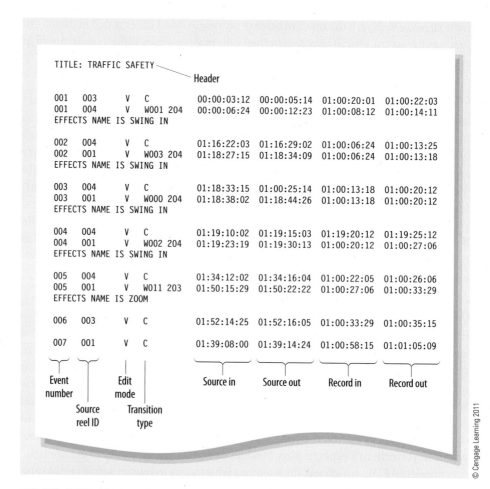

12.19 FINAL EDIT DECISION LIST

The final EDL usually lists the names of the shots (or of the clips in nonlinear editing), their time code in- and out-numbers, the length of each shot, the major transitions and effects, the location of video and audio track numbers, and other technical information.

The on-line postproduction facilities for linear editing normally consist of a single multiple-source editing system located in the on-line suite. In comparison you can have a high-powered nonlinear editing setup in a corner of your study.

You can do modest NLE projects with a laptop computer, appropriate software, and headphones. To meet fairly complex nonlinear editing demands, however, you need a slightly more elaborate setup with dual monitors, good loudspeakers, an audio console, a server, and a high-speed computer with a high-capacity hard drive. **SEE 12.20**

In an instructional setting, you will find several editing bays side-by-side in a single room. The advantage of such an arrangement is that when you are working with other people on a similar, or the same, project, you can readily consult one another without having to run from room to room. Also, the instructor can more easily

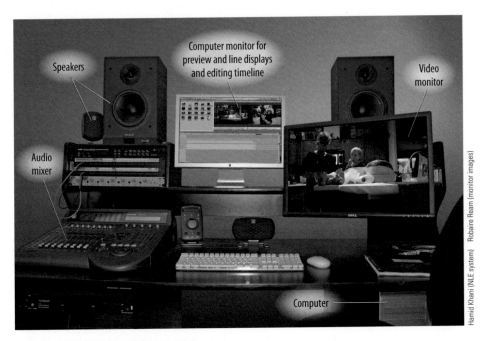

Hamid Khani (NLE system)   Robaire Ream (monitor images)

12.20 NONLINEAR EDITING SETUP

The nonlinear setup normally has a high-speed, high-capacity computer; a keyboard; a display for the editing interface and one for viewing the edited sequences; a small audio mixer; and speakers for stereo sound.

supervise a class and provide quick help when needed. The disadvantage is that the audio will spill from one bay to the next, unless everybody wears headphones.

Two final points: Editing is always more time-consuming than you initially thought and budgeted for; and despite the great assistance from edit controllers and nonlinear computing power, it is still you who has to make the choices about which shot goes where. How to make the right aesthetic decisions is the subject of chapter 13.

M A I N   P O I N T S

▶ **Nonlinear Editing**

The basic principle of nonlinear editing (NLE) is file management. The NLE system uses computers with high-capacity hard drives and associated video and audio for all three editing phases: capture (importing) of all source clips; editing, the selection and the sequencing of clips and their audio; and exporting the edited version to the final edit master media (usually videotape or disc).

▶ **Linear Editing**

The use of videotape recorders (VTRs) designates linear editing, whether the recording is analog or digital. The basic principle of linear editing is copying sections of the source tapes in the desired sequence to the edit master tape.

▶ ***Single- and Multiple-Source Systems***

The simplest linear editing system consists of a source VTR and a record VTR. The source VTR provides the selected clips in a specific order, and the record VTR records them on the edit master tape. Single-source VTR editing systems are limited to cuts-only transitions. Dissolves, wipes, and other special-effects transitions are possible only with multiple-source editing systems, which use at least two source VTRs. The pulse-count and address-code systems aid in finding a specific clip or frame, and the edit controller assists in sequencing them.

▶ ***Linear Assemble and Insert Editing***

In assemble editing, an entire source clip is transferred to the edit master tape. Assemble edits are often unstable because the edit master tape is prone to breakups at the edit points, where the control track may not match up properly with that of the previous shot. Assemble editing does not permit split edits. Insert edits are highly stable. The source clips do not transfer their own control track but use the prelaid control track of the edit master tape. Insert editing allows split edits.

▶ ***Production Tips for Postproduction***

Efficient postproduction starts in the production phase. It includes shooting for continuity, properly slating each take, leaving edit margins, recording background sounds for masking edits, recording cutaways for smooth vector continuity, and, of course, keeping a field log that lists all takes, good and bad.

▶ ***Postproduction Preparations***

The most important step before editing is to make protection copies of all of the source footage. You can do this during the capture phase. The next steps include adding time code (if necessary), making a window dub, and reviewing and logging all recorded source clips by time code in- and out-numbers. This becomes your VR log. When using logging software, you also need to name each clip. Noting the various vectors in the vector column helps identify each shot's principal screen directions. Although time-consuming, transcribing the entire audio text will greatly facilitate the editing process.

▶ ***Pre-Edit Decision-Making***

This phase includes selecting the relevant clips and putting them in a preliminary sequence. This activity is called paper-and-pencil editing.

▶ ***Off-Line and On-Line Editing***

Linear and nonlinear off-line editing refer to a preliminary, lower-quality edit intended only for critical review. Off-line linear editing produces a preliminary edit decision list (EDL) or a rough-cut. On-line linear editing produces the final edit master tape. In nonlinear editing, off-line refers to the capture of source footage and file manipulation at low picture resolution. On-line refers to recapturing the off-line footage at a higher resolution according to the EDL. The resulting footage is exported to an appropriate edit master media, such as videotape, a DVD, or some other digital storage device.

Z E T T L ' S   V I D E O L A B

For your reference or to track your work, the *Zettl's VideoLab* program cues in this chapter are listed here with their corresponding page numbers.

KEY TERMS

complexity editing Building an intensified screen event from carefully selected and juxtaposed shots. Does not have to adhere to the continuity principles.

continuing vectors Graphic vectors that extend each other, or index and motion vectors that point and move in the same direction.

continuity editing Preserving visual continuity from shot to shot.

converging vectors Index and motion vectors that point toward each other.

cutaway A shot of an object or event that is peripherally connected with the overall event and that is relatively static. Commonly used between two shots that do not provide good continuity.

diverging vectors Index and motion vectors that point away from each other.

jogging Frame-by-frame advancement of a recorded shot sequence, resulting in a jerking motion.

jump cut An image that jumps slightly from one screen position to another during a cut. Also, any gross visual discontinuity from shot to shot.

mental map Tells us where things are or are supposed to be in on- and off-screen space.

vector line An imaginary line created by extending converging index vectors or the direction of a motion vector. Also called the *line of conversation and action,* the *hundredeighty* (for 180 degrees), and, simply, the *line.*

Editing Principles

Once you feel comfortable with the basics of linear and nonlinear editing systems and their use in postproduction editing, you will discover that the real challenge of editing is not necessarily in mastering the equipment but in telling a story effectively and, especially, in selecting shots that compose a smooth shot sequence. A master editor must know not only how to operate the machines but especially how to tell a story and make a shot sequence flow. But what does this mean? This chapter acquaints you with some of the basic aesthetic editing principles.

- **EDITING PURPOSE**
  Why we edit
- **EDITING FUNCTIONS**
  Combining, condensing, correcting, and building
- **AESTHETIC PRINCIPLES OF CONTINUITY EDITING**
  The mental map, vectors, on- and off-screen positions, and cutting on action
- **AESTHETIC PRINCIPLES OF COMPLEXITY EDITING**
  Intensifying the event and supplying meaning

EDITING PURPOSE

Editing means selecting certain portions of an event or events and putting them into a meaningful sequence. The nature of such sequencing depends on the specific editing purpose: to cut a 20-minute video recording of an important news story to 20 seconds to make it fit the format; to join a series of close-up details so that they make sense and flow without any visual bumps; or to juxtapose certain shots so that they take on added meaning.

Basically, we edit to tell a story that makes sense and has impact. All editing equipment is designed to make the selection of clips, and their joining through transitions, as easy and efficient as possible. But whether you work with simple cuts-only videotape-editing equipment or a highly sophisticated nonlinear editing system, the functions and the basic aesthetic principles of editing remain the same.

> **KEY CONCEPT**
> Editing means selecting significant event details and putting them into a sequence to tell a story with clarity and impact.

■ EDITING FUNCTIONS

The specific editing functions are combining, condensing, correcting, and building. Although these functions frequently overlap, there is always a predominant one that determines the editing approach and style—the selection of shots, their length and sequence, and the transitions with which they are joined.

Combine

The simplest kind of editing is combining program portions. For instance, you may want to combine the segments you video-recorded during your vacation so that they are in chronological sequence on the edited version. Your carefully kept field log will aid you greatly in locating the source media and the specific clips. Because you simply hook the video-recorded pieces together, there is no need for transitions; it can be "cuts-only." The more aware you are of the desired sequence during the actual shooting, the easier it will be to combine the shots in this postproduction phase.

Condense

Often you edit to condense the material—to reduce the overall length of the program or program portion. The most drastic condensing is done in television news. As an editor of news footage, you are often called upon to cut extraordinary stories to unreasonably brief segments. It is not unusual to have to shorten a 30-minute speech to 10 seconds, the 20 hours of a rescue operation to a mere 20 seconds, or the 50 minutes of graphic war footage, video-recorded by a daring camera crew, to a mere 5 seconds. The infamous "sound bites" are a direct outgrowth of such drastic editing. Statements by public officials are tailored to a series of brief and memorable catchphrases rather than sensible narrative, very much in the spirit of advertising slogans.

But even in less drastic editing, you will find that it is often hard to part with some of the footage, especially if it took extra effort to record. As an editor, try to detach yourself as much as possible from the preproduction and production efforts and concentrate simply on what you need to show and say rather than what you have available. Don't use three shots if you can communicate the same message with one. Such editing requires that you identify the essence of an event and use only those shots that best serve the process message.

> **KEY CONCEPT**
>
> The condensing function of editing requires recognizing the event essence and selecting shots that best serve the process message.

Correct

Editing to fix production mistakes can be one of the most difficult, time-consuming, and costly postproduction activities. Even simple mistakes, such as the company president's misreading a word during her monthly address, can present a formidable problem when trying to match the body positions and the voice levels of the old (before the mistake) and new (after the mistake) takes. A good director will not pick up the speech exactly where the mistake was made but will go back to where a new idea is introduced in the speech so that a change in shots is properly motivated. Starting the "pickup" (new shot) from a different point of view (a tighter or looser shot or a different angle) will make the cut and a slight shift in voice level appear deliberate and ensure continuity.

More serious production problems, such as trying to match uneven colors and sound, can be a real headache for the editor. White-balancing the camera in each new lighting environment and watching the VU meter while listening carefully to the sound pickup are certainly easier than trying to "fix them in post."

Such seemingly minor oversights as the talent's wearing her coat buttoned while standing up but unbuttoned when sitting cannot be fixed in post even by the most experienced editor; they call for costly retakes. Again, meticulous attention to all preproduction details and keeping a close watch on every aspect of production can reduce many of the costly "fixing in post" activities.

> **KEY CONCEPT**
>
> Careful attention to preproduction and production details can obviate most corrective editing.

Build

The most satisfying editing is done when you can build a show from a great many carefully recorded shots. Some postproduction people think—not without cause— that the video recording during the production provides merely the bricks and mortar and that it is up to the editor to construct the building—to give the raw material shape and meaning. Regardless of whether editing is done to show an event as clearly as possible or to reveal its intensity and complexity—or a combination of the two—you need to apply one or both of the major aesthetic editing principles: continuity and complexity. **ZVL1** EDITING→ Functions→ select | combine | correct | try it

■ AESTHETIC PRINCIPLES OF CONTINUITY EDITING

Continuity editing means creating seamless transitions from one event detail to the next so that the story flows even though a great deal of information is purposely omitted. The aesthetic principles of continuity editing are concerned not so much with the logic of the story line and its narrative flow but with how the pictures and the sound from one shot carry over to the next.

Unlike the painter or still photographer, who is concerned with the effective composition of a single image, as a video editor you must compare the aesthetic elements of one picture with those of another and determine whether they lead smoothly from one to the other when seen in succession. Over the years of filmmaking, certain ways of achieving visual continuity became so firmly established that they matured from conventions to principles and now apply equally to video production.

The major principles of continuity editing are the mental map, vectors, on- and off-screen positions, and cutting on action.

Mental Map

Every time we watch television or a film, we automatically try to make sense of where things are and in what direction they move on and off the screen. In effect, we construct a *mental map* of such on- and off-screen positions and directions. For example, if you see somebody looking screen-left in a two-shot, he should also be looking screen-left in a close-up. **SEE 13.1**

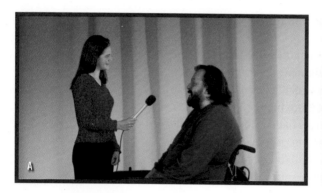

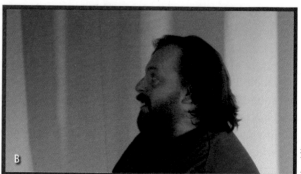

13.1 MENTAL MAP

To help establish the mental map of where things are in off-screen space, you need to be consistent with where people look.

A When someone looks screen-left in a medium shot . . .

B . . . he should look in approximately the same direction in a close-up.

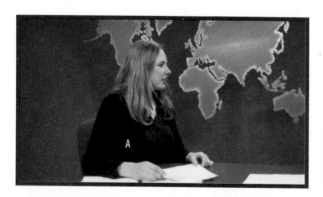

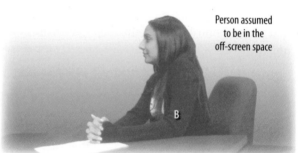

Person assumed
to be in the
off-screen space

13.2 MENTAL MAP OF RIGHT OFF-SCREEN POSITION

If you show person A looking and talking screen-right in a medium shot, we assume person B to be located in the right off-screen space, looking screen-left.

Person assumed
to be in the
off-screen space

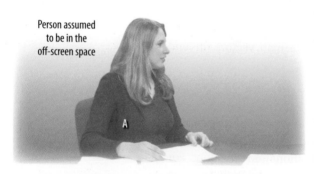

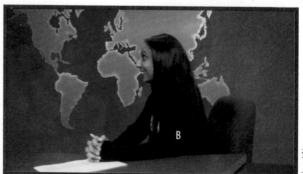

13.3 MENTAL MAP OF LEFT OFF-SCREEN POSITION

When we now see person B in a medium shot looking and talking screen-left, we assume person A to be in the left off-screen space.

If you see a news anchor in a medium shot looking screen-right during a two-way conversation, your mental map suggests that the other person is located somewhere in the right off-screen space. **SEE 13.2** According to the established mental map, the next shot must show the partner looking screen-left, with the first person having moved into the left off-screen space. **SEE 13.3** To show both persons looking in the same direction in subsequent shots would go against the mental map and suggest that both are talking to a third person. **SEE 13.4**

If, during a three-way conversation, you see one of three news anchors in a medium shot first looking screen-right and then screen-left, you expect somebody to be sitting on both sides of her rather than two people on one side or the other. **SEE 13.5** But if you see the anchor in a medium shot consistently looking screen-right during the three-way conversation, you expect the two other people to be sitting

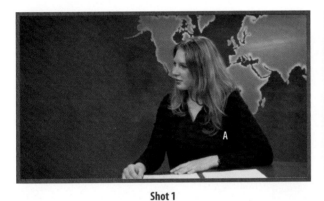

Shot 1   Shot 2

13.4 DIFFERENT MENTAL MAP OF OFF-SCREEN POSITION
Showing persons A and B looking in the same direction in subsequent shots would suggest that both are talking to a third person.

13.5 PERSON LOOKING SCREEN-RIGHT AND SCREEN-LEFT
When a person in a medium shot looks screen-right in shot 1, then screen-left in shot 2, we expect the other people to be sitting on both sides of her.

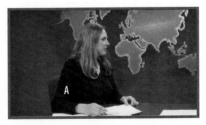
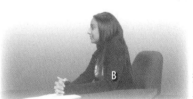

Shot 1

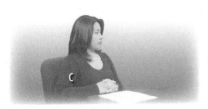
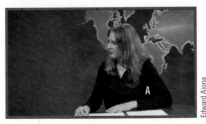

Shot 2

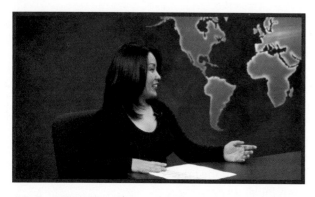

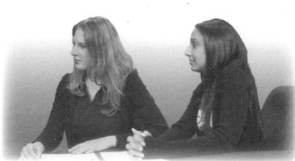

13.6 PERCEIVED SCREEN-RIGHT POSITION OF ANCHORS

When the news anchor continues to look screen-right during a three-way conversation, we expect her two partners to be sitting in the right off-screen space.

13.7 ACTUAL SCREEN POSITIONS

When seen in a long shot, the mental map of off-screen space coincides with the actual positions of the three people.

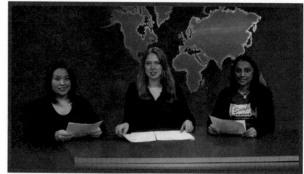

screen-right of her, although we cannot actually see them. **SEE 13.6** A three-shot of all the speakers shows that your mental map was accurate. **SEE 13.7**

As you can see, the mental map covers not only on-screen space but also off-screen space. Once such a mental map is established, you must adhere to it unless you purposely want to shake the viewers out of their perceptual expectations. Applying continuity principles will keep the map intact. **ZVL2** EDITING→ Continuity→ mental map

Vectors

As you recall from chapter 6, vectors are directional forces that lead our eyes from one point to another on the screen and even off it. They can be strong or weak, depending on how forcefully they suggest or move in a specific direction. Keeping the mental map intact requires proper vector continuity. **ZVL3** EDITING→ Continuity→ vectors

Continuity of graphic vectors   If you shoot a scene with a prominent graphic vector as the horizon line, such as a skyline, the ocean, a desert, or a mountain range, you need to make sure that the height of the horizon line is consistent in subsequent

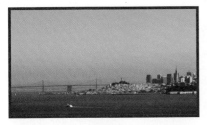
Shot 1

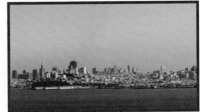
Shot 2

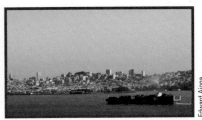
Shot 3

Edward Aiona

13.8 GRAPHIC VECTOR CONTINUITY
To prevent the horizon line from jumping up and down during subsequent shots, you need to make sure that it forms a continuous graphic vector from shot to shot.

shots and that it does not jump up or down. **SEE 13.8** You can accomplish this vector continuity simply by marking the horizon line of the first shot with a piece of tape on the viewfinder and aligning all subsequent shots according to the tape.

Directions of index and motion vectors   Index and motion vectors can be continuing, converging, or diverging.

 Continuing vectors follow each other or move or point in the same direction. **SEE 13.9** They must "continue"—point in the same screen direction—even if shown in separate shots. **SEE 13.10** If you show one of the people looking in the opposite direction in the close-up, you will jolt the established continuity. Instead of the

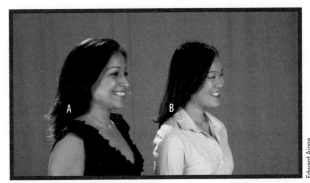
Edward Aiona

13.9 CONTINUING INDEX VECTORS IN A SINGLE SHOT
Continuing vectors point or move in the same direction. The continuing index vectors of these two people suggest that they are looking at the same target object.

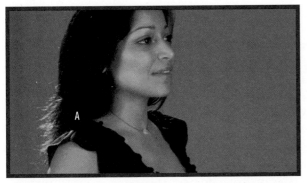
Shot 1

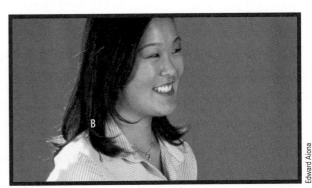
Shot 2

Edward Aiona

13.10 CONTINUING INDEX VECTORS IN SUCCESSIVE SHOTS
Even when seen in two successive close-ups (shots 1 and 2), these continuing index vectors suggest that the two persons (A and B) are looking at a common target object.

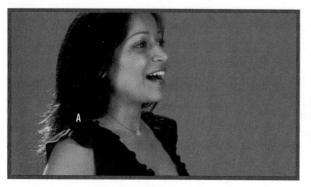 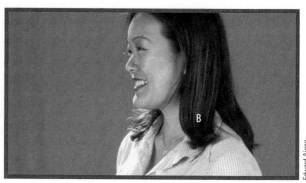

Shot 1   Shot 2

13.11 INDEX VECTOR REVERSAL IN SUCCESSIVE SHOTS
By reversing one of the index vectors (shot 2), we assume that the two persons (A and B) are looking at each other instead of at a common target object.

13.12 CONVERGING INDEX VECTORS IN A SINGLE SHOT
Converging vectors point or move toward each other. The index vectors of the two people (A and B) looking at each other converge.

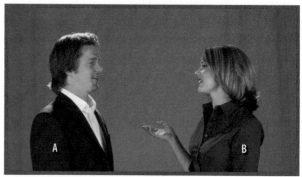

two people looking in the same direction, the mental map now tells us that they must be looking at each other. **SEE 13.11**

    Converging vectors move or point toward each other. **SEE 13.12** To maintain the mental map, you must maintain their direction in subsequent single shots. **SEE 13.13**

    Diverging vectors move or point away from each other. **SEE 13.14** Again, subsequent close-ups must maintain the diverging vector direction. **SEE 13.15**

    Vectors, of course, can change their directions in a single shot. In that case, the follow-up shot must continue the index or motion vector as seen just before the cut. For instance, if you show somebody running screen-left who then turns midscreen and runs screen-right, the subsequent shot must show the person continuing to run screen-right.

    Someone looking directly into the camera or walking toward or away from it constitutes a z-axis index or motion vector. As you recall, the z-axis is the depth dimension or the imaginary line that stretches from the camera to the horizon. Whether we perceive a series of z-axis shots as continuing, converging, or diverging depends on the event context. If you follow a two-shot that shows two people looking at each other with successive close-ups of each person looking into the camera, we perceive their successive z-axis vectors as converging: they are still looking at each other. **SEE 13.16**

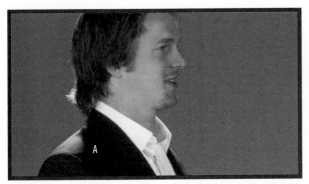

Shot 1　　　　　　　　　　　　**Shot 2**

13.13 CONVERGING INDEX VECTORS IN SUCCESSIVE SHOTS
When seen in successive close-ups (shots 1 and 2), the index vector of person A must converge with that of person B.

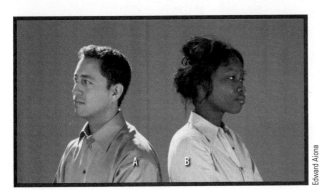

13.14 DIVERGING INDEX VECTORS IN A SINGLE SHOT
When two persons (A and B) look away from each other in a two-shot, their index vectors diverge.

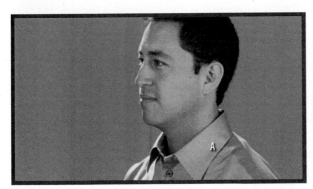

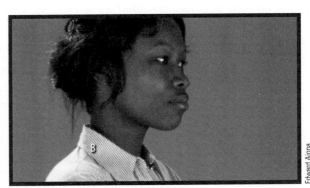

Shot 1　　　　　　　　　　　　**Shot 2**

13.15 DIVERGING INDEX VECTORS IN SUCCESSIVE SHOTS
To show that the index vectors are diverging in successive close-ups (shots 1 and 2), the index vectors of persons A and B must reflect the two-shot (figure 13.14).

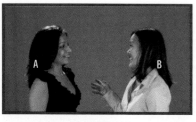
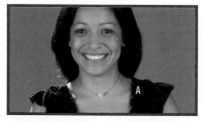
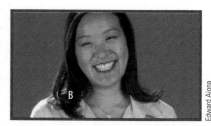

Shot 1   Shot 2   Shot 3

Edward Aiona

13.16 CONVERGING Z-AXIS INDEX VECTORS

Shot 1 establishes the index vectors of persons A and B as converging. By establishing that the vectors converge (shot 1), we perceive the subsequent z-axis close-ups of A and B in shots 2 and 3 also as converging.

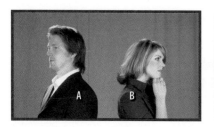
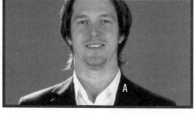
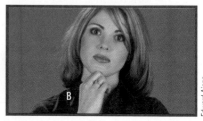

Shot 1   Shot 2   Shot 3

Edward Aiona

13.17 TWO-SHOT WITH DIVERGING INDEX VECTORS

If the context in shot 1 establishes that the two people (A and B) are looking away from each other, the vectors in the subsequent z-axis shots (2 and 3) are also perceived as diverging.

If the context (two-shot) shows that the two people are looking away from each other, we perceive the identical z-axis close-ups as diverging index vectors. **SEE 13.17**

On- and Off-Screen Positions

As shown in figures 13.1 through 13.7, we tend to create a mental map that helps us tell where people are located even if we can't see them. Such an off-screen map helps preserve visual continuity and ultimately stabilize the environment. In vector terms, we place a person off-screen wherever the on-screen index vector points. The same is true for on-screen positions: once we establish person A on screen-left and person B on screen-right, we expect them to remain there even if we cut to a different point of view. Such position continuity is especially important in over-the-shoulder and cross-shots. **SEE 13.18** In shots 1 and 2, person A remains screen-left and person B remains screen-right. Our mental map would be disturbed if we saw A and B change places in shot 3—we would perceive them as playing musical chairs. **SEE 13.19**

Vector line The navigation device that helps maintain on-screen positions and motion continuity is called the ***vector line***, the line of conversation and action, the hundredeighty (for 180 degrees), or, simply, the line. The vector line is an extension of converging index vectors or of a motion vector in the direction of travel. **SEE 13.20**

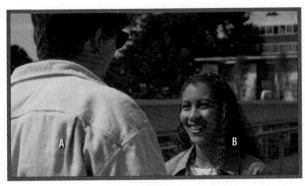

Shot 1

Shot 2

13.18 PRESERVING ON-SCREEN POSITIONS

When person B is first seen screen-right (shot 1), we expect her to remain there even when cutting to a different point of view, as in this over-the-shoulder sequence (shot 2).

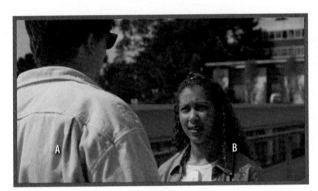

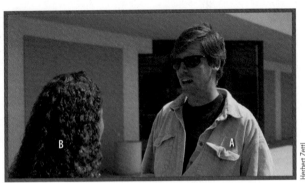

Shot 1

Shot 3

13.19 REVERSING ON-SCREEN POSITIONS

Our mental map is disturbed when person B appears screen-left in the over-the-shoulder shot (shot 3).

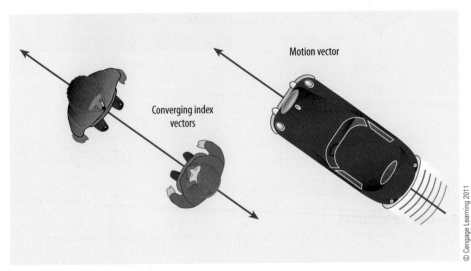

13.20 FORMING THE VECTOR LINE

The vector line is formed by extending converging index vectors or by extending a motion vector.

Motion vector

Converging index vectors

To maintain on-screen positions during over-the-shoulder shooting (with person A screen-left and person B screen-right), you must keep the cameras on the same side of the vector line. **SEE 13.21** Crossing the line would result in a musical chair–like switch of A and B. **SEE 13.22** Although you may argue that you would not confuse A and B even if they switched screen positions, crossing the line would definitely disturb the mental map and generate a big continuity bump; at best, it would inhibit optimal communication.

A similar problem occurs if you shoot two side-by-side people from the front and the back along the z-axis. Such a sequencing problem is common when covering a wedding, when you show the bride and the groom first from the front and then from

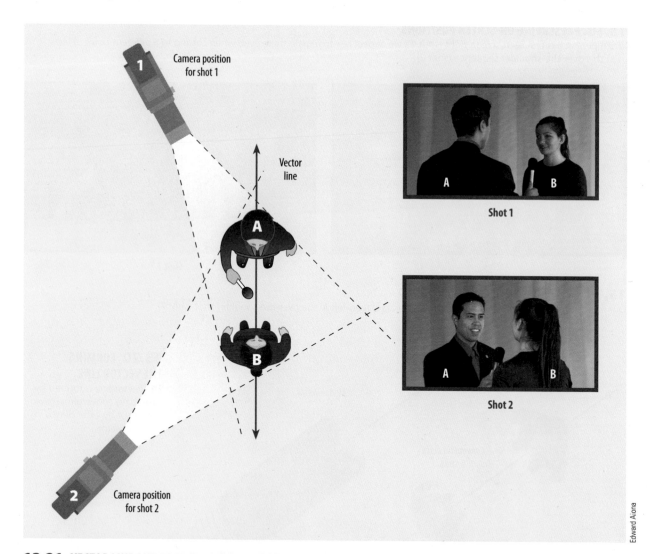

13.21 VECTOR LINE AND PROPER CAMERA POSITIONS
To maintain the screen positions of persons A and B in over-the-shoulder shooting, the cameras must be on the same side of the vector line.

the back while walking down the isle. When cutting the two shots together, the two people switch positions. **SEE 13.23**

To get around this "wedding switch," you can move to the side with the camera when the couple walks by and see them change positions within the shot. When cutting to the shot from behind, they have already switched positions.

When cross shooting, crossing the line will change the properly converging index vectors to improperly continuing vectors. Instead of having two people look at and talk with each other, they seem to be talking to a third person. **SEE 13.24**

When placing cameras on both sides of the motion vector line, the object motion will be reversed with each cut. **SEE 13.25** To preserve the direction of the object

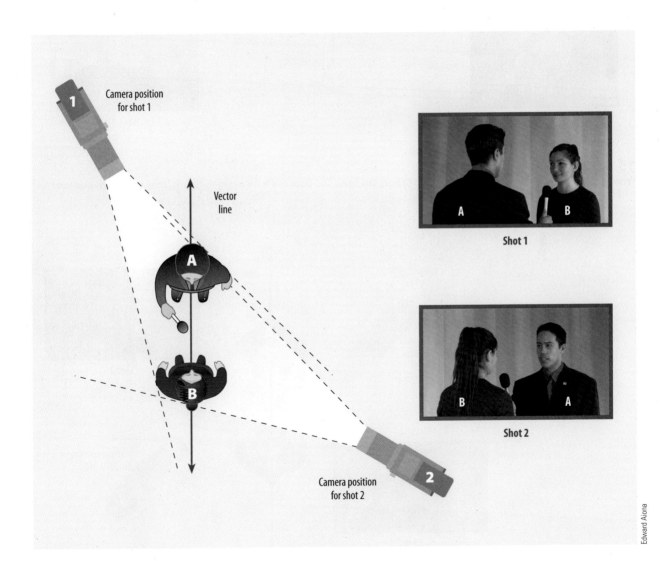

Edward Aiona

13.22 CROSSING THE VECTOR LINE
Crossing the vector line with one of the two cameras will result in a position switch of persons A and B. They will seem to play musical chairs.

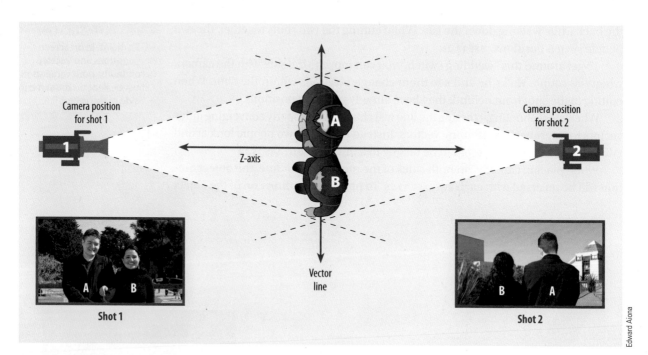

13.23 Z-AXIS POSITION SWITCH
When you shoot two people side-by-side (A and B) from the front and from the back along the z-axis, they will switch positions when the shots are edited together.

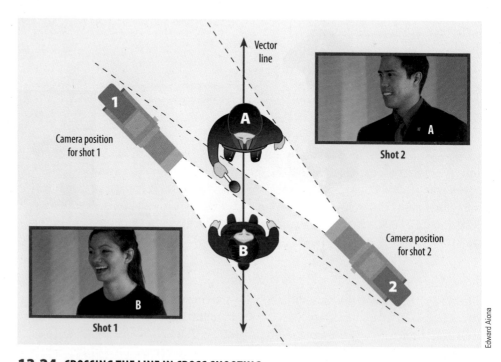

13.24 CROSSING THE LINE IN CROSS SHOOTING
When you cross the line in cross shooting, persons A and B seem to be looking in the same direction. The converging index vectors have become continuing ones.

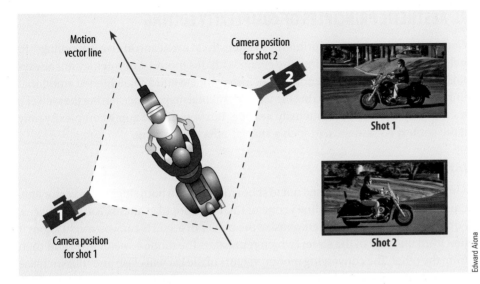

13.25 CROSSING THE MOTION VECTOR LINE
When crossing the motion vector line, the object motion will be reversed with each cut.

Edward Aiona

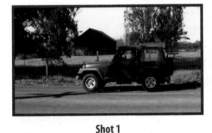

Shot 1

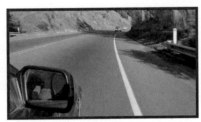

Shot 2

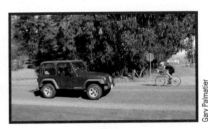

Shot 3

Gary Palmatier

13.26 CUTAWAY
If you want to show that a subject continues to move in the same direction although the successive shot shows it moving in the opposite direction (shots 1 and 3), you can establish a continuing motion vector by inserting a neutral cutaway (shot 2).

motion, you need to position both cameras on the same side of the motion vector line. (Covering a football game from both sides of the field is not a good idea.)

If you need to convey that an object moves in a single direction although two successive shots show it moving in opposite directions, you can insert a *cutaway*— a thematically related, usually nonmoving, shot that separates the two opposing motion vectors. **SEE 13.26** `ZVL4` EDITING→ Production guidelines→ cutaways

Cutting on Action

Always try to cut on action rather than right before or after. For example, if you have to cut from a close-up to a loose medium shot of somebody getting up from a chair, wait until he starts to rise, then cut to the medium shot just before he stands. This will be a much smoother transition than if you were to cut from his sitting to just before he stands or, worse, after he finishes getting up.

AESTHETIC PRINCIPLES OF COMPLEXITY EDITING

Complexity editing is done primarily to intensify an event and to give it meaning—to help us gain deeper insight into the event. With this motivation you may not always follow the rules of continuity editing but instead opt to edit for heightened emotional impact, even at the risk of jarring the viewer's mental map. In fact, jarring the viewer's mental map is one way to intensify a scene. But you should apply complexity only if the context is conducive to such a special-effects treatment.

Intensifying an Event

Although you were just advised not to shoot motion from both sides of the vector line, crossing the motion vector line is one of the more popular intensification devices. For example, if you want to emphasize the power of a sports car, you might shoot it first from one side of the street (which represents the motion vector line) and then from the other. The converging motion vectors of the car will clash and thus increase the aesthetic energy of the sequence. Because this is the only car in the two shots, we are not likely to perceive a switch in direction or see two cars racing toward each other. **SEE 13.27**

Crossing the vector line   Many music videos show rapid switching of screen directions, such as dancers or singers who flip frenetically from looking and moving in one screen direction to the opposite one. You probably noticed that this effect is accomplished by purposely crossing the vector line with the camera. When shooting from both sides of the line, you reverse the performer's index and motion vectors every time you cut. The purpose of crossing the vector line is to increase the energy of the sequence, just in case the high-volume sound, pulsating lights, and the singer's jumping up and down are not enough for you. The more rapid the switching, the more frantic the sequence appears.

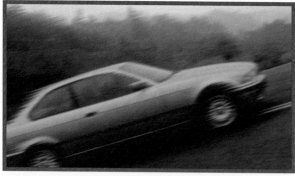

Shot 1

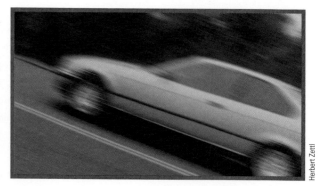

Shot 2

Herbert Zettl

13.27 INTENSIFICATION THROUGH CONVERGING MOTION VECTORS

Juxtaposing two converging motion vectors of a single prominent object, such as a powerful sports car, will intensify the object motion without destroying its vector continuity. Note that here the pictures of the car create index rather than motion vectors.

Jump cut   If you first frame a person standing next to the left screen edge, then in the succeeding shot near the right screen edge, the subject seems to vault magically from screen-left to screen-right. Such a drastic position change is aptly called a *jump cut*. You may inadvertently get a jump cut with a very slight position change. This often happens when you try to align the camera and the subject in exactly the same positions when setting up subsequent shots. Unfortunately, neither the camera nor the subject will remain in precisely the same place but will inevitably shift positions ever so slightly. When two such shots are cut together, the subtle shift appears as a sudden and highly noticeable jump. **SEE 13.28** To prevent jump cuts, always change the angle or the field of view, getting a looser or tighter shot, or insert a cutaway (see figure 13.26).

Although the jump cut is undesirable in continuity editing, it has now become fashionable through newscasts. When video editors of news footage did not have time to insert appropriate cutaways when editing interviews, they simply took a few interesting spots on the sound track and cut them together regardless of the video. Because most news interviews are shot with a single camera that is focused on the

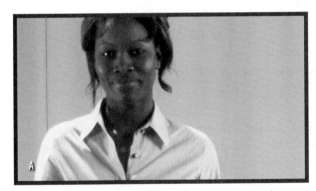

Shot 1

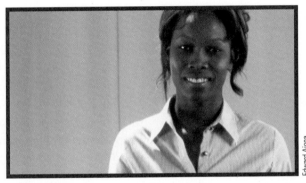

Shot 2

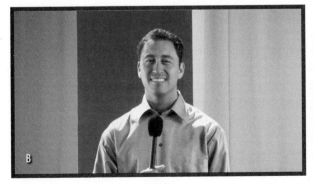

Shot 3

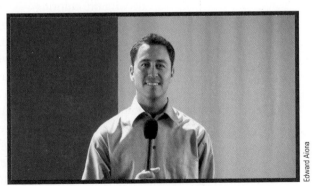

Shot 4

13.28 **JUMP CUT**

A The jump cut is caused by an extreme position change from shot 1 to shot 2.

B A relatively subtle position change from shot 3 to shot 4 results in an equally obvious jump cut.

guest throughout, the final edited version of the interview shows a series of jump cuts. Traditionally considered an aesthetic offense, jump cuts were eventually accepted by viewers because they gave some indication of where the interview had been trimmed. The jump cut is now used in commercials and even dramatic situations—not so much as an indicator of condensing time but rather as a prodding device. Like crossing the line, the jump cut jolts us out of our perceptual complacency.

Jogging   Producing a similar jolt to visual continuity, *jogging* consists of a sloweddown frame-by-frame advance of a motion, which is normally used to locate a specific frame for editing. When shown within a high-intensity scene, it draws attention to the motion itself and can heighten the drama of the shot.

Sound track   The sound track is, of course, one of the most effective and widely used intensifiers. There is hardly a car chase that—besides the squealing tires—is not accompanied by high-energy, highly rhythmic music. As you have undoubtedly experienced at rock concerts or other musical performances, it is primarily the beat and the volume of the music that supply its fundamental energy. We mentally transfer this basic sound energy readily to the video event. Low, rhythmic beats or sustaining sounds often continue even through long stretches of dialogue. When the thumps make the dialogue unintelligible, however, the intensification device has definitely misfired. There is no magic formula for just how much sound intensification you should use; all you can do is rely on your aesthetic sensitivity.

Supplying Meaning

You can create meaning not only through the actual content of a scene but also with a shot sequence. For example, if we see in the first shot a police officer struggling with a person and then, in the second shot, the person running across the street, we presume that the culprit has escaped. If we see the person running first, however, and then the police officer struggling with him, we believe that the officer has caught up with the culprit. **ZVL5** EDITING→ Functions→ quiz

You can supply additional meaning by juxtaposing the primary event with either related or contrasting events. For example, by showing how the homeless seek shelter in the city plaza and then switching to a scene of limousines driving up and elegant people entering the opera house across the street, you will not only intensify the plight of the homeless but also imply the idea of social injustice. Such a juxtaposition is called a collision montage. A montage is a carefully calculated juxtaposition of two or more separate event images that, when shown together, combine into a larger and more intense whole.[1]

You can also create audio/video montages in which the audio event either parallels or counters the basic theme of the video, such as a slow-motion battle scene accompanied by symphonic music as though it were an elegantly choreographed ballet.

> **KEY CONCEPT**
>
> A montage is a juxtaposition of two or more images that, when shown together, combine into a larger and more intense whole.

---

1. See Herbert Zettl, *Sight Sound Motion: Applied Media Aesthetics,* 6th ed. (Boston: Wadsworth, 2011), pp. 386–90. See also Steven D. Katz, *Film Directing Shot by Shot* (Studio City, CA: Michael Wiese Productions, 1991).

Complexity editing does not imply that there are no sequencing rules. Ignoring the conventions of continuity editing will not automatically lead to event intensification but more likely to viewer confusion. Exactly when and how to break the rules of continuity for effective complexity editing requires, first and foremost, a thorough knowledge of the rules plus your deliberate judgment.

With a firm grasp of the vector concept, you will be ahead of many editors who do their editing more or less intuitively. There is nothing wrong with this so long as everything goes right. But when something goes wrong, intuition might not be sufficient to fix the problem. In any case, knowledge of basic editing aesthetics will give you confidence in making optimal shot selections and sequencing choices the first time around.

MAIN POINTS

▶ **Editing Purpose and Functions**

Editing means selecting significant event details and putting them into a sequence to tell a story with clarity and impact. The basic editing functions are to combine various shots, condense footage, correct production mistakes, and build a show from selected shots.

▶ **Continuity Editing**

Continuity editing means to create seamless transitions from one event detail (shot) to the next. You do this by applying a few specific rules that make the cuts appear seamless.

▶ **Mental Map**

Editing must help the viewer construct and maintain a mental map of where things are, where they should be, and where they are going, even though only certain parts of the scene are shown in successive shots.

▶ **Vectors**

Graphic, index, and motion vectors play an important part in establishing and maintaining continuity from shot to shot. Index and motion vectors can be continuing (pointing or moving in the same direction), converging (pointing or moving toward each other), or diverging (pointing or moving away from each other).

▶ **Vector Line**

The vector line is established by extending converging index vectors or a motion vector. To maintain position and directional continuity, the camera must shoot from only one side of the vector line. In multicamera productions all cameras must shoot from the same side of the vector line.

▶ **Complexity Editing**

Complexity editing frequently violates the principles of continuity, such as crossing the vector line, to intensify the screen event. The jump cut, jogging, and the sound track are employed as energizing devices.

Z E T T L ' S   V I D E O L A B

 For your reference or to track your work, the *Zettl's VideoLab* program cues in this
chapter are listed here with their corresponding page numbers.

Production Environment: Studio, Field, and Synthetic

When you look at some of the clips you shot with an HDTV pocket recorder at your friend's home, you probably wonder why we still use studios. After all, the highly portable camcorders and lights and the wireless microphones make it possible to originate a video program anywhere, indoors or out—even in outer space. In tandem with portable transmission equipment and satellite uplinks, you don't need to re-create a street corner in the studio—you can go to the actual street corner as the background for your interview. This is true so long as it doesn't rain, the street noise doesn't obliterate your guest's answers, and you don't have kids making faces in the background of your shot.

Studios provide optimal production control and efficiency. It is, after all, much easier to cut between interviewer and guest with a switcher than to take two camcorders on-location and then do extensive editing to insert close-ups and reaction shots. On the other hand, you would have a hard time fitting a football game into even a large studio. In this case, you need to pack much of the studio's control equipment into a truck and bring it to the stadium.

Part V explains the relative advantages of the studio and field production environments and briefly touches on synthetic, computer-generated imaging.

cyclorama A U-shaped continuous piece of canvas or muslin for backing of scenery and action. Also called *cyc*. Hardwall cycs are permanently installed in front of one or two of the studio walls.

flat A piece of standing scenery used as a background or to simulate the walls of a room. There are hardwall and soft-wall flats.

floor plan A diagram of scenery, properties, and set dressings drawn on a grid.

IFB Stands for *interruptible foldback* or *feedback*. A prompting system that allows communication with the talent while on the air. A small earpiece worn by on-the-air talent carries program sound (including the talent's voice) or instructions from the producer or director.

ingest The selection, coding, and recording on a large server of various program feeds.

intercom Short for *intercommunication system*. Used for all production and engineering personnel involved in a show. The most widely used system has telephone headsets to facilitate voice communication on several wired or wireless channels. Includes other systems, such as IFB and cellular telephones.

master control Controls the program input, storage, and re-trieval for on-the-air telecasts. Also oversees the technical quality of all program material.

monitor High-quality video display used in the video studio and control rooms. Cannot receive broadcast signals. Also refers to flat-panel camera viewfinders.

PL Stands for *party line, phone line,* or *private line*. Major inter-communication device in video studios.

props Short for *properties*. Furniture and other objects used by talent and for set decoration.

SA Stands for *studio address system*. A public address loud-speaker system from the control room to the studio. Also called *studio talkback* and *PA* (public address) *system*.

studio control room A room adjacent to the studio in which the director, producer, production assistants, technical di-rector, audio engineer, and sometimes the lighting director perform their production functions.

Production Environment: Studio

The video production studio provides an environment that is independent of the weather and the restrictions of an outdoor location. It affords optimal production control. The studio facilitates the coordination and the effective use of all major production elements—cameras, lighting, sound, scenery, and the actions of production personnel and performers—making video production highly efficient.

After visiting a few studios in television stations, independent production houses, or colleges, you will soon discover that despite their differences in size and layout they all contain similar installations and equipment. Television studios are designed to facilitate the interaction of the installations and the team members for a great variety of production activities. Knowing about how a studio and its facilities function will help you make optimal use of them.

▶ **VIDEO PRODUCTION STUDIO**
   Physical layout and major installations

▶ **STUDIO CONTROL ROOM**
   Image control and sound control

▶ **MASTER CONTROL**
   Automated workflow and quality control, content ingest, and storage and archiving

▶ **STUDIO SUPPORT AREAS**
   Scenery and property storage, and makeup and dressing rooms

▶ **SCENERY, PROPERTIES, AND SET DRESSINGS**
   Softwall and hardwall flats; modules, drops, and set pieces; set and hand props; and set dressings

▶ **SET DESIGN**
   Process message, floor plan, prop list, and setup

■ VIDEO PRODUCTION STUDIO

Video production studios are designed not only for multicamera productions and teamwork but also to provide an optimal environment for single-camera video and digital cinema productions. Most studios are fairly large rectangular rooms with smooth floors and high ceilings from which the lighting instruments are suspended. They have a number of other technical installations that facilitate a great variety of productions and help make them highly efficient. **SEE 14.1**

Physical Layout

When evaluating a production studio, you should look not only at the electronic equipment it houses but also at its physical layout—its size, floor and ceiling, doors and walls, and air-conditioning.

Size   If you do a simple interview or have a single performer talk to the audience on a close-up, you can get by with amazingly little studio space. But if you plan a more ambitious project, such as a large panel discussion or the video-recording of a music show or drama, you need a larger studio. In general, it is easier to produce a small show in a large studio than a large show in a small one. But you will quickly learn that large studios are usually harder to manage than small ones. Somehow large studios require more energy to get a production started than do smaller ones; they necessitate longer camera and audio cables, more lighting instruments, and usually more crew. If you have a choice, use a studio that fits your production needs.

Floor and ceiling   A good studio must have a hard, level floor so that cameras can travel freely and smoothly. Most studio floors are concrete that is polished or covered with hard plastic or seamless linoleum.

14.1 VIDEO PRODUCTION STUDIO
A well-designed studio provides optimal control for multicamera and single-camera video productions. It facilitates teamwork and the coordination of all major production elements.

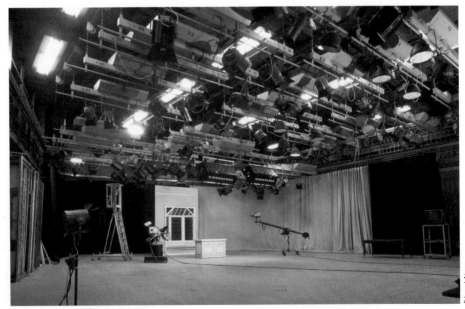

Edward Aiona

One of the most important design features of a good studio is adequate ceiling height. The ceiling must be high enough to accommodate normal 10-foot scenery and to provide enough space for the lighting grid or battens. Although you may get by with a minimum ceiling height of 14 feet for a very small studio, most professional studios have ceilings that are 30 or more feet above the studio floor. Such a high ceiling makes it possible to suspend the lighting instruments above even tall scenery and leaves adequate space above them for the heat of the lighting instruments to dissipate.

Doors and walls   Studio doors seem rather unimportant until you have to move scenery, furniture, and large equipment in and out. Undersized studio doors can cause a great deal of frustration for the production crew and frequently damage to equipment and scenery. Good studio doors must also be soundproof enough to keep all but the loudest noises from leaking into the studio.

The studio walls and ceiling are normally treated with sound-absorbing material to "deaden" the studio. A fairly "dead" studio minimizes reverberation, which means that it keeps the sounds from bouncing indiscriminately off the walls.

At least two or three sides of the studio are normally covered with a ***cyclorama***, or cyc—a continuous piece of muslin or canvas suspended from a pipe or heavy curtain track. The light-gray or light-beige cyc serves as a convenient neutral background for a variety of setups. It should be light enough so that you can tint it with colored lights. A ground row, which is a curved piece of scenery placed on the studio floor in front of the cyc, helps blend the vertical cyc into the studio floor to form a seamless background. **SEE 14.2**

Some cycloramas are suspended from a double track, with the front track holding a variety of additional curtains, called drops. The most frequently used drops are the chroma-key backdrop, which consists of a large chroma-key blue or green piece of cloth, and the black drop, used for special lighting effects.

Many studios have a built-in hardwall cyc, which covers part of a studio wall. The ground row is part of the hardwall cyc. **SEE 14.3** The advantages of a hardwall cyc are that it does not wrinkle or tear even after longtime use and it can easily be repainted. The disadvantages are that it has a high degree of sound reflectance, often causing unwanted echoes, and it takes up considerable studio space.

Air-conditioning   Many studios suffer from air-conditioning problems. Because the lighting instruments generate so much heat, the air-conditioning system must work overtime. When operating at full capacity, all but the most expensive systems create air noise, which is inevitably picked up by the sensitive studio mics and duly amplified in the audio console. You must then decide whether to keep the air-conditioning going despite the noise it makes or to turn it off and make talent, crew, and equipment sweat.

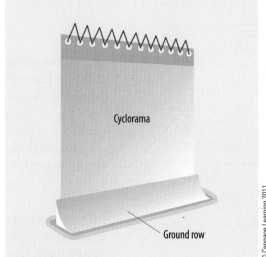

Cyclorama

Ground row

© Cengage Learning 2011

14.2 GROUND ROW
The ground row is a curved piece of scenery that is placed on the studio floor in front of the cyclorama to blend the two into a seamless background.

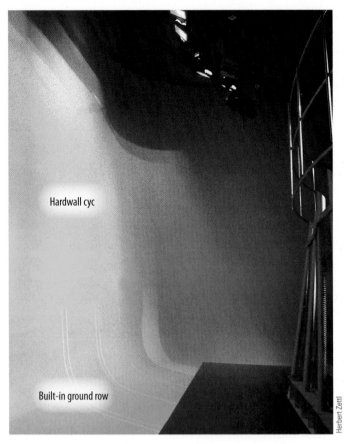

Hardwall cyc

Built-in ground row

Herbert Zettl

14.3 HARDWALL CYC

The hardwall cyc is constructed of fiberboard and placed in front of one of the studio walls. The ground row is built-in.

Major Installations

Regardless of size, all studios have similar basic technical installations, which include lights, electrical outlets, intercommunication systems, monitors, and studio speakers.

Lights   Most of the lighting instruments used in a video production studio are suspended from a lighting grid or movable battens, as shown in figure 14.1. Hanging the lighting instruments above the scenery and action keeps the lights out of camera range, allows the cameras and the people to move about freely, and, if it is a permanent set, minimizes the time needed for lighting it.

Some studios still have a physical lighting patchboard (which routes lights to specific dimmers) and even the actual dimmer controls in the studio itself. When using computerized lighting control units, you may find the main control unit in the control room and an additional remote lighting control in the studio. The one in the control room is used for the actual studio production; the one in the studio is for setup and rehearsals. The patching—the assignment of lighting instruments to dimmers—is usually done with computer software.

Electrical outlets   You may not consider wall outlets an important factor in studio design until you discover that there are not enough of them or that they are in the wrong places. There should be several groups of outlets for cameras, microphones, monitors, intercommunication headsets, and regular AC power distributed along all four walls. If all the outlets are concentrated on only one wall, you will have to string long power cables and extension cords throughout the studio to get the equipment into the desired positions around the scenery.

All outlets must be clearly marked so that you do not plug equipment into the wrong outlet. This labeling is especially important when the outlets are behind the cyc, where it is usually dark and there is little space to maneuver.

Intercommunication systems   Reliable *intercom* systems are one of the most important technical installations. Normal studio intercoms use PL and IFB systems. The *PL* (party line, phone line, or private line) system allows all production and engineering personnel to be in constant voice contact with one another. Each member of the production team and the technical crew wears a headset with a microphone for efficient communication. Such systems can be wired (through the camera cables or separate intercom cables) or, in larger studios, wireless. Most PL systems operate on at least two channels so that different groups can be addressed separately.

Producers and directors make frequent use of the *IFB* (interruptible foldback or feedback) system, which allows them to communicate directly with the talent, who wear tiny earpieces instead of headsets while on the air. Such instant communication from the control room to the talent is especially important during news and interviews.

Monitors As you recall, a *monitor* is a high-quality video display that cannot receive broadcast signals. You need at least one fairly large monitor in the studio that shows the line-out pictures—the video that goes to the video recorder (VR) or transmitter—to everyone on the floor. By viewing the line-out picture, the crew can anticipate a number of production tasks. For example, the operator of the camera that is not on the air can vary its shot so that it does not duplicate that of the on-the-air camera; the floor manager can see how close he can be to the talent for the necessary hand signals without getting into camera range; and the microphone boom operator can test how far the mic can be lowered before it gets into the shot.

News- and weathercasters often work with several studio monitors that carry not only the line-out pictures but also the remote feeds and the video playbacks. Because the weathercaster actually stands in front of a plain chroma-key backdrop when pointing to the (nonexistent) weather map, the monitor, which shows the complete key including the map, is essential for guiding the talent's gestures. For audience participation shows, you need several monitors to show the audience what the event looks like on-screen. When the camera is on the audience, it always entices some people watching the monitors to wave at themselves, probably to confirm that they are indeed on television.

Studio speakers The studio speakers do for the program sound what the video monitors do for the picture portion. The studio speakers can feed the program sound or any other sounds—music, telephone rings, crashing noises—into the studio to be synchronized with the action. They can also be used for the *SA* (studio address system, also called PA, for public address system), which allows the control room personnel (usually the director) to talk to the studio personnel who are not on headsets. The SA is obviously not used on the air, but it is helpful for calling the crew back to rehearsal, reminding them of the time remaining to air time, or advising them to put on their PL headsets.

◼ STUDIO CONTROL ROOM

The *studio control room*, housed in a separate area adjacent to the studio, is designed to accommodate the people who make the decisions while production is under way as well as the equipment necessary to control the video and audio portions of the production.

The people normally working in the control room are the director, the producer, and their associates; the technical director (TD); the CG (character generator) operator; the audio engineer; and sometimes the lighting director (LD) and even the video operator (VO).

The control room equipment is designed and arranged to coordinate the total production process. Specifically, it facilitates the instantaneous editing (selection and sequencing) of video images, the selection and the mixing of sound inputs, and the lighting control. The control room of news studios also houses the control equipment for robotic cameras. Some control rooms have windows that let the control room personnel see what is going on in the studio. More often, however, you will find that the only way you can see what's happening in the studio is by watching the monitors that show the various camera points of view. A studio that is used primarily for instruction, however, should have a large window. Such a window will greatly help students translate what appears on the control room monitors into actual studio traffic.

> **KEY CONCEPT**
>
> The control room is designed to coordinate the studio production process.

Image Control

The image control section contains the equipment necessary to select and sequence the video inputs, to coordinate the video with the audio, and to communicate with the production people, technical crew, and talent. In news studios it also includes the operation of robotic cameras (see figure 10.14).

Monitors   Recall for a moment the video switcher (explored in chapter 10). Each of the buttons on the program bus represents a separate video input. But how can you tell which pictures to choose from all the inputs? Wouldn't you need a separate monitor for each major video input? Yes, indeed. This is why a control room requires a large bank of monitors. **SEE 14.4**

Even a small control room requires a surprising number of monitors. Let's count them and identify their functions. **SEE 14.5**

Preview	1	
Line	1	
Air	1	If an on-the-air or cable station studio, this monitor will show what the home viewer sees
Camera preview	4	One for each camera; camera 4 can also be switched to remote
VRs	3	One for each playback VR
CG	1	
Electronic still store system	1	
Special effects	1	
Remote	1	Remote feeds; can also be used for additional camera
Total	14	Monitors

These monitors are stacked in a variety of configurations in front of the director and the TD. The preview (or preset), line, and air monitors are generally larger than the rest of the preview monitors. They usually have the wide-screen 16 × 9 HDTV (high-definition television) aspect ratio, even if the rest of the preview monitors

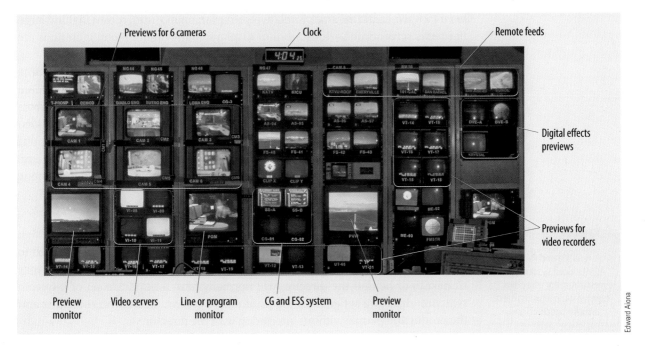

Previews for 6 cameras — Clock — Remote feeds

Digital effects previews

Previews for video recorders

Preview monitor — Video servers — Line or program monitor — CG and ESS system — Preview monitor

Edward Aiona

14.4 CONTROL ROOM MONITOR STACK

The control room monitors show all available video sources, such as the studio cameras, remote video, video recorders, servers, CG, electronic still store (ESS) system, and special effects. The large color monitors show the preview video (the upcoming shots) and the line-out (what is being sent to the VR and/or the transmitter).

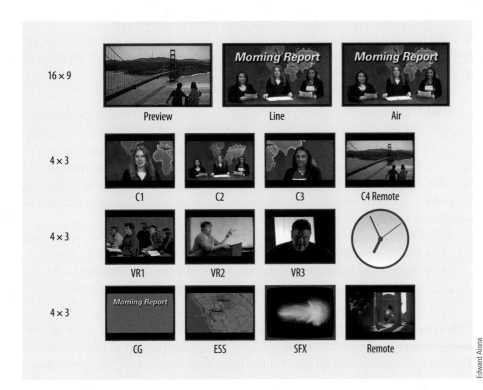

16 × 9 — Preview — Line — Air

4 × 3 — C1 — C2 — C3 — C4 Remote

4 × 3 — VR1 — VR2 — VR3

4 × 3 — CG — ESS — SFX — Remote

Edward Aiona

14.5 SIMPLE MONITOR STACK

Even this simple control room display requires 14 monitors: three large 16 × 9 monitors for preview, line, and air; four camera previews, one of which is switchable to remote; three for VRs; and one each for CG, ESS, special effects, and remote. Except for the 16 × 9 preview, line, and air monitors, all are 4 × 3 displays.

have 4×3 screens. If the stack is relatively simple, some control rooms divide a large flat-panel screen into various monitor displays. Many different configurations are possible with such a multiview display.

You may wonder how anybody can ever watch all these monitors at the same time during a multicamera show. Actually, you don't pay full attention to all of them all the time; you scan the active ones, much like looking at your rearview mirrors while driving, and then focus your attention on the monitors that carry the video most important to you. Nevertheless, you must always be aware of what the rest of the monitors are showing. After some practice you will be able to see more and more monitors, much like a maestro's reading a complex score while conducting an orchestra.

Intercom   The director also has easy access to a variety of intercom switches that control the PL, SA, and IFB systems. The associate director (AD), who sits next to the director in large productions, uses the same switches. The producer, who may sit next to or behind the director, will normally have a duplicate set of intercom switches; this extra set enables the producer to communicate with the talent and the production people without interfering with the director.

Program sound   In addition to watching the preview monitors, giving instructions to production people, and listening to the PL, the director must also listen to the program audio to coordinate the video portion with the sound. A separate volume control enables the director to adjust the control room speakers, called audio monitors, without affecting the volume of the program sound that goes to the line-out. You will find that listening to the program sound while doing all the other things is one of the hardest tasks for a rookie director. (We discuss directing more thoroughly in chapter 17.)

Switcher   You already learned that the video switcher is located next to the director's position. But why? This proximity enables the TD (technical director, who is normally doing the switching) to use the same monitor stack as the director and remain in close contact. Sitting close together helps the director and the TD communicate not only through the PL system but also through hand signals. For instance, by moving an arm at a certain speed, the director can indicate to the TD how fast a dissolve or wipe should be. **SEE 14.6** ZVL1 SWITCHING→ Switching introduction

When fast cutting is required, some directors snap their fingers rather than call for a take once a shot has been readied. Such physical cues are faster and more precise than verbal ones. In smaller productions directors may do their own switching (labor unions permitting), a practice not recommended for complex shows.

Character generator   The CG and the CG operator are also located in the control room. Although most of the titles are usually prepared ahead of time, there are always changes to be made. Especially during live or live-recorded productions, such as sports, the CG operator must update the scores and prepare statistics

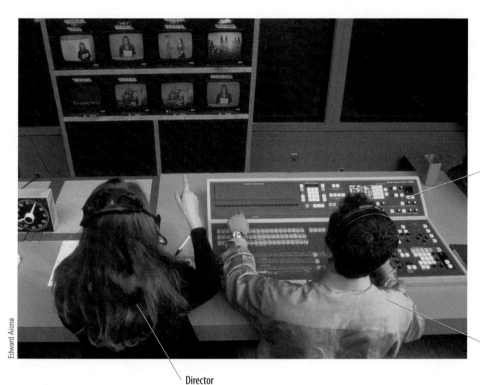

Edward Aiona

Director

14.6 DIRECTOR/ TD PROXIMITY IN CONTROL ROOM
The production switcher is located next to the director's position for optimal communication between director and TD.

Production switcher

TD operating switcher

during the game; or the producer or director may call for titles that have not been preprogrammed. With the CG operator in the control room, such changes are readily communicated and quickly made.

Clocks and stopwatches   These timing tools are essential in broadcast operations, where programs are aired according to a second-by-second schedule. But even if your productions are video-recorded for postproduction, the clock will tell you whether the recording session is going according to the production time line, and the stopwatch will guide you when inserting other recorded material. Digital stopwatches—actually little clocks—give you a choice of running forward from the start of the program or backward from the end-time. When running backward the stopwatch will display the time actually left in the program. Some directors prefer the analog clock and stopwatch because they can "look ahead" by watching the hands of the clock moving and thus pace the remaining program more accurately.

Lighting control and CCUs   Some control rooms house the lighting control (dimmers) and/or the CCUs (camera control units) for each camera. The advantage of having this additional equipment in the control room is that all image control is in a single location, helping communication among the various technicians. The disadvantage is that the control room gets quite crowded with additional equipment and people.

14.7 AUDIO CONTROL BOOTH

The television audio control booth contains a variety of audio control equipment, such as the control console, a patchbay, various digital record and play equipment, loudspeakers, intercom systems, and a video line monitor.

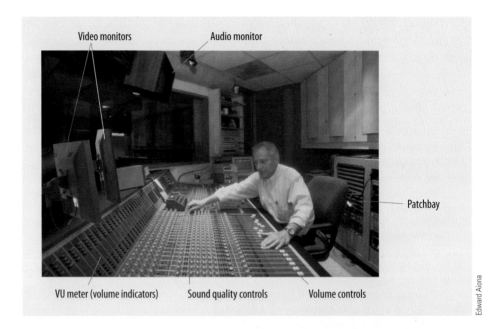

Video monitors · Audio monitor · Patchbay · VU meter (volume indicators) · Sound quality controls · Volume controls

Edward Aiona

Sound Control

The sound control is the audio booth attached to the video control room. It is usually isolated from the video control room so that the audio engineer is not disturbed by all the talk. Most audio booths have a window that allows the audio engineer to see the activities in the control room and, ideally, even the director's preview monitors. Well-equipped audio booths have both a preview and a line monitor. The preview monitor aids the audio engineer in anticipating and executing tight audio cues. The audio engineer is further aided by a marked script or show format, whose cue lines prepare him for upcoming audio and help him react more quickly to the director's cues.

The audio booth normally contains an audio console, a patchbay, a computer, and various digital recording and playback devices. The audio engineer can listen to the director via a PL headset or a small cue speaker and can talk to the control room and the studio through the PL and SA systems. The program sound is monitored though high-quality program speakers. **SEE 14.7**

■ MASTER CONTROL

If you use the studio strictly for producing video-recorded programs, you don't need a master control room, assuming that the CCUs are located somewhere in the studio control room. But all television stations and most larger nonbroadcast production houses have an equipment and communication center called ***master control***. If you are in the business of telecasting programs over the air or on cable or via Internet streaming, master control becomes an essential electronic nerve center.

The basic functions of master control in broadcast operations are overseeing the automated workflow and the technical quality of all program material slated for transmission, the content ingest from various internal and external program sources, and the storage and archiving of recorded content.

Master control normally houses the studio CCUs, video recorders, video servers, ESS systems, and various routing switchers and installations that monitor the technical quality of every second of programming that is broadcast on the air, though cable, or via Internet streaming. Master control for nonbroadcast operations may contain equipment that is usually housed in a studio control room, such as CCUs, video recorders and servers, and monitors and intercom systems.

Workflow and Quality Control

Master control monitors every studio production and supplies additional video clips from both stored and external sources. Its main function is to select for each program day specific live feeds or content from video servers, check their technical integrity, and route the selected programs to the transmitter, cable, or other distribution channel, such as the Internet.

The daily program sequence is dictated by the program log, which lists what programs go on the air at what time. The program log shows every second of programming aired on a particular day as well as other important information, such as the title and the type of each program and its origin (local live, server, or network or satellite feed). The log is distributed throughout the station via computer and sometimes also as hard copy. **SEE 14.8**

The actual on-the-air switching of broadcast content is mostly done by computer. In case the computer system goes down, however, an operator monitors

HSE NUMBER	SCH TIME	PGM	LENGTH	ORIGIN VID	AUD
N 3349	10 59 40	NEWS CLOSE	015	VR4	VR4
S11	10 59 55	STATION BR	005	ESS	CART20
E 1009	11 00 00	GOING PLACES 1	030	VR5	VR5
C5590	11 00 30	FED EX	010	VR2	VR2
C 9930-0	11 00 40	HAYDEN PUBLISHING	010	VR18	VT18
C 10004	11 00 50	SPORTS HILIGHTS	005	ESS	CART21
PP 99	11 00 55	STATION PROMO SPORTS	005	SVR2	SVR2
E 1009	11 01 00	GOING PLACES CONT 2	1100	VR5	VR5
C 9990-34	11 12 00	HYDE PRODUCTS	030	VR34	VR34
C 774-55	11 12 30	COMPESI FISHING	010	VR35	VR35
C 993-48	11 12 40	KIPPER COMPUTERS	010	VR78	VR78
PS	11 12 50	RED CROSS	005	ESS	CART22
PP 1003	11 12 55	STATION PROMO GOOD MRNG	005	SVR2	SVR2
E 1009	11 13 00	GOING PLACES CONT 3	1025	VR5	VR5
C 222-99	11 23 25	WHITNEY MOTORCYCLE	020	VR33	VR33
C 00995-45	11 23 45	IDEAS TO IMAGES	010	VR91	VR91
PS	11 23 55	AIDS AWARENESS	005	ESS	CART02
E 1009	11 24 00	GOING PLACES CONT 4	100	VR5	VR5
N 01125	11 25 00	NEWSBREAK ***LIVE	010	ST1LV	ST1
C 00944-11	11 25 10	ALL SEASONS GNRL FOODS	030	VR27	VT27
N 01125	11 25 40	NEWS CONT***LIVE	200	ST1LV	ST1
C 995-89	11 27 40	BLOSSER FOR PRESIDENT	020	VR24	VR24
PP 77	11 28 00	NEXT DAY	010	VR19	VR19

© Cengage Learning 2011

14.8 PROGRAM LOG
The program log is a second-by-second list of all programs telecast during a broadcast day. It shows the scheduled (start) times, program title and type, video and audio origin (server, tape, live, or feed), house number, and other pertinent broadcast information.

14.9 MASTER CONTROL SWITCHING AREA

Master control serves as the final video and audio control for all program material before it is broadcast or distributed by the station's transmitter, a satellite, cable, or the Internet. Computers run most master control functions, with the master control technician overseeing the automated functions and assuming manual control in case of system failure.

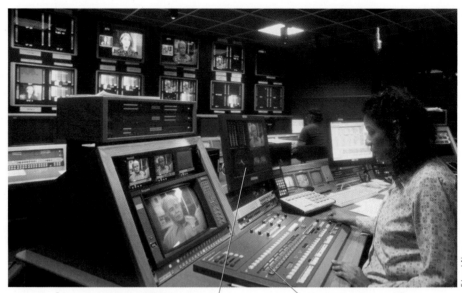

Computer log display   Manual master control switcher

Edward Aiona

the automatic switching and is ready to press into service the manual master control switcher. **SEE 14.9**

Content Ingest

Content **ingest** refers to program input. Somehow the industry fell in love with this term, which stuck against all odds and respect for language. Master control keeps track of all incoming content, regardless of whether it arrives via satellite, cable, Internet, or mail. As ingest operator, you are responsible for logging all incoming program feeds, giving them identification codes (occasionally still called "house numbers"), and recording the priority feeds on a video server. Fortunately, much of this work is automated by computer. Isn't ingest a form of capture? Yes, but *capture* refers more to transferring camera source footage onto the hard drive of a nonlinear editing program, whereas *ingest* refers to selecting relevant programs from the various program feeds, translating them into specific data files, and storing them on high-capacity hard drives of large video servers.

Storage and Archiving

You have probably noticed that storing all of the videotapes, CDs, and DVDs you have collected is already quite difficult, especially if you want to quickly find a specific disc. Just think how challenging that job must be for a television station that deals with hundreds of pieces of new program content every day. Much of such content needs to be cataloged and stored for easy retrieval. Also, somebody must take care of archiving the ever-growing video library so that a specific piece of content, such as the president's latest speech, can be quickly retrieved if necessary for the evening newscast. Fortunately, these activities are also made somewhat more manageable by workflow software.

STUDIO SUPPORT AREAS

No studio can function properly without support areas that house scenery, properties, and makeup and dressing rooms. Unfortunately, even large and relatively new studios usually lack sufficient support areas. As a consequence the studios themselves become partial storage areas for scenery and sometimes even serve as makeup and dressing rooms.

Scenery and Property Storage

One of the most important aspects of scenery and property storage is ease of retrieval. The floor crew must be able to find and pull each piece of scenery without having to dig it out from under all of the others. The prop areas and the storage boxes must be clearly labeled, especially if they contain small hand props.

Makeup and Dressing Rooms

Wherever you apply makeup, it must be done in lighting conditions that are identical to those in the studio. Most makeup and dressing rooms have two types of illumination: indoor lighting (with a color temperature standard of 3,200K) and outdoor lighting (5,600K). Because the indoor standard has a warmer, more reddish light than the cooler, more bluish light of outdoors, you should always check your makeup on-camera in the actual performance area before the dress rehearsal and again before the performance. (Color temperature is explained in chapter 8.)

SCENERY, PROPERTIES, AND SET DRESSINGS

You may wonder why the networks have such gigantic news sets for a single anchor, who usually appears on a loose close-up throughout the newscast. Although you see the whole set for only a few seconds during the opening and the closing, it is supposed to signal that the news department is large, well equipped, and high-tech and that the news the anchor delivers is significant. Yes, you could certainly do the same newscast just as successfully on a much smaller set.

Nevertheless, scenery and properties are used primarily to create a specific environment in which the action takes place, but they also reflect the nature of the event. The bookcases filled with matching volumes in an interview set may be a cliché, but they instantly communicate a lawyer's office. When dealing with scenery and properties in video production, you must always keep in mind that it is the camera that looks at the scenic environment, not the crew or the casual studio visitor. The set must be detailed enough to withstand the close-up scrutiny of an HD (high-definition) camera yet plain enough to avoid clutter that can detract from the performers. Careful attention to set detail is especially important when using HDTV cameras. The high resolution of HDTV makes even background detail more visible. The set must also allow for optimal camera movement and angles, microphone placement and mobility, appropriate lighting, and maximum action by the talent. It is also a major factor in setting style.

> **KEY CONCEPT**
>
> Scenery must create a certain environment and allow for optimal lighting, audio pickup, and camera movement.

Scenery

Although the design and the construction of scenery require specific training and skills, you should know what standard set units are and how to use them for creating simple environments. Here we discuss softwall flats; hardwall flats; set modules; seamless paper and painted drops; and set pieces, platforms, and wagons.

Softwall flats   A ***flat*** is a freestanding piece of scenery used as a background or to simulate the walls of a room. Softwall flats are background units constructed of a lightweight wood frame covered with muslin. The wood frame consists of 1 × 3 lumber that is glued together and reinforced at the corners by ¼-inch plywood pieces. To keep the frame from twisting, it is further strengthened by two diagonal braces and a toggle rail in the middle. If the studio floor is hard, you can put metal or plastic gliders on the bottom rail of the flat so that you can push it around without damaging the flat or the floor or yourself. **SEE 14.10**

The traditional and still most practical way to tie softwall flats together is by using lashlines. When joining flats, you actually lash two pieces of scenery together with a clothesline that is attached to the right top rail of each flat and pulled through cleats, similar to lacing the hooks of a boot. **SEE 14.11** Flats are supported by jacks—wood braces that are hinged, tied, or fastened to the flats with C-clamps—and are weighted down and held in place with sandbags or metal weights.

Standard softwall flats have a uniform height but various widths. The height is usually 10 feet, or 8 feet for small sets or studios with low ceilings; width ranges from 1 to 5 feet. When two flats are permanently hinged together, they are called twofolds or books (because they open like a book); three flats hinged together constitute a threefold.

Softwall flats are easy to move, assemble, and store, but their simple construction is also a disadvantage: they tend to shake when you close a door or window on

14.10 SOFTWALL FLATS
Softwall flats are made of
1 × 3 lumber and covered
with muslin.

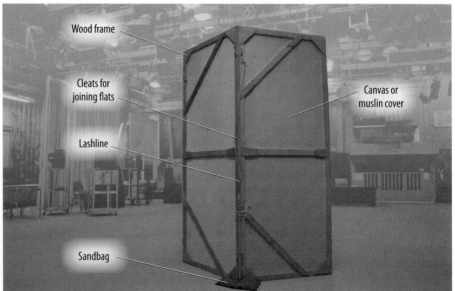

Wood frame

Cleats for
joining flats

Canvas or
muslin cover

Lashline

Sandbag

Herbert Zettl

the set or if someone or something brushes against them. They are ideal for rehearsal and for less demanding productions.

Hardwall flats   Most professional video production sets are constructed with hardwall flats. They are usually built for a specific set and do not always conform to the standard dimensions of softwall scenery. Although there is no standard way to build hardwall scenery, most flats are constructed with a sturdy wood or slotted-steel frame (which looks like a big erector set) and covered with plywood or pressed fiberboard. Most hardwall scenery is moved with the help of built-in casters and joined with bolts or C-clamps. **SEE 14.12**

The advantage of hardwall scenery is that it is extremely sturdy; if a scene calls for slamming the door, you can do so without fear of shaking the whole set. You can also attach pictures or posters the way you would on a real wall. The disadvantages of hardwall flats are that they are expensive to build, difficult to move and set up, and even harder to store. Hardwall scenery is also apt to reflect sound and cause unwanted reverberations.

Set modules   Smaller video production companies, whose scenery demands are usually limited to news, interviews, office sets, or environments in which products are displayed and demonstrated, often use set modules. A set module is a series of hardwall flats and three-dimensional set pieces whose dimensions match whether they are used vertically (right-side up) or horizontally (on their sides). They can be assembled in different combinations, similar to building blocks. For example, you might use a modular hardwall set piece as a hardwall flat in one production and as a desktop in the next. Or you might dismantle a modular desk and use the boxes (representing the drawers) as display units. A wide variety of set modules are commercially available.

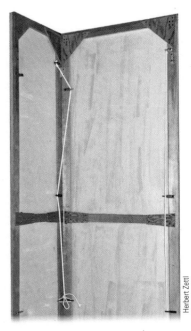

14.11 FLATS JOINED BY LASHLINE
Softwall flats are connected by lashing them together with a clothesline, called a lashline. The lashline is woven around alternating metal cleats and secured with a slipknot.

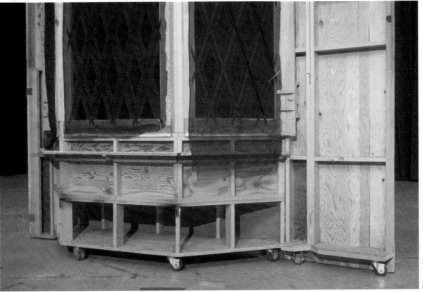

14.12 HARDWALL SCENERY
Hardwall scenery is built with a sturdy wood or metal frame that is covered with plywood or fiberboard. Most hardwall scenery has built-in casters or is placed on small wagons for mobility. This is the back of a windowseat.

Seamless paper and painted drops   As you recall, the cyclorama is a large, plain, seamless drop that serves as a neutral background (see figure 14.2). In the absence of a cyc, you can construct a limited neutral area with a roll of seamless paper (usually 9 feet wide by 36 feet long) simply by unrolling it and stapling it horizontally on softwall flats. Seamless paper rolls come in a variety of colors and are relatively inexpensive. Painted drops, on the other hand, usually refer to rolls of paper or canvas with realistic or, more often, stylized background scenes painted on them. You can also create believable backgrounds electronically. (Synthetic environments are discussed in chapter 15.)

Set pieces, platforms, and wagons   Set pieces consist of freestanding three-dimensional objects, such as pillars, pylons (which look like three-sided pillars), sweeps (large, curved pieces of scenery), folding screens, steps, and periaktoi (plural of *periaktos*). A periaktos is a three-sided standing unit that looks like a large pylon; it moves and swivels on casters. **SEE 14.13** Set pieces are often constructed in modular dimensions so that they can be fitted together in different combinations. Some set pieces, such as pillars and pylons, are unstable and must be secured so that they do not tip over when bumped by crew, talent, or equipment. It is always better to overbrace than underbrace a set.

Platforms are elevation devices. Normal platforms are 6 inches, 8 inches, or 12 inches high and can be stacked. Platforms are often used for interview and panel discussion sets so that the cameras see the participants straight-on rather than look down on them. When used for interviews, the entire platform should be covered

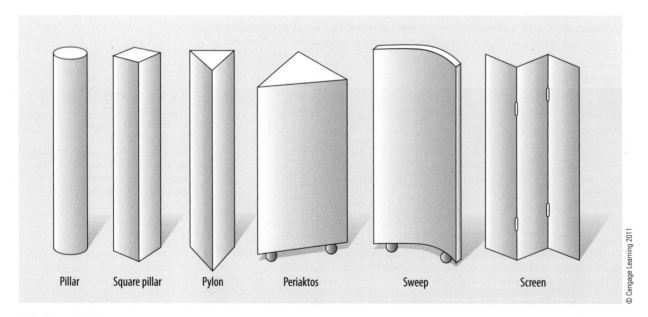

Pillar   Square pillar   Pylon   Periaktos   Sweep   Screen

© Cengage Learning 2011

14.13 SET PIECES
Set pieces are freestanding three-dimensional scenic objects used as background or foreground pieces.

with carpeting. As well as making the set more attractive, the carpeting absorbs the hollow sounds from people moving on the platform. You can further deaden such sounds by filling the platform interior with foam rubber or foam spray. Some 6-inch platforms have four heavy casters, converting the platforms into wagons that can support and move scenery from one place in the studio to another.

Properties

In video production properties—**props** for short—and set dressings are often more important than the background scenery for signifying a particular environment. You will work with two kinds of properties: set props and hand props.

Set props   Set props include the furniture you use on a set, such as the chairs for an interview, the table for a panel discussion, the desk from which the corporate manager delivers her weekly address, the bookcase and the file cabinet for the office set, and the inevitable couch in situation comedies.

When choosing set props, look for functional furniture that can be used in a variety of settings. Small, simple chairs, for example, are more useful and versatile than large upholstered ones. Most regular couches are too low and make sitting down and getting up look awkward on-camera. You can easily remedy this problem by padding the seats or elevating the entire couch. Some set props, such as news desks or panel tables, are custom-made. As with the news set, do not go overboard with such custom furniture, especially if most of the scenes show only medium shots or close-ups of the performers.

Hand props   Hand props are items actually handled by the talent—cell phones, laptop computers, dishes, silverware, books, magazines, glasses, and flowers. Hand props must work and they must be real. A bottle that doesn't open on cue can cause costly production delays. Because hand props are an extension of the talent's gestures and actions, and because of the close scrutiny of the video camera, you cannot get by with fake props. A papier-mâché chalice that looks regal on the theater stage looks ridiculous on the video screen. Equally silly is laboring under the weight of an empty suitcase. Whereas the theater audience may have some sympathy for your toil, the television viewer will more likely consider it a comic routine or a production mistake.

If you have to use a handgun, never use an actual firearm; try to get a prop gun. Shooting blanks at close range can be as deadly as if you were to use a bullet. This is one place where you can pretend; rather than pull the trigger, you can simply add a popping sound by pricking a balloon. The balloon pop is uncomfortably similar to the sound of a handgun going off and can be more accurately synchronized with the action than a recorded effect. If you add the sound in postproduction, you can quite readily match the pop with the action.

When using food, make certain that it is fresh and that the dishes and the silverware are meticulously clean. Liquor is generally replaced with water (for clear spirits), tea (for whiskey), or soft drinks (for white and red wine). With all due respect for realism, such substitutions are perfectly appropriate.

Set Dressings

Set dressings include things that you would place in your own living quarters to make them look attractive and to express your taste and personal style. Although the flats may remain the same from one type of show to another, the dressing gives each set its distinguishing characteristics and helps establish the style of the environment. Set dressings include curtains, pictures, sculptures, posters, lamps, plants, decorative items for a desk and bookshelves, or a favorite toy that survived childhood. Secondhand stores and flea markets provide an unlimited source for such things. In case of emergency, you can always raid your own living quarters or office. As with props, set dressings must be realistic so that they can withstand even the probing eye of an HD camera.

■ SET DESIGN

Although you may never be called upon to design a set, you will certainly have to tell the set designer what environment you envision and why. You will also have to know how to interpret a set design so that you can evaluate the set relative to the program objective and the technical requirements, such as lighting, audio pickup, and camera and talent movement.

Process Message

Once again, a clear statement of the desired process message will guide you in designing the appropriate environment. For example, if the objective of an interview is to have the viewer get to know the guest as intimately as possible and probe her feelings and attitudes, what kind of set do you need? Because you should show the guest in close-ups throughout most of the show, you don't need an elaborate interview set. Two simple chairs in front of an uncluttered background will do just fine.

On the other hand, if the objective is to have the viewer see how the guest uses the physical environment of her office to reflect her power, you had better conduct the interview on-location from the guest's actual office or on a studio set that closely resembles it.

As with all other medium requirements, in designing or evaluating a set you must have a pretty good idea of what it is you want the viewer to see, hear, and feel. Once you have interpreted the process message as to scenic requirements, you need to translate the scene design into a floor plan of an actual studio set.

Floor Plan

The **floor plan** is a diagram of scenery and set properties drawn on a grid, called a floor plan pattern, that resembles the usable floor space in the studio. To help you locate a certain spot on the studio floor, the floor plan pattern normally has the lighting grid superimposed, much like the orientation squares of a map. By using the lighting grid, the floor plan pattern can also be used for drawing a light plot.

Elaborate set designs are always drawn to scale, such as the common ¼ inch = 1 foot. There are templates with in-scale cutouts for typical set pieces, such as tables, sofas, chairs, beds, and dressers. You can also use one of the many computer programs on the market for architectural layouts or interior design.

If the setup is relatively simple, the art director may make only a rough sketch that shows the background scenery, set props, and approximate location of the set, leaving it up to the floor manager to place the set in the most advantageous spot in the studio. **SEE 14.14** The floor plan should indicate all scenery, including doors and windows, as well as the type and the location of set props and major hand props. **SEE 14.15**

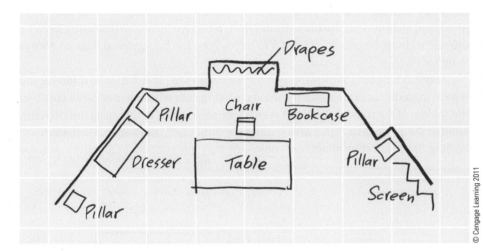

14.14 SIMPLE FLOOR PLAN SKETCH
The floor plan grid (often the lighting grid) helps locate the positions of scenery and set props.

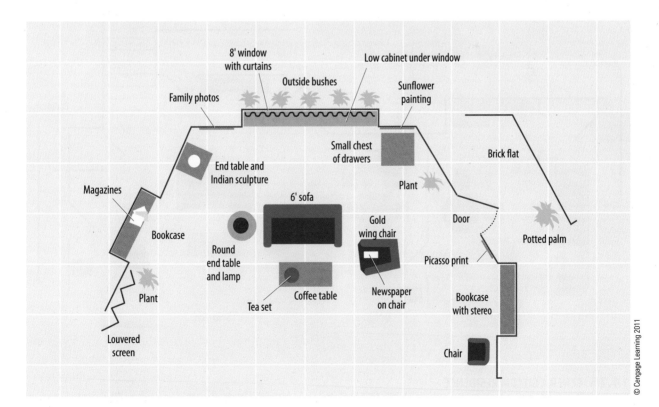

14.15 FLOOR PLAN WITH SET AND HAND PROPS
Elaborate floor plans indicate the type and the position of set props (furniture, lamp, sculpture, and paintings) and major hand props (newspaper, tea set, and magazines).

When drawing a floor plan, keep in mind that the set must be workable for the cameras—it must provide adequate backing for different camera angles. A common mistake of inexperienced set designers is to show inadequate backing for the set props and the talent action. Another frequent mistake is a set that exceeds the floor area actually available. As mentioned earlier, the cyc and the items stored in the studio can radically reduce the usable floor space. To help the lighting people direct the back lights at the performance areas at not too steep an angle and avoid unwanted shadows on the background flats, all active furniture (furniture used by the talent) must be placed at least 6 to 8 feet from the background flats, as shown in figure 14.15.

Some floor plans indicate a generic set. **SEE 14.16** This set design has all the typical ingredients of a situation comedy: a living area with the inevitable couch in the middle of the room, a door to a second active set area (in this case, the kitchen), another door to an imaginary area (hallway or front yard), and a staircase in the back, leading to yet another imaginary room—usually a bedroom. In a generic set, the

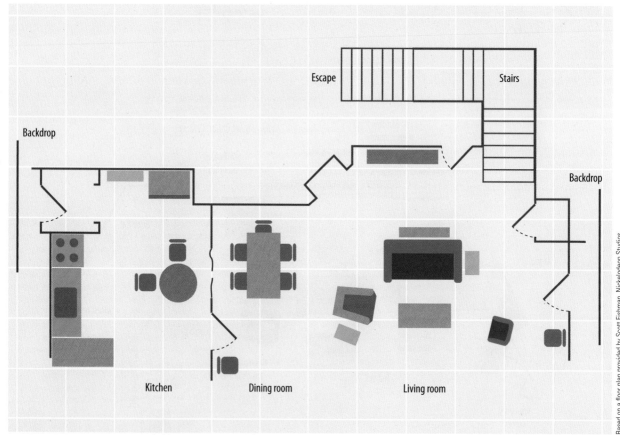

14.16 GENERIC SITCOM RESIDENCE
This set is designed so that four cameras, situated side-by-side in front, can pick up the action. It can be easily changed to other environments by using different set props.

basic setup remains the same but can be individualized by different props and set dressings. Note the "escape" behind the stairs, which helps the actors get back down to the studio floor, and the two backdrops on either side that display the imaginary extended space, such as a hallway or front yard on the right and a patio on the left.

Prop List

Even if the floor plan shows some of the major set and hand props, all props must be itemized on a prop list. Some prop lists itemize set props, set dressings, and hand props separately, but you can combine them on a single list, provided you don't forget anything. Assuming that you are the floor manager, confirm with the property manager that the props you requested are actually available when you need them, and inspect each one to see whether it fits the intended scene design. For example, a Victorian chair would certainly look out of character in an otherwise modern office set, unless it is to suggest an eccentric office manager. Verify that all listed props are delivered to you and that they are not damaged in any way before taking them into the studio.

Using the Floor Plan for Setup

A floor plan is useless if you can't translate it into an actual set and performance environment. You must acquire some of the skills of an architect or builder, who can look at a blueprint of a building and visualize what it will look like when erected and how people will move through and function in it. The following figure shows how a simple floor plan translates into the corresponding setup. **SEE 14.17**

 The ability to read a floor plan is a necessary skill for all production personnel. A good floor plan helps the floor manager and the crew put up and dress the set fairly accurately, independent of the designer. The director can map out the major talent positions and blocking and also design the principal camera shots, positions, and

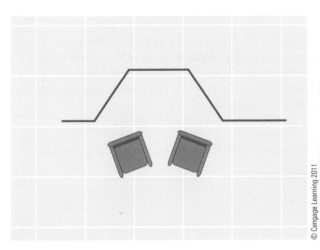
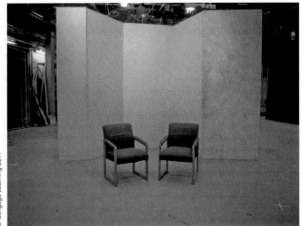

© Cengage Learning 2011

Herbert Zettl

14.17 FLOOR PLAN AND ACTUAL SETUP
The floor plan on the left translates into the simple set in the photo on the right.

movements before setting foot in the studio. The lighting director can lay out the basic light plot, and the audio engineer can determine mic placement. Also, by knowing how to read a floor plan, you can catch and often solve production problems before they occur. Because the floor plan is such a critical factor in production efficiency, you should insist on having one drawn even if the new set and the production are relatively simple.

M A I N   P O I N T S

▶ ***Video Production Studio***

Video production studios are designed for multicamera productions and teamwork. Important features include sufficient floor space, a smooth floor for camera travel, adequate ceiling height so that the lights can be suspended, large doors, acoustically treated walls, and relatively quiet air-conditioning.

▶ ***Major Studio Installations***

The major studio installations include a lighting grid or movable battens, adequate electrical outlets, an intercommunication system between the studio and the control room, studio video monitors, and studio speakers.

▶ ***Studio Control Room***

The studio control room is designed and arranged to coordinate the total production process. It usually comprises the image control—with the switcher, CG (character generator), monitor banks, intercom lines, and sometimes the lighting control board—and the sound control, which contains an audio console and recording and playback equipment.

▶ ***Director and TD***

The director and the technical director (TD) must sit next to each other to share the monitors and react quickly to physical signals.

▶ ***Master Control***

Master control is the nerve center for television stations. Its basic functions are overseeing the automated workflow and the technical quality of all program material slated for transmission, the content ingest from various internal and external program sources, and the storage and archiving of recorded content. Much of such program acquisition and control is automated.

▶ ***Studio Support Areas***

Studio support areas include the scenery and property storage and the makeup and dressing rooms.

▶ ***Scenery, Properties, and Set Dressings***

Scenery consists of softwall and hardwall flats, a cyclorama and various drops, set pieces, platforms, and wagons. Properties include set props (such as furniture), hand props (items actually used by the talent), and set dressings (artwork, lamps, and decorative plants). Scenery must convey a certain environment and allow for optimal lighting, audio pickup, and talent and camera movement.

▶ ***Floor Plan***

The floor plan is a diagram of scenery and set props that facilitates the setup of scenery, set decoration, and lighting and the preplanning of shots.

Z E T T L ' S   V I D E O L A B

For your reference or to track your work, the *Zettl's VideoLab* program cue in this chapter is listed here with its corresponding page number.

ZVL1 SWITCHING→ Switching introduction   304

KEY TERMS

big remote A production outside the studio to televise live and/or live-record a large scheduled event that has not been staged specifically for television. Examples include sporting events, parades, political gatherings, award ceremonies, and government hearings. Also called *remote*.

contact person A person who is familiar with, and can facilitate access to, the remote location and the key people. Also called *contact*.

electronic field production (EFP) Video production done outside the studio that is usually shot for postproduction (not live).

electronic news gathering (ENG) The use of portable camcorders, lights, and sound equipment for the production of mostly unscheduled daily news events. ENG is usually done for live transmission or immediate postproduction.

field production Production activities that take place away from the studio.

remote survey An inspection of the remote location by key production and engineering personnel so that they can plan for the setup and the use of production equipment. Also called *site survey*.

remote truck The vehicle that carries the production control room, audio control, video-recording section, video control section, and transmission equipment.

synthetic environment Electronically generated settings, either through chroma key or computer.

uplink truck The vehicle that sends video and audio signals to a satellite.

virtual reality Computer-simulated environment with which the user can interact.

Production Environment: Field and Synthetic

Field production refers to any video production that happens outside the studio. It includes documentaries that are shot on-location as well as elaborate remotes for sporting events and the Thanksgiving Day parade.

When taking video equipment outside the studio, the world is your stage. The tradeoff for moving out of the studio and into the field is control. In field productions you cannot create and control a specific production environment but must adapt to one. If a shoot takes place outdoors, the weather is always a potential hazard; if you are indoors, the room may not be to your liking or conducive to effective video and audio pickup. Still you can make the environment work for you instead of against you.

This chapter gives you some guidance about how to work effectively in the field, including electronic news gathering, electronic field production, and big remotes. From the field we move to a production environment in which the computer plays a central role: postproduction and synthetic image creation.

▶ **ELECTRONIC NEWS GATHERING**
News gathering and transmission

▶ **ELECTRONIC FIELD PRODUCTION**
Preproduction, including the remote survey and the location sketch; production, including the equipment checklist and shooting outdoors and indoors; and the postproduction wrap-up

▶ **BIG REMOTES**
The remote truck and remote transmission

▶ **SYNTHETIC ENVIRONMENTS**
Computer-generated settings, virtual reality, and computer-controlled environments

◼ ELECTRONIC NEWS GATHERING

By their very nature, the time, specifics, and location of most news events cannot be planned. Neither can the coverage of such events, called *electronic news gathering (ENG)*. All you can do is run after the breaking story and cover it as best you can. This does not mean that you give up all control over production procedures. Preproduction in ENG entails having your equipment ready to go at any time and functioning properly regardless of where you are and under what conditions you are working.

News Gathering

As a news videographer, also called a shooter, you are responsible not only for video-recording the story but also for making the decisions on just how to tell it. In a breaking story, you must be able to assess the situation, operate the equipment, and capture the essence of the event—all in a matter of minutes. You rarely have time to consult your producer or anyone else about what is going on or how to shoot it. But even in intense situations, experienced videographers are able to deliver well-composed shots that can be edited into a smooth sequence.

If you are covering a story with a reporter, the news-gathering process is slightly less hectic. You usually have some flexibility in placing the field reporter for a standup report in a location that tells part of the story (city hall, college campus, county hospital) and in selecting the most effective shots.

Whenever possible have the reporter stand in a shaded area rather than in direct sunlight or, worse, in front of a brightly lit building. As explained in chapter 8, bright sunlight will cause unflattering fast falloff and dense shadows, and the bright background will cause the reporter to be seen in silhouette. Even if you have a reflector handy to slow down the falloff, you probably won't have anybody to hold it. You will find that the quickest and easiest way to avoid fast falloff is to place the reporter in a shaded area. Do not forget to white-balance the camera for every new lighting situation. Watch what is behind the reporter so that you do not have street signs, trees, or telephone poles appear to be growing out of the reporter's head. **ZVL1** LIGHTS→ Field→ outdoor | use of reflectors

Be mindful of the audio requirements. Don't have the reporter deliver a report on the windiest corner of the street; find a location that is relatively protected. Small rooms or corridors with bare walls have a tendency to produce unwanted echoes and make reporters sound as though they are speaking from inside a barrel. Take an audio level before each video recording. Always turn on the camera mic to record ambient sound on a second sound track of the videotape or other recording media. At the end of the report, record at least one minute of ambient sound to help the editor bridge the sound shifts at the edit points.

Transmission

As you well know, some big stories have been shot and transmitted to a station or network solely with a cell phone. In such cases the content is more important than the picture and sound quality. You can of course also capture source footage on a laptop and transmit it to the station via the Internet. In normal news operations, however,

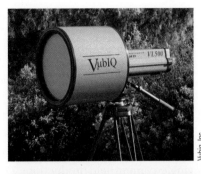

15.2 SMALL MICROWAVE TRANSMITTER
Small microwave transmitters are used when cable runs prove too unwieldy to connect a camera to the remote truck. This tripod-supported transmitter has a reach of about 1,600 feet (500 meters).

Vubiq, Inc.

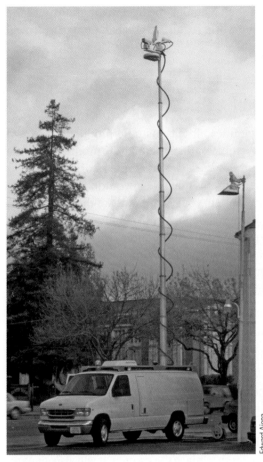

Edward Aiona

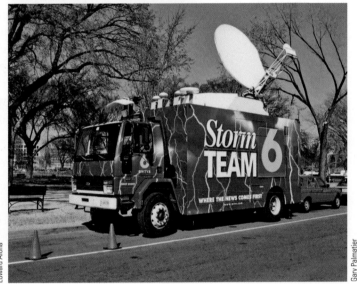

Gary Palmatier

15.1 ENG VAN
For ENG and routine productions, a large car or sport utility vehicle can serve as a production van. If the signal must be relayed to the station for live transmission or video recording, a vehicle that contains video-recording equipment, generators, and microwave transmission equipment is used.

15.3 SATELLITE UPLINK TRUCK
The satellite uplink truck is a portable station that sends the video and audio signals to a specific satellite.

you use a van with recording and transmission equipment to relay the video and audio signals back to the station and ultimately to the transmitter or satellite. **SEE 15.1**

The signal can be sent from the camera to the van by ordinary camera cable or via a small microwave transmitter attached to the camera. A more reliable way is to connect the camera to a tripod-mounted transmitter. **SEE 15.2** From the van the signal can be further relayed by microwave to the transmitter. If the signal must be directly uplinked to a communications satellite (positioned 23,300 miles above the earth), an *uplink truck* that contains the satellite transmitting equipment is used. **SEE 15.3** The satellite then amplifies the signal and sends it back to the receiving earth station or stations, called downlinking.

Although signal transmission is always done by qualified engineers, you should at least know what is needed to get the live signal from the camera to the station transmitter. Broadcasting the casual chitchat among the host in the studio and the guests located in different corners of the world requires a great amount of technical equipment and know-how.

▋ ELECTRONIC FIELD PRODUCTION

Electronic field production (EFP) includes all out-of-studio productions except news and the big remotes that more resemble multicamera studio productions than single-camera field productions. Documentaries, magazine news stories, investigative reports, travel shows, and exercise programs that are shot outdoors are all EFPs.

Because all field productions are planned, you can prepare for them in the preproduction phase. The more preproduction that goes into an EFP, the more likely it is to succeed. In fact, EFP needs the most careful preparation. Unlike in the studio, where most of the equipment is already installed, in EFP you must take every single piece of equipment to the shoot. A wrong or missing cable can delay the production for hours or even cause its cancellation.

Preproduction: Remote Survey

In ENG you may be sent at a moment's notice to a location you have never seen in your life; when doing a field production, on the other hand, it makes sense to look at it before showing up with talent, crew, and production gear.

A field inspection is called a ***remote survey*** or site survey. You should do a remote survey even if the field production is relatively simple, such as interviewing someone in a hotel room. Looking at the room beforehand will help you decide where to position the guest and the interviewer and where to place the camera. It will also give you important technical information, such as specific lighting and sound requirements.

For example, the small table and the two chairs may be adequate for getting optimal shots of the interviewer and the guest, but the large picture window behind the table will certainly cause lighting problems. If you shoot against the window, the guest and the interviewer will appear in silhouette. Drawing the curtains would require lighting the interview area with portable instruments. **ZVL2** LIGHTS→ Color temperature→ light sources

Are there enough electrical outlets for the lighting instruments? Are they convenient? Perhaps you can move the table and the chairs away from the window or use the window as fill or even side-back light. Will the new setup still be workable for the interviewer and the guest and, most importantly, the camera? Will the background be reasonably interesting, or will it interfere with the shots? Now listen to the room. Is it relatively quiet, or do you hear noises through the door or window or from the air-conditioning? Can you disconnect the telephone so that it won't ring during the interview? As you can see, even this relatively simple field production will benefit a great deal from a preproduction remote survey.

For complex productions, careful remote surveys are essential. You need to find out what the event is all about, where it is to take place, how to adapt the environment to the medium requirements, and what technical facilities are necessary for video-recording or telecasting the event. For a relatively simple field production, the director and/or the producer usually make up the survey team. For elaborate productions, you need to add a technical expert—the technical director (TD) or the engineering supervisor. If possible, have a contact person accompany you on the initial remote survey.

Contact person   The ***contact person***, or contact, is someone familiar with the remote location who can help you adapt the environment to the production requirements. For the hotel room interview, for example, the contact person should not be the guest you are about to interview but rather someone who has the knowledge and the authority to get certain things done in the hotel. If you overload a circuit with the lighting instruments, the contact should be able to call the hotel engineering or maintenance department immediately and have the circuit breaker reset. To prevent the telephone from ringing during the interview, the contact should be able to have the hotel operator hold all calls or a maintenance person disconnect the phone line temporarily. The contact might even find you an empty hotel room that is better suited for video-recording the interview than the one the guest actually occupies.

If the field production involves the coverage of a scheduled event over which you have no real control, such as a parade or sports match, the contact person must be thoroughly familiar with the event and supply you with vital information, such as names and the order of the parade entries. Most importantly, the contact should help you gain access to restricted areas or to facilities at times when they are ordinarily locked. Always get the contact's full name, title, postal and e-mail addresses, and pager, cell, fax, business, and home phone numbers. Also establish an alternate contact and have one or the other accompany you on the initial remote survey. This is especially important if the EFP is scheduled during off-hours or on a weekend.

Conducting the survey   Whenever possible, try to conduct the survey at the same time of day as the scheduled field production so that you can see just where the sun will be. The position of the sun will ultimately determine camera placement when shooting outdoors—as well as indoors when large windows are in camera view.

Be sure to prepare a location sketch, which is similar to a studio floor plan. The location sketch should show the major streets and structures of the outdoor production environment as well as the main features of the indoor production space, such as hallways, doors, windows, and principal furnishings. Even if the field production happens in an actual field, make a sketch that indicates the approximate size of the production area, the major crossroads, and the location of the sun. Include such details as parking areas, location of the EFP vehicle or remote truck, and the closest toilet facilities. **SEE 15.4 AND 15.5** The following table lists the major survey items and the key questions you should ask. **SEE 15.6**

If you have scheduled a field production outdoors, what will you do if it rains or snows? Obviously, it is a good idea to have alternative dates for a field production, unless the event is going on regardless of weather conditions, such as a football game or the Thanksgiving Day parade.

15.4 OUTDOOR LOCATION SKETCH

An outdoor location sketch should show the main streets, buildings, and facilities of the immediate production area. It should also indicate the location of the EFP vehicle and the nearest toilet facilities. Also note the position of the sun during the scheduled production period.

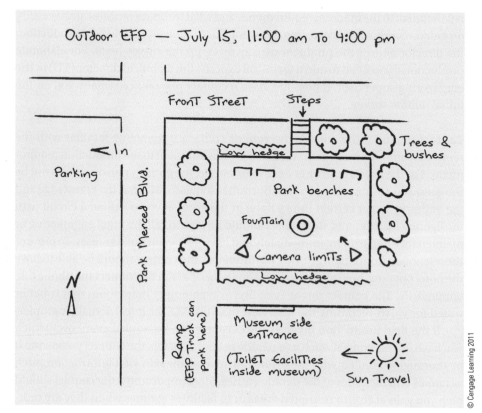

15.5 INDOOR LOCATION SKETCH

The indoor location sketch should show the principal production areas (room and hallway), windows and doors, and major furnishings, such as desks, chairs, plants, and file cabinets.

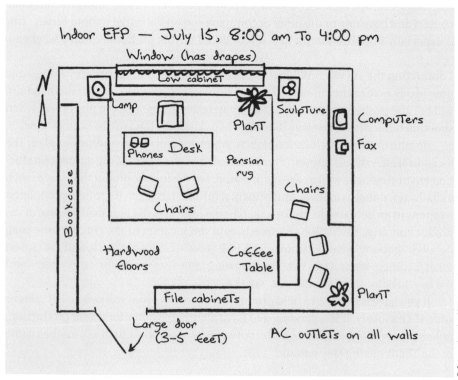

15.6 REMOTE SURVEY

SURVEY ITEM	KEY QUESTIONS
Contact	Who is the principal contact? Title; postal and e-mail addresses; and business, cell, home, pager, and fax numbers. Who is the alternate contact? Title; postal and e-mail addresses; business, cell, home, pager, and fax numbers.
Place	What is the exact location of the telecast? Street address, telephone number. Where can cast and crew park and eat? Where are the closest toilet facilities?
Time	When is the remote telecast? Where is the sun at the beginning and the end of the telecast?
Event	What type of action can you expect? Where does the action take place?
Cameras (stationary)	Where are the major positions of the camcorder? When doing a multicamera remote, how many cameras do you need to cover the event? Try to use as few as possible. What are the locations of the cameras? Do not shoot from, or place the cameras on, opposite sides of the action. In general, the closer together the cameras are, the easier and less confusing the cutting will be. Shoot with the sun, not against it. Try to keep the sun behind or to the side of the cameras for the entire telecast. Use an umbrella or large card behind you to prevent the sun from washing out the foldout monitor. Are there any large objects blocking the camera view, such as trees, telephone poles, or billboards? Will you have the same field of view during the actual time of the telecast? Spectators may block a camera's field of view, although at the time of the survey the view was unobstructed. Do you need camera platforms? How high? Where? Can the platforms be erected at this particular point? If a camera is connected to a power outlet or camera control unit (CCU), what is its action radius? How long a cable run do you need? What camera mounts do you need? For which cameras?
Lighting	If you need additional lighting, what kind, and where? Can you use reflectors? Can the lighting instruments be conveniently placed? Can you place back lights so that they are out of camera range? Are there windows that let in a large amount of daylight? Can they be covered or filtered so that they do not cause silhouette or color temperature problems? How many watts can each circuit handle?
Audio	What type of audio pickup do you need? Where do you need to place the microphones? Which mics are appropriate? What is the exact action radius so far as audio is concerned? Which are stationary mics and which are handled by the talent? Do you need wireless microphones? Otherwise, how long must the mic cables be? Do you need to make special arrangements for the audio, such as audio foldback or a speaker system that carries the program audio to the location? Do you need long-distance mics for sound pickup over a great distance? Where should the mics be located?
Power	What is the power source? Even if you run the camcorders by battery, what about the lights? Does the contact person have access to the power outlets? If not, who does? Make sure that the contact is available at the times of the remote setup and the actual production. Do you need extension cords or power cables? Do the extension cords fit the power outlets at the remote location? Do you need a power generator?
Intercommunications	What type of intercom system do you need? In a multicamera production, you need to set up a system that is similar to the studio intercom. How many I.F.B. channels and/or stations do you need, and where should they go? Do you need walkie-talkies to coordinate the crew efforts? Do you need a cell phone hookup?
Location of production vehicle	If you need a large production vehicle, such as a remote truck, where can you park it? Is it close enough to the event location? Does the production vehicle block traffic? Make sure that parking is reserved for the production vehicle and the cars of talent and crew.
Miscellaneous	Will you need the assistance of the local police or other security service to control vehicle and pedestrian traffic or to secure parking?

Production: Outdoors and Indoors

Each field production has its own requirements and challenges. Although your careful preproduction survey should have eliminated most of the potential problems, here are a few considerations that are not part of the remote survey: equipment checklist, outdoor field production, indoor field production, and general production reminders.

Equipment checklist   The success of the field production depends a great deal on thorough preproduction and how well you have prepared the time line. Contrary to the studio, where all major installations and equipment are readily available, you need to transport every single piece of equipment to the EFP site.

Prepare a checklist that includes all of the equipment and verify every item that is loaded onto the EFP vehicle. Use the same list when reloading the equipment for the return trip. The type and the amount of equipment you need depends on the production requirements and, specifically, on the preproduction survey. Check the following list of equipment items you need to consider for EFP.

CHECKLIST: FIELD PRODUCTION EQUIPMENT

☑ **Camcorders** How many do you need? If a spare camera is available, take it along, even if it is of lower quality. In case of emergency, a properly lighted interview shot with a digital consumer camcorder will certainly be better than having no camcorder at all.

☑ **Camera mounts** Always take along a tripod, even if you intend to work the camera from your shoulder. Do you need special camera mounts, such as tripod dollies, jib arms, or beanbags?

☑ **Recording media** Do you have the proper media for the camcorders and the video recorders (VRs)? Not all ¼-inch videotape cassettes fit all digital camcorders. If the new 60-minute cassette has little tape on its supply reel, you can be sure that it will not give you the recording time stated on the box. Note that not all camcorders accept mini-cassettes. If you use memory cards or optical discs, do they fit the camcorder, and do you have enough of them for extended recording periods? Do you need an additional external VR? This is especially important if you use a DSLR camera for the shoot.

☑ **Power supply** How will you power the camcorder? Are the batteries fully charged? Take several along. If you use an AC/DC power supply, do you have enough AC extension cords to reach the AC outlet? You also need extension cords for portable lighting instruments and a field monitor. If the monitor or external light is battery-powered, do you have the right battery? Is it fully charged? Do you have a spare battery along or the appropriate charger?

☑ **Audio** In addition to lavalier microphones, bring at least one shotgun mic and one hand mic. For a more ambitious EFP, you need to match the mics to the acoustics of the location. Are the mic cables long enough to reach the camcorders or audio mixer? If you intend to use wireless mics, do the transmitter and the receivers work properly? All remote mics, including lavaliers, need windscreens. Shotgun mics need additional windsocks. Test them before leaving for the remote location and again before the video recording. Do you need mounting equipment, such as clamps, stands, or fishpoles? Do you need a mixer or an additional audio recorder? Do you need an XLR pad? Don't forget earphones for the fishpole operator and the audio-recording technician.

☑ **Cables and connectors** Do you have the appropriate cables and connectors? Most professional equipment operates with BNC connectors for the video coaxial cables and XLR connectors for balanced audio cables (see figures 4.23 and 7.26). Some camcorders use RCA phono and mini connectors instead of XLR connectors, also shown in figure 7.26. Bring along some adapters for video and audio cables. Double-check all connectors and adapters. If you need to connect the camera to an RCU (remote control unit), you also need an external monitor. Do you have enough camera cable with the proper connectors?

☑ **Monitor and test equipment** Be sure to take along a monitor for playback. If you do a multicamera EFP with a switcher, each camera input needs a separate preview monitor unless you have a portable switcher unit with a flat-panel multiscreen preview. If a narrator is describing the action, you must provide a separate monitor for him or her. In field productions that require high-quality pictures, you need test equipment, such as a waveform monitor and a vector scope, which tests the Y and C signals. Ordinarily, the technical crew chief (usually the TD) is responsible for such items, but you should still see to it that they are part of the equipment package.

☑ **Lighting** More often than not, you will need at least one or two portable lighting kits, each containing several lighting instruments, barn doors, diffusers, light stands, and spare bulbs. Use floodlights (softlights) or diffusion tents and umbrellas for large-area lighting. Do the spare bulbs actually fit the lighting instruments? Do they burn with the desired color temperature (3,200K or 5,600K)? Use light-blue and amber gels on the lighting instruments if you need to raise or lower the color temperature, unless the lights come with color temperature filters. White diffusion material is always needed to soften key lights. Reflectors (white cards, foam core, aluminum foil, or professional collapsible reflectors) are essential for outdoor productions. Even when shooting indoors, reflectors are often much easier to manipulate than additional instruments.

The lighting package should also include: a piece of muslin to cover an off-camera window; a piece of black cloth to cut down on unwanted reflections; diffusion umbrellas; a light meter; extra light stands; and clamps and sandbags for securing the light stands. Unless you have access to expandable battens, take along some 1 × 3 lumber for constructing supports for small lighting instruments. Pack a roll of aluminum foil for making reflectors, heat shields, or makeshift barn doors. You will also need a few wooden clothespins to attach the diffusion material or gels to the barn doors of the lighting instruments. Take enough AC extension cords and adapters that fit household outlets. `ZVL3` LIGHTS→ Field→ indoor

☑ **Intercom** In small field productions, you do not need elaborate intercom setups, but you should always leave a telephone number at home base where you can be reached in case of an emergency. A cell phone is a must if you do primarily EFP. Do not use a cell phone near a wireless mic, however; it will add a high-pitched tone to your recorded audio. For larger field productions, you need a small power megaphone or walkie-talkies to reach a dispersed crew. If you use a multicamera and switcher system, you need to set up a regular PL intercom.

☑ **Miscellaneous** Here is what you should also take along on every EFP: extra scripts and time lines to be posted; field VR log forms; a slate or clapboard; several large rain umbrellas and "raincoats" (plastic covers) to protect equipment and crew in case of rain; a white card for white-balancing; a large newsprint pad and markers for writing cue cards or other information for the talent while on the air or recording; if necessary, a remote teleprompter with batteries and cables; several rolls of gaffer's tape and masking tape; white chalk; wooden clothespins to hold things in place, even if you don't use any lighting instruments; a makeup kit; a large bottle of water; a small plastic bowl; paper towels; a broom and trash bags; and plenty of sandbags.

Test all equipment before loading it onto the EFP vehicle. At the very least, do a brief test recording with the camcorder to check that video and audio can be properly recorded. If you don't have a battery tester, attach the batteries one by one to the camera to see that they are properly charged. Test each mic and each lighting instrument before loading it. All of this checking may seem like a waste of time—until you get stuck far from your production facility with a malfunctioning camcorder, mic, or light that you neglected to test.

Outdoor field production The production environment for an outdoor EFP is pretty much determined by the production location. All you can do is decide which portions of the environment you want to show.

Weather When outdoors you are at the mercy of the elements. Always be prepared for bad weather. As mentioned, take raincoats along for the cameras (a plastic tarp will do in a pinch) and rain gear for yourself and the crew. As old-fashioned as it may seem, a large umbrella is still one of the most effective means of keeping rain off people and equipment.

If you move from a chilly outside location to indoors, let the camcorder warm up a bit. The extreme temperature change could cause condensation in the recording section, shutting down its operation automatically. Such a shutdown will certainly put a crimp in the shooting schedule. In extremely cold weather, zoom lenses and even the video-recording transport in camcorders have a tendency to stick. Keep the camera in a vehicle and run the camcorder for a while when it is exposed to the cold temperature to prevent the lens and the recording mechanism from sticking. If possible, take a car-battery-powered hair dryer along to speed up the defrosting. Some mics refuse to work properly in extremely low temperatures unless protected by a windscreen or windsock. Always have a backup plan in case it rains or snows.

Most importantly, watch the weather for shot continuity. If video-recording a brief scene of two people talking to each other requires several takes that stretch over an hour or so, you may have a cloudless sky as the background for the first few takes and a cloudy one for the last takes. The sudden appearance of clouds or rain between question and answer does not exactly contribute to good continuity. So long as you are aware of the problem, you can try to choose a background that does not show the time progression, or arrange the time line so that the time change does not jeopardize postproduction editing.

Foreground With a prominent foreground piece in the shot—a tree, fencepost, mailbox, or traffic sign—you can dramatically improve the scene, make the composition more dynamic, and give it depth. If there is no natural foreground piece, you can often plant one. Instead of looking for a convenient foreground tree, you can simply handhold and dip a tree branch into the shot. The viewer's mind will fill in the rest and perceive the whole tree.

Background Always look beyond the main action to avoid odd juxtapositions between foreground and background. You must also be careful to maintain background continuity in postproduction editing. For instance, if you show a prominent tree in the background of shot 1 but not in the following shot with a similar background, the tree will seem to have mysteriously disappeared when the two shots are edited together. A similar problem might occur if you lock down the camera for shot 1 and continue shot 2 from the same camera position. Because the camera will most likely have shifted a little between the two shots, the background tree seems to jump ever so slightly from one position to another. An alert editor will probably rule against editing such shots together. You can easily prevent jump cuts by changing the angle or field of view (how close you show the scene) between the two shots. **ZVL4** CAMERA→ Composition→ background

> **KEY CONCEPT**
>
> Watch the weather and the background for shot continuity when shooting outdoors.

Indoor field production   When shooting indoors you may have to rearrange the furnishings and (more often) the pictures on the wall to get optimal shots. Before you start moving things around, always make a record of what the room looks like, by drawing a sketch, photographing the scene with a digital still camera, or video-recording the room with a camcorder. Even if you have a detective's memory, such a record will come in handy when you have to put things back where they belong.

Lighting   Be especially aware of the lighting requirements. Again, check the available outlets. Be careful when placing lights inside a room. Do not overload the circuits. Turn off the lights whenever you don't need them. Sandbag all light stands and make heat shields with aluminum foil, especially when a lighting instrument is close to curtains, upholstered furniture, books, or other combustible materials.

Even on a cloudy or foggy day, the color temperature of the light coming through an outside window is considerably higher than that of indoor light. In this case, you must decide whether to boost the color temperature of the indoor light or lower the color temperature of the daylight coming through the window. It is usually simpler to gel the indoor lights (with a light-blue color media) than the window. **ZVL5** ▸ LIGHTS→ Field→ indoor **ZVL6** LIGHTS→ Color temperature→ white balance

Audio   Except for simple interviews, good audio always seems to be a bigger problem than good video. This is because the microphones are often placed at the last minute without adequate consideration of the acoustics of the room or the specific sound pickup requirements. You should include a brief audio rehearsal in the EFP time line so that you can listen to the sound pickup before beginning the video recording. If you have brought along several types of mics, you can choose the one that sounds best in that environment.

As you recall, it is better to record the principal sounds and the ambient sounds on separate tracks rather than mix them in the field. You may find, however, that this separation is difficult, if not impossible, in most EFP situations. In this case try to record a good portion of the background sounds without the principal sounds after the scenes have been recorded. If necessary, you can then mix the background sounds into the scene during postproduction. If careful mixing between foreground and background sounds is required, you can do it much better in the postproduction studio. If you mix the sounds in the field, you pretty much eliminate the option of further adjustment in postproduction.

General production reminders   Very much like the routines developed for the studio—striking the sets, rolling up the cables, putting the cameras back in their regular parking places, and sweeping the floor—there are some general guidelines for EFP.

Respecting property   Whenever you are on someone else's property, be mindful that you are a guest and are actually intruding with your video gear and production people. Working in video does not give you license to invade people's homes, upset their routines, and make unreasonable demands on them. When you shoot a documentary in somebody's well-kept garden, don't trample on carefully tended plants just to get a good camera position. Dragging equipment dollies or camera cases along polished floors or valuable rugs is not appreciated by the owner. Even if pressed for time, do not get so caught up in the production activities that you lose your common sense.

Safety As in studio productions, in EFP you need to be constantly aware of safety precautions. Don't be careless with extension cords, especially if you string them outside in damp weather. Tape all connections so that they become waterproof and don't pull apart. If you have to lay cables across corridors or doorways, tape them down with gaffer's tape and put a rug or rubber mat over them. Better yet, try to string them above so that people can walk below them unhindered. Ask the police to assist you when shooting along a freeway or in downtown traffic.

Logging During the shoot keep an accurate field log of all takes, good and bad. Label all recording media and boxes and put them in a container used solely for transporting the video-recorded material. Activate the cassette protection devices so that the source media cannot be accidentally erased. Keep the hard drive cassettes and memory cards away from magnetic fields.

Strike and cleanup Put everything back the way you found it. Consult your documentation of where things were before you rearranged them. When you are finished, verify that everything is back as it was. Remove all gaffer's tape that you may have used to secure cables; pick up all extension cords, sandbags, and especially empty soft drink cans and other lunch remnants. An EFP team that had finally gained access to an old and venerable family ranch after weeks of pleading by the show's producer was invited back with a smile for the follow-up show because one of the production people had brought along a broom and swept the area clean.

Loading the equipment When loading the equipment onto the remote vehicle after the shoot, pull out the checklist again. Check off every item that is loaded up for the return trip. Look for missing items right away; it is usually easier to find them right after the production than days or weeks later. Check that all source media are properly labeled and that the field logs match the labels. Keep them close to you until you return to home base.

KEY CONCEPT

After the production make sure that you leave the location the way you found it and that you bring back everything you took to the field.

Postproduction: Wrap-Up

The first order of business is to make protection copies of all source material, especially if you can't perform the capture by the nonlinear editing (NLE) system right away. Check whether all source footage displays a time code. If not, you need to add one. You can make window dubs while transferring the source footage to the hard drive of the NLE system.

You now need to review the copies of the source footage and prepare an accurate VR log. Recall that such a log must list all shots by in- and out-numbers, identify good and bad takes, indicate predominant vectors, and list the principal audio for each shot. Then it is up to the postproduction people to put it all together into a comprehensive message that ideally will convey the program objective.

◼ BIG REMOTES

While learning basic video production, you will probably not be called upon to participate in a big remote, but you should have at least some idea of what a remote is all about and what equipment it requires. A **big remote** is the field production of a large, scheduled event done for live transmission or the uninterrupted recording of a live event.

Big remotes are devoted to the coverage of major events that are not staged specifically for video (at least not obviously); these include parades, sporting events, awards shows, significant international occasions, and political gatherings. Big remotes resemble multicamera studio productions in every respect, except that the "studio" is now a remote location: the plaza in front of city hall, the sports stadium, or the Senate chambers.

All big remotes use high-quality field cameras (studio cameras with lenses that can zoom from an extreme long shot to a tight close-up) and EFP cameras, which are normally connected to the remote truck by cable. The **remote truck** represents a compact studio control room and equipment room. It contains an image control center with preview and line monitors; a switcher with special effects; a character generator (CG); intercom systems (PL, PA, and elaborate IFB systems); an audio control center with a fairly large audio console, digital audio-recording and playback equipment, monitor speakers, and an intercom; a video-recording center with several high-quality VRs that can handle regular recordings as well as instant replays, slow-motion, and freeze-frames; and a technical center with CCUs, technical setup equipment, and patchbays for camera, audio, intercom, and light cables. **SEE 15.7**

Although remote trucks can draw power from available high-capacity electrical sources, most engineers prefer to use portable generators. Because big remotes are often done live, remote trucks have microwave transmission facilities that range from small links from camera to truck, to larger ones that transmit the signal from truck to transmitter. Some large remote trucks have their own satellite uplink; others connect to an uplink truck if a direct satellite feed is necessary. In very big remotes, one or more additional trailers may be used for supplemental production and control equipment, such as slow-motion and instant-replay facilities.

> **KEY CONCEPT**
>
> Big remotes resemble multicamera studio setups except that the event takes place outside the studio, and the control room is located in a truck.

◼ SYNTHETIC ENVIRONMENTS

Not all environments are lens-generated (photographed by the video camera); they can be synthetic as well. **Synthetic environments** are generated electronically.

You can create a great variety of backgrounds with a chroma key, which you recall uses a specific color (usually blue or green) for the backdrop into which various still or moving images can be keyed. The actual foreground action then appears to be playing in the keyed environment. Because you can use any photograph, video recording, or computer-generated effect as a chroma-key source, your choices of background are unlimited. **SEE 15.8**

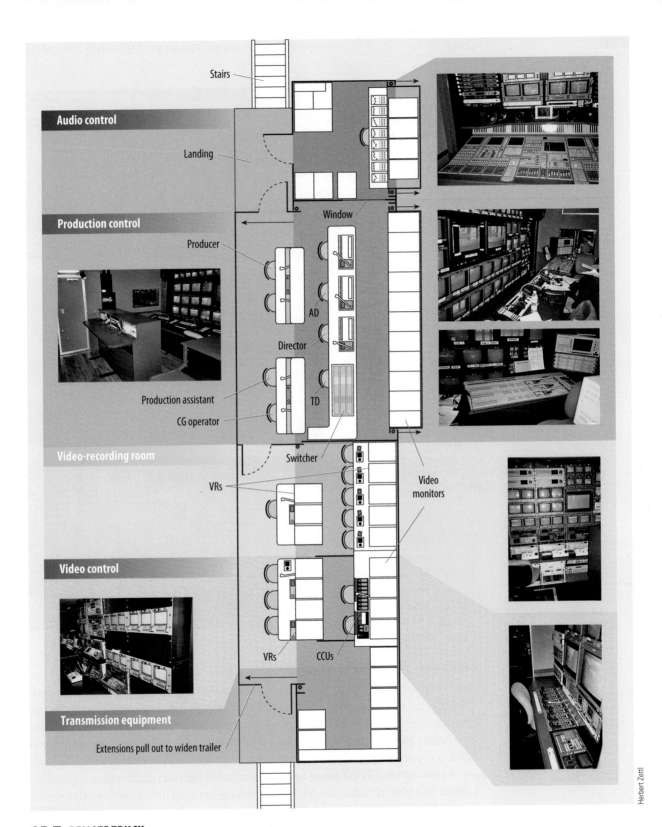

Stairs

Audio control

Landing

Window

Production control

Producer

AD

Director

Production assistant

TD

CG operator

Video-recording room

Switcher

VRs

Video monitors

Video control

VRs

CCUs

Transmission equipment

Extensions pull out to widen trailer

Herbert Zettl

15.7 REMOTE TRUCK
The remote truck is a studio control center on wheels. It contains the audio, production, and video control centers; a number of VRs; and transmission equipment.

15.8 CHROMA KEY

A The source for this background image is a video frame of the museum exterior from the electronic still store system.

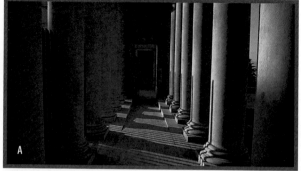

B The studio camera focuses on the actor playing a tourist in front of the blue chroma-key backdrop. The lighting must match the environment of the background.

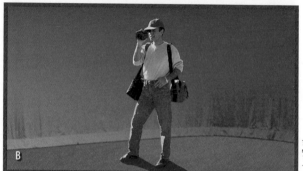

C All blue areas are replaced by the background image; the tourist appears to be in front of the museum.

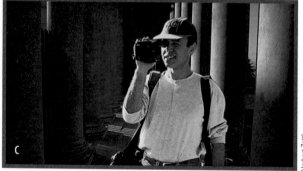

Computer-Generated Settings

Despite all the skills you may have acquired in adapting a real environment to your video needs, the computer offers novel alternatives. Outdoor landscapes can be computer-generated, which you have seen many times in fantasy landscapes. But even highly realistic settings are often easier to compose with the computer than to build in the studio.

As you can see in following figure, the actor in the red windbreaker is standing in front of a blue chroma-key backdrop, resting her arm on a small wooden frame that is also painted chroma-key blue. **SEE 15.9** When chroma-keying the actor into the computer-generated background picture, all blue areas (the backdrop and the wooden frame) drop out and are replaced with the computer image of the lighthouse.

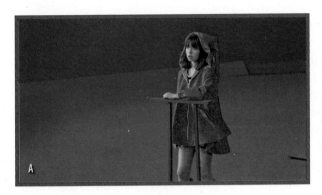 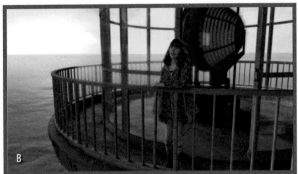

15.9 COMPUTER-GENERATED SET

A The blue areas of this chroma-key set, including the armrest, will be keyed out and replaced with the computer-generated image of a lighthouse.

B The finished effect places the actor in a convincingly realistic location.

Because she was positioned exactly right in relation to the virtual background set, she now appears to be standing on the lighthouse platform, resting her arm on the railing, and looking out to sea.

If all of this is possible, couldn't we have actors move about in front of a chroma-key backdrop and then key them into the lighthouse platform? Yes, that is certainly possible. There is, however, the problem of a changing perspective when the real foreground figures (the actors) move against the static background, although sophisticated computer programs can compensate for such a perspective shift. The real problem with such a setup is not technical but human: it is extremely difficult for even experienced actors to operate in a horizonless, undefined space. You can easily get disoriented simply by stepping into such a limitless blue-screen or green-screen environment.

Virtual Reality

Virtual reality consists of computer-generated environments and events that are animated. You could, for example, change the peaceful scene of vacationers traveling happily along a sun-drenched road into a frightening event by replacing the fluffy white clouds with a huge computer-generated twister. You can also generate objects, animals, or even people and place them in, or have them move through, this virtual environment. There are synthetic environments that appear to be three-dimensional, provided you wear 3D glasses when viewing the video screen.

Whenever you combine a chroma-key or virtual reality environment with real performers, you must pay particular attention to the lighting so that the shadows of the synthetic environment correspond with the ones in the actual scene (see figure 15.8). The size and motion relationships between foreground and background are also a major concern. Unless you want to achieve a special effect, the synthetic environment should fit the dimensions of the people keyed into it and change according to the camera angles.

Computer-Controlled Environments

Computer-aided design (CAD) programs can produce from a floor plan an actual scenic environment. Once the virtual scenery is set up, you can try out a number of color schemes and textures for the walls, doors, windows, and floor. For example, you can try out a blue rug, change it to red or beige, and take it out again—all with the click of a mouse. You can also put virtual furniture into the set and dress it with properties of your choice. You use the mouse to select the items from a menu and drag them into the desired positions. If you don't like what you selected, simply delete the images and try new ones.

Other such programs let you light the set, with a menu offering an assortment of lighting instruments that you can drag onto the set and aim at the elements of the virtual production environment. You can test different lighting setups until you are satisfied. Finally, you can have a virtual camera move through this virtual space to show you what shots you can get from various angles and lens settings. Some sophisticated programs let you generate virtual performers and move them through the synthetic space. ZVL7 LIGHTS→ Triangle lighting→ try it

> **KEY CONCEPT**
>
> Synthetic environments can be built partially or entirely by computer.

Even if you do not use the virtual sets as the "actual" environment for your production, such interactive displays of setups, colors, and camera and talent positions are an invaluable preproduction aid.

When combined with live action, virtual environments can yield startling effects.

MAIN POINTS

▶ **Field Production**

A field production is any production that happens outside the studio, including ENG (electronic news gathering), EFP (electronic field production), and big-remote telecasts.

▶ **Electronic News Gathering**

ENG involves newspeople and equipment for reacting quickly to a news event. The event is either video-recorded and edited for a regularly scheduled broadcast or, if important enough, transmitted live. Normally, preproduction amounts to being ready to go anywhere at a moment's notice rather than conducting a remote survey.

▶ **Electronic Field Production**

EFPs, which occur away from the studio, are thoroughly planned in preproduction. They include documentaries, magazine news stories, investigative reports, and on-site interviews. One of the most important steps is the remote, or site, survey. In EFP you cannot create an environment but must adapt to one.

▶ **Preproduction**

A remote survey is necessary for all field productions except ENG. It supplies important information about such technical aspects as power availability, lighting, and sound requirements, and it gives the director an idea of where to place the camera or cameras. Establishing a reliable contact person is an important part of preproduction.

▶ **Production: Outdoors and Indoors**

Use a checklist when taking the equipment into the field and bringing it all back. When shooting outdoors, changing weather conditions and random sounds are a constant hazard and must be carefully monitored. Be aware of changing lighting conditions, which may seriously influence editing continuity. Be careful not to place lighting instruments too close to combustible materials. Respect people's property and take safety precautions at all times. Carefully monitor the audio pickup.

▶ **Big Remotes**

Big remotes are devoted to the live coverage or the video-recording of large scheduled events, such as parades, sports, and award shows. Big remotes resemble multicamera studio setups and are coordinated from the remote truck. The remote truck houses a complete production control room, primarily devoted to image control, audio control, elaborate intercom facilities, video-recording and video control sections, various other technical facilities, and transmission equipment.

▶ **Synthetic Environments**

Environments can be electronically generated through chroma keys of video-recorded or computer-generated backgrounds. Interactive virtual reality programs can create entirely synthetic, computer-generated environments. Some CAD programs can also simulate production situations (camera positions, scenery colors, or lighting), which can be manipulated to find the most effective combinations. Such a simulation is a valuable preproduction aid.

Z E T T L' S   V I D E O L A B

For your reference or to track your work, the *Zettl's VideoLab* program cues in this chapter are listed here with their corresponding page numbers.

Production Control: Talent and Directing

Now that you have acquired the basics of video production, you need to learn more about the people who work in front of the camera—the talent—and what they must do to convey the intended message. It is, after all, the people who appear on-camera who do the communicating with the viewers, not the ones who work behind the scenes to make the communication possible. Once you work as a video professional, you are bound to be asked to appear on-camera from time to time, as either a guest or a host. And, as a director, before you can tell the talent what to do, you must have some idea of what to expect from a good performer or actor.

Part VI explains what you need to know about performing in front of the camera—whatever your focus in video production—and prepares you for the culminating experience of multicamera directing from the control room and for single-camera film-style directing.

KEY TERMS

actor A person who appears on-camera in dramatic roles. The actor always portrays someone else.

blocking Carefully worked-out positioning, movement, and actions by the talent and for all mobile video equipment used in a scene.

cue card A large hand-lettered card that contains copy, usually held next to the camera lens by floor personnel.

foundation A makeup base, normally done with water-soluble cake makeup; it is applied with a sponge or sprayed on the face and sometimes all exposed skin areas.

IFB Stands for *interruptible foldback* or *feedback*. A prompting system that allows communication with the talent while on the air. A small earpiece worn by on-the-air talent carries program sound (including the talent's voice) or instructions from the producer or director.

moiré effect Color vibrations that occur when narrow, contrasting stripes of a design interfere with the scanning lines of the video system.

performer A person who appears on-camera in nondramatic shows. The performer does not assume someone else's character.

talent Collective name for all performers and actors who appear regularly in video.

teleprompter A prompting device that projects moving copy over the lens so that the talent can read it without losing eye contact with the viewer.

Talent, Clothing, and Makeup

The incredible amount of equipment and effort that goes into making even a relatively simple production, such as somebody's announcing on-camera the latest company news, is generally lost on viewers. All they judge the show by is whether the person on-screen is likable and whether he or she is doing a credible job. Similarly, viewers attribute the success of a talk show primarily to the host, not to how the show is lighted, how the cameras are handled, or whether the director shows a reaction shot at the right moment.

Video *talent* refers (not always accurately) to all people performing in front of the camera. We divide talent into two groups: performers and actors. *Performers* are primarily engaged in nondramatic activities. They portray themselves and do not assume the role of other characters; they are aware of the viewers and usually communicate directly with them by addressing the camera lens. *Actors*, on the other hand, always portray someone else; they assume a character role, even if the role is close to their own personality. They normally do not acknowledge the presence of the viewers but interact with other actors. Because performance and acting requirements differ in several major ways, they are discussed separately here. Specifically, this chapter focuses on the techniques of appearing in front of the camera, what to wear, and how to do basic makeup for the television camera.

> **KEY CONCEPT**
>
> Talent refers to video performers and actors. Performers portray themselves; actors portray someone else.

▶ **PERFORMING TECHNIQUES**
Performer and camera, audio and lighting, and timing and prompting

▶ **ACTING TECHNIQUES**
Environment and audience, close-ups, and repeating action

▶ **AUDITIONS**
How to prepare

▶ **CLOTHING**
Texture, detail, and color

▶ **MAKEUP**
Technical requirements and materials

■ PERFORMING TECHNIQUES

As a performer you are always aware of the viewers. Your goal is to establish as much rapport as possible with them and to have them share in what you do and say. Because video is normally watched by individuals or small groups of people who know one another, your performance techniques must be adjusted to this kind of communication intimacy. Always imagine that you are looking at and talking with someone you know, seated a comfortably short distance from you. Some performers prefer to imagine that they are talking to a small group or family; in any case, don't envision yourself at a mass rally, addressing "millions of viewers out there in videoland." When viewers watch you at home, it is you who is "out there"—not they. They are not visiting you; you are visiting them.

To help you establish this intimate viewer contact and perform effectively in front of the camera, you need to familiarize yourself with some production aspects of performer and camera, audio and lighting, and timing and prompting.

Performer and Camera

As a performer you have a communication partner—the video camera. It represents the viewer with whom you are talking. You may find it difficult at first to consider the camera your communication partner, especially when all you actually see while talking is the camera and the red tally light or the screen of the prompting device, some lights shining in your eyes, and perhaps the dim outlines of a few production people who are more interested in operating the equipment than in what you have to say.

Eye contact   To establish eye contact with the viewer, you need to look at the lens, not at the camera operator or the floor manager. In fact, good performers keep constant eye contact with the lens and seem to look *through* it rather than merely at it. When pretending to look through the lens, you will more readily extend your glance through the screen—toward the viewer—than if you simply stare at the camera. Also, you must maintain eye contact with the lens much more directly and constantly than when engaged in a real interpersonal conversation. Even a small glance away from the lens will be highly distracting for the viewer; it will not be seen as a polite relief from your stare but as an impolite loss of concentration or interest on your part.

If two or more cameras are used while you demonstrate a product, you need to know which of the two will remain on you and which will take the close-up of the product. Keep looking at the camera (or, rather, through the camera lens) that is focused on you, even when the director switches to the close-up camera that is focused on the product. This way you will not get caught looking in the wrong direction when your camera is switched back on the air.

If both cameras are on you and switched according to the director's cues, you must shift your view from one camera to the other to maintain eye contact. A good floor manager will assist you greatly in this task. He or she will warn you that a switch is coming up by pointing on the director's "ready" cue to the camera you are addressing and then motioning you over to the other camera on the "take" cue. On the floor manager's cue, shift your glance quickly but smoothly in the new direction. Unless told otherwise, always follow the floor manager's cues (shown in figure 16.1) and not the tally light that indicates the hot camera.

If you discover that you are talking to the wrong camera, look down as if to collect your thoughts, then look up into the on-the-air camera. Such a shift works especially well if you use notes or a script as part of your on-camera performance. You can simply pretend that you are consulting your notes while changing your view from the wrong camera to the correct one.

Close-ups   On video you will be shown more often in a close-up (CU) than in a medium or long shot. The camera scrutinizes and magnifies your expressions and your every move. It does not politely look away when you scratch your ear or touch your nose; it reveals faithfully the nervous twitch or mild panic when you have forgotten a line. The close-up also does not give you much room to maneuver. In a tight CU, a slight wiggle of the product you are holding will look as though an earthquake has struck. The close-up also accelerates your actions. If you lift up a book at normal speed to show its cover, you will most certainly yank it out of the close-up camera's view. Here are a few important rules for working with close-ups:

- When on a close-up, do not wiggle—remain as steady as possible.

- Keep your hands away from your face, even if you feel your nose itching or perspiration collecting on your forehead.

- Slow down all movements.

- When demonstrating small objects, keep them as steady as possible in one position. Better yet, keep them on a display table.

- If they are arranged on a table, do not pick them up. You can point to them or tilt them a little to give the camera a better view.

There is nothing more frustrating for the camera operator, the director, and especially the viewer than when a performer snatches the object off the table just as the camera is getting a good close-up of it. A quick look at the studio monitor will tell you whether you are holding or tilting the object for maximum visibility.

Also, don't ask the camera to come a little closer to get a better look at what you are demonstrating. As you well know, the camera operator can get a close-up not just by dollying in with the camera but much more quickly and easily by zooming in. You will not make the director very happy by asking for specific shots when the shot is already on the air or when there are technical problems that prevent the director from calling up the desired material. Talent—however eager they may be to look good on the air—should not try to outdirect the director.

Audio and Lighting

A clear, resonant voice alone will not make you a good performer. Besides having something to say and saying it clearly and convincingly, you need to be aware of the more technical audio requirements.

Microphone techniques   At this point you should briefly review the use of microphones in chapter 7. Here is a short recap of the basic mic techniques of concern to you as a performer:

KEY CONCEPT

Eye contact with the camera lens establishes eye contact with the viewer.

KEY CONCEPT

When on a close-up, keep your gestures small and slow.

■ Treat all microphones gently. They are not props but highly sensitive electronic devices that respond to minute vibrations of air.

■ If you work with a lavalier microphone, don't forget to put it on. If not assisted by the floor manager, run the cable underneath your jacket or shirt and fasten the mic to the outside of your clothing. Unless you are wearing a wireless lavalier, once "wired" you have a highly limited action radius. Don't forget to remove the mic and lay it gently on the chair before walking off the set. When using a wireless mic, check the power switch on the transmitter belt pack. It should be on when going on the air but off whenever you are on a break.

■ When using a wired hand mic, see how far the mic cable will let you move. In normal situations hold the hand mic chest high and speak *across* it, not into it. In noisy surroundings hold it closer to your mouth. When interviewing a guest with a hand mic, hold it near you when speaking and toward the guest when he or she responds. Gently pull the mic cable with your free hand when moving around. If you need both hands for something else, tuck the mic under your arm. A wireless hand mic will make your movements less restricted but adds the liability of losing the mic signal on its way to the receiving station.

■ Once a desk mic has been placed by the audio engineer, don't move it. Check with the engineer if you think it should be closer to you or pointing more toward you. Talk toward it, not away from it.

■ When using a stand mic, adjust the height of the stand so that the mic is a little below your chin, pointing toward your mouth.

■ When a fishpole or boom mic is used, be aware of where the mic is when you are moving, but don't look at it. Move slowly and avoid fast turns. If you see that the boom operator can't follow you with the mic, stop, then move on when the problem is fixed.

Taking a level   When asked to test the mic or to take a level, don't blow into it; say your opening remarks at the volume you will use when on the air. Performers who rapidly count to 10 or speak with a low voice off the air and then blast their opening remarks when on the air will not win points with the audio engineer.

Do not speak louder simply because the camera moves farther away from you. Although you correctly assume that the camera is the viewer with whom you are communicating, the camera distance has nothing to do with how close the shot actually is. More importantly, the distance of the camera has nothing to do with how close the mic is. If you wear a lavalier, you are heard at the same level and with the same presence regardless of whether the camera is 2 or 200 feet away from you.

Checking lighting   Although as a performer you need not be concerned with lighting, it doesn't hurt to quickly check the lighting on the monitor before going on the air. When outdoors, don't stand against a brightly lighted background unless you want to be seen in silhouette. When in the studio, if there is no light hitting your eyes, you are not in the lighted area. Ask the director where you should stand so that you will be properly lighted. In a play, when you happen to get off the rehearsed blocking into a dark area, move a little until you feel the heat of the lights or see the lights hitting you. Such concern for lighting should not encourage you to take over the director's function. Always check with the director if you have any questions about the technical setup and your activities within it.

Timing and Prompting

As a performer you need to be acutely aware of time, whether or not you are on the air. Even nonbroadcast video programs are packaged according to a rigid time frame. Because the audience has no idea about your time restrictions, you need to appear relaxed and unhurried when you have only 2 seconds left or you have to fill unexpectedly for an additional 15 seconds. Experienced performers can accurately judge a 10-second or 30-second duration without looking at a clock or stopwatch. Radio professionals can teach you a lot in this respect. They seem to be totally relaxed and never hurried, even when working up to the last second of the segment. Such timing skills are not inborn but acquired through practice. Don't put too much trust in your instincts; use a clock or stopwatch for precise timing. In any case, respond immediately to the floor manager's time cues.

IFB system   As a performer you must rely on—or put up with—a variety of prompting devices. The most direct prompting device is the **IFB**—interruptible foldback or, as it is also called, interruptible feedback—system. You have probably seen performers or interview guests in remote locations touch their ear as though they were adjusting a hearing aid. That is exactly what they are doing.

When using interruptible foldback, you wear a small earpiece that carries the total program sound, including your own remarks, unless the producer or director (or some other production member connected to the IFB system) interrupts the program sound with specific instructions. For example, if you interview the CEO of a new Internet company, the producer may cut in and tell you what question to ask next, to slow down, to speed up, or to tell the guest that she has only 15 seconds to explain the latest multiplatform software. The trick is to not let the viewer know that you are listening to somebody other than the guest.

If you conduct an interview long-distance, with the guest in a remote location, he or she may also wear an IFB earpiece that transmits your questions on a separate IFB channel. You may find that guests may experience some problem with the IFB system, especially when the location is relatively noisy. Try to test the IFB system in advance to make sure the guest is comfortable using it.

Floor manager's cues   The time, directional, and audio cues are usually given by the floor manager. As a performer you will quickly learn that the floor manager is your best friend during the production. A good floor manager will always be in your vicinity, telling you whether you are too slow or fast, whether you are holding the product correctly for the close-up camera, and whether you are doing a good job. Unlike prompting devices, the floor manager can react immediately to your needs and to unforeseen performance problems. Normally, the floor manager cues you with a system of hand signals. **SEE 16.1**

16.1 FLOOR MANAGER'S CUES

Because the microphone is live during production, the talent must rely on visual time cues, directional cues, and audio cues from the floor manager.

CUE	SIGNAL	MEANING	SIGNAL DESCRIPTION
TIME CUES			
Standby		Show about to start.	Extends hand above head.
Cue		Show goes on the air.	Points to performer or live camera.
On time		Go ahead as planned (on the nose).	Touches nose with forefinger.
Speed up		Accelerate what you are doing. You are going too slowly.	Rotates hand clockwise with extended forefinger. Urgency of speed-up is indicated by fast or slow rotation.
Stretch		Slow down. Too much time left. Fill until emergency is over.	Stretches imaginary rubber band between hands.

16.1 FLOOR MANAGER'S CUES *(continued)*

CUE	SIGNAL	MEANING	SIGNAL DESCRIPTION
TIME CUES			
Wind up		Finish up what you are doing. Come to an end.	Similar motion to speed-up, but usually with arm extended above head. Sometimes expressed with raised fist, good-bye wave, or hands rolling over each other as if wrapping a package.
Cut		Stop speech or action immediately.	Pulls index finger in knifelike motion across throat.
5 (4, 3, 2, 1) minute(s)		5 (4, 3, 2, 1) minute(s) left until end of show.	Holds up five (four, three, two, one) finger(s) or small card with number on it.
30 seconds (half minute)		30 seconds left in show.	Forms a cross with two index fingers or arms. Or holds card with number.
15 seconds		15 seconds left in show.	Shows fist (which can also mean wind up). Or holds card with number.
Roll VR or server (and countdown) 2, 1, take VR or server		VR is rolling. VR or server insert is coming up.	Holds extended left hand in front of face, moves right hand in cranking motion. Extends two, one finger(s); clenches fist or gives cut signal.

16.1 FLOOR MANAGER'S CUES *(continued)*

CUE	SIGNAL	MEANING	SIGNAL DESCRIPTION
DIRECTIONAL CUES			
Closer		Performer must come closer or bring object closer to camera.	Moves both hands toward self, palms in.
Back		Performer must step back or move object away from camera.	Uses both hands in pushing motion, palms out.
Walk		Performer must move to next performance area.	Makes a walking motion with index and middle fingers in direction of movement.
Stop		Stop right here. Do not move anymore.	Extends both hands in front of body, palms out.
OK		Very well done. Stay right there. Do what you are doing.	Forms an *O* with thumb and forefinger, other fingers extended, motioning toward talent.

Edward Aiona

16.1 FLOOR MANAGER'S CUES *(continued)*

CUE	SIGNAL	MEANING	SIGNAL DESCRIPTION
AUDIO CUES			
Speak up		Performer is talking too softly for current conditions.	Cups both hands behind ears or moves hand upward, palm up.
Tone down		Performer is too loud or too enthusiastic for the occasion.	Moves both hands toward studio floor, palms down, or puts extended forefinger over mouth in *shhh*-like motion.
Closer to mic		Performer is too far away from mic for good audio pickup.	Moves hand toward face.
Keep talking		Keep on talking until further cues.	Extends thumb and forefinger horizontally, moving them like a bird's beak.

Edward Aiona

As a performer you must react to the floor manager's cues immediately, even if you think that a cue is inappropriate. Good performers don't try to run the show all by themselves: they react to the floor manager's cues quickly and smoothly.

Don't look around for the floor manager when you think that you should have received a time cue; he or she will make sure that you see the signal without having to break eye contact with the lens. As you just learned, even a brief glance away from the lens will tend to interrupt the connection you have established with the viewer. Once you have seen a cue, don't acknowledge it in any way. The floor manager can tell by your subsequent actions whether you received the cue.

KEY CONCEPT

Always respond promptly to the floor manager's cues.

16.2 TELEPROMPTER

The teleprompter consists of a small video display that reflects the copy onto a slanted glass plate directly in front of the lens. The talent can see the copy clearly while it remains invisible to the camera.

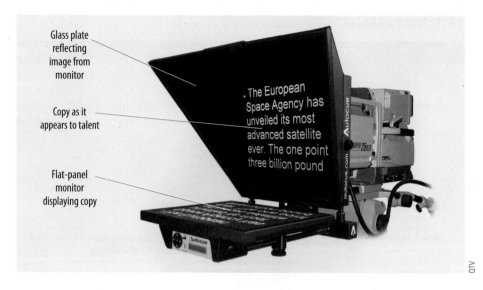

Glass plate reflecting image from monitor

Copy as it appears to talent

Flat-panel monitor displaying copy

The European Space Agency has unveiled its most advanced satellite ever. The one point three billion pound

Teleprompter   The ***teleprompter*** enables you to read copy without taking your eyes off the lens. The teleprompter projects the copy off a small, usually flat-panel monitor or computer screen (such as an iPad) onto a slanted glass plate mounted directly in front of the lens. **SEE 16.2** While you read the copy on the glass plate, the lens can view the scene through the plate without seeing the lettering. All newscasters and hosts of shows with a newslike format use teleprompters, as do people who deliver on-camera speeches. The copy itself is normally generated by a word-processing program and sent by a desktop computer to the teleprompter monitor on each camera that focuses on you. The computer scrolls the copy from the bottom of the teleprompter screen to the top exactly at your reading speed. If you have to change your pace to stay within the allotted time, the scrolling speed can be adjusted accordingly by the floor manager or the teleprompter operator.

When you are using a teleprompter, the camera should be far enough away that the viewers don't see your eyes moving back and forth while reading yet close enough that you can clearly see the copy. Experienced performers still manage to look through the lens and make eye contact with the viewer even while reading the copy in front of the lens. Not an easy job by any means!

For the small teleprompters that can be used in the field, the copy originates from a laptop computer that also controls the speed of the scroll. Simple field prompters use a paper roll that projects hand-lettered copy over a glass plate in front of the lens. On some field prompters, the paper roll is mounted below or to the side of the lens. The roll is battery-powered and can operate at various speeds. If nothing else is available, read the copy off your script or notebook.

Cue cards   One of the simplest yet most highly effective cueing devices is ***cue cards***—sheets of paper or posterboard on which the copy is hand-lettered with a marker. The size of the cards depends on how well you can see and how far away the camera is when you're reading the copy. A floor person must hold the cards as close to the lens as possible so that you don't have to glance too far away and thereby lose eye contact with the viewer. You must read the copy out of the corner of your

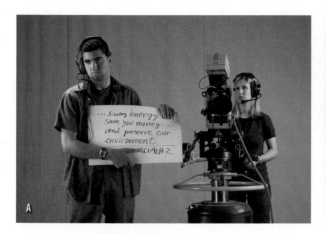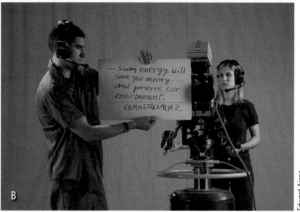

16.3 HANDLING CUE CARDS

A This is the wrong way to hold cue cards. The card is too far away from the lens. The floor person is also covering part of the copy, is not reading along with the talent, and is therefore unable to change cards when necessary.

B This is the correct way to hold cue cards. The cards are as close to the lens as possible, and the floor person reads along with the talent to facilitate smooth card changes.

eye while looking through the lens. Decide on an optimal distance, then check that the cards are in the right order and that the floor person holds them close to the lens without covering the copy. **SEE 16.3** Ask the floor person to practice changing cards with you. A good floor person will change the card while you are reading the last few words and have the new card up while you are still delivering the last word from the previous card. He or she will not dump the used cards on the floor but put them quickly and quietly on a nearby chair.

ACTING TECHNIQUES

To become a good video or television actor, you must first learn the art of acting. Whereas performers always portray themselves, actors assume somebody else's character and identity. Even the best stage and film actors must adjust their acting style and methods to the requirements of the video medium. Some of the major requirements are working in a technical environment without an audience, adjusting to the relatively small video screen and the frequent use of close-ups, and repeating the action.

Environment and Audience

As a video actor, you will be surrounded by much more technical equipment than if you were on-stage. Worse, you do not have an audience whose reaction you can see, hear, and feel. Unless there is a studio audience, all you see are lights, cameras, and production people who do not pay much attention to you. In fact, you will often feel neglected even by the director. But realize that, in a multicamera production, the director has to coordinate numerous pieces of equipment and a great many personnel and that some of the technical operations may need more of the director's attention than you do.

You may feel even more abandoned because of the lack of a live audience. Unlike in the theater, where the audience remains in a fixed place and gives you direct and indirect feedback, the camera does not respond to your performance but stares at you impassively and moves quietly all around you. It may look at your eyes, your back, your feet, your hands, or whatever the director chooses for the viewer to see. It is a little like acting for theater-in-the-round, except that in video all viewers, as represented by the cameras, sit at arm's length and even join you on-stage to get a better look at you.

Because the viewer is in such close virtual proximity, you need not, and should not, project your actions and emotions to somebody sitting in the last row. The camera, which is doing the projecting for you, can convert a small gesture into a grand act. When on a close-up, there is no need for you to act out your role; instead you must feel it. Internalizing your role is a key factor in acting for video.

The intimacy of video also influences the way you speak. You must reduce the customary stage declamation and voice projection to clear but normal speech. Good writers help you in this task. Instead of having you, as Oedipus, dramatically request, "Who planned the crime, aye, and performed it, too?" on video you would simply ask, "Who did it?" Exaggerated voice projection is one of the hardest things for stage actors to unlearn when switching over to the video medium. In video (as in radio) precise enunciation is more important than volume and projection.

Most importantly, you must be able to memorize your lines quickly and accurately. Although there may be a variety of prompting devices available (mainly cue cards), you cannot and should not rely on them if you want to be convincing in your role. Because many of your lines serve as important video and audio cues that trigger all sorts of production activity, you cannot afford to ad-lib. Ad-libbing a cue line will inevitably cause chaos in the control room and prompt a retake of the scene.

Close-Ups

The frequent use of close-ups does not give you much wiggle room. Sometimes you must stand uncomfortably close to other actors or move much more slowly than normal without appearing to do so to stay within camera range. The close-up also limits your gestures. If, when seated, you lean back or move forward unexpectedly, you may fall out of focus, and weaving sideways just a little may take you right out of the frame.

The close-up shots require that you be extremely exact in following the rehearsed *blocking*—the carefully worked-out stage positions, movements, and actions relative to other actors and the camera. If you stray even a few inches from the rehearsed blocking, you may be out of camera range or obstructed by another actor. To help you remember the critical blocking positions, the floor manager will usually mark the floor with chalk or masking tape.

If you or another actor is off the mark in an over-the-shoulder shot, you may be obstructed from camera view by the other actor. You can tell whether the camera sees you simply by looking for the camera lens. If you see the lens, the camera can see you; if you don't see the lens, you aren't being seen. If you can't see the lens, inch to one side or the other without obviously searching for it. Although the camera can be adjusted to get the proper over-the-shoulder shot, it is usually easier to adjust your position than the camera's.

KEY CONCEPT When acting for the video medium, you must feel the role rather than act it out.

To remember blocking, you may want to establish a mental road map that has prominent landmarks, for example: "First stop, the left corner of the table. Second landmark, couch. Move to the couch and sit on the right. Third landmark, telephone. Get up and move behind the telephone table facing the center camera. Pick up the phone with the left hand."

Although good directors will block you as much as possible so that your movements are natural, you will occasionally be in a position that seems entirely wrong to you. Do not try to correct this position until you have consulted the director. A certain shot or special effect may very well warrant such blocking.

> **KEY CONCEPT**
> Meticulously follow the rehearsed blocking during each take. If you can't see the camera lens, you won't be in the shot.

Repeating Action

Unlike the theater, where your performance is continuous and according to plot progression, video acting—like acting for digital cinema—is usually done piecemeal. You may have to switch from the happy opening scene to the intensely sad closing scene, merely because both play in the friend's living room. By remembering the exact blocking, you can also help preserve continuity. For instance, if you held the telephone receiver in your left hand during the medium shots, don't switch it to your right hand for the close-ups.

In single-camera productions, it is normal to repeat the same scene over and over again. Such repetitions are done to get a variety of camera angles or close-ups or to correct major or minor technical problems. In repeats not only must you duplicate exactly the lines and the blocking for each take, you must also maintain the same energy level throughout. You cannot be "on" during the first takes and "off" during the later close-ups.

◾ AUDITIONS

Auditions are a test of your ability as a performer—and of your self-confidence. Not getting the part does not mean that you gave an inferior performance but that somebody else was thought to be more suitable. Take all auditions equally seriously, whether you are trying out for a starring role in a big television drama or for a one-line off-camera utterance for a product demonstration; but don't take them so seriously that you begin to suffer from depression because you didn't get the part.

Although you may not know beforehand what will be asked of you in an audition, you can still prepare for it. Be properly groomed and wear something that's appropriate and that looks good on-camera. Arrive on time, bring your résumé, and don't be intimidated by either the number or the caliber of people auditioning with you. You all have an equal chance; otherwise you would not have been called to try out for the part. Have a brief monologue ready that shows your range of ability. Keep your energy up even if you have to wait half a day before being asked to perform.

If you get a script beforehand, study it carefully. If the script calls for you to talk about or demonstrate a specific product, such as a new computer, familiarize yourself with the product ahead of time. The more you know about the product, the more confidence shows in your delivery. Ask the person conducting the audition what shots the camera will take. If close-ups predominate, slow down your actions and avoid excessive movements. Remember that you are not addressing a large audience but an individual or a small family seated near you.

As an actor be sure that you understand the character you are to portray. If you are not sure what the segment you are to read or the character you are to portray is all about, ask the person conducting the audition (casting director or producer)—but don't ask for the proper motivation. As a professional actor, you are expected to motivate yourself. Be inventive but don't overdo it. When working in video, little mannerisms, such as a specific way of keeping your eyeglasses from slipping down your nose, playing with keys, or using a slightly rusty fingernail clipper while engaged in a serious conversation, tend to sharpen your character more readily than simply working up to a high emotional pitch.

■ CLOTHING

What you wear depends not only on your preference and taste but also on how the camera sees your clothing. Because the camera can look at you from extremely close range or from a distance, you need to consider the overall line of your clothes as well as the texture and the accessories.

The video camera has a tendency to add a few pounds. Clothing that is cut to a slim silhouette usually looks more favorable than something loose and baggy. Avoid horizontal stripes; they emphasize width instead of length and make you look wider around the middle.

Texture and Detail

Because of the frequent close-ups in video and the extremely sharp image of the high-definition television (HDTV) camera, you need to pay special attention to texture and detail. Textured material and ties look better than plain so long as the texture is not too busy or contrasting. Even the best video cameras have a difficult time handling closely spaced and highly contrasting patterns, such as black-and-white herringbone weaves or checks. The electronic scanning of the video image can't accommodate the frequency of the high-contrast pattern, causing the camera to create a new, highly distracting frequency that shows up on-screen as vibrating rainbow colors and patterns, called a ***moiré effect***. **SEE 16.4**

Prominent, high-contrast horizontal stripes may also extend beyond the clothing fabric and bleed through surrounding sets and objects as though you were superimposing venetian blinds. On the other hand, extremely fine detail in a pattern will either look busy or, more likely, show up on-screen as smudges even in high-definition video.

You can always provide the necessary texture by adding such details as jewelry or a tie or scarf. Although you will undoubtedly prefer wearing jewelry that you like, refrain from overly large or too many pieces. Too much tends to look gaudy on a close-up, even if the jewelry is of high quality.

Color

Again, the colors you select are not entirely up to you but must fulfill certain technical requirements. If the set you work in is primarily beige, a beige dress or suit will certainly get lost in it. Avoid wearing blue if you are part of a chroma-key effect that uses blue as the backdrop. The chroma-key process renders transparent everything

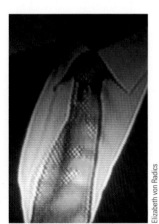

Elizabeth von Radics

16.4 MOIRÉ EFFECT
The vibrating rainbow colors on the white shirt and gray tie of this performer were caused by narrow rows of reflective dots that crashed with the scanning of the video image.

blue and lets the background show through. If you wear a tie or suit whose blue color is similar to that of the chroma-key backdrop, you will see the keyed background image in place of the clothing. Of course, if the chroma-key color is green, you can wear blue but not green.

Although you may like red, most video small cameras—and some home television sets—don't. Even fairly good video cameras may show highly saturated reds as vibrating and bleeding into other areas. Such video problems, called artifacts, are especially noticeable in low-light conditions. But even if the camera can handle the brilliant red of your dress or sweater, your home receiver is apt to display vibration or bleeding effects.

Most high-quality cameras, especially HDTV cameras, can tolerate a relatively high brightness contrast. But, again, you will make the lives of the lighting director and the VO (video operator) much easier if you reduce the contrast of your clothing.

You should therefore avoid wearing colors of high-contrast brightness, such as dark blue and white, or black and white. If you wear a black jacket over a reflecting white shirt, the camera or the VO does not know whether to adjust for the high brightness values of the white or the low values of the black. If the VO tries to lighten the black areas to see some shadow detail, the white areas become overexposed and begin to "bloom." If the VO tries to control the overly bright areas to show more picture detail, the shadows become uniformly dense. Your skin tones will also get a few shades darker. Obviously, if you are a dark-skinned performer, you should not wear a starched white shirt (unless the occasion demands it). If you wear a dark suit, reduce the brightness contrast by wearing a pastel shirt rather than a white one.

As you remember from chapter 4, this contrast problem is especially noticeable when the camcorder is on automatic iris. The auto-iris will seek out the brightest spot in the picture and close down the aperture to bring this excess light under control. As a consequence all other picture areas darken accordingly. If, for example, you wear a brilliantly white jacket while standing in a relatively dark restaurant set, the auto-iris will close to darken the brightness of the jacket and, unfortunately, the already dark set as well. What you will get is a properly exposed jacket in front of an underlighted set.

■ MAKEUP

All makeup is used for three reasons: to enhance appearance, to correct appearance, and to change appearance.

Most video productions require makeup that accentuates the features rather than changes them. For female performers, normal makeup does just fine on-camera; male performers may need some makeup primarily to reduce light reflections off the forehead or bald spots and perhaps to cover some wrinkles and skin blemishes. In both cases, makeup must be adjusted to the technical requirements of the HDTV camera and the scrutiny of the close-up.

Technical Requirements

The video camera prefers warmer (more reddish) makeup colors over cooler (more bluish) ones. Especially under high-color-temperature lighting (outdoor or fluorescent lighting, which is bluish), bluish red lipsticks and eye shadow look unnaturally blue. Warm makeup colors, with their reddish tint, look more natural and provide sparkle, especially on dark skin.

Regardless of whether you are a dark-skinned or light-skinned performer, you should use *foundation* makeup that matches your natural skin color. This foundation is available in various types of cake or spray-on makeup. If you perspire readily, you should use a generous amount of foundation; although it won't prevent your perspiration, it will make it less visible to the camera.

Because you will be seen in close-ups, your makeup must be smooth and subtle. This requirement is the reverse of theatrical makeup, which you need to exaggerate as much as possible for the spectators sitting some distance from the stage. Good video makeup should accentuate your features but remain invisible, even on an HDTV close-up. Most talent who appear on high-definition shows prefer spray-on make-up. This make-up comes in liquid form that is applied to the face with an airbrush (an atomizer using compressed air). Be careful, however, that you don't spray too much on your face. Too much foundation makeup will make your face look pasty or even mask-like, especially when the lighting is rather flat (slow falloff).

Always apply makeup under the lighting conditions of the performance area. If you apply your makeup in a room that has bluish fluorescent (high-color-temperature 5,600K) lights and then perform under normal studio lights (with a lower color temperature of 3,200K), your makeup will be excessively reddish and your face will look pink. The opposite is true if you apply your makeup under lights with the indoor standard of 3,200K and then move into a location that is illuminated with the outdoor standard of 5,600K: your makeup will look unnaturally bluish.

If possible, check your makeup on-camera: have the camera take a close-up of you in the performance area. You may consider this method a frivolously expensive mirror, but it will benefit you during the performance.

If you need to use makeup to change your appearance, enlist the services of a professional makeup artist.

Materials

You can easily find a great variety of excellent makeup materials for video. Most large drugstores carry the basics for improving a performer's appearance. Women performers are generally experienced in using cosmetic materials and techniques; men may, at least initially, need some advice.

The most basic makeup item is the foundation that covers minor skin blemishes and cuts down light reflections from oily skin. Water-based cake makeup foundations are preferred over the more cumbersome grease-based foundations. The Max Factor or Kryolan pancake series is probably all you need for most makeup jobs. The colors range from a warm light ivory for light-skinned performers to a very dark tone for dark-skinned performers. For critical HDTV makeup, you may try the Dinair Airbrush Foundation, or Kryolan's HD micro foundation, which is sprayed on and looks smooth even in an extreme CU with a digital cinema camera.

Women can use their own lipsticks or rouge, so long as the reds do not contain too much blue. Other materials, such as eyebrow pencils, mascara, and eye shadow, are generally a part of every performer's makeup kit. Additional materials, such as hairpieces and even latex masks, are part of the professional makeup artist's inventory. They are of little use in most nondramatic productions.

Regardless of whether you will be on-camera as a reporter, a performer, or an actor, a solid knowledge of basic video production techniques will aid you greatly not only when working behind the camera but also when working in front of it. In fact, talent who know basic production techniques seem more relaxed in front of the camera and more prepared to cope gracefully with the technical commotion and the unexpected problems while on the air than performers who know little or nothing about video production. Likewise, knowing how to perform and act in front of the camera will make you a better behind-the-camera production person. As a director, such knowledge is essential.

M A I N P O I N T S

▶ *Talent*

Talent are people who work in front of the camera. Talent include performers, who are primarily engaged in nondramatic activities, and actors, who portray someone else.

▶ *Performing Techniques*

The performer must imagine the video camera as his or her communication partner, keep eye contact with the lens when addressing the viewer directly, handle the microphone for optimal sound pickup, and use prompting devices discreetly, without making the viewer aware of it.

▶ *Close-Ups*

When on a close-up (CU), move slowly and keep all gestures small.

▶ *Prompting Devices*

In addition to the floor manager's cues, the major prompting devices are the IFB (interruptible foldback or feedback) system, the studio or field teleprompter, and cue cards.

▶ *Cues*

Always respond promptly to the floor manager's cues.

▶ *Acting Techniques*

Good video actors learn how to work well within a highly technical environment, adjust to frequent close-ups, and repeat certain actions in the same way and with the same intensity.

▶ *Blocking*

Meticulously follow the rehearsed blocking during each take. If you can't see the camera lens, you won't be in the shot.

▶ *Clothing*

On-camera clothing should have a slim silhouette, with textures and colors that are not too busy or contrasting. The camera does not like closely spaced, high-contrast herringbone weaves or checks because they cause the camera to produce moiré effects. Try to avoid highly saturated reds, especially if you're using small camcorders.

▶ *Makeup*

Makeup is used to enhance, correct, and change appearance. Always apply makeup under lights that have the same color temperature as those in the performance area.

KEY TERMS

angle The particular approach to a story—its central theme.

blocking Carefully worked-out positioning, movement, and actions by the talent and for all mobile video equipment used in a scene.

camera rehearsal Full rehearsal with cameras and other pieces of production equipment. Often identical to the dress rehearsal.

dry run Rehearsal without equipment, during which the basic actions of the talent are worked out. Also called *blocking rehearsal*.

fact sheet Script format that lists the items to be shown on-camera and their main features. May contain suggestions of what to say about the product. Also called *rundown sheet*.

multicamera directing Simultaneous coordination of two or more cameras for instantaneous editing (switching). Also called *control room directing* and *live-switched directing*.

news script Fully scripted text with video information on page-left and news copy on page-right. The copy (spoken text) can also be in a large center column that contains some additional information.

program objective The desired effect of the program on the viewer. The defined process message.

script Written document that tells what the program is about, who says what, what is supposed to happen, and what and how the audience will see and hear the event.

shot The smallest convenient operational unit in video and film, usually the interval between two transitions. In cinema it may refer to a specific camera setup.

shot sheet A list of every shot a particular camera has to get. It is attached to the camera to help the camera operator remember a shot sequence.

single-camera directing Directing a single camera (usually a camcorder) in the studio or field for takes that are recorded separately for postproduction.

single-column drama script Traditional script format for television plays. All dialogue and action cues are written in a single column.

take Any one of similar repeated shots taken during video-recording and filming.

time line A breakdown of time blocks for various activities on the actual production day, such as crew call, setup, and camera rehearsal.

trim handles Recording additional footage before and after the major shot content for precise editing. Also called *edit margins* and *pads*.

two-column A/V script Traditional script format with video information (V) on page-left and audio information (A) on page-right for a variety of video scripts, such as for interviews, documentaries, and commercials. Also called *two-column documentary script*.

visualization The mental image of a shot. May also include the imagining of verbal and nonverbal sounds. Mentally converting a scene into a number of key video images and their sequence.

walk-through/camera rehearsal A combination of an orientation session for talent and crew and a follow-up rehearsal with full equipment. This combination rehearsal is generally conducted from the studio floor.

Putting It All Together: Directing

Directing is where everything you have learned so far comes together. The job description is relatively simple: all you need to do is tell people behind and in front of the camera what to do and how to do it. The difficulty is that you must know exactly what you want them to do before you can direct them to do it.

Of course, reading about directing or listening to somebody explain it can take you only so far. The real test is when you sit in the studio control room and literally call the shots. Once you feel comfortable with directing multiple cameras from the control room, you can adjust relatively easily to single-camera directing—in the studio or in the field.

Before you dash into directing by reserving cameras, drawing a storyboard, and marking up a script, you must ask yourself what the intended program is all about. Recall the discussion from chapter 1 about the production model: moving from the idea to ***program objective***—the desired effect on the viewer, then backing up to the specific medium requirements to achieve the process message—the actual effect. Fortunately, most scripts and program proposals state the program objective or purpose on the cover page or in the general introduction to the project.

You should also be clear about the angle with which the topic is approached. The ***angle*** of the program—its central theme and major storytelling approach or framework—is often buried in the script itself. The angle is usually provided by the writer or producer, but sometimes it is up to you, the director, to find one. The angle will then dictate your visual approach to the program.

Now it is time to learn about the various script formats, how to visualize and "hear" the scripted information as audio and video images, and finally how to coordinate your team to accomplish the actual production steps efficiently and reliably.

▶ **SCRIPT FORMATS**
   Fact, or rundown, sheet; news script; two-column A/V script; and single-column drama script

▶ **VISUALIZATION**
   Visualization of image, sound, context, and sequence

▶ **PREPARING FOR A MULTICAMERA STUDIO PRODUCTION**
Floor plan, talent blocking, camera positions, and script marking

▶ **CONTROL ROOM DIRECTING**
Terminology, time line, rehearsals, and directing the multicamera show

▶ **SINGLE-CAMERA DIRECTING**
Differences between multicamera and single-camera studio directing, and directing a single-camera production in the field

SCRIPT FORMATS

The *script* interprets the show idea into what the viewers should actually see and hear when watching the program. It is similar to a recipe in that it lists the major ingredients of the program and how they must be mixed to get the desired result. In the language of the production model, the script helps you translate the program objective into specific medium requirements. As a director you must know the basic script formats used in video production so that you can make this translation process as efficient and effective as possible.

Despite considerable variations, there are four basic script formats for video productions: the fact, or rundown, sheet; the news script; the two-column A/V script; and the single-column drama script.

Fact, or Rundown, Sheet

The *fact sheet* format is used for simple demonstrations by a show host. Also called a rundown sheet, it normally lists the major features of a product that the host should mention, although the presentation itself is ad-libbed. The director may write in the cameras used for the demonstration, but the cutting from one to the other depends on the host's actions. The rundown script format may also be used for routine shows, such as the morning show sequence of program segments that repeat Monday through Friday. **SEE 17.1**

News Script

The only thing that news scripts from different newsrooms have in common is that they are, more or less, two-column. In a **news script** format, every word spoken by the anchorperson is fully scripted. You may find news scripts that have two equally sized columns: The right column contains the spoken news copy plus the out-cues of the words of prerecorded segments, called packages. The left column contains cues to who is talking; the name, number, and length of the prerecorded clips, CG (character generator) copy, and effects; some shot designations; and whether the prerecorded insert is to be played with a voice-over (V/O) of the anchor describing what is happening on the video insert or with SOS (sound on source) or SOT (sound on tape)—the actual sounds that are recorded on the sound track of the news package. At other times the news copy takes center-stage and is written as a single-column text, with the nontext information squeezed into a narrow left-margin column or

```
Zettl's VideoLab 4.0 DVD-ROM COMMERCIAL
SHOW:
DATE:


PROPS:
Laptop computer running Zettl's VideoLab 4.0.
VideoLab package with disc as hand props.

FEATURES TO BE STRESSED:

1.   New multimedia product by Wadsworth/Cengage Learning.

2.   Sensational success.

3.   Was nominated for prestigious Codie Award.

4.   Designed for both the production novice and the video
     professional.

5.   Truly interactive. Provides users with a video studio in
     their own home. Easy to use.

6.   Users can proceed at their own speed and test their progress
     at any time.

7.   Will operate on both Windows and Macintosh platforms.

8.   Special introductory offer. Expires Oct. 20. Hurry. Available
     from all major software and bookstores. For more information
     or the dealer nearest you, visit www.academic.cengage.com.
```

17.1 FACT SHEET
The fact, or rundown, sheet lists the major points of what the talent is to do and show. The talent ad-libs the demonstration, and the director follows the talent's actions. No specific audio or video cues are listed.

embedded in the center column. In the latter case, the nontext information is clearly separated from the spoken copy by lines and/or a different typeface. **SEE 17.2**

A news package is a brief, prerecorded, self-contained story by the field reporter that is inserted into the newscast after the news anchor's lead-in. There are usually several packages in a newscast.

What news writers don't seem to agree on is just how to format the audio column. Many use uppercase letters for the spoken words, but some prefer upper- and lowercase letters; others use a combination of both. Reading from a printed page seems easier when the copy is in upper- and lowercase letters; when using a teleprompter, however, all-caps copy seems easier to read. In fact, some of the larger news services change all types of news scripts into an all-caps format when used as teleprompter copy.

Two-Column A/V Script

The two-column A/V (audio/visual) script is also called the two-column documentary script or, simply, documentary format, although it may be used for a variety of nondramatic programs, such as interviews, cooking shows, and commercials. In a

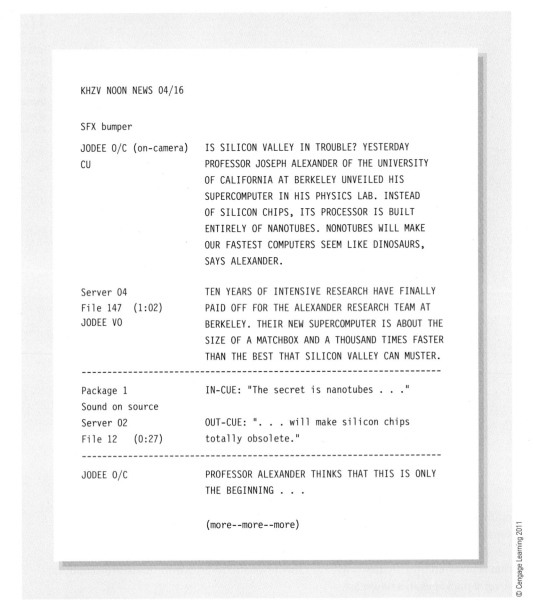

```
KHZV NOON NEWS 04/16

SFX bumper

JODEE O/C (on-camera)      IS SILICON VALLEY IN TROUBLE? YESTERDAY
CU                         PROFESSOR JOSEPH ALEXANDER OF THE UNIVERSITY
                           OF CALIFORNIA AT BERKELEY UNVEILED HIS
                           SUPERCOMPUTER IN HIS PHYSICS LAB. INSTEAD
                           OF SILICON CHIPS, ITS PROCESSOR IS BUILT
                           ENTIRELY OF NANOTUBES. NONOTUBES WILL MAKE
                           OUR FASTEST COMPUTERS SEEM LIKE DINOSAURS,
                           SAYS ALEXANDER.


Server 04                  TEN YEARS OF INTENSIVE RESEARCH HAVE FINALLY
File 147   (1:02)          PAID OFF FOR THE ALEXANDER RESEARCH TEAM AT
JODEE VO                   BERKELEY. THEIR NEW SUPERCOMPUTER IS ABOUT THE
                           SIZE OF A MATCHBOX AND A THOUSAND TIMES FASTER
                           THAN THE BEST THAT SILICON VALLEY CAN MUSTER.
---------------------------------------------------------------------
Package 1                  IN-CUE: "The secret is nanotubes . . ."
Sound on source
Server 02                  OUT-CUE: ". . . will make silicon chips
File 12    (0:27)          totally obsolete."
---------------------------------------------------------------------
JODEE O/C                  PROFESSOR ALEXANDER THINKS THAT THIS IS ONLY
                           THE BEGINNING . . .


                           (more--more--more)
```

17.2 NEWS SCRIPT

In this two-column news script format, the left margin contains such production information as who is on-camera, the type and the length of the video inserts, and special effects. The right or center column shows every word to be spoken by the newscaster as well as the audio in- and out-cues of the video-recorded inserts.

two-column A/V script, the left column contains all of the video information, and the right column lists all of the audio information. **SEE 17.3** Review the content of the script in figure 17.3, as well, as it is the basis of your control room directing assignment later in this chapter. **ZVL1** PROCESS→ Ideas→ scripts

Note that all audio cues in the audio column, including the names of the talent speaking the lines, are in uppercase letters. All spoken words are in upper-/lowercase style. The instructions in the video column use both upper- and lowercase. Some

```
LIGHT AND SHADOWS Series
Program No. 4: High- and Low-Key Lighting


VIDEO                              AUDIO

VR standard opening                SOS

Mary on camera                     MARY

                                   Hi, I'm Mary, your LD. Today I will
                                   show the differences between high-key
                                   and low-key lighting. No, high-key and
                                   low-key has nothing to do with how
                                   high or low the key light hangs but
                                   rather with how much light is on the
                                   scene. High-key has plenty of light on
                                   the scene. Low-key uses only a few
                                   instruments to illuminate specific
                                   areas. But high- and low-key make us
                                   feel differently about a situation.
                                   Let's watch.


Susan sitting on bench             OPEN MICS. SFX: DISTANT TRAFFIC SOUNDS.
waiting for bus                    OCCASIONAL CARS GOING BY.


Key titles


John walks to telephone


Freeze-frame                       SFX OUT - MARY (VO)

                                   This is a high-key scene. It is obviously
                                   daylight. There is plenty of light on
                                   the set with fairly prominent shadows.
                                   But the faces of the people have enough
                                   fill light to slow down the falloff and
                                   make the attached shadows transparent.
                                   Now let's see what John and Susan are
                                   up to.
```

17.3 TWO-COLUMN A/V SCRIPT

In the two-column A/V (audio/video) script format, the left column contains all of the video information, and the right column shows all of the audio information. The dialogue or narration is fully scripted.

VIDEO	AUDIO
John by the phone, looking for change	SFX: DISTANT TRAFFIC SOUNDS. OCCASIONAL CARS GOING BY.
John approaches bench	JOHN Excuse me. Could you please change a five-dollar bill? I need to make a call and . . .
Susan gets up and walks toward curb	SUSAN No!
Freeze-frame	MARY (VO) Oops. They don't seem to be hitting it off too well. In the meantime, note that the high light level helps give the scene a great depth of field. Although Susan and John are relatively far apart on the z-axis, they are both in sharp focus. Sorry about the interruption. Let's see how this plot develops.
CU John	JOHN I didn't mean to startle you. But I really need to make this call. You wouldn't have a cell phone I could borrow?
Susan studies the bus schedule; she looks through her purse	SUSAN No, I am sorry.

17.3 TWO-COLUMN A/V SCRIPT *(continued)*

```
VIDEO                          AUDIO

CU John                        JOHN
                               You wouldn't use pepper spray on me,
                               would you?

Susan moves to the lamp
post; John steps closer
                               SFX: BUS APPROACHES AND STOPS
                               POLICE SIREN COMING CLOSER
                               SUSAN
                               I'm not so sure . . .

Susan boards the bus           SFX: BUS PULLS AWAY

                               JOHN
                               Thanks a lot.
```

The scene will be repeated under low-key lighting. Mary now comments over the freeze-frames on the specifics of low-key lighting. She emphasizes the change in how we feel about the situation under high-key and low-key lighting.

```
Mary O/C                       MARY
                               I would certainly prefer to have John
                               ask me for change in the high-key scene
                               than in this low-key scene. Wouldn't
                               you? With all those ominous cast shadows
                               around and such sparse street lighting,
                               I wouldn't have taken a chance with him
                               either. Poor John!

Freeze-frame of                MUSIC
low-key scene

Closing credits

Fade to black
```

17.3 TWO-COLUMN A/V SCRIPT *(continued)*

scriptwriters maintain the all-caps convention because these words are not spoken. Because upper-/lowercase lettering is much easier to read, however, you will find that most scripts use that style for the video column.

Partial two-column A/V script   If there is considerable ad-libbing to be done by the talent, the audio column indicates only who is speaking and the general topic; such a script is generally called a partial two-column A/V script. **SEE 17.4** This partial A/V script format is often used for instructional shows, even if they contain some dramatic scenes.

VIDEO	AUDIO
CU of Katy	KATY But the debate about forest fires is still going on. If we let the fire burn itself out, we lose valuable timber and kill countless animals, not to speak of the danger to property and the people who live there. Where do you stand, Dr. Hough?
CU of Dr. Hough	DR. HOUGH (SAYS THAT THIS IS TRUE BUT THAT THE ANIMALS USUALLY GET OUT UNHARMED AND THAT THE BURNED UNDERBRUSH STIMULATES NEW GROWTH.)
MS of Katy and Dr. Hough	KATY Couldn't this be done through controlled burning? DR. HOUGH (SAYS YES BUT THAT IT WOULD COST TOO MUCH AND THAT THERE WOULD STILL BE FOREST FIRES TO CONTEND WITH.)

17.4 PARTIAL TWO-COLUMN A/V SCRIPT
The partial two-column A/V script format shows all of the video information in the left column but only partial dialogue or narration in the right column. The questions are usually fully scripted, but the answers are paraphrased.

Single-Column Drama Script

The *single-column drama script* format contains the complete dialogue, narration over video, and all major action cues in one column. **SEE 17.5** As you can see, all names of characters ("ALAN" and "VICKY") and audio cues ("THEME #2") are in uppercase letters. All spoken dialogue (or narration over a scene) is in upper-/lowercase. Specific delivery cues ("surprised") and directions ("getting an extra chair for Alan") are also in upper-/lowercase but are clearly isolated from the dialogue either by double-spacing or by parentheses or brackets. You will, however, find scripts in which these instructions are in all-caps. If you aspire to be a scriptwriter, don't ever include camera instructions. Specific descriptions of shots should always be omitted and left for the director to add in the visualization and script preparation phases.

> **KEY CONCEPT**
>
> The four basic script formats are the fact, or rundown, sheet; the news script; the two-column A/V script; and the single-column drama script.

■ VISUALIZATION

Take just a moment and pretend that you see your mother on television. Just how do you picture her? In a close-up (CU) or a medium shot (MS)? Seated or moving around? Do you see her indoors or out? What is she wearing? What is she doing? Reading? Getting ready for work? Cooking? Sweeping the front steps? Now imagine your dream car. What color is it? Is it parked in your garage or tearing up a winding country road? What sounds do you hear in these scenes?

What you just did is called visualization. In video production *visualization* means creating a mental image of a shot or a sequence of shots. A *shot* is the smallest convenient operational unit in video and film, usually the interval between two transitions. In a wider sense, visualization also includes imagining the sounds that go with the pictures. For the director visualization is an indispensable preproduction tool.

Image If the script gives you only general visualization cues, such as "young woman waiting at the bus stop" or "bus stop in an isolated part of town," you need to fill in the details to make a specific person out of the "young woman" and to give the bus stop a certain look (refer to the script in figure 17.3). You would certainly have different visualizations if the scene were to take place at midday than if it were played on a deserted street late at night. Providing such details is an important part of the director's job.

Sound Though you may find it difficult at first, you should always try to "hear" the sounds simultaneously with the pictures you are visualizing. For example, what sounds do you imagine at a brightly lit bus stop scene and at a dimly lit one? You probably think of different sounds in the two scenes. Assuming that you will support the lighting shifts with audio, we should probably hear more traffic sounds in the daytime scene than in the nighttime one. But the few traffic sounds in the low-key scene should be more penetrating. Similarly, we should hear the steps of the person approaching the young woman much more distinctly (higher volume) in the nighttime scene than in the daytime one. If music is used, the nighttime scene should have ominous music and, for good measure, be mixed with a faint police siren. It is usually easier to establish the emotional context of a shot or scene with the sound track than with the pictures.

```
SCENE 6

SKY ROOM. TABLE BY THE BANDSTAND.

THEME #2

We hear the last bars of dance music. The band is taking a break.
ALAN and YOLANDA are coming back to their table to join STUART, who
has been watching them dance. During their dance, VICKY joined STUART
and is now sitting in ALAN'S chair.

                          ALAN
                       (surprised)
                  You're sitting in my chair.


                          VICKY
           Oh, it's YOUR chair? No wonder it felt so good.
           But I didn't see any name on it. You know--reserved
                    for . . . what's your name again?


                          ALAN
                          Alan.


                          VICKY
                        Alan who?


                          ALAN
               Alan Frank . . . like in frank!


                          VICKY
                Reserved for Mr. Alan Frank!


                         STUART
                     Dr. Alan Frank.


                          VICKY
           Oh, DOCTOR! What are you a doctor of?


                         STUART
               (getting an extra chair for Alan)
                 He's a doctor of philosophy.


                          VICKY
                       (laughing)
          A doctor of philosophy? You look like one!
```

17.5 SINGLE-COLUMN DRAMA SCRIPT

The single-column drama script format contains every word of characters' dialogue and occasional descriptions of their major actions.

Context   Besides the program objective and the angle, your visualization is ultimately determined by the prevailing context in which a scene plays. For example, in the nighttime scene you would probably work with more tight close-ups of the young woman and have the man approach her more aggressively. But even if you kept the shots pretty much the same for both lighting scenes, the sound tracks could readily establish their different contexts.

Sequence   Your visualization must include not only the key shots but also a shot sequence. Unless you are dealing with a static setup and little camera movement, such as in news or studio interviews, your visualization must include how to get from one shot to the next. This is where your knowledge of vectors and the mental map comes in handy. A good storyboard can also be of great help in planning shots and sequencing. As you recall from chapter 12, the storyboard shows a number of carefully framed shots and their sequence (see figure 12.15). Such a sequence illustration is especially important for maintaining shot continuity when shooting out of sequence for postproduction editing.

KEY CONCEPT

A storyboard helps translate the director's key visualizations into effective shots and shot sequences.

But even in seemingly simple directing assignments, such as video-recording the monthly campus report by the college president, shot continuity must be foremost in your mind. Recall from chapter 13 how to preserve continuity when somebody misreads a word during a recording session. This advice is important enough to repeat here. If, for example, the college president mispronounces a name, stop the video recorder (VR) or camcorder and inform her of the problem. Do not resume the recording just before the mistake was made; ask her to go back to a point where a new idea—a new paragraph—is introduced. You can then start with a different camera angle or a tighter or looser shot, or have her look up from her notes, thus making the edit look natural and properly motivated.

A good rule is to keep your visualization simple. Don't be afraid to use conventional approaches; they are conventions because they have proved effective. As pointed out earlier, there is nothing wrong with a steady close-up of a "talking head" so long as the head talks well and has something worthwhile to say. Using conventional approaches is different from stereotyping, which deliberately seeks out event details that reinforce prejudices. Creativity in directing does not mean doing everything differently from all other directors; it means adding subtle touches that intensify the message and that give your visualization personality.

PREPARING FOR A MULTICAMERA STUDIO PRODUCTION

With your understanding of the program objective and the angle, you must now interpret the script for its medium requirements. This implies visualizing the shots; working out major talent and equipment positions and moves, or ***blocking***; and marking the script with cues to the talent and the crew.

Unless you are directing soap operas or dramatic specials right away, most of your initial directing assignments will not involve complicated shots or the blocking of complex scenes. More often you will have to coordinate where an interview

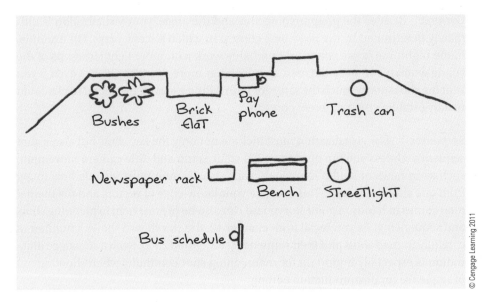

17.6 BUS STOP FLOOR PLAN
This floor plan shows the principal scenery and props for simulating a bus stop.

set should be located for optimal lighting, making sure that the audio is functioning properly and that the cameras are positioned for the best shots. Nevertheless, let's revisit the lighting-show script of the bus stop scene (figure 17.3); it is a bit more complicated than setting up an interview, but it will help you learn to read a floor plan, block talent and cameras, and mark a script.

Reading the floor plan   A floor plan will greatly assist you in visualizing key shots, determining the lighting and audio requirements, and blocking the talent and the cameras. Let's take a brief look at the floor plan sketch for the bus stop scenes. **SEE 17.6**

This bus stop floor plan will make your job relatively easy. You have four major action areas: Susan's bench, John's telephone, the bus stop sign and schedule, and the streetlight. Both cameras can be positioned for z-axis blocking of John and Susan in the bench and streetlight areas. The four areas offer a good opportunity for demonstrating selective low-key lighting. The audio is best handled by two wireless lavaliers, which eliminates any problems with unwanted shadows during the low-key scene.

Blocking the talent   Although the script has already given you basic visualization and action cues, such as "Susan sitting on bench" and "John walks to telephone," you need to be specific about exactly where on the bench Susan will sit and just where John will be at the pay phone. You can probably come up with several blocking ideas, but try to keep them simple. According to the program objective, you are not demonstrating clever blocking but the difference between high-key and low-key lighting. **SEE 17.7**

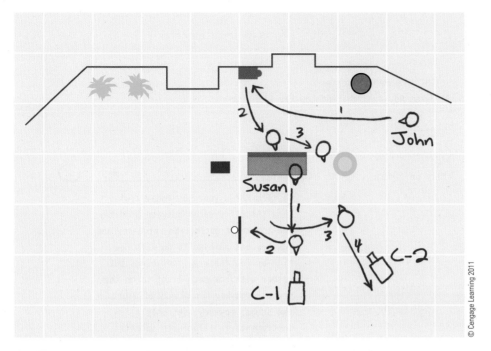

17.7 TALENT BLOCKING AND CAMERA POSITIONS
With a floor plan, the director can block the major moves of the talent and the cameras.

Positioning the cameras   Note that whenever possible you should block the talent first, then place the available cameras in optimal shooting positions. This will achieve a more natural flow than if you move the talent to accommodate the cameras. Of course, there are many circumstances in which camera positions are established before you can do any talent blocking. Don't forget that you are essentially blocking for the cameras, not for a stage performance. In this directing assignment, two cameras should be sufficient. Both are positioned to cover z-axis blocking and effective over-the-shoulder shots (see figure 17.7). With minor reblocking you could even do this scene with a single camera.

Marking the script   Unless you have a photographic memory, you need to mark your script for multicamera directing. Although there is no universal standard for marking a script, over the years certain conventions have been developed that make the job easier. The key to good script marking is to keep it consistent and to a minimum. Because every command should have a ready or standby cue preceding it, you don't need to mark the ready cues. A circled number 2 not only designates camera 2 but also implies the "Ready 2" cue. The worst thing you can do is overmark your script: While you are trying to read all your scribbles, you won't be able to watch the preview monitors or listen to the audio. Before you know it, the talent is a page or two ahead of you. As you can see in the next figure, some of the cues that were included in the script are reinforced, but most of the other essential cues are marked by the director. **SEE 17.8**

```
LIGHT AND SHADOWS Series
Program No. 4: High- and Low-key Lighting


VIDEO                          AUDIO

(VR) standard opening          SOS

Mary on camera              Q  MARY                    1        MS    (2)

                               Hi, I'm Mary, your LD. Today I will
                               show the differences between high-key
                               and low-key lighting. No, high-key and
                               low-key has nothing to do with how
                               high or low the key light hangs but
                               rather with how much light is on the
                               scene. High-key has plenty of light on
                               the scene. Low-key uses only a few
                               instruments to illuminate specific
                               areas. But high- and low-key make us
                               feel differently about a situation.
                               Let's watch.          2  Susan  CU  (1)


Susan sitting on bench         OPEN MICS. SFX: DISTANT TRAFFIC SOUNDS.
waiting for bus                OCCASIONAL CARS GOING BY.      ZOOM OUT

(Key titles)

John walks to telephone                          Q John walk

(Freeze-frame)                 SFX OUT - (MARY (VO))

                               This is a high-key scene. It is obviously
                               daylight. There is plenty of light on
                               the set with fairly prominent shadows.
                               But the faces of the people have enough
                               fill light to slow down the falloff and
                               make the attached shadows transparent.
                               Now let's see what John and Susan are
                               up to.
```

17.8 MARKED SCRIPT

This script has been marked by the director. Note that the markings for the field of view (how close a shot appears) are written by the director, not the scriptwriter. Many script-marking symbols have become standardized, but you can use your own system so long as you are consistent. The ready cues are not written but implied.

VIDEO	AUDIO
John by the phone, looking for change	(SFX:) DISTANT TRAFFIC SOUNDS. OCCASIONAL CARS GOING BY. *3 John CU ②*
John approaches bench	JOHN *4 z-axis ①* Excuse me. Could you please change a five-dollar bill? I need to make a call and . . .
Susan gets up and walks toward curb	SUSAN No!
(Freeze-frame)	*Q* MARY (VO) Oops. They don't seem to be hitting it off too well. In the meantime, note that the high light level helps give the scene a great depth of field. Although Susan and John are relatively far apart on the z-axis, they are both in sharp focus. Sorry about the interruption. Let's see how this plot develops. *5 John CU ②*
CU John	JOHN I didn't mean to startle you. But I really need to make this call. You wouldn't have a cell phone I could borrow? *6 follow ① Susan*
Susan studies the bus schedule; she looks through her purse.	SUSAN No, I am sorry. *7 CU Purse ②* *8 John CU ①*

17.8 MARKED SCRIPT *(continued)*

VIDEO   AUDIO

CU John   JOHN
                                         You wouldn't use pepper spray on me,
                                         would you?

Susan moves to the lamp
post; John steps closer
                                         (SFX:) BUS APPROACHES AND STOPS
                                         POLICE SIREN COMING CLOSER
                                         SUSAN └─────────── 9 ─────── ②
                                         I'm not so sure . . .

Susan boards the bus   (SFX:) BUS PULLS AWAY └── *10* ①
Walks past C-2
                                         JOHN
                                         Thanks a lot. └── *11*   *Zoom out*
                                                                   FREEZE

> The scene will be repeated under low-key lighting. Mary now comments over the
> freeze-frames on the specifics of low-key lighting. She emphasizes the change in how
> we feel about the situation under high-key and low-key lighting.

Mary O/C   (Q) MARY └──── *12*   *Mary MS* ②
                                         I would certainly prefer to have John
                                         ask me for change in the high-key scene
                                         than in this low-key scene. Wouldn't
                                         you? With all those ominous cast shadows
                                         around and such sparse street lighting,
                                         I wouldn't have taken a chance with him
                                         └either. Poor John! *13 DISS* ① *FREEZE*

Freeze-frame of   (MUSIC)
low-key scene

(Closing credits)

(Fade to black)

17.8 MARKED SCRIPT *(continued)*

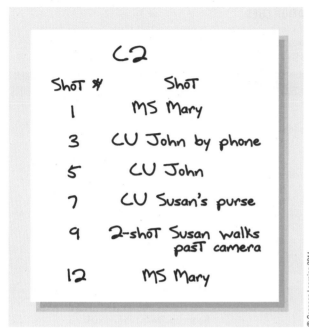

17.9 SHOT SHEET
This shot sheet shows the shot sequence for camera 2.

© Cengage Learning 2011

Make the markings big enough that you can see them clearly in the dark control room. Try to keep all of the camera markings in one row so that you can easily grasp the sequencing cues without having to read all of the lines. If there are many shots, you should number them in ascending order as they occur in the script. You can then prepare a ***shot sheet*** for each camera. **SEE 17.9** Don't number the shots for each camera with 1, 2, 3, etc. Rather, copy the shot number that you assigned each camera in the script.

■ CONTROL ROOM DIRECTING

Now you are ready to step into the studio to rehearse before going into the control room and video-recording the show. To communicate effectively with talent and crew and to make efficient use of your assigned time, you now must learn about the director's terminology, the time line, directing rehearsals, standby procedures, and on-the-air procedures.

Terminology

Most of the director's commands and cues have become pretty well standardized. The following five tables introduce you to the basic visualization, sequencing, special-effects, audio, and video-recording cues. **SEE 17.10–17.14**

Time Line

All studio productions must be done within a tight time frame. The overall production schedule, which lists the deadlines for the production, is usually prepared by

17.10 DIRECTOR'S VISUALIZATION CUES

The visualization cues are directions for the camera to achieve certain shots. Some of these visualizations can be achieved in postproduction (such as an electronic zoom through digital magnification), but they are much more easily done with proper camera handling.

ACTION	DIRECTOR'S CUE
To reveal what is in the upper off-screen space or to increase headroom	**Tilt up.**
To reveal what is in the lower off-screen space or to decrease headroom	**Tilt down.**
To center an object	**Center it.**
To reveal right off-screen space	**Pan right.**
To reveal left off-screen space	**Pan left.**
To raise the camera height	**Pedestal up.** *or:* **Boom up.** [with a jib or crane]
To lower the camera height	**Pedestal down.** *or:* **Boom down.** [with a jib or crane]
To move the camera closer	**Dolly in.**
To move the camera farther away	**Dolly out.**
To move the camera in a slight left curve	**Arc left.**
To move the camera in a slight right curve	**Arc right.**
To zoom to a tighter shot	**Zoom in.** *or:* **Push in.**
To zoom to a looser shot	**Zoom out.** *or:* **Pull out.**
To move the camera to the left with the lens pointing at the scene	**Truck left.**
To move the camera to the right with the lens pointing at the scene	**Truck right.**
To tilt the camera sideways to the left	**Cant left.**
To tilt the camera sideways to the right	**Cant right.**

17.11 DIRECTOR'S SEQUENCING CUES

The sequencing cues help get from one shot to the next. They include the major transitions.

ACTION	DIRECTOR'S CUE
Cut from camera 1 to camera 2	**Ready two — take two.**
Dissolve from camera 3 to camera 1	**Ready one for dissolve — dissolve.**
Horizontal wipe from camera 1 to camera 3	**Ready three for horizontal wipe** [over 1] **— wipe.** *or:* **Ready effects number *x*** [the number being specified by the switcher program] **— effects.**
Fade in camera 1 from black	**Ready fade in one — fade in one.** *or:* **Ready up on one — up on one.**
Fade out camera 2 to black	**Ready black — go to black.**
Short fade to black between cameras 1 and 2	**Ready cross-fade to two — cross-fade.**
Cut between camera 1 and clip 2 from server	**Take clip two.** [Sometimes you simply call the server number. If , for example, the server is labeled 6, you say: **Ready six — take six.**]
Cut between VR and CG	**Ready CG — take CG** *or:* **Ready effects on CG — take effects.**
Cut between CG titles	**Ready change page — change page.**

17.12 DIRECTOR'S SPECIAL-EFFECTS CUES

Special-effects cues are not always uniform, and, depending on the complexity of the effect, directors may invent their own verbal shorthand. Whatever cues are used, they need to be standardized among the production team.

ACTION	DIRECTOR'S CUE
To super camera 1 over camera 2	**Ready super one over two — super.**
To return to camera 2	**Ready to lose super — lose super.** *or:* **Ready to take out one — take out one.**
To go to camera 1 from the super	**Ready to go through to one — through to one.**
To key the CG over the base picture on camera 1	**Ready key CG** [over 1] **— key.**
To key the studio card title on camera 1 over the base picture on camera 2	**Ready key one over two — key.**
To have a wipe pattern appear over a picture, such as a scene on camera 2, and replace a scene on camera 1	**Ready two diamond wipe — wipe.**

Many complicated effects are preset and stored in the computer. The retrieval goes by numbers. All you do to activate a whole effects sequence is call for the number: **Ready effects eighty-seven — take effects.**

17.13 DIRECTOR'S AUDIO CUES

Audio cues involve cues for microphones, starting and stopping audio sources such as CD players, and integrating or mixing those sources.

ACTION	DIRECTOR'S CUE
To activate a microphone in the studio	**Ready to cue talent.** [Or something more specific, like **Mary — cue her.** The audio engineer will automatically open her mic.] *or:* **Ready to cue Mary — open mic, cue her.**
To start music	**Ready music — music.**
To bring the music under for an announcer	**Ready to fade music under — music under, cue announcer.**
To take the music out	**Ready music out — music out.** *or:* **Fade music out.**
To close the microphone in the studio (announcer's mic) and switch over to the sound on source, in this case, a clip from the server	**Ready SOS** [sound on source] **— close mic, track up.** *or:* **Ready SOS — SOS.**
To roll an audio recording (such as a clip or CD)	**Ready audio recorder, clip two** [or **CD two**]. **Roll audio.** *or:* **Ready audio clip two — play.**
To fade one sound source under and out while simultaneously fading another in (similar to a dissolve)	**Ready cross-fade from** *[source]* **to** *[other source]* **— cross-fade.**
To go from one sound source to another without interruption (usually two pieces of music)	**Ready segue from** *[source]* **to** *[other source]* **— segue.**
To increase program speaker volume for the director	**Monitor up, please.**
To play a sound effect from a CD	**Ready CD cut** *x* **— play.** *or:* **Ready sound effect** *x* **— play.**
To put slate information on the recording media (either open floor manager's mic or talkback patched to the VR)	**Ready to read slate — read slate.**

17.14 DIRECTOR'S VIDEO-RECORDING CUES

These cues are used to stop or start the recording mechanism (VR, optical disc, hard drive, or video server), to slate a video recording, and to switch to the recording output.

ACTION	DIRECTOR'S CUE
To start recording a program	**Ready to roll VR one — roll VR one.** [Now you have to wait for the "in-record" or "speed" confirmation from the VR operator.]
To "slate" the program after the VR is in the record mode. The slate is on camera 2 or on the CG; the opening scene is on camera 1. (We are assuming that the color bars and the reference level audio tone are already on the recording media.)	**Ready two [or CG], ready to read slate — take two [or CG], read slate.**
To put the opening 10-second beeper on the audio track and fade in on camera 1. (Do not forget to start your stopwatch as soon as camera 1 fades in.)	**Ready black, ready beeper — black, beeper.** **Ten — nine — eight — seven — six — five — four — three — two — cue Mary — up on one.** [Start your stopwatch.]
To stop the recording on a freeze-frame	**Ready freeze — freeze.**
To roll the recording out of a freeze-frame	**Ready to roll VR three — roll VR three.**
To roll the recording for a slow-motion effect	**Ready VR four slo-mo — roll VR four.** *or:* **Ready VR four slo-mo — slo-mo four.**
To roll a VR as a program insert while you are on camera 2; sound is on source. Assuming a 2-second roll.	**Ready to roll VR three, SOS — roll VR three.** **Two — one, take VR three, SOS.** If you do not use a countdown because of instant start, simply say: **Ready VR three, roll and take VR three.** [Start your stopwatch for timing the VR insert.]
To return from VR to camera and Mary on camera 1. (Stop your watch and reset it for the next insert.)	**Ten seconds to one, five seconds to one.** **Ready one, ready cue Mary — cue Mary, take one.**

the producer. The ***time line*** for the single production day is your—the director's—responsibility; it assigns each production activity a block of time in which the specific job must be accomplished. Initially, you will feel that the allotted time is much too short to even get through the basic rehearsals, or you may allocate too much time for one activity and too little for another. With some experience, however, you will quickly learn how long the individual production activities take and what you can accomplish in a certain period. The time line in the following figure allows generous time blocks for your lighting-show assignment. **SEE 17.15**

17.15 TIME LINE
The time line shows a breakdown of the major activities on the production day.

6:45 a.m.	Crew call
7:00–10:00 a.m.	Setup and lighting; dry run in rehearsal room
10:00–10:30 a.m.	Talent and crew meeting; trim lighting
10:30–11:30 a.m.	Camera and talent blocking in studio
11:30–11:45 a.m.	Notes and reset (correction of minor problems)
11:45 a.m.–12:15 p.m.	Lunch
12:15–1:15 p.m.	Camera (dress) rehearsal
1:15–1:30 p.m.	Notes and reset
1:30–1:35 p.m.	Break
1:35–3:00 p.m.	Recording
3:00–3:30 p.m.	Spill (grace period to fix whatever needs fixing)
3:30–4:00 p.m.	Strike

Once you have a realistic time line, you must stick with it. Novice directors tend to spend an inordinate amount of time polishing the first takes and then have to rush through the better part of the show before having to clear the studio. (Recall that a *take* is any one of similar repeated shots during video-recording and filming.) When rehearsing, good directors move on to the next activity according to the time line, even if they are not quite done with the current one. They usually gain enough time to pick up the skipped part at the end of the rehearsal.

Rehearsals

For most nondramatic shows, you probably need only two rehearsal methods: the dry run and the walk-through/camera rehearsal combination. The best way to explain these two methods is to apply them to your lighting-show assignment.

Dry run   You use the *dry run*, or blocking rehearsal, to work out the basic actions of the talent—where they stand and walk and what they do. If you have worked out such blocking on the floor plan, you simply test your blocking schematic in a real situation. For the dry run of your lighting show, any room will do because you don't need an actual set. You can use masking tape on the floor to indicate the sidewalk and use three chairs for the bus stop bench, another chair for the pay phone, a fifth chair for the sign with the bus schedule, and a trashcan for the streetlight. Your eyes will substitute for the cameras.

Watch the blocking first from camera 1's point of view (POV), then from camera 2's POV. In a complicated scene, you may want to use a director's viewfinder (an optical device that is similar to a monocular with which you can set aspect ratios and zoom lens positions) or a small camcorder to check the approximate shot framing. Effective dry runs usually include some or all of the following points:

- Start with the more complicated blocking, but don't get hung up on details. In the lighting show, you can block Susan first, then John, then both of them. If time is limited, you can block both talent simultaneously. Have Susan seated on the bench, anxiously looking for the bus. Enter John from camera-right and have him go to the pay phone and look for change. Susan gets up and walks toward camera 1, and so forth. Check especially the z-axis positions so that the camera can get good over-the-shoulder shots.

- Be as precise with your cues as possible. Don't just say, "Susan, sit on the bench," but, "Susan, sit on the left side—your left—of the bench." Your cue to the floor manager would be: "Have Susan sit on the camera-right side of the bench."

- Whenever possible, run through the scenes in the order they will be recorded. This will help the talent prepare for the sequence. More often than not, the scene sequence is dictated by location and necessary talent rather than narrative development.

- Call out the cues, such as, "Ready two, cue John—take two," and so on. This will enable you to get used to the cues and will help the talent anticipate them.

- If timing is critical, do a rough timing for each scene.

Walk-through/camera rehearsal   To rehearse a routine show, such as a standard interview in a permanent set, you can go straight to the control room. From there you ask the cameras to line up their shots, ask the audio engineer to check the audio levels of host and guest, have the video-record operator calibrate the VR with the audio console, and ask the CG operator to run through the titles and the credits for a final check of proper sequence and correct spelling of names.

If the show is a special event, you need to do a walk-through and a separate camera rehearsal. If you have enough time (a rare occurrence), you can do one after the other. In a walk-through you have the talent repeat the rehearsed blocking on the actual set, and you give the technical people some idea of what you expect them to do during the show. Then you go to the control room and conduct a ***camera rehearsal***, which should approximate the on-the-air or recording sessions as closely as possible except that the signal goes only as far as the line-out monitor.

More often than not, you won't have time for separate walk-throughs and camera rehearsals, so you must combine them to stay within the allotted rehearsal time. Here are some recommendations for conducting a ***walk-through/camera rehearsal*** combination:

- Always conduct such a rehearsal from the studio floor, not the control room. To change some minor blocking or camera positions, you can simply walk to the spot where you want the talent or camera to be. Explaining such corrections over the intercom would take up too much valuable rehearsal time. Use a headset or a wireless lavalier to communicate with the control room.

- If possible, have the technical director (TD) show a split feed of all cameras used on the studio monitor. (You may have to discuss such a split-screen display with the TD prior to the rehearsal.) This way you can preview the cameras from the studio floor. If this is not practical, have the TD switch as usual and feed the line-out signal to the studio monitor.

- Have all talent and crew who are actively involved in the rehearsal take their positions. On the studio floor, this includes the floor manager and the floor persons, all camera operators, and the fishpole mic operator. In the control room, you should have the TD, the audio engineer, and, if necessary, the LD (lighting director), standing by to adjust the lighting.

- Give all cues as you would in the control room. The TD will execute your switching calls and feed them to the studio monitor (assuming you don't have a split-screen setup).

- Have the floor manager do all the cueing, as though you were giving the instructions from the control room. The more you involve the floor manager in the walk-through/camera rehearsal, the better prepared he or she will be when you give the cues from the control room during the actual recording.

- Once the talent has moved into a new position or you are satisfied with an especially demanding camera maneuver, skip to the next section. Do not get hung up on a minor detail while neglecting to rehearse more important parts. For example, in the lighting show, don't waste time rehearsing John standing at the pay phone, looking for change. Instead, rehearse his walk from the phone to the bench while Susan walks to the curb.

- If you encounter some minor problems, don't stop the rehearsal. Have the AD (associate director) or the PA (production assistant) take notes. The time line should have notes and reset time scheduled at least twice for this rehearsal (see chapter 2).

- Allow some time for yourself in the control room to rehearse the most critical parts of the show. At least go through the opening of the show and the opening cues to the talent.

- Stay calm and be courteous to everyone, even if things don't go as well as expected. Give the talent and the crew a brief break before the video recording. Rehearsing right up to airtime rarely contributes to a better performance.

KEY CONCEPT

All but routine multicamera shows require a dry run and a walk-through/camera rehearsal combination.

Directing the Multicamera Show

You are finally ready to undertake **multicamera directing**, also known as control room directing and live-switched directing; that is, to use switching to coordinate two or more cameras from the control room and edit their output while the show is in progress. Live recording does not necessarily mean that you must do the entire show in a single take but that you video-record fairly long, uninterrupted sequences that require no, or only minor, postproduction editing. Normally, such editing consists of joining the video-recorded segments in their correct sequence.

Once you are in the control room, your directing job becomes largely a matter of coordinating and cueing the production crew to instantly execute their assigned tasks. The following lists give some pointers about standby and on-the-air procedures. Of course, such lists are no substitute for actual control room experience, but they can help avoid common mistakes when first sitting in the director's chair.

Standby procedures   Use these procedures immediately preceding the on-the-air or live-recorded show. Use the SA (studio address) system and have every crewmember put on a PL (private line) headset. Call on each crewmember and ask whether he or she is ready. This includes the TD, audio technician, VR operator, CG operator, teleprompter operator (if necessary), floor manager, camera operators, audio boom or fishpole operator, and lighting technician (if light changes occur during the segment).

■ Ask the floor manager whether the talent and the rest of the floor crew are ready. Tell the floor manager who gets the opening cue and which camera will be on first. The floor manager is now your essential link between the control room and the studio.

■ You can save time by having the TD and the VR operator prepare the video leader. Have the VR operator do a test recording, including a brief audio feed of the talent's opening remarks.

■ Announce periodically the time remaining until the telecast or recording.

■ Alert everyone to the first cues and shot sequence. Ready the VR operator to start the recording, the CG operator to bring up the opening titles, the audio engineer to fade in the opening music, and the TD to fade in the opening shot.

■ Have the floor manager get the talent into position.

On-the-air procedures   You now need to use the director's terminology as explained in figures 17.10 through 17.14. When giving standby and on-the-air cues, speak clearly and precisely. Do not chatter on the intercom to show how relaxed you are; you will only encourage the crew to do the same. Don't shout, even if something goes terribly wrong. Keep your cool and pay particular attention to these matters:

■ Call for the VR start and wait for the confirmation that the VR is actually in the record mode. A VTR (videotape recorder) needs a few seconds to reach full tape speed so that you won't experience picture breakup for the first few frames. The VR operator will call out "speed" or "in-record" when the system is ready.

- Unless done by the AD or TD, start the recording with the leader information. Otherwise, start with the recording of the program.

- Fade in the camera that has the opening shot and key the opening titles.

- Cue talent by name. Don't just say, "Cue her"; say, "Cue Susan."

- Cue the talent *before* you fade in the camera. By the time the floor manager has relayed your cue to the talent and the talent begins to speak, the TD will have faded in the picture.

- Talk to the cameras by number, not by the name of the operator.

- First call the camera before you give the instructions: "Three, when we come to you, dolly in. One, stay on the close-up."

- Do not pause too long between your ready and take cues. The TD may no longer be ready by the time you get to the action cue.

- Do not pause between the "take" and the number of the camera. Do not say, "Take [pause] one." The TD may punch up your camera at the take cue.

- If you change your mind after your ready cue, cancel the cue by saying, "No" or "Cancel" or "Change that." Then give the correct ready cue.

- Try to watch the camera preview monitors as much as possible while reading the script. Large but clear script markings make this juggling act easier.

- Do not do one take after another to get the first scene right at the expense of the rest of the show. Realize that the crew and the talent may lose energy and interest if you require too many takes.

- If you must stop the recording because of a technical problem, ask the floor manager to inform the studio crew and the talent of the nature of the problem. If solving the problem takes more than a few minutes, have the crew and the talent relax until you call for the video-recording to resume.

- If timing is critical, keep an eye on the clock and the stopwatch.

- After fading to black at the end of the show, call for a "Stop VR" and give the all-clear signal. Have the VR operator spot-check the recording before dismissing the talent and calling for a scenery strike.

But we are not there yet. It's time to go into the control room and do the show.

Standby. Ten seconds to VR one roll. Ready VR. Roll VR [if using a VTR, wait for the in-record confirmation]. Bars and tone. Ready slate. Take slate. Read slate [done by the AD or audio technician; this will give you an additional audio slate]. Black. Countdown [done by the AD or audio technician; the numbers from 10 to 2 flash by each second]. Ready server 2.12. Roll it, take it, sound up. Two on Mary. One on Susan. Ready two. Cue Mary. Take two. Ready one. Take one. Cue Susan [this is strictly an action cue]. Traffic sounds. Open mics. Ready key. Key. Change page [new title from CG]. Lose key. Cue John [action cue for John to walk]. Ready freeze-frame. Ready to cue Mary voice-over . . .

You are on your way. Don't bury your face in the script; by now you are pretty familiar with it. As much as possible, keep your head up and watch the preview monitors. Listen to what is being said but especially to the cue lines. Unless something went wrong, stop the recording only after the daylight segment is finished. You can use this break for a brief notes session, and the lighting people can use the opportunity to fine-tune the nighttime lighting. Give everyone a short break before recording the nighttime scene, but tell them the exact time to be back in the studio.

This time around you don't need a new VR leader, but you should have a new slate indicating that you are now doing the low-key scene. Before you restart the VR, make sure that Mary's V/O script includes the commentary for the low-key lighting segment. Fade in camera 1 (with Susan sitting on the bench), key the low-key scene titles, cue John to walk to the phone, freeze the long-shot frame, and cue Mary for her voice-over segment.

When you have about one minute left, get ready for the closing (shot 9, two-shot on C2):

Thirty seconds. Ready bus effect [sound effect of the bus pulling up]. Ready to cue Susan. Bus effect one. Cue Susan [she delivers her last line, turns, and walks past C2]. SFX police siren low under. Bus effect two [sound effect of bus closing door and driving off]. Ready one on John. Cue John. Take one. Zoom out. Slowly. Freeze. Ready two on Mary. Cue Mary. Take two. Ready dissolve to one. Ready CG credits and music. Dissolve. Music. Roll credits. Key. Lose key. Fade music. Fade to black. Stop VR. Hold everything. Check tape. All clear. Thank you all. Good job.

> **KEY CONCEPT**
>
> When in the control room, give all your calls with clarity and precision.

If everything goes that smoothly, you have indeed done a superior job. But don't be discouraged if you need to stop down to repeat a portion of the scene or even reblock a shot. Just don't spend an inordinate amount of time polishing a specific shot while the clock ticks right into the next time line segment. If you have postproduction time and a good editor, you can have the editor add all sound effects (traffic, bus, police siren), do the freeze frame and titles, and insert a few segment you had to retake. **ZVL2** SWITCHING→ Advanced lab→ try it #1 | try it #2 | try it #3 | quiz

▇ SINGLE-CAMERA DIRECTING

In **single-camera directing**, you need to observe all the continuity principles of multicamera directing except that you are video-recording the shots piecemeal and not necessarily in the order of the script. Let's first look at some of the more obvious differences between single-camera (film-style) and multicamera directing and then demonstrate these differences briefly with the lighting-show example.

Major Differences

When switching from multicamera to single-camera directing, you will find major differences in the way you conduct rehearsals and in how and when to engage performers and actors. Continuity becomes a prime consideration, as well.

Rehearsals   Single-camera scenes are easier to rehearse than multicamera scenes because you can walk through and rehearse the talent and the crew immediately before the actual video recording. The performers can quickly review their lines, and you can give detailed instructions to the crew as to the nature of the upcoming shot and the specific lighting and audio requirements. Because of the short time lapse between rehearsal and recording, your directions will be fresh in the minds of talent and crew for each take.

Rehearsing single-camera scenes can also be more difficult, however, because you need to reconstruct the preceding and following shots for each take to maintain continuity of action, emotion, and aesthetic energy. This is why many movie directors like to work from carefully worked-out storyboards. The storyboard helps them recall what happened before and should happen after the specific shot they are rehearsing.

Performing and acting   Single-camera production puts an added strain on the performers. Because the video-recording sequence is not governed by the narrative continuity of the script, the talent cannot build or maintain a specific emotional level but must often switch from one extreme to another. Also, many repetitions of a single take to get a variety of camera angles and close-ups require the actors to deliver identical performances each time. As a director you need to make sure that the talent not only repeat the same blocking and actions but also maintain the same rhythm and energy level during each subsequent take.

Continuity   One of the major challenges for the director in single-camera shooting is maintaining continuity from shot to shot. Because the shots are almost always video-recorded out of sequence, you need to maintain a mental map of how they will cut together for good continuity. In the absence of a detailed storyboard, marking the field log with principal vector symbols can greatly facilitate your lining up shots for proper continuity. For example, if in the lighting show you want to imply in a CU that Susan is watching John walk to the phone, Susan's index vector must converge with John's screen-left motion vector. The field log would simply show $i\rightarrow$ (for Susan's CU) and $\leftarrow m$ (for John's walk). This notation will be enough for you to remember John's shot even if the actual takes are fairly far apart.

An experienced director of photography (DP), who might also be operating the camera, or the AD can be of great assistance in continuity matters, such as continuity of vectors, sound, and general aesthetic energy. Don't be afraid to ask them if you are not sure whether your next shot will provide the necessary continuity. To make the editor's job a little easier, ask the camera operator to start the camera before you call for action and to let it run for a few seconds after the action is finished. These ***trim handles*** (ample "leaders" and "tails") will give the editor some wiggle room to

> **KEY CONCEPT**
>
> In single-camera directing of out-of-sequence shots, watch for continuity of vectors, action, sound, and aesthetic energy.

cut precisely on action and dialogue. At this point it might be worthwhile for you to revisit the discussion of field production in chapter 15.

Single-Camera Studio Directing

Most directors do single-camera directing from the studio floor, similar to a walk-through/camera rehearsal. If you direct the single-camera production from the studio floor, you can have the AD in the control room, handling all the operational activities such as rolling the VR, putting on the leader, calling for the slate, and keying the titles. The AD or the PA can also keep the field log. You, as the director, are then free to watch the line monitor on the studio floor and call for action to get the first take recorded.

For practice, let's direct the first three "scenes" of the lighting show. Strictly defined, they are actually shots, but for logging they count as scenes. The first scene in the lighting program is Mary's intro: "Hi, I'm Mary . . ."

The AD rolls the VR and calls for the slate: *Scene 1, take 1 (Mary)*. After Mary says, "Let's watch," have her stand there quietly for a moment before calling "cut"—to stop the action. This will make the exact edit-out point more flexible. "Cut" in this context means to stop the action and the camera.

Because Mary did such a good job, you can now move on to the next scene, John's walk to the pay phone. The slate should now read: *Scene 2, take 1 (J walk)*. On your "action" call, John walks to the phone and the camera pans with him. John stops at the phone and waits for your "cut." Both John and the camera operator did a great job, but you must call for another take. Why? Because your cut to a CU of John looking for change would not allow the editor to cut on action—a fundamental requirement for smooth continuity in postproduction editing. John must start to reach into his pocket while still on the wide or medium shot and then repeat the action on the close-up. The editor can now cut from an LS to a CU *during* the action, not before or after it. This way the cut will remain virtually invisible to the audience. For the second take of John's walk, the slate now reads: *Scene 2, take 2 (J walk)*.

Next you can line up the camera on the z-axis shot that includes Susan in the foreground and rehearse John's approach to the bench. Now the slate should read: *Scene 3, take 1 (J and S)*. Again, start the scene with John looking for coins before approaching Susan, to give the editor the necessary trim handles and the opportunity to cut on action. Susan blocks John while he's walking to the curb, so you need to retake the scene. The slate now reads: *Scene 3, take 2 (J and S)*.

Although not in the script, an essential shot would be a CU of Susan watching John walk to the phone. You decide to do this reaction shot, so the slate reads: *Scene 3, take 3 (S CU)*.

What happened to the traffic sounds, the occasional cars going by, and the police siren? Shouldn't the AD have cued the sound engineer to mix John's walking sounds and the brief dialogue between John and Susan with the traffic sounds? No. That audio will be laid in later in postproduction mixing. That way you can keep the background sounds continuous through John's walk, fishing for coins, and talking to Susan.

Single-Camera Field Production

Your single-camera production changes radically if you were to take the lighting show on-location—to an actual bus stop. In effect, you would now be directing a single-camera electronic field production (EFP). The major change would be in the script breakdown, that is, how the scenes are arranged for video recording.

The order of the shooting script is no longer determined by narrative progression (Susan waiting for the bus and John walking to the phone) but by location. Location here refers to the action areas of the bus stop. All shots are exterior—outdoors and, in this case, at a real bus stop. This is how the script might read:

Daytime Shot Breakdown

1. **Location:** *Bus stop. Bus pulls up. Susan boards bus. Bus drives off.* This shot is listed first because you need to adhere to the bus schedule to get a variety of angles. The timing of all the other shots is under your control.

2. **Location:** *Pay phone and bench. John walks to phone and bench.* Show John walking to the phone and to the bench from several angles. Get CUs of him looking for change and glancing at Susan. Ordinarily, you would do a pickup of close-ups after shooting most of the long shots and medium shots. In this case, however, the continuity of lighting is crucial, so you should get the close-ups right away.

3. **Location:** *Bench. Susan sitting on the bench.* Susan performs moves 1 through 4 in combination with John's blocking and, depending on the angle, without John (seated on the bench, looking for the bus, and watching John; walking toward the curb and looking back at John; looking at the bus schedule, looking through her purse, moving to the lamp post, and talking to John; and moving toward the curb to board the bus).

4. **Cutaways:** *Bus pulling up and departing, the bus schedule, the pay phone, the newspaper rack, and the bench.* Shoot additional cutaways of whatever other event details could serve as transitions and intensifiers.

5. **Audio:** You will have ample background sounds of traffic and cars going by whether you like it or not, but this can be a disadvantage, especially if the street noise overpowers the talent's lines. Wind noise is always a potential hazard. Be sure to audio-record a generous amount of such sounds after you are done with the actual production. This will help the postproduction editor establish shot continuity through ambient sound. The police siren can be supplied by the sound-effects (SFX) library.

The real problem is that all of these shots must now be repeated as closely as possible for the nighttime scene. Night shooting is always difficult because of the additional lighting requirements. Also, as pointed out earlier, the audio requirements change (fewer traffic sounds). In this case the postproduction sound manipulation is becoming more difficult.

As you can see, the single-camera EFP of the lighting show is getting more complicated. What at first glance seemed to be the easier aspect of the production assignment turns out to be a much more formidable job than the multicamera studio production.

Isn't shooting on-location a rather clumsy way of doing the lighting show, especially if it can be done more efficiently with multiple cameras in the studio? Yes, in a way, it is. This is where the producer's judgment comes in. A relatively simple production, such as the lighting show, is much more efficiently done as a multi-camera studio production than a single-camera EFP. But bigger projects are often more easily and effectively done film-style with a single camera, even if it doesn't seem that way considering the many takes it may require just to get a simple action right. Fortunately, neither video production nor filmmaking is locked into one or the other approach.

Many digital cinema productions use multiple cameras simultaneously, not just for spectacular one-time-only shots—like blowing up a building—but also for ordinary scenes. Video too uses both approaches, depending on the nature of the production. There are two EFP formats that are almost always produced with a single-camera setup: the interview with a single guest and various forms of documentary.

Interview   The standard formula for setting up an interview for a host and a guest is to position the camera next to the host (interviewer), pointed at the guest (interviewee), who is sitting or standing opposite the host. **SEE 17.16** If the emotional context requires a close-up, zoom in. You can replace the zoom later in postproduction with a reaction shot of the interviewer. If you interrupt the interview, start the next take with a different angle or field of view (a tighter or looser shot). At the end of the interview, place the camera next to the guest's chair or where the guest was standing and get some reaction shots of the host.

In this reaction shot session, watch that you don't cross the vector line with the camera in the new setup. If the host sports an automatic smile when on-camera, be

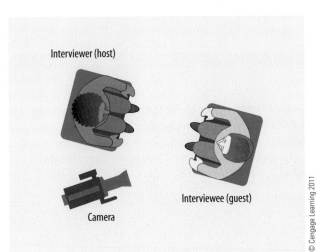

Interviewer (host)

Camera

Interviewee (guest)

© Cengage Learning 2011

17.16 STANDARD SINGLE-CAMERA INTERVIEW SETUP

In the standard single-camera interview setup, the interviewer (host) sits opposite the interviewee (guest). The camera is placed next to the interviewer.

careful that he or she doesn't smile in all reaction shots, especially when the interview had some serious moments. To show the host asking some of the questions, you can have him or her repeat them. Try to match the CU sizes of guest and host—don't make one or the other CU noticeably larger. The editor will insert the reaction and question shots in the spots you designate.

Because camcorders have become smaller and less expensive while maintaining high quality, you should try to use two cameras in over-the-shoulder setups on the same side of the vector line. In this way you will have one recording of the guest and another recording of the host; you can then mix the source material in various ways in postproduction, provided you have striped both media with identical time codes.

Documentary   When shooting a documentary, you cannot and should not direct the event itself but simply the coverage of it. Although you usually have a basic objective or angle in mind before you start recording, don't try to predetermine shots before you see the actual event. Directors who draw up detailed scripts and storyboards before they have seen at least part of the event they are to document often fail to see the event essences but instead seek shots that fit their preconception of what the event should look like. Ultimately, they document their prejudices rather than the true event.

A good initial approach is to "take notes" with the camera before doing the actual EFP. If you are open-minded and sensitive to what is going on, you may not only refine your initial objective but also develop an idea for an effective angle.

In any case, get some shots that best express the essence of the event; then get some environmental shots that establish the location and the atmosphere, as well as plenty of cutaways. Remind the camera operator or DP to shoot tight: inductive sequencing with plenty of close-ups packs a more powerful punch than a series of medium and long shots, regardless of screen size.

Your real directing skills may have to come into play during postproduction, when you work with the video and sound editors. If you have a specific idea of what the show should look like, do a paper-and-pencil rough-cut for the editor that will help communicate your idea.

MAIN POINTS

► **Script Formats**

The fact, or rundown, sheet simply lists the major points to be covered by the talent and the director. The news script and the two-column A/V (audio/video) script contain the video and some directing information on page-left and all spoken words and additional audio information on page-right. The single-column drama script contains all spoken dialogue, major character behaviors, and action cues in a single column.

► **Visualization**

A principal task of the director is translating the script into video images and sound. Visualization is one of the techniques employed. It means creating a mental image of a shot or a series of shots. It also includes the mental imaging of sound, context, and sequence.

▶ *Floor Plan*

A floor plan can help the director visualize key shots, determine lighting and audio requirements, and decide on blocking for talent and cameras.

▶ *Script Marking, Director's Terminology, and Time Line*

Easy-to-read script markings, consistent terminology, and a realistic time line are essential to successful multicamera directing.

▶ *Rehearsals*

A dry run, or blocking rehearsal, is used to block the movements of the talent—where they stand and walk and what they do. In a walk-through/camera rehearsal, the director explains to talent and crew what is happening on the set before doing a run-through with full equipment. The initial walk-through/camera rehearsal should be conducted from the studio floor.

▶ *Multicamera Directing*

When directing from the control room, the director communicates all major cues to the crew via PL (private line) headset. The director's cues and procedures must be consistent.

▶ *Single-Camera Directing*

In single-camera directing, production efficiency rather than script narrative dictates the order of shots. Utmost care must be taken that the out-of-order shots will enable seamless continuity in postproduction editing. Always provide the editor with usable cutaways and trim handles.

Z E T T L ' S   V I D E O L A B

 For your reference or to track your work, the *Zettl's VideoLab* program cues in this chapter are listed here with their corresponding page number. ZVL2 is designed as an advanced switching exercise; however, you will benefit from hearing a director call shots.

ZVL1 PROCESS→ Ideas→ scripts   364

ZVL2 SWITCHING→ Advanced lab→ try it #1 | try it #2 | try it #3 | quiz   387

Epilogue

nough of my preaching! It's now up to you to apply these techniques and principles effectively and efficiently—but I cannot help but give you one more bit of advice: You are now in command of a powerful means of communication and persuasion. Use this power wisely. Treat your viewers with respect and compassion regardless of whether they are third-graders, the local university alumni association, corporate employees, or a worldwide audience. Whatever role you play in the production process—pulling cables or directing a complex show—do the very best you can muster. With the readily available Internet as a distribution device, your video accomplishments, big and small, can reach a worldwide audience. This brings opportunity but also mandates responsibility. The opportunity is to make a difference and to help all of us see the world with heightened awareness and joy; the responsibility is to keep this goal in mind, however modest your contributions may seem.

Glossary

480i/480p A scanning system of digital television. The *i* stands for *interlaced,* and the *p* stands for *progressive.* Each complete television frame consists of 480 visible lines, usually in the 4 × 3 aspect ratio, that are scanned as two interlaced fields (480i) or one after the other (480p). This system is generally referred to as *digital SDTV* (standard-definition television).

720p A scanning system of digital television. The *p* stands for *progressive,* which means that each complete television frame consists of 720 visible lines that are scanned one after the other. An HDTV (high-definition television) standard.

1080i A scanning system of high-definition television. The *i* stands for *interlaced,* which means that each complete television frame consists of two interlaced scanning fields. A high-end HDTV system.

1080p A scanning system of high-definition television. The *p* stands for *progressive,* which means that each complete television frame consists of 1,080 visible lines that are scanned one after the other. A high-end HDTV system.

above-the-line personnel *See* **nontechnical production personnel**

AB-roll editing Creating an edit master tape from two source VTRs, one containing the A-roll and the other containing the B-roll. Transitions other than cuts, such as dissolves and wipes, are possible.

academy leader *See* **video leader**

actor A person who appears on-camera in dramatic roles. The actor always portrays someone else.

AD Stands for *associate* or *assistant director.* Assists the director in all production phases.

additive primary colors Red, green, and blue. Ordinary white light (sunlight) can be separated into the three primary light colors. When these three colored lights are combined in various proportions, all other colors can be reproduced.

address code An electronic signal that marks each frame with a specific address. *See* **SMPTE time code**.

advanced television (ATV) *See* **digital television**

AGC Stands for *automatic gain control.* Regulates the volume of the audio or video levels automatically, without using pots.

ambience Background sounds.

analog A signal that fluctuates exactly like the original stimulus.

angle The particular approach to a story—its central theme.

aperture Iris opening of a lens; usually measured in *f*-stops.

arc To move the camera in a slightly curved dolly or truck.

aspect ratio The ratio of the width of the television screen to its height. In STV (standard television), it is 4 × 3 (4 units wide by 3 units high); for HDTV (high-definition television), it is 16 × 9 (16 units wide by 9 units high). Mobile media devices have various aspect ratios, including vertical ones.

assemble editing In linear editing, adding shots on videotape in consecutive order without first recording a control track on the edit master tape.

ATR Stands for *audiotape recorder.*

attached shadow Shadow that is on the object itself. It cannot be seen independent of (detached from) the object.

ATV Stands for *advanced television. See* **digital television.**

audio track The area of the videotape used for recording the audio information.

auto-focus Automatic focusing system on most consumer camcorders and some ENG/EFP cameras.

auto-iris Automatic control of the aperture (lens opening).

background light Illumination of the set pieces and the backdrop. Also called *set light.*

back light Illumination from behind the subject and opposite the camera; usually a spotlight.

barn doors Metal flaps in front of a lighting instrument that control the spread of the light beam.

baselight Even, nondirectional (diffused) light necessary for the camera to operate optimally. Refers to the overall light intensity.

beam splitter Optical device within the camera that splits the white light into the three additive primary light colors: red, green, and blue.

below-the-line personnel *See* **technical production personnel**

big remote A production outside the studio to televise live and/or live-record a large scheduled event that has not been staged specifically for television. Examples include sporting events, parades, political gatherings, award ceremonies, and government hearings. Also called *remote.*

binary digit (bit) The smallest amount of information a computer can hold and process. A charge is either present, represented by a 1, or absent, represented by a 0. One bit can describe two levels, such as on/off or black/white. Two bits can describe four levels (2^2 bits); 3 bits, eight levels (2^3 bits); 4 bits, 16 (2^4 bits); and so on. A group of 8 bits (2^8) is called a *byte.*

blocking Carefully worked-out positioning, movement, and actions by the talent and for all mobile video equipment used in a scene.

blocking rehearsal *See* **dry run**

book *See* **twofold**

boom (1) *Audio:* microphone support. (2) *Video:* part of a camera crane. (3) To move the boom of the camera crane up or down; also called *crane.*

bump-down Copying a videotape to a lower-quality tape format. Also called *dub-down.*

bump-up Copying a videotape to a higher-quality tape format. Also called *dub-up.*

calibrate the zoom lens To preset a zoom lens to stay in focus throughout the zoom.

camcorder A portable camera with the video recorder built into it.

camera chain The camera and the associated electronic equipment, consisting of the power supply, sync generator, and camera control unit.

camera control unit (CCU) Equipment, separate from the actual camera, that allows the video operator to adjust the color and brightness balance before and during the production.

camera rehearsal Full rehearsal with cameras and other pieces of production equipment. Often identical to the dress rehearsal.

cant To tilt the camera sideways.

cap (1) Lens cap: a rubber or metal cap placed in front of the lens to protect it from light, dust, and physical damage. (2) Electronic device that eliminates the picture from the camera CCD.

capture Moving video and audio from the recording media to the hard drive of a computer with a nonlinear editing program. Analog video signals must be converted to digital before they can be imported by a computer.

cardioid Heart-shaped pickup pattern of a unidirectional microphone.

cast shadow Shadow that is produced by an object and thrown (cast) onto another surface. It can be seen independent of the object.

CCD Stands for *charge-coupled device.* One of the popular imaging devices in a studio camera or camcorder. *See* **sensor.**

C channel *See* **chrominance channel**

C-clamp A metal clamp with which lighting instruments are attached to the lighting batten.

CCU *See* **camera control unit**

CD Stands for *compact disc.* A recording media that contains audio and/or video information in digital form.

CG *See* **character generator**

character generator (CG) A computer dedicated to the creation of letters and numbers in various fonts. Its output can be directly integrated into video images.

chip *See* **CCD** and **sensor**

chroma key Key effect that uses a color (usually blue or green) for the key source backdrop. All blue or green areas are replaced by the base picture during the key.

chrominance channel Contains the RGB video signals or some combination thereof. Also called *color,* and *C, channel.*

close-up (CU) Object or any part of it seen at close range and framed tightly. The close-up can be extreme (extreme or big close-up) or rather loose (medium close-up).

closure *See* **psychological closure**

CMOS Stands for *complementary metal-oxide semiconductor.* A high-quality imaging device similar to a CCD. *See* **sensor**.

codec Stands for *compression-decompression.* Can be one of several compression systems of digital video, graphics, and audio files.

coding To change the quantized values into a binary code, represented by 0's and 1's. Also called *encoding.*

color bars A color standard used in video production for the alignment of cameras and videotape recordings. Color bars can be generated by most professional portable cameras.

color channel *See* **chrominance channel**

color media *See* **gel**

color temperature Relative reddishness or bluishness of white light, as measured on the Kelvin (K) scale.

The norm for indoor video lighting is 3,200K; for outdoors, 5,600K.

complexity editing Building an intensified screen event from carefully selected and juxtaposed shots. Does not have to adhere to the continuity principles.

component system *See* **RGB component video**, **Y/C component video**, and **Y/color difference component video**

composite video A system that combines the Y (luminance, or black-and-white) and C (color—red, green, and blue) video information into a single signal. Also called *NTSC.*

compression The temporary rearrangement or elimination of redundant picture information for easier storage and signal transport.

condenser microphone A high-quality, sensitive microphone for critical sound pickup.

contact person A person who is familiar with, and can facilitate access to, the remote location and the key people. Also called *contact.*

continuing vectors Graphic vectors that extend each other, or index and motion vectors that point and move in the same direction.

continuity editing Preserving visual continuity from shot to shot.

contrast The difference between the brightest and the darkest spots in a video image.

control room directing *See* **multicamera directing**

control track The area of the videotape used for recording synchronization information.

control track system *See* **pulse-count system**

converging vectors Index and motion vectors that point toward each other.

crane To move the boom of the camera crane up or down. Also called *boom.*

cross-shot (X/S) Similar to the over-the-shoulder shot except that the camera-near person is completely out of the shot.

CU *See* **close-up**

cue card A large hand-lettered card that contains copy, usually held next to the camera lens by floor personnel.

cut (1) The instantaneous change from one shot (image) to another. (2) Director's signal to interrupt action (used during rehearsal).

cutaway A shot of an object or event that is peripherally connected with the overall event and that is relatively static. Commonly used between two shots that do not provide good continuity.

cyc *See* **cyclorama**

cyc light *See* **strip light**

cyclorama A U-shaped continuous piece of canvas or muslin for backing of scenery and action. Also called *cyc*. Hardwall cycs are permanently installed in front of one or two of the studio walls.

delegation controls Controls that assign a specific function to a bus on a switcher.

depth of field The area in which all objects, located at different distances from the camera, appear in focus. Depends primarily on the focal length of the lens, its *f*-stop, and the distance from the camera to the object.

diffused light Light that illuminates a relatively large area and creates soft shadows.

digital Pertaining to data in the form of binary digits (on/off pulses).

digital television (DTV) Digital systems that generally have a higher image resolution than standard television. Sometimes called *advanced television (ATV)*.

digital versatile disc (DVD) The standard DVD recording media can store 4.7 gigabytes of video and/or audio information.

digital video effects (DVE) Video effects generated by an effects generator in the switcher or by a computer with effects software. The computer system dedicated to DVE is called a *graphics generator*.

digitize Necessary step with analog source material whereby the analog signals are converted to digital signals prior to capture.

dimmer A device that controls the intensity of light by throttling the electric current flowing to the lamp.

directional light Light that illuminates a relatively small area and creates harsh, clearly defined shadows.

diverging vectors Index and motion vectors that point away from each other.

documentary script *See* **two-column A/V script**

dolly To move the camera toward (dolly in) or away from (dolly out) the object.

downstream keyer (DSK) A control that allows a title to be keyed (cut in) over the picture (line-out signal) as it leaves the switcher.

dress (1) What people wear on-camera. (2) Decorating a set with set properties. (3) Set dressing: set properties. *See also* **dress rehearsal**.

dress rehearsal Final rehearsal with the cast fully dressed and all facilities operating. The dress rehearsal is often video-recorded.

drop Heavy curtain suspended from a track (usually in front of the cyc). A painted drop is a large piece of canvas with a background scene painted on it.

dry run Rehearsal without equipment, during which the basic actions of the talent are worked out. Also called *blocking rehearsal*.

DSK *See* **downstream keyer**

DSLR camera Stands for *digital single-lens reflex camera*. Basically a still-photo camera that can also produce video footage. It has an optical viewfinder that permits viewing through the lens for still pictures. In the video mode, it switches to an electronic image.

DTV *See* **digital television**

dub The duplication of an electronic recording. The dub is always one generation away from the recording used for dubbing. In analog systems, each dub shows increased deterioration.

dub-down *See* **bump-down**

dub-up *See* **bump-up**

DVD *See* **digital versatile disc**

DVE *See* **digital video effects**

DVR Stands for *digital video recorder*.

dynamic microphone A relatively rugged microphone. Good for outdoor use.

edit controller A machine that assists in various linear editing functions, such as marking edit-in and edit-out points, rolling source and record VTRs, and integrating effects. It can be a desktop computer with editing software. Also called *editing control unit.*

edit decision list (EDL) Consists of edit-in and edit-out points, expressed in time code numbers, and the nature of transitions between shots.

editing control unit *See* **edit controller**

editing log *See* **VR log**

edit master The videotape or disc that contains the final version of an edited program. Subsequent copies are struck from the edit master.

EDL *See* **edit decision list**

effects bus Row of buttons on the switcher that can select the video sources for a specific effect. Usually the same as a mix bus that has been switched to an effects function.

effect-to-cause model *See* **production model**

EFP *See* **electronic field production**

EFP team Usually a three-person team consisting of the talent, a camcorder operator, and a utility person who handles lighting, audio, and/or video recording, and, if necessary, the microwave transmission back to the studio.

electron beam A thin stream of electrons, which is generated by the electron gun in back of the video tube and strikes the photosensitive color dots at the face of the tube.

electronic field production (EFP) Video production done outside the studio that is usually shot for postproduction (not live).

electronic news gathering (ENG) The use of portable camcorders, lights, and sound equipment for the production of mostly unscheduled daily news events. ENG is usually done for live transmission or immediate postproduction.

electronic still store (ESS) system Stores still video frames in digital form for easy random access.

encoding *See* **coding**

ENG *See* **electronic news gathering**

ENG/EFP camera Highly portable, high-end self-contained camera for electronic field production.

ESS *See* **electronic still store (ESS) system**

essential area The section of the television picture that is seen by the home viewer, regardless of minor loss during signal transmission or signal processing by the television receiver. Also called *safe title area.*

establishing shot *See* **long shot**

fact sheet Script format that lists the items to be shown on-camera and their main features. May contain suggestions of what to say about the product. Also called *rundown sheet.*

fade The gradual appearance of a picture from black (fade-in) or disappearance to black (fade-out).

fader A volume control that works by sliding a button horizontally along a scale. Identical in function to a pot. Also called *slide fader.*

fader bar A lever on the switcher that activates buses and can produce superimpositions, dissolves, fades, keys, and wipes of different speeds. Also called *T-bar.*

falloff The speed (degree) with which a light picture portion turns into shadow areas. *Fast falloff* means that the light areas turn abruptly into shadow areas and there is a great difference in brightness between light and shadow areas. *Slow falloff* indicates a very gradual change from light to dark and a minimal brightness difference between light and shadow areas.

fast lens A lens that permits a relatively great amount of light to pass through at its largest aperture (lowest *f*-stop number). Can be used in low-light conditions.

fc *See* **foot-candle**

field One-half of a complete scanning cycle, with two fields necessary for one television picture frame. In analog (NTSC) television, there are 60 fields, or 30 frames, per second.

field dolly A plywood platform supported by four wheels with pneumatic tires. Used for moving a tripod-mounted camera on a rough surface.

field log A record of each take during the video recording.

field of view The portion of a scene visible through a particular lens; its vista. Expressed in symbols, such as CU for close-up.

field production Production activities that take place away from the studio.

fill light Additional light on the opposite side of the camera from the key light to illuminate shadow areas and thereby reduce falloff; usually done with floodlights.

film-style *See* **single-camera production**

fishpole A suspension device for a microphone; the mic is attached to a pole and held over the scene for brief periods.

flash drive *See* **memory card**

flat A piece of standing scenery used as a background or to simulate the walls of a room. There are hardwall and softwall flats.

floodlight A lighting instrument that produces diffused light.

floor director *See* **floor manager**

floor manager In charge of all activities on the studio floor, such as setting up scenery, getting talent into place, and relaying the director's cues to the talent. In the field, basically responsible for preparing the location for the shoot and for cueing all talent. Also called floor director and *stage manager.*

floor plan A diagram of scenery, properties, and set dressings drawn on a grid.

focal length With the lens set at infinity, the distance from the iris to the plane where the picture is in focus. Normally measured in millimeters or inches.

foldback The return of the total or partial audio mix to the talent through headsets or IFB channels. *See* **IFB**.

foot-candle (fc) The unit of measurement of illumination, or the amount of light that falls on an object. One foot-candle is 1 candlepower of light (1 lumen) that falls on a 1-square-foot area located 1 foot away from the light source. *See also* **lux**.

foundation A makeup base, normally done with water-soluble cake makeup; it is applied with a sponge or sprayed on the face and sometimes all exposed skin areas.

fps *See* **frame rate**

frame A complete scanning cycle of the electron beam. In interlaced scanning, two partial scanning cycles (fields) are necessary for one frame. In progressive scanning, each scanning cycle produces one complete frame. *See* **interlaced scanning** and **progressive scanning**.

frame rate The time it takes to scan a complete frame; usually expressed in frames per second (fps). In analog (NTSC) television, there are 60 fields, or 30 frames, per second. HDTV can have variable frame rates for acquisition, editing, and delivery.

frame store synchronizer Image stabilization and synchronization system that has a memory large enough to store and read out one complete video frame. Used to synchronize signals from a variety of video sources that are not locked to a common sync signal.

Fresnel spotlight One of the most common spots, named after the inventor of its lens, which has steplike concentric rings.

ƒ-stop The scale on the lens, indicating the aperture. The larger the ƒ-stop number, the smaller the aperture; the smaller the ƒ-stop number, the larger the aperture.

gel Generic name for color filter put in front of spotlights or floodlights to give the light beam a specific hue. *Gel* comes from *gelatin,* the filter material used before the invention of much more heat- and moisture-resistant plastic material. Also called *color media.*

generation The number of dubs away from the original recording. A first-generation dub is struck directly from the source media. A second-generation tape is a dub of the first-generation dub (two steps away from the original media), and so forth. The greater the number of nondigital generations, the greater the loss of quality.

graphics generator A computer specially designed for creating a variety of images and colors. Also called *paint box. See also* **digital video effects**.

hand props Objects, called *properties*, that are handled by the performer or actor.

HDTV *See* **high-definition television**

headroom The space between the top of the head and the upper screen edge.

high-definition television (HDTV) Includes the 720p, 1080i, and 1080p scanning systems.

high-key lighting Light background and ample light on the scene. Has nothing to do with the vertical positioning of the key light.

hundredeighty *See* **vector line**

hypercardioid Very narrow unidirectional pickup pattern with a long reach. The mic is also sensitive to sounds coming directly from the back.

IFB Stands for *interruptible foldback* or *feedback*. A prompting system that allows communication with the talent while on the air. A small earpiece worn by on-the-air talent carries program sound (including the talent's voice) or instructions from the producer or director.

imaging device In a video camera, converts the optical image into electric energy—the video signal. Also called *chip, pickup device,* and *sensor*.

incident light Light that strikes the object directly from its source. To measure incident light, point the light meter at the camera lens or into the lighting instruments.

ingest The selection, coding, and recording on a large server of various program feeds.

insert editing Produces highly stable edits for linear editing. Requires the prior laying of a continuous control track by recording black on the edit master tape.

instantaneous editing *See* **switching**

interactive video A computer-driven program that gives the viewer some control over what to see and how to see it. It is often used as a training device.

intercom Short for *intercommunication system*. Used for all production and engineering personnel involved in a show. The most widely used system has telephone headsets to facilitate voice communication on several wired or wireless channels. Includes other systems, such as IFB and cellular telephones.

interlaced scanning The scanning of all the odd-numbered lines (first field) and the subsequent scanning of all the even-numbered lines (second field). The two fields make up a complete television frame. *See also* **frame**.

iris Adjustable lens-opening mechanism. Also called *lens diaphragm*.

jack (1) *Audio:* a socket or receptacle for a connector. (2) *Scenery:* a brace for a flat.

jib arm A small camera crane that can be operated by the cameraperson.

jogging Frame-by-frame advancement of a recorded shot sequence, resulting in a jerking motion.

jump cut An image that jumps slightly from one screen position to another during a cut. Also, any gross visual discontinuity from shot to shot.

Kelvin (K) The standard scale for measuring color temperature, or the relative reddishness or bluishness of white light.

key An electronic effect in which the keyed image (figure—usually letters) blocks out portions of the base picture (background) and therefore appears to be layered on top of it.

key bus Row of buttons on the switcher used to select the video source to be inserted into the background image.

key light Principal source of illumination; usually a spotlight.

lavalier A small microphone that is clipped to clothing. Also called *lav*.

leadroom The space in front of a laterally moving object or person.

LED lights *LED* stands for *light-emitting diodes*. A solid-state device that changes electric energy into light energy. Most computer screens use LEDs as the light source.

lens Optical lens, essential for projecting an optical image of the scene onto the front surface of the camera imaging device. Lenses come in various fixed focal lengths or in a variable focal length (zoom lenses) and with various maximum apertures (lens openings).

lens diaphragm *See* **iris**

level (1) *Audio:* sound volume. (2) *Video:* video signal strength.

light intensity The amount of light falling on an object that is seen by the lens. Measured in lux or foot-candles. Also called *light level. See* **foot-candle** and **lux**.

light level *See* **light intensity**

light plot A plan, similar to a floor plan, that shows the type, size (wattage), and location of the lighting instruments relative to the scene to be illuminated and the general direction of the light beams.

lighting triangle *See* **photographic principle**

line *See* **vector line**

line monitor The monitor that shows only the line-out pictures that go on the air or to the video recorder.

linear editing system Uses videotape as the editing medium. It does not allow random access of shots.

line-level input Input channel on a mixer or an audio console for relatively high-level audio sources. *See also* **mic-level input**.

line of conversation and action *See* **vector line**

line-out The line that carries the final video or audio output.

live recording The uninterrupted video recording of a live show for later unedited playback. Also called *live-on-tape* even if other recording media are used.

live-switched directing *See* **multicamera directing**

location sketch A rough, hand-drawn map of the locale for a remote telecast. For an indoor remote, the sketch shows the dimensions of the room and the locations of furniture and windows. For an outdoor remote, the sketch indicates the buildings and the location of the remote truck, power source, and the sun during the time of the telecast.

long-focal-length lens *See* **telephoto lens**

long shot (LS) Object seen from far away or framed very loosely. The extreme long shot shows the object from a great distance. Also called *establishing shot.*

lossless compression Rearranging but not eliminating pixels during digital storage and transport.

lossy compression Throwing away redundant pixels during digital compression. Most compression is the lossy kind.

low-key lighting Fast-falloff lighting with dark background and selectively illuminated areas. Has nothing to do with the vertical positioning of the key light.

LS *See* **long shot**

luma *See* **luminance**

luma channel *See* **luminance channel**

lumen The light intensity power of one candle (light source radiating in all directions).

luminance The brightness (black-and-white) information of a video signal. Also called *luma* to include the gray-scale information.

luminance channel Contains the black-and-white part of a video signal. It is mainly responsible for the sharpness of the picture. Also called *luma,* or *Y, channel.*

lux European standard unit for measuring light intensity. One lux is 1 lumen (1 candlepower) of light that falls on a surface of 1 square meter located 1 meter away from the light source. 10.75 lux = 1 foot-candle. Most lighting people figure roughly 10 lux = 1 foot-candle. *See also* **foot-candle**.

master control Controls the program input, storage, and retrieval for on-the-air telecasts. Also oversees the technical quality of all program material.

matte key The key (usually letters) is filled with gray or a color.

MD *See* **mini disc**

M/E bus Row of buttons on the switcher that can serve mix or effects functions.

medium requirements All personnel, equipment, and facilities needed for a production, as well as budgets, schedules, and the various production phases.

medium shot (MS) Object seen from a medium distance. Covers any framing between a long shot and a close-up.

memory card A read/write solid-state portable storage device that can download, store, and upload a limited amount of digital audio and video information. Also called *flash drive.*

mental map Tells us where things are or are supposed to be in on- and off-screen space.

mic Short for *microphone.*

mic-level input Input channel on a mixer or an audio console for relatively low-level audio sources such as microphones. *See also* **line-level input**.

mini disc (MD) An optical disc that can store one hour of CD-quality audio.

mini plug Small audio connector.

mix bus Row of buttons on the switcher that permits the mixing of video sources, as in a dissolve or a super.

mixing (1) *Audio:* combining two or more sounds in specific proportions (volume variations) as determined by the event (show) context. (2) *Video:* combining two shots as a dissolve or superimposition via the switcher.

moiré effect Color vibrations that occur when narrow, contrasting stripes of a design interfere with the scanning lines of the video system.

monitor High-quality video display used in the video studio and control rooms. Cannot receive broadcast signals. Also refers to flat-panel camera viewfinders.

monochrome One color. In video it refers to a camera or monitor that produces a black-and-white picture.

mounting head A device that connects the camera to its support. Also called *pan-and-tilt head.*

MPEG A digital compression technique developed by the Moving Picture Experts Group for moving pictures.

MPEG-2 A digital compression standard for motion video.

MS *See* **medium shot**

multicamera directing Simultaneous coordination of two or more cameras for instantaneous editing (switching). Also called *control room directing* and *live-switched directing.*

multicamera production The use of two or more cameras to capture a scene simultaneously from different points of view. Each camera's output can be recorded separately (iso configuration) and/or fed into a switcher for instantaneous editing.

multimedia Computer display of text, sound, and still and moving images. Usually recorded on CD-ROM or DVD.

narrow-angle lens *See* **telephoto lens**

news script Fully scripted text with video information on page-left and news copy on page-right. The copy (spoken text) can also be in a large center column that contains some additional information.

NLE *See* **nonlinear editing (NLE) system**

noise (1) *Audio:* unwanted sounds that interfere with the intentional sounds, or unwanted hisses or hums inevitably generated by the electronics of the audio equipment. (2) *Video:* electronic interference that shows up as snow.

nonlinear editing (NLE) system Allows random access of shots. The video and audio information is stored in digital form on computer disks. Usually has two external monitors, small loudspeakers, and an audio mixer.

nonlinear recording media Storage of video and audio material in digital form on a hard drive, memory card, or read/write optical disc. Each single frame can be instantly accessed by a computer.

nontechnical production personnel People concerned primarily with nontechnical production matters that lead from the basic idea to the final screen image. Includes producers, directors, and talent. Also called *above-the-line personnel.*

noseroom The space in front of a person looking or pointing toward the edge of the screen.

NTSC Stands for *National Television System Committee.* Normally refers to the composite video signal, consisting of the Y signal (luminance, or black-and-white information) and the C signal (red, green, and blue color information). *See also* **composite video**.

off-line editing In linear editing it produces an edit decision list or a rough-cut not intended for broadcast. In nonlinear editing the selected shots are captured in low resolution to save computer storage space.

omnidirectional Pickup pattern of a microphone that can hear equally well from all directions.

on-line editing In linear editing it produces the final high-quality edit master for broadcast or program duplication. In nonlinear editing the shots listed on the edit decision list are recaptured at a higher resolution.

over-the-shoulder shot (O/S) Camera looks over the camera-near person's shoulder (shoulder and back of head included in shot) at the other person.

O/S *See* **over-the-shoulder shot**

PA Production assistant.

P.A. system *See* **SA**

pads *See* **trim handles**

paint box *See* **graphics generator**

pan To turn the camera horizontally.

pan-and-tilt head *See* **mounting head**

party line *See* **PL**

patchbay A device that connects various inputs with specific outputs. Also called *patchboard*.

patchboard *See* **patchbay**

pedestal To move the camera up or down using a studio pedestal.

performer A person who appears on-camera in nondramatic shows. The performer does not assume someone else's character.

photographic principle The triangular arrangement of key, back, and fill lights. Also called *triangle,* or *three-point, lighting*.

pickup device *See* **imaging device**

pickup pattern The territory around the microphone within which the mic can hear well.

PL Stands for *party line, phone line,* or *private line*. Major intercommunication device in video studios.

pocket recorder Small camcorder, such as a cell phone, that fits into a shirt pocket. Records exclusively on memory cards. Also called *mobile media*.

point of convergence (POC) The point where z-axis vectors of the right and left 3D lenses meet, resulting in a perfect overlap of the right-eye and left-eye images.

polar pattern The two-dimensional representation of the microphone pickup pattern.

pop filter A wire-mesh screen attached to the front of a mic that reduces breath pops and sudden air blasts.

postproduction Any production activity that occurs after the production. Usually refers to video editing and/or audio sweetening.

postproduction editing The assembly of recorded material after the actual production, in contrast to instantaneous editing with the switcher.

postproduction team Normally consists of the director, a video editor, and, for complex productions, a sound designer who remixes the sound track.

pot Short for potentiometer, a sound-volume control. *See* **fader**.

preproduction The preparation of all production details.

preproduction team Comprises the people who plan the production. Normally includes the producer, writer, director, art director, and technical director. Large productions may include a composer and a choreographer. In charge: producer.

preroll To start a videotape and let it roll for a few seconds before it is put in the playback or record mode to give the electronic system time to stabilize.

preset bus *See* **preview bus**

preset the zoom lens *See* **calibrate the zoom lens**

preview bus Row of buttons on the switcher that can direct an input to the preview monitor at the same time another video source is on the air. Also called *preset bus*.

preview monitor Any monitor that shows a video source, except for the line and off-the-air monitors.

process message The message actually perceived by the viewer in the process of watching a video program.

producer Creator and organizer of video programs.

production The actual activities in which an event is recorded and/or televised.

production model Moving from the idea to the program objective and then backing up to the specific medium requirements to achieve the program objective.

production schedule A calendar that shows the preproduction, production, and postproduction dates and who is doing what, when, and where. *See also* **time line**.

production switcher Switcher designed for instantaneous editing, located in the studio control room or remote truck.

production team Comprises a variety of nontechnical and technical people, such as producer and various assistants (associate producer and production assistant), director and assistant director, and talent and production crew. In charge: director.

program bus Row of buttons on the switcher, with inputs that are directly switched to the line-out.

program objective The desired effect of the program on the viewer. The defined process message.

progressive scanning The consecutive scanning of lines from top to bottom. *See also* **frame**.

properties *See* **props**

props Short for *properties*. Furniture and other objects used by talent and for set decoration.

psychological closure Mentally filling in missing visual information that will lead to a complete and stable configuration. Also called *closure*.

pulse-count system An address code that counts the control track pulses and translates that count into time and frame numbers. It is not frame-accurate. Also called *control track system*.

quantizing A step in the digitization of an analog signal. It changes the sampling points into discrete numerical values (0's and 1's). Also called *quantization*.

quick-release plate A mechanism on a tripod that makes it easy to mount and position the camera so that it is perfectly balanced each time.

radio mic *See* **wireless microphone**

RCA phono plug Connector for video and audio equipment.

reflected light Light that is bounced off the illuminated object. To measure reflected light, point the light meter close to the object from the direction of the camera.

refresh rate The number of complete scanning cycles per second. Also expressed in frames per second (fps). *See also* **frame**.

remote A production of a large, scheduled event done for live transmission or live-on-tape recording. *See also* **big remote**.

remote survey An inspection of the remote location by key production and engineering personnel so that they can plan for the setup and the use of production equipment. Also called *site survey*.

remote truck The vehicle that carries the production control room, audio control, video-recording section, video control section, and transmission equipment.

RGB Stands for *red, green,* and *blue*—the basic colors of television.

RGB component video A system in which all three color signals are kept separate and recorded separately on videotape. Often called *RGB system*.

RGB system *See* **RGB component video**

ribbon microphone A high-quality, highly sensitive microphone for critical sound pickup in the studio, usually for recording string instruments.

rough-cut A preliminary edit.

rundown sheet *See* **fact sheet**

SA Stands for *studio address system*. A public address loudspeaker system from the control room to the studio. Also called *studio talkback* and *PA* (public address) *system*.

safe title area *See* **essential area**

sampling Taking a number of samples (voltages) of the analog video or audio signal at equally spaced intervals.

scanning The movement of the electron beam from left to right and from top to bottom on the video screen.

scene Event details that form an organic unit, usually in a single place and time. A series of organically related shots that depict these event details.

scenery Background flats and other pieces (windows, doors, pillars) that simulate a specific environment.

scoop A scooplike floodlight.

scrim A heat-resistant spun-glass material that comes in rolls and can be cut with scissors like cloth; it is attached to a scoop to diffuse the light beam.

script Written document that tells what the program is about, who says what, what is supposed to happen, and what and how the audience will see and hear the event.

sensor A solid-state imaging device in a video or digital cinema camera that converts the optical image into electric energy—the video signal. Also called *CCD, chip,* and *CMOS.*

sequencing The control and the structuring of a shot sequence.

server *See* **video server**

set light *See* **background light**

shader *See* **video operator (VO)**

shot The smallest convenient operational unit in video and film, usually the interval between two transitions. In cinema it may refer to a specific camera setup.

shot sheet A list of every shot a particular camera has to get. It is attached to the camera to help the camera operator remember a shot sequence.

shotgun microphone A highly directional mic with a shotgunlike barrel for picking up sounds over a great distance.

shutter speed A camera control that reduces the blurring of bright, fast-moving objects. The higher the shutter speed, the less blurring occurs but the more light is needed.

single-camera directing Directing a single camera (usually a camcorder) in the studio or field for takes that are recorded separately for postproduction.

single-camera production All of the video is captured by a single camera or camcorder for postproduction editing. Similar to the traditional film approach. Also called *film-style.*

single-column drama script Traditional script format for television plays. All dialogue and action cues are written in a single column.

site survey *See* **remote survey**

slate (1) To identify, verbally or visually, each video-recorded take. (2) A blackboard or whiteboard upon which essential production information is written, such as the title of the show, date, and scene and take numbers. It is recorded at the beginning of each video-recorded take.

slide fader *See* **fader**

slow lens A lens that permits a relatively small amount of light to pass through (relatively high *f*-stop number at its largest aperture). Requires higher light levels for optimal pictures.

SMPTE Stands for *Society of Motion Picture and Television Engineers.*

SMPTE time code A specially generated address code that marks each video frame with a specific number (hour, minute, second, and frame). Named for the Society of Motion Picture and Television Engineers, this time code is officially called *SMPTE/EBU* (for *European Broadcasting Union*).

sound perspective People (or other sound-producing sources) sound farther away in long shots than in close-ups.

source VTR The videotape recorder that supplies the program segments to be edited by the record VTR.

spotlight A lighting instrument that produces directional, relatively undiffused light.

stage manager *See* **floor manager**

Steadicam A camera mount that allows the operator to walk and run, with the camera remaining steady.

sticks *See* **tripod**

storyboard A series of sketches of the key visualization points of an event, with the corresponding audio information given below each visualization.

strike To remove certain objects; to remove scenery and equipment from the studio floor after the show.

strip light Several self-contained lamps arranged in a row. Used mostly for illumination of the cyclorama. Also called *cyc light.*

studio camera Heavy, high-quality camera and zoom lens that cannot be maneuvered properly without the aid of a pedestal or some other type of camera mount.

studio control room A room adjacent to the studio in which the director, producer, production assistants, technical director, audio engineer, and sometimes the lighting director perform their production functions.

studio pedestal A heavy camera dolly that permits raising and lowering the camera while on the air.

studio production Production activities that take place in the studio.

studio talkback *See* **SA**

super Short for *superimposition*. A double exposure of two images, with the top one letting the bottom one show through.

Super Hi-Vision A video system that produces extremely high-resolution video images. Generally used for digital cinema.

S-video *See* **Y/C component video**

sweep Curved piece of scenery, similar to a large pillar cut in half.

sweetening The postproduction manipulation of recorded sound.

switcher (1) A panel with rows of buttons that allow the selection and the assembly of multiple video sources through a variety of transition devices as well as the creation of electronic effects. (2) Production person who is doing the switching.

switching A change from one video source to another and the creation of various transitions and effects during production with the aid of a switcher. Also called *instantaneous editing*.

sync generator Part of the camera chain; produces electronic synchronization pulses.

synthetic environment Electronically generated settings, either through chroma key or computer.

take Any one of similar repeated shots taken during videorecording and filming.

talent Collective name for all performers and actors who appear regularly in video.

tally light Red light on the camera and inside the camera viewfinder, indicating when the camera is on the air (switched to the line-out).

tapeless systems Refers to the recording, storage, and playback of audio and video information via digital storage devices other than videotape.

TBC *See* **time base corrector**

TD Stands for *technical director*. The TD usually operates the switcher.

technical personnel People who operate the production equipment, including camera operators, floor persons, and video and audio engineers. Also called *below-the-line personnel*.

telephoto lens Gives a close-up view of an event relatively far away from the camera. Also called *long-focal-length*, and *narrow-angle, lens*.

teleprompter A prompting device that projects moving copy over the lens so that the talent can read it without losing eye contact with the viewer.

threefold Three flats hinged together.

three-point lighting *See* **photographic principle**

tilt To point the camera up or down.

time base corrector (TBC) An electronic accessory to videotape recorders that helps make videotape playbacks electronically stable. It keeps slightly different scanning cycles in step.

time code *See* **SMPTE time code**

timeline *Nonlinear editing:* shows all video and audio tracks of a sequence and the clips they contain. Each track has individual controls for displaying and manipulating the clips.

time line *Production:* a breakdown of time blocks for various activities on the actual production day, such as crew call, setup, and camera rehearsal.

tongue To move the boom with the camera from left to right or from right to left.

track *See* **truck**

triangle lighting The triangular arrangement of key, back, and fill lights. Also called *three-point lighting* and *photographic principle*. *See* **photographic principle**.

triaxial cable Thin camera cable in which one central wire is surrounded by two concentric shields.

trim handles Recording additional footage before and after the major shot content for precise editing. Also called *edit margins* and *pads*.

tripod A three-legged camera mount. Also called *sticks*.

truck To move the camera laterally by means of a mobile camera mount. Also called *track*.

two-column A/V script Traditional script format with video information (V) on page-left and audio information (A) on page-right for a variety of television scripts, such as for interviews, documentaries, and commercials. Also called *two-column documentary script*.

two-column documentary script *See* **two-column A/V script**

twofold Two flats hinged together. Also called *book*.

two-shot Framing of two people in a single shot.

unidirectional Pickup pattern of a microphone that can hear best from the front.

uplink truck The vehicle that sends video and audio signals to a satellite.

variable-focal-length lens *See* **zoom lens**

vector A directional screen force. There are graphic, index, and motion vectors.

vector line An imaginary line created by extending converging index vectors or the direction of a motion vector. Also called the *line of conversation and action,* the *hundredeighty* (for 180 degrees), and, simply, the *line*.

video leader Visual and auditory material that precedes any color videotape recording. Also called *academy leader*.

video operator (VO) In charge of the camera setup and picture control during a production. Also called *shader*.

video-record operator In charge of video recording. Also called *VR operator* and *VTR operator*.

video server A large-capacity hard-drive array that can ingest, store, and play back a great amount of audio and video information. It can be accessed by several users simultaneously.

video track The area of the videotape used for recording the video information.

viewfinder A small video screen or flat-panel display on a camera that shows the black-and-white or color picture the camera generates. The flat-panel displays are also called *monitors*.

virtual reality Computer-simulated environment with which the user can interact.

visualization The mental image of a shot. May also include the imagining of verbal and nonverbal sounds. Mentally converting a scene into a number of key video images and their sequence.

VO *See* **video operator**

volume-unit (VU) meter Measures volume units, the relative loudness of amplified sound.

VR log A record of each take on the source media. Also called *editing log*. When the recording media is videotape, the shot record is also called *VTR log*.

VR operator *See* **video-record operator**

VTR operator *See* **video-record operator**

VU meter *See* **volume-unit (VU) meter**

walk-through/camera rehearsal A combination of an orientation session for talent and crew and a follow-up rehearsal with full equipment. This combination rehearsal is generally conducted from the studio floor.

waveform Graphic representation of a sound that occurs over a period of time.

white-balance To adjust the color circuits in the camera to produce white color in lighting of various color temperatures (relative reddishness or bluishness of white light).

wide-angle lens A short-focal-length lens that provides a large vista.

wind jammer *See* **windsock**

window dub A dub of the source tapes to a lower-quality tape format with the address code keyed into each frame.

windscreen Acoustic foam rubber that is put over the entire microphone to cut down wind noise.

windsock A moplike cloth cover that is put over the windscreen to further reduce wind noise in outdoor use. Also called *wind jammer.*

wipe A transition in which one image seems to "wipe off" (gradually replace) another from the screen.

wireless microphone A system that sends audio signals over the air rather than through microphone cables. The mic is attached to a small transmitter, and the signals are sent to a receiver connected to the audio console or recording device. Also called *radio mic.*

XLR connector Professional three-wire connector for audio cables.

X/S *See* **cross-shot**

Y/C component video A system that keeps the Y (luminance, or black-and-white) and C (color—red, green, and blue) signals separate. Y and C are combined again when recorded on a specific media. Also called *Y/C system* and *S-video.*

Y channel *See* **luminance channel**

Y/color difference component video Video-recording system wherein the three signals—the luminance (Y) signal, the blue signal minus its luminance (B–Y; in digital, Pb), and the red signal minus its luminance (R–Y; in digital, Pr)—are kept separate during the transport and recording process.

Y/C system *See* **Y/C component video**

z-axis Indicates screen depth. In standard two-dimensional video space, it extends from the screen (camera lens) to the background (horizon). In three-dimensional video space, it also extends from the screen to the viewer.

zoom To change the focal length of the lens through the use of a zoom control while the camera remains stationary.

zoom lens Variable-focal-length lens. All video cameras are equipped with a zoom lens.

zoom range How much the focal length can be changed from a wide shot to a close-up during a zoom. The zoom range is stated as a ratio, such as 20:1. Also called *zoom ratio.*

zoom ratio *See* **zoom range**

Index